TAR

Ata Servati

> To obtain more information about the writer, go to
> www.eeiff.com

Copyright@ 2007 Library of the congress of USA.
Registrations # TXu 2-021-337

ISBN print: 978-1-7358163-2-6
ISBN eBook: 978-1-7358163-3-3
WGAW NO: 514370 1989/

All right reserved. No part of this book maybe reproduced or transmitted in any form or by any means, electronic or mechanical, including photocopying, recording, or by any information storage and retrieval system, without permission in writing from the copyright owner.

This book was released in 2022.

This book was printed and bound in the United State of America

To my high school friend, the late Hussein Navab Safavi, who stood and died for what he believed in and was unjustly executed by the recent regime. He chose to give up his life for his beloved country, Iran. And to Pary and all the others who have shed their blood for freedom and for their homeland, Iran. My prayers go out to them.

Ata Servati.

ALSO, BY ATA SERVATI

I AM A LOTUS – I AM NEDA
(Spiritual Poems From the Heart.)

IN SEARCH OF HEAVEN
(The Howard Baskerville story)

IN SEARCH OF LOVE
(Base on a true story)

MARRIED TO THE WELL
(INCLUDES 3 volumes)

ASYEH
(Volume 1)

THE SILENT BEGGER
(Volume 2)

THE SHRINE
(Vallum 3)

========

Plays (In Farsi)

OVER THE BRIDGE, BOTTOM OF THE RIVER
The Window

Table of Contents

Foreword x

Chapter 1

When You Are Forced to Choose Between the Love of Your Land and the Loves of Your Life... 1

Chapter 2

The Only Real Defeat Is Hopelessness... 10

Chapter 3

Too Late to Question Decisions Waking up in Iran, the World of the Unknown 16

Chapter 4

Finding Your Daughter – When the American Embassy Is Your Only Hope... 29

Chapter 5

When You Cannot Trust Your Own Shadow... 37

Chapter 6

New Country, Different Rules. Their Eyes Met and It Was the Birth of a New, Forbidden Love... 45

Chapter 7

The Birth of a New Incomprehensible Bond of Friendship with Your One-Time Enemy... 60

Chapter 8

When Your Most Trusted Friend Betrays You... 66

Chapter 9

When You Give in To Your Enemy for the Goodness of Others..............75

Chapter 10

Alone in a Brightly Lit, Stark, Interrogation Room, Fearing for Your Life..............81

Chapter 11

When You Are in a Car with Savak and Wondering, is it Your Turn to Die?
..............86

Chapter 12

Following an Unchartered Journey, in an Unknown Land called Persia...
..............100

Chapter 13

Two Cultures Clash as Two Generations Face One Another over What is Done and Not Done ... .109

Chapter 14

When You Cross the Line Drawn and Challenge Your Own Culture, Hoping No One is Watching 113

Chapter 15

When You are Bored with Your Host's Customs and Culture..............121

Chapter 16

Explorations of the Heart, of Old Iranian Cultures and Unexpected Tragedy..............127

Chapter 17

When the Past and Present Meet Through the Arrival of an Unexpected Guest... 132

Chapter 18

When Your Unexpected Guest Shatters the Wall between Past and Present... 140

Chapter 19

When a man of experience risks his life to save loved ones 150

Chapter 20

One by One, They Disappear... 166

Chapter 21

Black Friday – The Turning Point of a Movement... 179

Chapter 22

A Fire Destroys a Way of Life... 203

Chapter 23

When Unexpected Violence and Anger Overpowers Peace and Takes Over the Nation... 210

Chapter 24

Conspiracy in France... Madness is Logic... 226

Chapter 25

When the Shadow of Death and Sadness moves the Light of Life Away from a Nation... and madness is Logic... 241

Chapter 26

Another struggle... When the Shadow of Misplaced Hope and Trust Moves the Light of Life Away from a Nation... 256

Chapter 27

Friends Now Executioners... 262

Chapter 28

A New Family... 280

Chapter 29

When Decisions for Your Future Are Made Behind Closed Doors and Without Your Knowledge, by Outsiders... 305

Chapter 30

What at First Seemed Noble, Replaced with Sadness, Fear and Futility 323

Chapter 31

If This Wasn't a Time to Cry... There Was No Other... 334

Chapter 32

When You Are Imprisoned by Your Own Convictions... 351

Chapter 33

When You Share More Than a History Together... 360

Chapter 34

Lost Everything You Have Known, with No Place to Go, in the Middle of a Revolution... with the Entire Revolutionary Execution Guard looking for you... 369

Chapter 35

Sad Old Jokes about Clergy; Trouble was on the Way... 374

Chapter 36

A Path to Heaven from A Trail of Blood... 385

Chapter 37

Hidden in a Place So Secret, No One Will Find You but Death... 398

Chapter 38

Willing to Do Anything to Protect Friends. Even Kill. Even Die... 401

Chapter 39
When the Silence is Kissed by its Haunting Melody... the Light Finally Shines... 420

Chapter 40
When Your Medicine, Your Peaceful elixir, is the One You Love... and Love is divided... 425

Chapter 41
Marrying Because of Guilt, to Stay Alive Under the Radar... 431

Chapter 42
When Life Doesn't Go as Planned...and Love is divided... 436

Chapter 43
The Purpose of Dreaming is to Give Life Direction Until Reality Sets Your Course. 444

Chapter 44
When You Have No Choice but to Beg For Help From Someone You Don't Trust... 447

Chapter 45
When You Have No Way Out, and You Are Forced to Face and Talk with Your Worst Enemy...? 453

Chapter 46
When the Hope for Survival Means Hiding the **Truth**... 462

Chapter 47
The Sound of the Tar Haunts a Soul... 480

Foreword

Ata Servati has written about a very elusive country. He lived through the 1979 revolution. His family, friends, and neighbors were directly affected by the events that led up to the political turmoil and the aftermath. When I first met Ata, he told me that the United States government was directly manipulating and directing policies in Iran. In my naivety, I was sure that he was exaggerating.

Now I can Google the 1979 revolution, and the information will come up in a matter-of-fact style explaining the United States government's extensive involvement. It is exposed, right there on the Internet, the huge mistake President Carter and his staff made during the Iranian Revolution and confirmation of the political games Republicans played behind the scenes to win the White House back.

The manifestation of TAR as a story began with Mummer Gaddafi, who financed the 1979 Iranian Revolution with 16 million dollars and knowledge, which in itself is priceless. He was able to do it with the help of American Colonel Sylvan, Sadegh Ghotbzadeh, Dr. Ebrahim Yazdi (who was married to an American from Texas and said he was affiliated with Bush's family), and CIA agent, Dorian MacGray. MacGray went to Iran at the age of 16 to work for the CIA. It was there she met Ayatollah Mohammad Beheshti, who was working for SAVAK, the Iranian secret police that was organized with help from the CIA. They develop interest, which later continued in Germany, and they eventually had a daughter. But she kept her relationship secret.

In fact, she is the one who singlehandedly brought the Shah of Iran to his knees, putting Khomeini in power. You could always find her. She was the American woman dressed in Islamic clothes who used to sit next to Khomeini at all his interviews. In fact, it was she who persuaded Khomeini to accept political asylum in France. Sadegh Ghotbzadeh, AbolHassan Banisadr, and Dr. Ebrahim Yazdi were the main advisors to Khomeini, as well as Khomeini's connection to the American, English, and Israeli government. And later, she was the one who helped Ayatollah Beheshti, the father of her own child, to be killed so Khomeini could retain power and lead the revolution, when in fact, Ayatollah Beheshti was supposed to take over the power from Khomeini, something she did not want.

No one has heard the story that Ata Servati has told in TAR. How it was that American officials traveled to Iraq to convince Khomeini to travel to France. And how, upon arriving in France, Bush and a somewhat unknown senator paid Khomeini's people a visit, handing over 750 million dollars to help him, expecting much in return!

Sometime later, it was Bush who made a deal with Rafsanjani (the second most powerful man in Iran after Khomeini, and closest adviser to Khomeini to continue to hold hostages in Iran until after the presidential election, (which resulted in the hostages being kept in Iran over 444 days.) The Republicans were afraid that the freeing of the hostages might give incumbent Jimmy Carter enough of an electoral boost to be re-elected. If you recall, the hostages were released immediately after Ronald Reagan became president and Carter was defeated. These newly built Republican relations eventually led to the Iran-Contra deal with Oliver North leading it.

This is a story about two countries that were lied to. TAR is a story about a women's search for her father in Iran. It is also a looking glass into how Iranians think, live, feel and search for their personal and ideological identity. We all deal with the balance of personal and civic responsibilities. How far would we go for our country? And once again - does the end justify the means?

While Roxanna is looking for her father in this new country, she holds a mirror up to her own life in California, where she had so many personal freedoms. Yet, she is haunted by one question, why does she feel so connected and loved in this new country? Perhaps because, in contrast, it offers perspective. I have always felt that you need to know another language to really comprehend your own, and a visit to another culture and way of life helps you define your life and your community.

TAR is a love story that becomes tangled and knotted as it ties itself into an integral part of the revolution. We see characters who live their lives with love as the central theme. Love of God, country, family, and friends. While on another level, we witness the personal and political corruption and games behind the scenes that manages to be both revolting and enticing, simultaneously. Ata's life has been dedicated to telling one of the premiere stories in his country's history. Digging deep into his memory for events that both he and his friends not only witnessed but also were involved in, Ata vividly describes these events and how they changed the course of the 1979 Iran Revolution.

TAR is exciting, breathtaking, entertaining, and informative. The author has given us a story that explains how the changes in Iran developed but disguises it as a romantic novel. The importance of this book lies in the fact it gives the reader a glimpse into another world, another culture that we would ordinarily not be privy to. To outsiders, appearances are based on false knowledge, not truth. With Ata's help, we are escorted through the haze created by ignorance into clarity. The reader begins to understand the people of Iran and their struggle to live a peaceful life if allowed. The forces that drive us as humans sometimes lead us in different directions, but ultimately to the same destination.

TAR is nonfiction. However, some of the character's names and locations have been changed. Ata has conjoined two different groups of friends into one to tell the story of all Iranians and their struggle to return to dynasties of Past Persian Emperors, which ruled before the thirteenth century.

Ata has written to express and show how ordinary everyday people react to what they hear through the Bayes theorem media or their friend, how they react to it in their day-to-day lives, and how they are being affected. So, in this matter, maybe some of the facts are intended to look somehow fictional and nonfictional, only because it is based on the false information people are getting from people at the top rank.

This also writes about people who are in the rank of political decision making and how they push their agendas and force it upon the innocent, naive, and uneducated people, and the only things they care about is what they want, and people mean nothing to them.

It is the story of a people longing to return to a life that existed before the invasion of the Arabs, a conquest, which has tumultuously changed the great nation and the great culture of Persia throughout history.

Ata Servati has put a mirror up to the people of Iran, reflecting their thoughts, feelings, and emotions during and after the revolution. In a delicate balancing act, he exposes both the average person and the government players whose games were played behind closed doors allowing each side to voice opinions based on personal experience.

On one of the occasions, quietly and thoughtfully, Ata whispered, "I hope the people, or the nations like the English, Arabs, Americans, and others, whose names and involvement mentioned or described in the past and/or recent Iranian revolutions in this book, will not be offended. I hope they understand I never had the intention to insult them or their cultures. It is only their policy, which is in question. I believe, right or wrong, I must stay honest with the events and feelings of the Iranian people and especially the group I wrote about, in regard to their involvement at the time of and during the 1979 Revolution and the effect their acts had in Iran and for the Iranian people in general.

Through exposing these truths, we as people and the nation can learn about our mistakes and resolve our differences. I truly have respect for all those nations and the people mentioned in this book, regardless [of] if their actions have brought mass harm upon the Iranian people. But I personally must blame our own Iranian people who were so naive as to let those nations play such political games, which resulted in harm upon them."

Of course, there is no question that Ata's own beliefs are reflected throughout the book. He stands for peace, love, tolerance, and forgiveness. He believes we all must forget the past wrongdoings and start a new thought by doing good deeds, having good thoughts, and good conversations. His ideology is reflected in his poetry, novels, and films.

And for these same reasons, he funded "The Lotus Light Children Charity" and "Love International Film Festival" to promote "Love, Peace..."

There is a saying, "The more you learn, the less you know." The more we learn about governments and the reasons behind their involvement in world politics, the more it makes us wonder... but the most important is we all as people look into the facts and accept them with no prejudice, and put ourselves in their shoes, in their place and look into the mirror and ask ourselves if we wish the same to happen to us, to me? I now wonder what the true motives are behind what's going on in Afghanistan and Iraq and the rest of the world, and if we will ever really know for sure.

"The soft, white tissue paper was beautifully painted with lime green, orange, and purple mosques imprinted on its delicate surface. Underneath it held a tar, a musical instrument, several hundred years old. Long, slim, austerely feminine hands gingerly wrapped the ancient Persian musical instrument. It now seemed as dead as all the time-worn hands that once made it sing. The paper shroud silenced the wooden face, concealing mysteries; its divine knowledge lost, forever..."

Kristy Ibbotson.

*****

Chapter 1

When You Are Forced to Choose Between the Love of Your Land and the Loves of Your Life...

Hopelessness hollows out the heart, leaving the spirit stranded and feeling alone. The year was 1952. Somewhere on the outskirts of Frankfurt, Germany, a gentle rain was drenching the tall trees, leaving their leaves touched with drops of transparent iridescence. The rain had washed away the dust, intensifying nature's palette. Droplets were joining a small river, its banks lined with green grass as far as the eye could see, tapping the water's surface, creating concentric circles that were small, and then grew larger before disappearing. The leaves were the instruments, the raindrops pinging against them, creating in fugue a repetitive, soothing song.

Standing alone amidst nature's symphony was a dark-haired man. Assad was Iranian, good-looking, trim, and in his early thirties. Every word issued from his mouth was deliberate, measured, and uttered with intent. Temporarily lost in his thoughts, Assad walked through the woods that had become so familiar to him, unaware of the soaked shirt draped languorously against his body.

He had a decision to make and hoped that somehow the daunting task that lay ahead would pass as quickly as the summer rains often did. The huge tree upon which he stopped and rested his head had been simultaneously a metaphor of both his family and his beloved country, Iran. Assad regarded the slow-moving river for a quiet, peaceful moment. All of a sudden, an inexorable feeling of despair came over him. He glanced toward home from the cover of his safe harbor in the woods. The cottage stood solidly, its dark blue, weathered, and worn shutters rising from the clay-tiled roof.

His eyes, the camera's lens, imprinted images that would forever be a part of him; his mind became the photo album, upon which he would often reflect in coming years. His attention drawn ahead, he saw the silhouette of his American wife, Linda, an exquisite work of art, framed by a window in the cottage.

Linda was in her thirties and quite lovely; she had small delicate features and a subtle strength that was the backbone of her character. Her full lips had an unusual hue and soft texture as if a ripe peach. She was extremely intelligent with a quick wit and was kind and gentle, the essence of love wrapped in a tough package.

Linda held baby Roxanna, their precious daughter, in her arms, rocking her gently in the small living room, softly singing, "Hush little baby, don't say a word, Baba's gonna buy you a mockingbird..." Radio BBC from London, as always, was echoing in the background. "You're listening to BBC from London. Good morning, Frankfurt. Our top story on the international scene: in Iran, thousands of demonstrators have taken to the streets shouting, 'Down with the Shah' and 'Long live Mosaddegh.'"

Revolution was looming. The words issued from the radio echoing with turbulence, the dread of a sea of change that seemed all but imminent. Mossadegh became a hero by winning an international lawsuit at The Hague against Britain. No longer would the natural treasures of Iran be stolen unceremoniously from its people. He envisioned an economically independent and democratic Iran, free of foreign influences.

Mossadegh had engineered the nationalization of Iran's oil industry, shattering the chains of British colonialism. The implications were profound; a new chapter was being written, a page at a time, reinventing this great country with a renewed sense of hope, a national self-sufficiency, and global respect. But, now people wanted their new hero to take over and were asking the Shah to leave. There was still blood to be shed.

The unsettling situation in Iran both saddened and frightened Linda. Her reaction was visceral, her concern great. What would follow? How would these events impact her small family? Linda was painfully aware of Assad's feelings regarding his homeland, and uneasiness crept into her mind as she contemplated how Assad would react to how the current events were unfolding in Iran.

Assad's eyes looked up on Linda at the window. She straightened and gazed out as if she were staring at him. He could hear Linda's voice in his thoughts, "Your daughter and your wife need you more. You are all we have, and there are millions of Iranians who can help your country!" He looked up again, and Linda was gone. The window was wide open, and the shutters started to rattle against the exterior walls of the cottage; as the rain began to pour down harder.-Linda reappeared long enough to pull the shutters closed, cutting off his view of her.

It was getting late in the day, and a sorrow hung over Linda; she could sense the struggle within Assad. They were so connected that she could always tell when he was conflicted. Feeling somewhat helpless, she found comfort in the familiarity of daily tasks. They both knew their relationship was reaching a turning point but avoided confronting the obvious by focusing their attention on Roxanna.

During one particularly tense dinner, made even more awkward because of the silence, their actions were all they dared to use to communicate. As if bracing himself against a winter storm, Assad balanced back in his chair, pushing his foot against the leg of the table, which creaked in defiance. Forks scraped against plates, and although Linda didn't realize she was doing it, she made a slow clicking noise with her spoon against the wooden surface of the table Assad had lovingly reinvented using an old barn door.

Assad studied Roxanna, sleeping in her crib as if he was afraid, she was going to evaporate into the breeze. He could almost feel himself holding her, rocking her, covering her with kisses. Suddenly he was desperate, wanting to wake her up and sing to her, play on the floor, change her diapers one more time before he left. Because he knew he would. No matter how much it hurt. He took a deep breath and looked away from his precious child, surveying everything he would leave behind.

Assad stopped looking around the room and focused on the delicious plate of food Linda had prepared for him. He felt embarrassed that he was in Germany, where food was plentiful when millions of people in his own country were hungry. In Iran, there were children who would go to bed with no food, suffering not only from the pain of hunger but from the hopelessness that accompanied it.

He asked himself a question. Can one judge the behavior of others when they, themselves, do nothing? He looked up, and his eyes locked with Linda's. He saw the tightness of her jaw, the sense of rejection in her eyes. Although she was screaming inside with frustration, she never said a word. Still, Assad could read the familiar look in her eyes. "Can you live with the guilt of abandoning us?"

They both stopped eating and grabbed each other in a tight embrace. They knew that the answer to that unspoken question would hurt them both. Neither of them wanted to commit to a decision until knowing they had the courage to follow through. Logical thinking didn't help them decide; it only led to emotional arguments full of passion and resentment. Assad heard her whisper, "We will both lose no matter what happens."

In Assad's embrace, Linda's mind shifted back in time to the defining moment that had been the beginning of their life together. Her father worked for the American Embassy, which afforded her the chance to study abroad while traveling with her family. Assad had come to West Germany to study, with the intention of returning to Iran.

The year was 1947; Linda was standing with a friend near the open patio where students gathered before and after class to socialize. As Linda looked upward and into Assad's piercing eyes, time stood still. Assad gazed down on her, pulling her even closer to him, and from that moment on, they could not be separated. After a few intense months of courting, they married. Linda held tight to this memory, cherishing it in the face of the uncertain future.

*****

Assad wished he had the ability to communicate the overwhelming love he had for his homeland in relation to the love he had for his beautiful wife and child. He struggled to find words that would convey he was Iran. Her soil ran through his veins. The motherland was calling to him, singing the sweet words of Omar Khayyam and Rumi. Each memory of his prior life intensified his unwavering desire to be part of the evolution, paving a new road map for his beloved Iran.

Assad was keenly aware of the sacrifices required and the profound impact his decision would have on his lovely wife and child. The tides would shift, life-changing decisions would be made, and the implications were such that nothing would ever be the same again.

Still, his heart remained torn between two shores; one, the land of his birth, the other, the land on which he now stood. Roxanna and the woman he loved were grounded in Germany. He was facing his first real moral dilemma; it was overwhelming. Do what's right or do what's comfortable. Unlike Assad, Linda had never uttered words of prayer in the name of Allah, upon the sweet land of Iran. How could he expect his beautiful wife to understand his love and commitment to a country she had never seen, never known, never touched?

He had grown up with the pride of being Persian, his country of birth, the cornerstone of civilization. He would wake up plagued by dreams of his family, old friends, and his country. Although three of his closest childhood friends kept him up to date on occurrences as they unraveled in Iran, not being witness and only getting information after they had occurred was torture for him.

*****

A surprise visit from Mehdi, his childhood friend, didn't help the situation; his attempt to convince Assad that Iran needed him only added fuel to the fire. His appearance took Assad back many years to a creek in Tehran. It had been raining softly. He was talking to his three best friends, Mohammad, Anvaar, and Mehdi, while eating feta cheese and sangak, the famous hot Iranian bread bought from the neighborhood bakery.

Assad was the leader of the four, probably because he was the strongest, at least financially. They were bragging about what they would become and what they would do when they grew up. Mohammad wanted to be a teacher, Mehdi wanted to be a wrestling champion, Anvaar wanted to be an engineer, and Assad wanted to go into politics.

But that was twenty, long years ago. Dreams of youth are frequently required to adjust as life makes demands of idealistic individuals, with unpredicted changes and turns of events leading the way. His three friends ultimately followed paths much different than planned.

Assad was luckier than the rest. His father had been a rich and prominent merchant at the Bazaar, allowing him the opportunity to go to Germany to study modern economics. In Iran at the time, the Bazaar controlled the entire economy in the country.

Most of the merchants had Islamic beliefs, and in reality, it was the Bazaar and the merchants that supported the religious leader financially. If you wished to obtain power in Iran, you needed the support and backing of the Bazaar, and the only way to get that was to have the backing of Assad's father, who was the most respected, powerful, and influential man in the Bazaar.

That was why a few weeks earlier, at the request of Mossadegh, Mehdi had gone to Germany. Knowing that Mehdi was Assad's favorite son, Mossadegh and his followers hoped he could convince his father to back Mossadegh and get him to return to Iran. For a week or more, Mehdi whispered into Assad's ear that his homeland needed him. Mehdi finally left Germany, hopeful but unsure of whether he had made a difference.

Little did he know that long after he was gone, his words remained behind, echoing in Assad's ears and heart, haunting him, forever changing his life. Mehdi did not know the information he had given Assad had turned him upside down. Especially about the intentions of the British after Mossadegh nationalized the British oil companies in Iran.

With the nationalization of the oil company, he cut off the hand of British colonialism, which for decades had been bribing Iranian politicians; they were paid off for signing contracts stating the British could take Iranian oil for almost nothing. The disgraceful contract caused a plundering of all of Iran's oil resources and wealth for several decades while the Iranian people lived in poverty and misery.

But Mossadegh knew the British would not be silent and give in so easy. He found out they were organizing a Coup against him, using their agents, and especially the mullahs. This is why he closed the British embassy and expelled all members of the embassy from Iran. Britain, which had lost for the first time in the world court, now saw that with the closure of its embassy, their way to rioting and ousting Mossadegh was blocked.

Thus the British used their power and connections to make a just as dirty move; they went to the Americans and asked them to oust Mossadegh for them. But Harry Truman objected and did not want the CIA to enter into the business of ousting governments. The British still did not want to back down. They began planning an attack; rumor was they were going to try to take over Iran in full, or just the south region where most of the oil resources were.

But again, Harry Truman, aware of the British's plan, came to Iran's aid and gave the British an ultimatum; that they would never allow Britain to enter Iran, and if they tried, there would be consequences. Thus, the Americans and Harry Truman saved Iran from invasion. Unfortunately, President Eisenhower, who was in office after Truman, ended up helping the British and ousted Mossadegh during the 1953 coup.

*****

Now the time came when Assad had to make the difficult decision to leave the life he had created, the wife and daughter he loved, and go back home to put his education to use by developing a more stable financial infrastructure within the economy. Certainly, revolution and the subsequent change in government and policy would lay the groundwork for new systems leading to prosperity, or that was the hope. Staying in Germany was never part of his plan, but the heart has never respected the plans of man.

It was another cold, rainy day in Germany as Assad walked along the riverbank, struggling with his ongoing internal conflict. He softly began to sing, "Hush, Little Baby." Gradually his legs gained speed, and soon he was running in the rain as he switched to Farsi, breathing hard and gasping for breath between words. "Allayed Koon morghake man, dokhtareh man."

As his thoughts wandered, he began singing a different song, "I want to go to the mountain, where is my gun? Where is my gun? I want to hunt the deer. Where is my gun? Where is my gun, my dear Roxy? Where is my gun?" His body was trembling as he continued singing and running.

Getting rid of the Shah would be the easy part, he thought. There had been a growing dissatisfaction with the Shah's government for some time. It had begun as a slow-burning ember, fueled by discontent and frustration, turning into a great wildfire. Regaining political stability, on the other hand, would be hard, almost impossible. With startling clarity, Assad knew that he could not turn his back on his homeland, no matter how small or large his role. He ran faster and harder, digging and pushing his feet into the soil, flinging mud everywhere. The rain was beating down, punishing him with heavy, stinging droplets.

His mind was now made up, with certainty. He could not stand idly by to witness foreign invaders who pulled the rose petals from the stem of the flower and left the thorns behind to cut and draw blood from the people who remained to tend the garden. Over and over again, swirling through his mind like the echo of a beating drum, were Mossadegh's words, "If I sit silently, I have sinned." Those powerful words changed the heading of Assad's compass. This was the moment in time, the precipice where the direction of history would shift.

But it was not easy for Assad to come to a decision whether to go back to Iran or not. He knew the time had come to choose between the love of his country and its people and the love of his family. Every time he looked at his beloved wife and his sweet angel, Roxanna, guilt captured his heart. He hated himself for thoughts of leaving, but life was cruel, and sacrifices would have to be made. He knew what he had to do.

His hand reached into his pocket, and he pulled out his pocket watch. He rubbed it with his finger to wipe away the rain before opening it. Inside was a picture of himself with Linda and baby Roxanna. The watch began to play, "Hush, Little Baby." The song mixed in Assad's mind with words that kept playing over from the BBC Radio, reporting about the riots in Iran, "Death to the Shah!"

*****

Chapter 2

The Only Real Defeat Is Hopelessness...

Almost thirty years later, in 1976, in Westwood, California, a pretty female flipped through a stack of old photos. In her twenties, the woman was beautiful and slim, with long dark brown hair. Her thick brows, deep dark eyes, and rosebud lips were easily attributed to her Persian heritage. In her slender hand, she held a photo of herself as a baby nestled between her mother, Linda, and her father, Assad.

Gazing at the photo, Roxanna tried to remember her childhood with her father but was unable to recall any memories of him. The walls of Roxanna's room were covered with pictures of Iran, and a map with Tehran circled in bright red. Beautiful hand-woven silk Persian rugs decorated her floor and miniature paintings, in ivory frames, hung on her back wall. A large hand-painted sign with the bold slogan "Persians Rule!" was hanging above her headboard.

Roxanna suddenly lunged toward the foot of her bed and picked up the remote control. Turning up the volume on her TV, she rewound the video, grabbed her peach, and, taking a big bite of the juicy fruit, settled cross-legged on her bed. After a few more clicks, the volume from the TV was nearly deafening.

"And now for a special report about American involvement in Iran," droned an anchorman, his tone serious and somber. "In 1972, the CIA informed Congress of its secret activities in other countries, geared at protecting American interests."

Roxanna was focused on the footage as a woman newscaster began reporting over the black and white footage. The film was sadly dilapidated, with streaks of silver running through its blurred images and missing frames. But it didn't matter. To Roxanna, the footage was priceless.

"Iran's democratically elected Prime Minister Mossadegh is overthrown in a coup organized by the CIA, clearing the way for close energy ties between Washington and Iranian Monarch Mohammad Reza Shah Pahlavi..."

On the screen, a storefront window in Tehran being shattered, a group of protesters leading a large dog down the street wearing a military helmet. In unison, the protesters are chanting, "Death to the Mossadegh!"

The anchorman's voice could be heard over the protesters, "Supporters who had returned to Iran to help Mossadegh have disappeared. There is speculation that some were jailed, and others executed, but many have just disappeared with no trace."

Roxanna was caught up in the moment, the news footage showing Mike Wallace interviewing Kermit Roosevelt. "Kermit Roosevelt, the second son of Theodore Roosevelt, was the CIA man who pleaded with the Iranian Prime Minister."

Mike Wallace asked, "You had a million dollars cash to run the coup?"

"That's right, and we used about sixty thousand dollars," Kermit Roosevelt responded.

Roxanna was transfixed as she watched the black and white footage.

She sighed, consumed by an overwhelming need to find out what had happened to her father. A moment later, her bedroom door was flung open, and her mother entered holding a lit cigarette-wearing a leopard leotard, her back slightly hunched from long years of stooping over, lowering herself, to accommodate conversations with people of a smaller stature. She was still tall and trim, with blond hair and eyes greener than hazel. Clearly, she struggled with aging and loneliness.

Linda peered inside Roxanna's room, seething with rage, her eyes narrowing as she gazed at the TV. "Is this the garbage you're being fed by your Persian boyfriend?" she demanded angrily.

Roxanna missed being raised in her father's culture and, as a way of compensating, was very drawn to all things from it. Her preference in men had always been dark hair and dark eyes. It should have been no surprise that she was attracted to a Persian man.

Roxanna paused the tape in the VCR. Several men being arrested were frozen in fear on the screen. After a long, tense silence during which mother and daughter glared at each other, searching for words, Roxanna finally spoke. "You're still in love with him, and you know it! It's just that your anger overshadows every other emotion and any good judgment!"

Linda didn't respond, her concern, understandable. She would do anything to protect her daughter from the same hurt she had suffered by falling in love with Assad. She tried to take the remote from Roxanna, but when she refused to give it up, Linda reached down and unplugged the cord. "For God's sake, I've told you to forget about your stubborn ass of a father! He's dead! His culture is dead! You are an American, damn it—a Caucasian!"

—"I am half-Persian. And where do you think Caucasians came from? The Caucus Mountains, which was part of Persia. The Aryan race, that's what Iranians are..." She smiled, sardonically, for a moment, "I just want you to stop lying to me! I am not a child anymore that you want to protect..."

Linda followed her into the kitchen, hurrying over to the sink to drop her cigarette ash. Realizing she wasn't going to make it, she dropped the whole thing into an old cup of cold coffee. It made a sizzling sound as it was extinguished. She spun abruptly and confronted Roxanna. "I gave him a choice—the Revolution or us. He left. We lost. What more is there to understand?"

"Why don't you understand? I want to know my father. I have a right to know my father. Why do you have to be so bitter and selfish? If you couldn't have him, nobody can?!"

Linda flinched, "Please don't talk to me like that. You have no idea what the reality is."

Roxanna changed her tactic, challenging her mother defiantly. "Mom, if Dad didn't care about us, why did he send us money and letters?" Roxanna bolted back into her bedroom and returned with a familiar box. Linda's heart ached, painfully, as her daughter turned the box upside down, and a pile of letters landed in a heap on the floor. "Why did you hide them from me? I gave up on ever hearing from him or seeing him. You made me think he hated us ... and then I found these! For the first time, I have hope!"

Linda had received many letters over the years. Her pain had been so overwhelming that it was impossible for her to deal with her heart-wrenching emotions. She'd held them to her face as she wept over each one. Each letter was smeared with lipstick and stained with tears mixed with old mascara; they were all she had of the man she had once adored. Each letter was carefully placed in the box, a cardboard coffin, where she had tried to lay to rest the agony that haunted her after all these years.

Roxanna, in defiance, picked up a letter and began to read: "My dear Roxanna and Linda, I have lost count of how many times I've written to you. Please let me know how you're doing. I'm terribly worried!" Linda grabbed the letter out of Roxanna's hand, her long fingers crumpling it in anger and frustration. Roxanna took another letter and began to read as she walked away from her mother.

"Dear Roxanna, I hope all is well. I miss you very much. I'm mailing this letter from Germany. I was denied a visa to the US, and I'm still dodging the Iranian government. It has been twelve years since I last had word from you. My greatest wish is to see you once more. Please let me know that you have received the money I've sent. Linda, stop this anger you hold against me, please write."

Trying to grab the letter, Linda lunged at Roxanna and accidentally knocked her over. They both fell to the floor, causing Linda to emerge with a bloody lip, her sad, pathetic eyes filling with tears as she sobbed, "What did you expect me to do? Go after him? Get kidnapped? Raped? They live in a different world than we do!"

"Why did you marry him?"

"I was young and stupid!" Linda snarled. Her lip began throbbing as blood started to drip down her chin. Roxanna leaned over, purposely putting her face directly in front of her mother's as she tried to help her up.

"You were in love! Just admit it, Mom. This has nothing to do with being Iranian or American. You were in love with him, and you still are! You're angry because he put his love for his country before you, before us. That's why you're so hateful! You can't get over him!" Roxanna swung her bedroom door shut behind her.

Linda slowly slipped back down to the floor, staring at the door, thinking back on her life. She had offered Assad roots. He had offered her wings. Now, middle-aged, she realized her daughter was crying for the man who had once been her own greatest joy. How could she deny her daughter the happiness of knowing and loving the same man she did? Her Father.

Feelings of love came rushing back to her as her mind traveled into the past. The intensity of those feelings of loss and abandonment hit her in the gut, and she felt as if she would vomit. She was overcome with worry, knowing it was about to happen again; she was going to lose Roxanna.

*****

The ball swished through the hoop as Hussein, alone on the court, hurried to retrieve it and attempt–another shot. He noticed Roxanna walking towards him and missed his shot as he glanced at her out of the corner of his eye. "You see, a good-looking woman walks in, and my aim goes to hell," he teased. He dribbled quickly then passed the ball to her.

"So, what's the good news?" she asked, passing the ball back to him. A sly grin came across Hussein's face, "I was going to tell you tonight at the apartment, but—"

"But what? Is he alive?" Roxanna interrupted him anxiously. Hussein stopped playing and looked directly at Roxanna. "Your father's alive. My sources say he escaped from jail and is now living under a different name somewhere in Iran. I have some friends willing to help you find him."

Roxanna's face lit up as she threw the ball into Hussein's stomach, feeling giddy. "What was that for?" he asked. She gave him a good, long, solid kiss and stole the ball from his grip. He smiled at her, "Thanks for the kiss."

*****

A man's hand wrapped two small machine guns in fabric and placed them inside a medium-sized suitcase under a stack of clothing. He shut and locked it,–quickly slipping the key into his pocket just as Roxanna reappeared from the bathroom. He smiled and placed the suitcase by Roxanna's other blue suitcases.

Hussein pointed to the suitcase he had just left by hers, saying, "I put in a few presents from me and you for my friends there. It will be a pleasant opening when you meet them. Just hand the suitcase to Pary or whoever picks you up."

Hussein considered how best to change the subject to take Roxanna's attention away from the suitcase with the machine guns inside and realized there was no better way than to start talking about her mother,

"So, who is going to break the news of your departure to your mother?"

Roxanna smiled as she responded, "You will ... after I'm gone."

Hussein gazed at her with a blank, concerned look on his face, "What?"

*****

Chapter 3

Too Late to Question Decisions Waking up in Iran, the World of the Unknown...

Like so many others, it was another sunny day at the University of California, Los Angeles, with students walking around the campus. Linda's BMW sports car was careening down the streets of Westwood, California. She entered the UCLA campus and came to a sharp stop, right in front of a fire hazard sign. Linda had been driving furiously. Her expression was threatening, her jaw-tight.

Jumping out of her car, she strode across the sidewalk with hard, angry steps that reverberated through her whole body, immediately catching the attention of two school police officers sitting in their car nearby. After studying her demeanor for a few moments, the officers nodded towards each other and got out of their car with the intention of following her.

Linda had no makeup on in public for the first time in years and had not even bothered changing out of her safari pajamas. She stormed into a building and down the hallway, her footsteps echoing loudly as she passed several classes in progress, peering into the windows, searching.

Her eyes landed on a good-looking, tall Persian man in his mid-twenties, giving a lecture. There was no doubt in her mind it was Roxanna's boyfriend, Hussein. She flung the door open with one kick, marched up to him, and slapped him across the face with all of the force she could muster.

The class watched in disbelief, waiting for a reaction from Hussein as Linda yelled at him incoherently. Her words flew out in a rapid stream that seemed unintelligible to anyone not familiar with the situation, "What have you done to her? I knew you had a plan for her all along! Where's my daughter?" Her voice had started with a piercing shriek and ended with a demanding crash like a deafening explosion.

There was total silence in the classroom while the students sat motionless, waiting for guidance from their professor. Fully aware of his bad temper, Hussein took several deep breaths, trying to calm himself before responding. He could feel his blood pressure rising.

"Where is my daughter?" Linda demanded. But Hussein would not say a word.

It was the moment Hussein had been dreading. Suddenly, without warning, he stood face-to-face with Roxanna's mother. Unable to find the words to tell her what had happened to her daughter, he was wise enough to keep his mouth shut. Nothing he could possibly say could make a difference. A campus policeman entered the classroom to find Hussein standing, motionless by his desk, patiently allowing Linda to ventilate.

She was shouting at him as if she were crazed. "I want you to know, if anything happens to her, I will kill you. I will kill you with my own hands." The presence of the campus police officer did nothing to calm her. She was desperate for a straight answer and was willing to do anything to get one out of Hussein.

The policeman started to approach Linda, but Hussein gestured for him to stay back. He did, but only after making sure Linda was not going to pounce on the instructor. Linda took a deep breath, looked around the room, and at last slowly gained her composure, fighting back tears. She gave Hussein one last helpless look and stormed out, past the officer before exiting the building.

Her body began to tremble as she collapsed on a nearby bench, so upset that she didn't notice Hussein had followed her out and was heading in her direction. He walked straight to the bench and sat down next to her without saying a word.

Finally, she looked up, making direct eye contact with the man she blamed for her daughter's disappearance. "Why do I have to pay for your struggle? I've already lost my husband. I'm not going to lose my daughter, too! Why did you do this to me? To her?" Linda's voice cracked with emotion as she pleaded for an answer.

Hussein couldn't explain, even if he wanted to. He was a member of an underground radical communist group against the Shah. Although known to be thoughtful and kind by his students, he was also a serious, stubborn man whom some considered to be very radical in his beliefs, one of the chiefs of the powerful underground political organization.

Still, he tried his best to sympathize with Linda and let her know he understood her feelings, the gripping fear that had paralyzed her, knowing she might lose her daughter. He wanted to reach over and hug her but was afraid she would hit him.

Watching Linda crying helplessly for her daughter, Hussein was reminded of his own childhood. Linda's tears became his mother's. He pictured his father lashing his mother over and over without mercy, covering her body with welts. The louder his mother would cry, the harder he would hit her. He had wanted to rise up and kill his father, but he was only a child and no match for his father's vile temper and heavy hand.

And now, watching Linda cry, Hussein's pain equaled hers. He wanted to comfort her by explaining what he was doing and what part her daughter would play in the bigger picture, but it was impossible. He couldn't even let Roxanna know how important she was to the future of his country. He was in no position to reveal the truth to anyone.

But seeing Linda now, he wished he had never set Roxanna up, using her to his own advantage while sending her to Iran in search of a ghost. He didn't recognize the manipulative person he had become. He looked at Linda; he wondered what had happened to the kind and good human being he had been in his youth.

Although Hussein was anti-Shah and strongly against the Iranian government, deep down in his heart, he was beginning to realize how complex the situation was. The Shah had done much for Iran. Regardless of the fact that life was not perfect, Iran had become progressively advanced under him. It had grown to be a rich, powerful country in a short time.

Despite the fact the Shah had become overconfident and felt that he was untouchable, everyone knew he loved his country and his people. The Shah decided that Iran would no longer give bribes to other countries. He wanted to lead Iran towards becoming one of the main powers in the region, an economic and military powerhouse able to stand on its own.

In fact, the country was almost there. There was only one thing standing between the Shah and his goal. The West, particularly the English and the Americans, were not going to let it happen. For the West, the only thing that was important was getting cheap oil. But none of this changed the fact that Linda was crying to find her daughter.

*****

On the other side of the world, completely unaware she was being set up, Roxanna could not wait for her plane to land in Tehran. She had no idea that she would soon find herself in the center of the political turmoil as she began her search for her father, the father that might not even continue to draw breath. For Roxanna, the plane was transporting her to a new and unfamiliar world, one she had dreamed of since she was a child. With a shudder, she remembered the saying that her mother often used: "Be careful what you wish for. It just might come true."

An Iranian stewardess had just made an announcement in preparation for landing and was walking through the cabin checking seatbelts. Roxanna had been flying for over 15 hours and was suddenly having feelings of apprehension. Everything was eerily quiet; most of the passengers were just waking and trying to shake the sleep from their eyes. The exhausting effects of the long flight showed on all their faces.

The stewardess stopped by Roxanna and touched her shoulder gently, pointing to her seatbelt. Roxanna fastened it and looked toward the window, hoping for a glimpse of some sign of Tehran below. Her eyes lit upon an Iranian woman, in her early sixties, sitting next to her.

The woman had been in a very deep sleep, her head bobbing up and down for the past few hours, and now saliva and lipstick had crusted at the edges of her mouth. When the stewardess gently shook her shoulder, she looked around sleepily. Along with the other women on the plane, she began to touch up her makeup. Seeing Roxanna looking at her, she smiled pleasantly.

Finally, Roxanna saw the landing lights in the distance, pointing the way to Mehrabad International Airport in Tehran. It was a bumpy, yet welcomed, landing. They rolled down the runway, stopping somewhere on the tarmac. Although asked to remain seated, impatient passengers all rose at the same time, hurrying to grab their belongings and get on with the tense process of going through customs.

Iran was so familiar to them; they moved with great ease, eager to meet loved ones and complete this last leg of the journey. This was where most of them were born and raised; their relatives spread out among Iran's varied landscape. Generation after generation of ancestors was buried in its soil.

Roxanna had listened with envy as the woman sitting next to her on the plane described what it was like for an Iranian coming home. A mob of family members would be waiting outside the door for them, eager for an affectionate embrace. Then they would be ushered into the car and rushed home for a hot meal, consisting of several courses of delicious stews, served with the famous sangak bread, hot rice with saffron, and kebabs made from lamb beef and chicken. There would be a mixture of green mints and plain yogurt mixed with dry mints and cucumber. Fresh fruit, nuts, and hot tea would follow this. It did not matter what time they arrived; it was always time for a feast.

Roxanna followed the crowd, feeling like a lost sheep. She was suddenly concerned about the decision she had made; going to a country, she had never been to without knowing anyone there. All of the passengers entered a bus that would take them across the tarmac to the front door of customs.

Finally, inside, Roxanna felt her first moment of relief as she approached customs, and the officer smiled and waved her through, welcoming her to Iran without even asking why she had come. She looked back at him easily, and she walked away to find her luggage.

A few minutes later, she was following an older porter as he pushed a cart through airport customs. The suitcase with the machine guns inside sat in plain view on top. As they reached the customs officer, the older porter went ahead of Roxanna, gesturing to the Officer as he spoke up in Farsi,

"American... America... good people... my family friend..."

The officer smiled and gestured to them to move on, welcoming Roxanna. She followed the older porter as they exited customs, having no idea that some of those porters were followers of Khomeini; too immersed in Islam, obsessed with heaven and hell.

Surprised how easily she passed through, Roxanna continued walking down a short corridor, following the porter as he pushed her cart up a walkway to the main lobby. The lobby was crowded with people waiting to get their first look at their arriving relatives or friends. Their chattering voices, echoing from the large slabs of white wall, were strange and foreign to Roxanna, like an unknown chant.

Feeling overwhelmed, Roxanna stepped out of the flow of traffic, looking around as the older porter left Roxanna's bags on the ground, putting the suitcase with the machine guns inside beside its twin. He then distracted Roxanna long enough for a young woman standing by the suitcase to grab the case with the guns inside. The young woman briefly made eye contact with the Porter and walked off. The older porter pushed the suitcase the woman left behind next to Roxanna's and smiled, saying goodnight, and walked away, pushing his cart.

The young woman carrying Roxanna's suitcase passed Nader, a muscular Iranian in his twenties, and exchanged smiles with him before promptly disappearing into the crowd. Nader, then, looked towards Roxanna, who was waiting, alone, with her suitcase.

She scanned her surroundings and was looking at the clock that read 2:00 A.M. when she noticed a couple of customs officers looking at her and couldn't help but feel nervous. Although she could tell the time, it had not occurred to her that the numbers on the face would be written in Farsi. She was surprised to see the display of the latest fashions in the crowd, with women out in miniskirts, even way past midnight.

Suddenly from behind, a voice with a heavy Iranian accent whispered softly into her ear. It was Nader. "You should watch your suitcases more carefully, or you may lose them." Roxanna spun around and saw a muscular Iranian man in his late twenties holding one in each hand. "Don't worry, I'm Nader, Hussein's friend. I came to pick you up. Welcome to Iran."

Roxanna was immediately uncomfortable, well aware that Hussein, her boyfriend back home, had told her that a woman named Pary would be meeting her. Noticing her concern, the young man continued, "Nothing to be worried about! You were expecting Pary. She is my sister, and she could not make it. So here I am to pick you up."

Although Roxanna felt the slightest sense of relief, she was not relieved enough to feel completely safe or comfortable with this stranger. She was annoyed that she was affected by the sheer sexuality of this man, and for that reason, she trusted him even less. He had a very deep, slow voice that was very deliberate. His skin was dark, and he had a powerful hooked nose. He was dressed casually in a thick beige sweater and jeans. He beckoned her to follow him and then strode away, carrying her suitcases. Although still uncomfortable, Roxanna had no choice but to follow.

They went outside into the cool air, and Nader flagged down a taxi. Roxanna watched in amazement as the taxi ran a red light, screeched to a halt, and then backed up on the very busy airport road, stopping directly in front of them. The driver jumped out and grabbed Roxanna's bags, tossing them in the trunk. Nader could tell that she was extremely uneasy.

They climbed into the back seat, and the driver pulled away, seeming to intentionally throw Roxanna against Nader. The driver laughed as both Nader and Roxanna looked down to cover their embarrassment. A half-hour out of the airport, the scenery started to change. The streets were quiet, and the surroundings seemed greener and even fresher than Los Angeles.

Roxanna looked out of the window at the unusual juxtaposition of tall buildings flanked by the green trees. It was not unusual for streets to be lit on both sides as the trees framed the road. There was also a small creek running parallel and on each side of the street, separating it from the sidewalks.

Roxanna was still questioning whether she had made the right decision to come to Iran. She knew her mother would be angry, but her mother was angry at the whole world, with no expectations and no joy. Roxanna told herself that was the reason she hadn't told her she was leaving; she neither wanted to add to her mother's anger nor be the recipient of it.

The taxi screeched to a halt in front of a small alley on the south side of Tehran. Nader settled with the driver and began to walk down the cold, narrow alley with Roxanna trailing close behind. She immediately wondered if she was still in the same Tehran she had observed as they were driving away from the airport. The streets were darker and not as clean or as lush with trees. The houses were rundown, not fancy or as well-kept as she had been seeing.

They paused in front of a-formidable entrance, an old wooden door with rusty brass knockers that gave Roxanna butterflies in her stomach. She had seen doors like that in movies and read about them in fantasy books. Nader placed the palm of his hand on it strategically, and it appeared to open as if by magic.

Roxanna carefully followed him down a few stairs into an open courtyard surrounded by homes that consisted of several small living spaces, joined together like a small hotel. They walked past a fountain in the middle of the courtyard with many goldfish inside and climbed the stairs along a back wall onto the second floor. They passed several doors and windows through which Roxanna could see people sleeping before Nader finally stopped. Thinking she saw a child, Roxanna glanced inside but realized it was a woman, small and frail, holding brown prayer beads, rocking back and forth in a fetal-like position, praying in the dark.

A beautiful young woman with long black hair and high cheekbones peeked through the window and opened the door, greeting Roxanna quietly with a big hug. She then kissed both sides of her cheeks and squeezed her hands, warmly. For the first time since landing in Iran, Roxanna felt safe. She had not expected such a warm welcome from a stranger. Nader turned to Roxanna, "This is my sister, Pary. She's an English major at the University of Tehran. Pary, this is Roxanna, Hussein's friend."

Roxanna felt awkward, yet relieved, as Pary invited her inside the dark room. It took her eyes some time to adjust, but when they did, she was able to distinguish a small table with a lamp on it in the center, and next to it a prayer rug where the childlike woman, who she suspected was Nader's mother, finished her prayers. Finally, the old woman got up and hugged and kissed Roxanna, making a big fuss over her as she dragged some food out of a cupboard.

Two small children were curled up on the floor next to each other, sleeping. Roxanna wasn't sure if they were boys or girls, but it didn't matter. All she could see were chubby little arms and peaceful faces in a deep slumber. Nader quietly leaned over and whispered, "Well, this is it! We'll have to find you a place to stay tomorrow."

Roxanna looked around, confused, wondering why Nader had brought her there instead of finding her a hotel right from the beginning. Before Roxanna could respond, one of the children woke up, followed quickly by the other. Surveying the room with sleepy eyes, they mobbed Nader, and he covered them with kisses, a boy and a girl, maybe around four and five years old. Overpowered by the children, they fell to the floor, shrieking and giggling in unison with his attackers.

Roxanna was confused when the little girl started to cry, her confusion deepening when the child's tears were followed by those of Nader's mother. Looking around, she then noticed that even Pary had tears in her eyes. Nader tried to disengage himself from all of the attention, but the children pulled him back down, and he succumbed to their wishes, rolling on the floor and defending himself from his attackers with a pillow. The kids stood back and then made another attempt at a second affectionate assault. Roxanna watched as Nader transformed himself into a big kid, giggling and shrieking with uncontrollable laughter.

Pary smiled kindly, "He just got back from an eight-month trip. Everyone cries here! They cry when you go, and they cry when you come, but they are tears of happiness. The children belonged to my late sister. She died in a car accident with their father. Our father also died at an early age. Now, Nader supports the family, and I help a bit, here and there, when I am not in school."

While everyone got to know each other, Nader's mother quickly fixed a warm meal while rubbing tears from her eyes throughout the preparation. Roxanna was embarrassed over the fuss Nader's mother was making but could see that it was done with love and accepted the delicious but simple food willingly. She had only been in Iran for a few hours, but she was already surrounded by a love purer and more honest than any she had ever felt.

Knowing he couldn't stay, Nader put the children back to bed on the floor next to the place his mother and Pary had made for Roxanna to sleep. After affectionately kissing them all, he left, saying he would be back in the morning. But before he left, he told Roxanna his mother would be insulted if she would not spend the night with them. Completely exhausted, both mentally and physically, Roxanna fell asleep to the hushed giggles of the children.

Roxanna woke a few hours later, brought out of her sleep by her need to use the bathroom. When she realized she had no idea where it was, she decided to wait rather than wake the entire family, searching for it. She lay on the floor, thinking about her situation.

As the sun rose, Roxanna was awakened by a tiny hand gently stroking her hair. She opened her eyes to find the precious little girl from the night before, with her wonderful smile and big peaceful, innocent black eyes, staring straight into hers. As Roxanna smiled back, she noticed the young boy was sitting in the corner, watching them shyly.

The smell of freshly baked bread filled the air as Pary and her mother prepared food just a few yards away from where she was sleeping. Their entire kitchen was nothing more than a small corner of the room, about five to six square feet, but Roxanna had finally fallen into such a deep sleep that even the delicate smells of warm bread and cheese hadn't wakened her.

It would take a lot to pull Roxanna away from tasting her first Iranian breakfast. In this case, it was her strong urge to use the bathroom. Pary, recognizing her frantic look, motioned for her to follow her outside onto the balcony, where she pointed downward towards several apathetic-looking tenants sitting around the murky fountain in the central courtyard.

Far into the distance, she noticed the flame of the Tehran refinery burning and dancing into the air. Oil was something that, for Iranians, was the only asset they had for a better life. But the welfare of Iran's masses was of no consequence to other oil-poor countries. The modus operandi of the west was to destabilize any country with oil resources, preventing them from organizing and increasing the price of oil.

Roxanna's attention was focused elsewhere. A line of people waiting to use the only bathroom snaked through the courtyard. Roxanna needed to be in that line. As she walked down the stairs, she could feel all eyes fixed on her, causing her to feel self-conscious. A man left the bathroom, and the little girl who had been waiting next in line turned to Roxanna, gesturing for her to take her turn next. The people in line copied her gesture.

At the same moment, an older man came running around the corner, holding his pants at the crotch, and rushed past the line, pushing the little girl out of his way as he dashed into the bathroom. Everyone was annoyed at the sudden jab of rudeness, and it quickly became the topic of conversation. However, all eyes remained on Roxanna as they tried to welcome her with kind, curious smiles. A woman approached and grabbed her hand and pulled her to the beginning of the line, while another offered Roxanna her half-eaten apple.

Pary was observing Roxanna closely. She could feel that Roxanna had different expectations of Iran and could see she was somewhat bewildered by the lifestyle. Roxanna had assumed that, since Iran was so rich in oil, all the people would be rich, or at least living in greater comfort. After what felt like forever to Roxanna, the old man walked out of the bathroom looking happier and much relieved. He looked around, wondering why no one went in after him. Realizing that he had shoved ahead of a guest, he gestured for Roxanna to use the bathroom next. When she hesitated, the people in line copied the old man's gesture.

Pary explained that she was a guest, and they would not use the bathroom until she did. Roxanna entered the bathroom, but before she closed the door, Pary pointed to a jar sitting inside underneath a small tub of water. "That is called an aftabeh," Pary said. "There is no toilet paper here. We always wash with water after relieving ourselves. Westerners are known as the people who wipe their butts with paper. It's better to be washed with water. It's more sanitary."

Pary's explanation held no condemnation, but still, Roxanna didn't know how to respond to such a statement. Noticing Roxanna's confusion, Pary walked in with her and went through the motions, showing her exactly how it was done. Roxanna smiled, realizing others were watching, amused by Pary's demonstration. "All bathrooms here, except for the houses on the North side of the city, have the same system," Pary said before stepping out. Roxanna smiled and entered, shutting the door behind her.

The bathroom floor was covered with white and gray tiles. In the middle was the bathroom stall, but it was much different from what she was accustomed to. She realized she had to crouch down on two feet; the toilet was underground. She worried about how she was going to squat and pee at the same time but figured it out. She then poured the water into the stall. As she left, she showed the empty aftabeh to everyone. Their smiles indicated that they would have a new, amusing story to share with friends and family.

A few minutes later, she was sitting around a tablecloth on the floor with Pary's family, taking in the elaborate presentation with all her senses. Breakfast consisted of hot milk, hot tea, fried eggs, butter, feta cheese, jelly, and, of course, fresh sangak bread.

Looking at Pary's family, she hated being the only child of a single mother and thought of all the nights she had tucked herself into bed, all alone in an empty house. Under the covers, she would wind up her musical doll and listen to "Hush, Little Baby" over and over. It's beautiful and comforting melody would flutter on her lashes like fairy dust, weighing down her eyelids, inducing a restful sleep. Surprised by the emotional intensity of her first day in Iran, tears appeared in the corners of Roxanna's eyes.

An hour after breakfast, Roxanna's heart sank. She was in a taxi with Pary, engrossed in the beauty and uniqueness of Tehran as they traveled through its streets, when Pary pointed to a rundown hotel in an alley and smiled, shattering all feelings of safety and love.

*****

Chapter 4

Finding Your Daughter – When the American Embassy Is Your Only Hope...

There was a beautiful sunrise over the hills of the Santa Monica Mountains in California. The sea breeze, with all its salty, briny smells, was quite pleasant to wake up to as it traveled through the palm trees from the Pacific Ocean. On a regular day, Linda would wake at six in the morning and begin her day with tea (no sugar), exercise, and a morning walk along the beach to clear her lungs.

Her chubby white Lhasa Apso, Tiger (a.k.a. Queen of the Concrete Jungle), loved to walk alongside her. Roxanna named her Tiger because she would frequently attack bigger dogs that were too polite to do anything but look down at her, perplexed.

Tiger had been a Christmas present from Roxanna to her mother, and despite the fact Linda had no interest in getting a dog, she absolutely fell in love with her little Tiger the second she set eyes on her. Tiger loved to jump on the bed and lick Linda's face in the morning to wake her up, and if Linda was sick, somehow, she would know, curling up right next to her to let her know she cared.

This particular morning Linda had no desire to get out of bed or go for her walk, her swollen eyes clearly revealing a sleepless night spent worrying about Roxanna and thinking about Assad. He was so full of love.

It had been so many years, over 27, since Assad had disappeared from their lives. To Linda, he was the kindest, most sensitive, caring, loving husband and father on the face of this Earth.

She had never dreamed of finding such happiness, and then, in one brief moment in time, that exact moment Assad made the decision to leave them behind and return to Iran, her happiness changed to hopelessness and heartache. How could any mother not do everything in her power to keep her daughter from suffering the same heartbreak? Even if it meant Roxanna would never understand or forgive her…

She tried to explain, but young love comes with a pair of blinders which obscures the bigger picture, and it was no different for Roxanna. There were men who loved women and men who loved something bigger, something more, their jobs, their children, their hobbies, or in Assad's case, his country. Those were the men to be wary of.

How typical of fate to intervene and put Roxanna in the arms of Hussein, her Iranian boyfriend. He was all it took for her to ignore everything her mother had taught her and become enthralled with Iran and the plight of her father. Hussein had filled her head with stories and images of Iran that fed her imagination and awakened her curiosity, fueling her desire to find her father and the love she had longed for.

And just as fast as Assad had disappeared from Linda's life, Roxanna was now gone, as far away from her mother as it was possible to be. What had been Linda's greatest fear was now a reality. In the short time since she had disappeared, Linda had already called everyone she could think of. The entire American Embassy in Iran knew of Linda Fatemi and her problem.

Her daughter, Roxanna, was somewhere in Iran, alone, searching for her father, who was probably dead. She had managed to talk to the active American ambassador in Tehran,-who had promised to look for Roxanna personally. Linda was debating whether to go to Iran or not, but during a sobering moment, she realized she would have absolutely no idea where or how to begin such a search on foreign soil, especially a political hotbed like Iran.

The American Embassy had assured her that there was no need for her to come, that Roxanna would be safe, and they would do everything in their power to keep her that way. The truth was that nothing was safe in Iran, and the last thing the Embassy wanted was for another American woman to enter the country in search of her daughter. They had more problems than they could handle as it was.

Although she heard the phone ring, she sat motionless, staring at it. A man's voice on the answering machine caused her to jump up. "Mrs. Fatemi? This is Fred Sullivan from the American Embassy in Tehran—" Linda had the phone in her hand.

"Yes, hello Fred, this is Mrs. Fatemi. Did you find my daughter?"

Fred's voice echoed in her ears. "Yes, Mrs. Fatemi, she is here. I'll put her on."

Tears poured down Linda's cheeks hearing Roxanna's voice crackle through the phone. "Mom, what's wrong with you? Why do you have to embarrass me? Why did you call the American Embassy? Please stop calling them. I promise to call you from the hotel tonight."

Linda could barely speak but managed to say, "I'm worried about you. I needed to know that you were okay. Please, please be careful."

"I'm okay! I'm safe. I'm fine! I'll call you later. I can't tie up the Embassy's phone any longer, Mom. I'll call you. I promise."

*****

As Roxanna hung up the phone, her eyes caught Fred's. She noticed the little gray that salted his temples gave him a distinguished look for a man in his late thirties. He was staring curiously, making her a bit uncomfortable.

She wondered why he had felt the need to give her a lecture about her safety when she arrived. "Thanks for your concern," she said, "but I'm not worried. I'm here because I'm hoping you can help me get some information about..."

Fred cut her off mid-sentence. "The father who abandoned you when he came to help Mossadegh in 1952." Roxanna was unable to hide her shock as this stranger verbalized the words that had played over and over in her mind. It was impossible that he could know her deepest feelings, but he did.

Fred was failing at any attempt of his own to hide his feelings; he felt extremely attracted to this beautiful young woman standing before him, willing to risk her life for her own cause. Could she really not know how much danger she was in?

Much like he had watched Fred acting with confidence like he was the head of the Embassy do during important meetings, Fred felt himself moving slower, pacing thoughtfully, in front of this vulnerable woman, in an attempt to appear powerful and more knowledgeable. He had learned long ago that verbal exchanges within the confines of a room were often won by intimidation. But more importantly, he knew that power was attractive, very attractive. And if he didn't have it, he would create it.

"Ms Fatemi, your mother has called us on more than one occasion. In fact, she's called quite a few times. She's worried about the intentions of your boyfriend, Hussein. She's convinced that he's using you and that your life is in danger. I hate to say it, but I think she's right."

Roxanna knew her mother would be livid when she found out what she had done, but she had never expected her to go this far. She continued to listen in stunned silence. "I cannot stress enough that these are strange times here. It looks like everything is calm, and that is exactly the facade we have hoped to create. But in reality, the situation in this country is far different, far more complicated. It is like smoke buried under ashes, the calm before the storm. When the winds of change blow in the wrong direction, ashes scatter, and smoke rises. And when that happens, many lives will be lost."

Roxanna listened in disbelief. How could her mother dare to call the Embassy and discuss her motives with this stranger? Instead of help, all she got was a lecture! She could feel her face flush with embarrassment. Her stomach tightened as her throat began to constrict. She was so mad it was impossible to focus on what Fred was saying. Something about smoke and ashes…and Iran not being safe and that it was dangerous for her to be there. He advised her to go back home. To her mother! How could she trust what anyone was saying? Nothing made sense to her.

It was all a jumble, a terrifying jumble. But none of it mattered. Roxanna didn't want to hear another one of her mother's speeches, no matter who was giving it. She took a moment to formulate her response. Finally, she looked at Fred with frightened and appreciative eyes, just the way she knew he expected her to, and then she let him know who was running the show.

"What a lovely way to tell me to go home and mind my own business. Thanks, anyway."

Before she could reach the door, Fred stepped in front of her, and as smoothly as if they were doing a slow waltz, Roxanna stepped around him and left.

" Ms. Fatemi. Ms. Fatemi! I'm here to help..."

*****

The American Embassy compound in Tehran was covered with broad-leafed trees and divided by a long, gated driveway leading to its formidable staircase, a welcome sight to visitors.

When Roxanna was convinced that Fred was no longer pursuing her, she sat down on the stairs to gather her thoughts. Why had she even gone to the Embassy? What had she thought she could achieve? What was she doing in Iran all by herself in the first place? She didn't expect to be asking herself such questions. She knew that focusing on her anger towards her mother would do nothing to solve her problems… But she did it anyway.

"Perhaps you're wondering if you made the right decision to come to Iran?"

A strikingly beautiful, long-legged American in her early forties, Dorian MacGray, stood behind her. It was obvious by her accent or lack of one to Roxanna that she was American. Roxanna took a moment to try and size her up, but it was impossible to tell by the way she was dressed whether she worked at the Embassy or was, perhaps, seeking help there. Just in case Fred had sent the woman, Roxanna decided to squint, menacingly, as if to warn her that she may bite. Amused, Dorian sat on the step next to her.

"There's no way to know so early in the game if you made the right or wrong decision. As long as you stand by your beliefs and never look back, you won't have any regrets. And that makes whatever path you take the right one. Your decision was based on passion. That's exactly what happened to me many years ago... and I'm still here..."

Roxanna was horrified that this complete stranger could know what she was thinking, "I take it Fred told you all about my mother and me?"

" Maybe I'm the one who told Fred about you..."

No matter how hard she tried not to laugh, Roxanna couldn't help herself. "Noooo, I can thank my mother for that."

" Fred and I actually do work together on some level, but he's pretty low on the totem pole. Like at the bottom. Don't tell him I said that! I wouldn't want to burst his bubble. I work with, not for, the Embassy here... advising Americans who travel to Iran on the best way to-... survive in a foreign country. Sounds simple, and it is if you keep us posted where you are 24/7."

Dorian took a piece of paper from a notepad and scribbled something down. "My number. Keep it in a safe place. This is a safe country, but at the same time, there are many dangerous undercurrents. It's easy to lose your footing and get in over your head. In fact, I'd say you can pretty much count on it. Just know I'm in and out of Iran, so that could be a problem. Oh, my name's Dorian. And you're-... Roxanna... Puts you pretty high on the totem pole, actually." Roxanna looked at her quizzically, but Dorian was already getting up to leave.

Back inside the Embassy, Dorian watched Roxanna's every move. Just as she had hoped, Roxanna hailed a taxi and gave the driver an address. He glanced towards the Embassy, his eyes searching for Dorian.

Then, as if sending some sort of message, he adjusted his mirror before disappearing with his passenger into the crowded streets of Tehran.

Satisfied with the way the situation was unfolding outside, Dorian reached for the thick file she had on Roxanna's father and started going through it. She knew damn well Hussein was placing Roxanna's life in danger by using her, but she was in no position to intervene. All she could do was wait and hope she would come to her senses and go back home. Back to America.

Nevertheless, it occurred to Dorian that Assad could be a great asset to her as far as achieving her own goals in Iran-... if only she could find him. Suddenly, she realized it was her turn to use Roxanna to accomplish her mission. But was it worth it to stand back, risking Roxanna's life in the hopes she would live long enough to lead her to Assad?

*****

It had been over a week since Roxanna first arrived in Tehran, and she was starting to settle in. People and places were beginning to look more familiar to her during her taxi rides to the hotel. Unfortunately, though, not much had changed in her life. She was still trying to get in touch with Hussein, who was either ignoring her or worse.

She thought for a minute, wondering if her mother had killed him. And as for Nader, he was nowhere to be found. It seemed as though the men in her life had washed their hands of all responsibility. Roxanna had hoped that Pary would stay in contact with her, at least until she was able to devise some sort of plan, but Pary had left her at the small hotel in the south of Tehran.

She had said she would come back and get her the next day but had failed to show up. Roxanna's decision to go to the Embassy and ask for assistance had not helped her. Her growling stomach reminded her that she had forgotten to eat all day. That thoughts of food slipped her mind.

It was almost dark when the driver pulled up in front of her hotel. She immediately got out after handing him the fare, not waiting for change. She was walking toward the entrance when an eerie feeling came over her.

She realized she had not told the driver the name of her hotel. How had he known where she was staying?

She bolted around, thinking it was too late to catch him, but he was casually sitting in his taxi, smoking a cigarette. He appeared to be a working-class man in his forties, with wrinkles and a twisted left brow; his face spoke of a hard life. Fear gripped her, and suddenly she felt nauseous. She was sure she was being followed. The driver sauntered over to her and held out her change, gesturing for her to take the money. He was trying to let her know she overpaid in Farsi, but she couldn't understand him.

"How did you know I was staying at this motel? I didn't tell you where I wanted to go!" Trying to communicate with him was all but impossible, with Roxanna not knowing Farsi and the taxi driver knowing very limited English. Once again, he repeated himself, telling her she overpaid-in Farsi.

A familiar young man working at the motel walked up to Roxanna and began to explain in broken English: "Miss Fatemi, he said you overpaid him. He said this is the hotel where most Americans stay. It was no mystery." Although Roxanna didn't understand Farsi well, it was obvious to her that the hotel manager, who she had considered a friend, was making it all up.

What she did understand was that the taxi driver had said something and then repeated it. He had not said half of what the man from the hotel implied he did. In an effort to convince Roxanna to believe him, the manager continued his explanations, saying that the taxi driver had passed by earlier in the day and saw her leaving the hotel. That much of the story Roxanna believed, as for the rest, she was doubtful. Making a mental note of the driver's looks, she took the change and smiled graciously, before walking quickly to her room.

*****

Chapter 5

When You Cannot Trust Your Own Shadow...

The ceiling fan was the only sound that could be heard in the motel room; Roxanna opened the window and let the breeze brush gently against her face, cooling her. She had become accustomed to sleeping in jeans and a huge T-shirt since arriving in Iran, and it made for some very warm evenings. She felt too vulnerable, sleeping in pajamas.

It was past midnight. Roxanna was lying on the hard, musty motel bed, staring at the ceiling fan as its blades cut through the streetlights, creating a flashing effect. Terror was creeping through her entire body, causing her legs to twitch. She was sure it was some sort of survival response, almost as if her body was reacting before her mind could catch up.

She bolted upright upon hearing a sound coming from her balcony... and then it stopped. Traffic had died throughout the sleeping city, magnifying every noise, and causing Roxanna to experience waves of dizziness with each faint sound. She lay back down, and within seconds fear drew her into a deep, unconscious state.

It was early dawn and still shadowy dark outside when she was awakened by an unsettling noise; something was knocking at her window. She lay frozen on the bed, waiting to hear if it would happen again or if it had simply been replaying in her mind all night. It did. She moved slowly, stealthily towards the curtain, determined to confront her fears, giving a huge sigh of relief when she realized the noise was being made by two pigeons perched on her window ledge, looking for food. Their presence meant no one else was in the vicinity, otherwise, they would have flown off.

She gazed out, hoping not to find the taxi driver. Thankfully, all she saw was an old man casually sweeping debris and sidewalk dust into the small water channel, the likes of which frequently appeared along the sides of the streets in Iran that separated-the sidewalk from traffic. On most streets, there were trees lining the channel, creating a beautiful, shaded walking path.

Roxanna was mesmerized by the old man, whose streetlights were his own personal spotlights. It was as if he was doing a pantomime, sharing his emotions silently, rhythmically, as if to music, through peaceful, repetitive movements. Roxanna looked, guardedly, for the taxi or for any signs of someone watching her but saw nothing.

Relieved, she felt as if the old man had helped cleanse her of her fears as he swept. She went back to bed, closed her eyes, and drifted back into a deep, necessary sleep; the rhythms of Iran, a background lullaby, accented by the fading sound of the wings of pigeons as they flew into the distance.

A ray of sunlight traveled through the window and lit upon Roxanna's face as she slept until a knock on the door abruptly woke her. She looked at the clock. It was ten in the morning. Still, in her street clothes, she walked to the door hesitating-before removing the chain.

A man was saying, "Ms. Roxanna... Ms. Roxanna... Telephone..." Recognizing the voice, she opened the door an inch and saw the night manager pointing to his ear, as if holding a phone, in an attempt to help her understand. "Telephone ..."

Roxanna followed him to the front desk and picked up the receiver. "Hello?" He watched closely as her expression changed from one of hopefulness to fear when she heard Hussein's voice on the other end. Although she didn't know it, he was calling from a military camp in Libya, a training camp for hired foreign mercenaries and religious fanatics to be trained and then used around the world. In this case, Hussein and a friend were attending with a specific goal; their mission to go back and fight against the Shah in Iran.

For some unknown reason, Hussein's voice triggered a multitude of uncomfortable feelings in Roxanna. His absence from her life from the time she arrived in Iran weighed heavily on her. It was his betrayal of her trust, his manipulating lies that had gotten her into the situation she was in, and she was filled with resentment. She was getting the feeling that Hussein had ulterior motives and that they were neither tied to her safety nor to helping her find her father. She already feared for her life, yet she had no idea there was a revolution in the air or that she was nothing more than a pawn.

"I'm sorry I didn't call sooner, but Nader and Pary had a death in their family, and I couldn't reach them. I had no way to find you… Then I went on vacation, and it was almost impossible to find a phone." Roxanna had no tolerance for him.

"Save your excuses. It was not just because of my father that you sent me to Iran! Is it?" Roxanna whispered.

"That is not true, Roxanna! Nader just got back and told me where you were!" It was obvious Hussein was trying to change the subject. His voice sounded muffled as if he was trying to block out the noise in the background. Roxanna thought it sounded like gunfire.

"Where are you? I hear guns! You're not in LA!"

Roxanna was suddenly distracted by the beautiful, young woman with long, black hair and a wonderful smile, dressed in a loose white dress, who had entered the motel and was walking toward her; concern and guilt written all over her tired body. She was positive it was Pary.

"Thank you, thank you! Thank you for coming for me!" Roxanna whispered, relieved, as Pary walked to her to give her a hug. For reasons unknown to her and having a knowledge Pary may be in this conspiracy with Hussein, still, she was so relieved and happy to see and hug Pary. They held each other tightly. Roxanna didn't realize she had hung up on Hussein without giving him a chance to concoct a believable story.

*****

Roxanna's suspicions about Hussein had been right. Soon after he had dropped her off at the airport, he boarded a plane, flew to Damascus in Libya, and was now at one of the military camps.

When he realized Roxanna was no longer on the phone, he hung up, walked outside, and prepared to join the hundreds of men to be trained as foreign mercenaries. Hussein himself-was there to be trained to prepare for his return to Iran to fight the Shah. As he walked towards the field, his eyes landed on Sadegh Ghotbzadeh several yards away, talking to three Iranian men. Not surprisingly, he could see a look of horror on their faces as they listened to the giant of a man standing in front of them.

It seemed Hussein had been tracking them, as he knew their story better than they did. Their names were Abdulreza Taghavynuia and Jamshid Naamani, and Mehdi Amir Husseini, and they were Iranian Homafar. Unlike Hussein, they had not come to Libya by their own free will. Remembering what Ghotbzadeh and they told him about the three Homafar he was watching, and they began to train with him, Hussein took off in their direction.

*****

In New York, the prior evening there Homafar, Abdulreza Taghavynuia and Jamshid Naamani, and Mehdi Amir Husseini had just arrived in the big apple from Long Island. They were there from Iran training at Kromann company, where F-14 fighters resided. They came to New York City to visit a friend on their way back to Iran and decided to all have a fun night out on the town.

Soon after, they were walking through Central Park by 5th Avenue. They ended up at a Mexican restaurant on 42nd street, and within minutes were drinking and conversing with three American blonde women, Judy,

Carol, and Sonya. The last thing they remembered was being invited to Sonya's apartment, and the party continued.

It was only when they groggily opened their eyes that they realized they had been kidnapped. They didn't know where the hell they were, but the cold, barren military-style room in the middle of nowhere was a wake-up call. They feared the worst and with good reason.

It wasn't as if they didn't know better. The women had been too beautiful, too easy. But at the time, the men were willing to take the risk, figuring the most they would lose would be their wallets. They held their heads in shame and complete agony.

They were still trying to adjust their eyes when the door opened and a man wearing an American Army jacket appeared, bigger than life, looming before them like the all-powerful being he was. He was Sadegh Ghotbzadeh, the man who would one day become the Iranian Foreign Minister and ultimately be executed by Khomeini, the man he helped put in power. Without saying a word, he escorted the men outside. Looking around in horror, they saw a group of several hundred Arab-looking men dressed in militia attire in the middle of training exercises. Ghotbzadeh couldn't hide the look of victory he wore on his face like a medal. The sounds of lethal weapons reverberating in the background punctuated his silence.

When he finally spoke, it was slow and deliberate, with confidence. "Welcome to Libya," Ghotbzadeh said, motioning to the three men who had, unbeknownst to them–had arrived for training, "You have two choices, join us and fight for truth, bring the Shah down, or…" He stopped long enough to let the first choice sink in before offering an alternative.

Finally holding their passports just out of reach, he continued. 'Or, if you would like, I can put you on a plane and send you to Tehran." Thinking this sounded like the best solution, the three grabbed for their passports, checking to make sure each had his own. Ghotbzadeh detected a sense of relief coming over them, exactly the reaction he had been fishing for. His grin grew even more sinister. 'I am sure Savak will be interested to know that you traveled from New York to Libya and then to Tehran."

A feeling of panic came over the three men as they, again, thumbed through their passports, dreading what they saw. Each had been stamped with a U.S. stamp and then, stamped again, upon entry into Libya. "…that alone will put you in jail. But perhaps you will be lucky and die a quick death. Or perhaps they will torture you, depending on how bored they are."

Confident he had made his point; he began to explain the details. "…or join us and from day one, we will deposit three times what your current salary is into your wives' accounts. And I assure you that after the Shah is gone, you will have a top position under the new Islamic force."

Ghotbzadeh's grin told the men that he was, again, about to say something they didn't want to hear. "Next time you wish to pick up beautiful blondes in bars, make sure they are not CIA agents. You see, America wants the Shah gone. The CIA has a profile on each and every Iranian student trained to be a Homafar in Texas, including you. You have been handpicked by those men to join us…it does not matter that you might not want to join. Only what American's liked to call "the best and the brightest" are selected for this particular job. You should feel honored. Your training will now be in Libya. You have a bright future with us… You have two choices. Go back to Iran, and Savak will put you in jail, and that means no job, no salary. Or join us, and we will put three times your salary in any account of your choice every month, "You have three days to decide if you want to work with us or put your life in the hands of the Savak."

Ghotbzadeh walked away, leaving them dumbfounded, feeling like they were free-falling out of an airplane, about to hit the ground. Then Abdulreza Chaychi, Saeed Rajai, Jaffar Shafizadeh, led by a Damascus intelligence officer ABDOUL SALAM who were trained terrorists, began to torture them. For more than a month, they went through Hell, tortured mentally, physically, and emotionally. They kept accusing them of murder. Finally, they broke down and complied.

What they never knew was who had kidnapped them. Some said a Libyan intelligence officer drugged and kidnapped them in New York and placed them in two wooden boxes and took them to Damascus to get info on F-14 Fighter. And some were saying the CIA was involved. Why?

Because how would their passport have had an American custom exiting stamp in the New York airport.

Their passports had been stamped by American customs when exiting at a New York airport, a stamp was given as well upon entering Libya. This was proof to them that the CIA had to know about and had likely orchestrated the kidnapping. Otherwise, how could three people be kidnapped and taken out of the country without the American government knowing about it? Knowing they had no choice but to comply, they agreed that staying and training was definitely a better option than death. Little did they know that in a few short weeks, they would become part of a much bigger team. Their assignment, along with about three to four hundred men from Syria and Libya, would be to go to France and personally guard Ayatollah Khomeini at his compound,-their past lives all but forgotten. By now there was no doubt within them that the CIA also kept a close eye on other groups of Iranians. Homafar was training on American soil, recruited like many to eventually go back to Iran as spy's and in this time to defeat the Shah.

Now sitting with Hussein, as they told him their story laughing about it. Hussein watched the reactions of confused and shocked men even after a month passed their arrival in Libya. Little did these three men know that Hussein, and few others, were there to study them, and watch in cause any doubts surfaced that made them feel the need to get rid of them.

Hussein himself and many of his friends–had been trained in firing machine guns in the Yuma Desert, in Arizona, and other locations throughout the state. There were many unanswered questions; How could it be possible that the FBI or the CIA didn't know about Iranian students training with machine guns throughout America in the middle of the day? How did they buy their machine guns? Who sold the guns to them when most were there on student visas? They were not even citizens! Who paid for them?

How could those guns pass through American customs without being caught? How could several Homafar get kidnapped and taken out of the country to Libya without the CIA or FBI knowing about it? The answer, of course, to all of these was that somebody told them to look the other way; the world of politics is beyond emotion. There is no mercy, and those in control will do anything to get what they want. They do not care if millions die.

It hadn't been until Hussein became involved with an Iranian lady named Soudabeh, who later introduced him to Dorian MacGray, that he realized the true extent of the CIA's involvement. She had helped his organization, telling them to pass their machine guns through American customs to Iran.

At first, Hussein didn't believe her when she told him she was part of the team established to overthrow The Shah and restructure the government in Iran, but when he was actually able to start getting machine guns into Iran, he realized who he was dealing with. Little by little, Hussein learned more about the American team that was formed to change the government in Iran, which included Dorian MacGray, Ramsey Clark, Colonel Edward Thompson, General Robert E. Huyser, and the American Ambassador to Iran, William H. Sullivan. Dorian, however, was then and would always remain a mystery. It was Soudabeh who kept in constant communication with Hussein and his team.

*****

Chapter 6

New Country, Different Rules. Their Eyes Met and It Was the Birth of a New, Forbidden Love...

Roxanna was greatly relieved that Pary had finally come for her. The taxi pulled up, and they climbed into the back seat, and the taxi took off. But a few minutes into the drive, there was a change in Roxanna's demeanor. It was obvious that something serious was going on in her head, as her happiness was giving way to something else. Suspicion?

Roxanna's eyes focused on a small rip in the cloth on the back of the driver's seat. It reminded her of something Tiger would have done to her mother's car, and suddenly, she was missing home. She longed for Tiger's unconditional love and her mother's obnoxious over-protectiveness. But it was more than just that... Roxanna was positive she had seen the same rip the last time she rode in a taxi, which meant this was the same taxi that had brought her to the motel the night before.

But it wasn't the same driver, which was in its own way even more unsettling. Pary, sensing her anxiety, reached out and grabbed her hand. "There is nothing to be worried about. You are in good hands, and we will find your father. But today, I will show you around. Tonight, I have a surprise for you." Roxanna welcomed Pary's thoughtfulness.

As the taxi traveled toward the northern part of Tehran, Roxanna could see a change in the appearance of the neighborhoods. It was obvious this was where the wealthy lived. The thought hit her that Pary and Nader had taken her purposely to the south, rather than the north, side first to make the contrast all the more vivid.

Unlike the area she had been staying in, the streets were spotless, paralleled on both sides by running creeks, and adorned with tall, beautiful trees. This area of Iran was lined with well-maintained streets, beautifully manicured lawns, and teahouses. The buildings were mostly modern, many with fancy restaurants and valet parking. A display of the most recent high-end fashions could be seen on mannequins in store windows.

Miniskirts were extremely short, and the high heels were high! The hairstyles were all outrageous. Pary was observing Roxanna's reaction to the exclusive stores and to the lifestyle so different than the one she had experienced when she first arrived, taking it all in as if she were a therapist gathering information about a patient.

Soon they were sitting in a modern coffee shop with unbelievably beautiful decor. It was unlike anything Roxanna had ever seen. There were Swarovski crystal chandeliers dripping from the ceiling and cowhides covering lounge chairs. The espresso-colored walls created an intimate atmosphere and set off all the gorgeous accents, pictures, and framed calligraphy that adorned them. Roxanna looked around, having to remind herself that she was in Iran. The long hair on the men and miniskirts on the young girls weren't much different than what students were wearing at UCLA.

Pary had obviously chosen to bring Roxanna to this place for a reason, but for the moment, she was keeping it to herself. Motioning for Roxanna to wait, she approached a man standing nearby who seemed to be waiting and watching. It was obvious that they were speaking Farsi, which made total sense but, for some reason, bothered Roxanna.

She tempered her paranoia by focusing on her surroundings and trying to memorize every minuscule detail so she would be able to recall how each of her senses had been challenged; the roughness of wood, the light beams dancing off the crystal chandelier, the harsh odor of treated cowhide, the warmth of candles, dizzying scents of fresh teas and exotic spices, strange noises, voices, and languages melding into a language all its own. Finally, able to let her guard down, she realized she was loving every second of this unique experience.

Pary returned far too soon but with good news. "We have been invited to a party tonight, on the north side in the hills, where the very rich live. A man will be there who may know your father."

Everything started later in Iran than Roxanna was used to. It was after 10:00 PM before she found herself in a taxi with Pary, traveling through another upscale area in Tehran filled with beautiful mansions, mostly built with marble. The taxi driver stopped in front of a very large estate, unable to hide the fact that even he was impressed by the opulence surrounding them. "You must have very wealthy friends."

The long driveway was lined with the latest and most expensive cars on the market, including a 1978 Peugeot 504 sedan, a Citroen DS, and a red Maserati Merak. As they walked between the two rows of cars towards the mansion, Roxanna was transfixed by the breathtaking landscape; statues and painted sculptures, a pool ornately decorated with aquamarine painted tiles, a built-in water fountain surrounded by various designer flowerbeds, and potted, blooming plants in reds and pinks.

Once inside, Roxanna was even more astounded by the wealth, beauty, and bright colors surrounding her. It felt like a palace, with its modern artwork and calligraphy displayed all through the house. Colorful marble pillars and paintings, along with weavings, Persian rugs, and chandeliers dripping with shimmering teardrops and crystal strings draped like necklaces, adorned the huge walkways.

The lavish surroundings took her breath away. Everywhere she looked, she gasped in sheer awe of such wealth, previously unimaginable to her. The mansion reminded her of a tour of Hearst Castle her mother had taken her on when she was little, only this mansion was a thousand times more opulent! She noticed that the guests were all young and beautiful, not one appeared to be in their thirties.

She wondered how it was possible for Pary and her entire family to live together in one room, while a stone's throw away, one person lived in this mansion under the intricate workmanship of its carved ceilings, surrounded by a kaleidoscope of opulence, all alone. The experience was unexplainable, like standing naked under a rainbow misted waterfall.

Pary once again signaled for Roxanna to wait. Hard rock music that had exploded in the 1970s, a combination of indigenous instruments and imported electric guitars, resonated throughout the mansion, piercing her ears. A young man with tight pants, sporting the long hair men were wearing at the time and accented by enormous earrings, interrupted Roxanna's thoughts by asking her to dance.

Intimidated by such ornate surroundings, her first reaction was to decline, but she changed her mind, concerned that it would be considered rude to refuse the invitation. Fortunately, the man started rocking back and forth, obviously high on drugs, providing Roxanna with an escape route. She politely walked away as if she hadn't heard and started looking for Pary to rescue her, or at the very least, for an escape route.

She noticed a handsome, rather thin young man surrounded by a group of friends who were cheering for some reason. He was entertaining them by trying to inhale a cigarette in one long breath. He succeeded and then burst out coughing, much to the amusement of those surrounding him.

Between coughs, the man, who she now realized was called Freydoon, managed to order more drinks for everyone.

Pary had been standing behind a large statue at the top of the marble staircase, hidden amongst the arched doorways and granite pillars. She appeared to be engaged in a serious conversation with a man while at the same time keeping one eye on Roxanna.

*****

Later that night, the taxi stopped abruptly in front of an intriguing, hidden restaurant. This time Pary paid him so he could leave. Roxanna followed her down several stairs into an underground shish kebab house.

Just as the mansion had been a new and exciting experience for Roxanna, these surroundings presented an experience of a totally different kind.

There were old farm tools attached to the walls and baskets of fresh bread on the tables. As they weaved their way through, Roxanna noticed that all the tables and chairs were mismatched, creating an effect as if they had been collected off the street, much like the people inside. None of the patrons were dressed within any kind of similarity.

Roxanna compared the restaurant to some of the artistically eclectic underground coffee shops found in California. There was a variety of artwork, paintings, and beautifully written calligraphic Farsi panels-on the walls. There were green, white, and blue light fixtures with pointed bottoms and octagon shades, giving off a soft, pleasant glow. These were crafted of etched brass with delicate holes carved in them to let light through.

Several plants hung around the room, giving the place a tropical cave-like feeling. Tobacco and hash smoke choked the air, music played, and a few people gyrated on the tiny dance floor. Several foreigners were present and seemed to be having a good time. As her eyes traveled around the room, absorbing her surroundings, that this was the gathering place for intellectuals, poets, and outcasts Pary had been telling her about. Finally, she felt comfortable.

A man stood and began yelling poetry verse. "My honor is my conscience!" His friends yanked him down as another man yelled out, "My patience makes me brave!" Another replied, "No gift exceeds forgiveness." Another man rose up, faced Pary and Roxanna, took a deep hit from his cigarette, and then released the smoke into the air. In a deep voice, he looked at Roxanna and announced, "The only defeat is hopelessness." Pary answered, "The only real mystery I know of his death." Pary turned to Roxanna, "See, they are trying to impress you."

Roxanna smiled shyly and followed Pary to a corner table, scanning the environment with wonder and curiosity. Her eyes stopped on Nader, standing by a group of men, oblivious to their surroundings. To say they were rowdy being an understatement. They were laughing, eating, and drinking, loud and fun-loving, the envy of everyone in the restaurant.

Roxanna's interest turned to one of the two young men, who seemed to be in a competition of some kind and made a mental note to find out his name. He had a short beard but appeared to be close to her age. He was dressed in jeans,-very casual, and his white shirt had a starched collar that he had lifted up around his dark neck. It was obvious that he was in good shape, rugged in a very sexy way.

He was sitting with a skinny man whose dark, deep-set eyes gave Roxanna the creeps. The two were racing with adolescent fervor to see who could eat more hard-boiled eggs, stuffing them in their mouths as others peeled and dropped more eggs into a bowl for them. Shells littered the table as onlookers encouraged them and took sides. Although she didn't know them, Roxanna was thankful for the comic relief they were bringing into her life.

Pary returned to the table with a plate of pastries and put them down in front of Roxanna. Sitting, she pointed directly towards the man in jeans and a white shirt who was laughing and desperately trying to swallow another egg without choking to death.

"That's Cyrus. His best is thirty eggs ... He is a writer and filmmaker whose work was banned by the government. Lucky for him, his brother is a big shot in the Savak; otherwise, he'd be in jail. Don't fall for him because he's wrapped up in his own life."

Roxanna got the feeling Pary sounded a little possessive, even territorial when she was telling her about the rugged man who had captured her attention. "The skinny one, Saeed, was studying to be a lawyer, but he just got out of jail and was suspended because of his political activities. Nader, Saeed, and Cyrus all went to high school with Hussein and are best friends."

Roxanna nibbled on a pastry as she watched Cyrus continue to stuff eggs into his mouth, as fast as Nader was handing him, a competitive look on his face, a twinkle in his eye. She was interrupted by a tall man, possibly American, casually dressed and very drunk, coming out of the kitchen with a bottle in his hand. He bellowed out a line from the Rubaiyat of Omar Khayyam:

"A like for those who for today prepare, And those that after tomorrow stare, a messenger from the Tower of Darkness cries, Fools! Your reward! Neither here nor there."

Roxanna was shocked to see an older, skinny American man reciting poetry in Farsi. Pary smiled at him with obvious affection and continued her simple introductions, "He's Peter. Peter 'the Priest.' He came here from America as a missionary but ended up in the missionary position— with a soon-to-be pregnant Iranian lady poet. She left him, and he left the church. Now he's a poet and owns this shish kebab house with Cyrus."

Roxanna never thought she would see an American priest in an underground restaurant in Tehran who spoke Farsi better than most and could quote Omar Khayyam's Rubaiyat poems at length. Happy and relieved to see another American, she made a mental note to ask him for advice.

A man approached Roxanna holding a red rose. "Let me present you with this tree of my heart, the color of my soul, which is as red and as passionate as this beautiful rose," he purred.

"Your tree is almost dead, and your rose has wilted." Roxanna heard an American voice and turned to see Peter standing behind her with the bottle and two glasses in his hands. He gestured at the man, who promptly faded back into the crowd.

"Let me guess," Peter said, smiling at Roxanna. "An American from New York?"

"California." Roxanna studied him with a slight smile.

Pary rose and gestured to her empty seat. "This is Roxanna. Take care of her for a few minutes." Peter smiled as he took Pary's place and poured her a drink.

The egg eating competition was getting so loud that it was impossible to do anything but join in. Roxanna and Peter sipped their drinks, laughing, as they watched the show. Saeed, drunk, stuffed, and defeated, spit the last unswallow egg onto the floor. Everyone cheered for Cyrus's victory.

Sitting alone, feeling isolated and unhappy in his defeat, Saeed leaned back and lit a cigar, glaring at Cyrus with undisguised animosity.

It was hard for Roxanna to imagine that the two could be best friends. Saeed's eyes roamed the room, coldly observing the crowd as he smoked his cigar and refilled his glass. There was something about the fact that he didn't do a double-take when he saw Roxanna that bothered her. She was an American and new to the scene; everyone else there found her a curiosity. Why not him?

Cyrus and his friends continued to cheer and laugh loudly, but Saeed seemed lost in his own thoughts, oblivious to their celebration. His stoic solitude made him stand out from the crowd. Roxanna was so intrigued by his abnormal behavior that she paid no attention to Peter's chatter. Thinking that Roxanna was unable to hear him, he yelled to Cyrus's group, "For God's sake! These are cultured people! Calm yourselves!" He shook his head, half amused. "What can you do with a bunch of kids? They are all a bunch of kids."

Roxanna took a sip of her drink. "So, should I call you 'Peter' or 'Father'? Or just, 'Old man?'"

Peter gave a smirk and exclaimed, "I'm Peter, and I'm a father! I am everything and nothing." Just then, Saaghi, a middle-aged woman holding a violin, approached the table and began to seduce him with a poem. Roxanna was sure, by the way, she moved her hips, that this was the woman who had enticed Peter from the church.

"Once I did live and drink…"

"And those passionate lips I kissed…"

"How many kisses might it take—before I'm quenched? Before my heart is content?"

Peter and Saaghi, his on-again/off-again girlfriend, had a long and checkered history. He had, indeed, left the church for her, only to have her desert him while she was pregnant. During her unexplained disappearance, she lost the baby in an accident, a terrible story that was unclear, even to Saaghi, who never really recovered from the devastating blow of losing her unborn child. One day she returned, as easily as she had disappeared, and they remained together until the next time she would leave, again. Although they never got married, Peter was her only refuge, and she was his.

Saaghi began to play a slow Sufi song. Her body swayed to the music, and she smiled as she danced, her eyes nearly shut. She had large round eyes and small rosebud lips, painted red. Her long black lashes gave her a cartoonish look.

Roxanna observed, with great interest, the smoky restaurant and the diverse characters within it. Nader, who had yet to acknowledge her, was sitting quietly on a couch, nodding his head to the music. Saeed was still sitting alone, morosely smoking his cigar and tossing back drink after drink. She could tell he was a loner and certainly in a foul mood, yet he and Cyrus, who seemed polar opposites, were the best of friends. How very strange…

Peter got up and began to do a samba around the table, an invitation for others to join in, their bodies moving with the music Saaghi was playing. But Roxanna didn't want to take her eyes off Cyrus. Seducing him in her mind, she was suddenly aware that she found the combination of raw smells strangely intoxicating. At that same moment, Cyrus noticed Roxanna and was immediately mesmerized by her eyes. The two gazed at each other, oblivious to the sounds of the bar around them.

Saaghi began to play an Iranian folk song while the crowd clapped and sang along in Farsi. Peter took Roxanna by the hand and pulled her up to dance with him, and although she joined in, dancing with the rest, she was hesitant and self-conscious.

One man after another cut in while several others waited for their opportunity to dance with the beautiful stranger. Roxanna spun around, startled to find herself nose to nose with Cyrus, staring into her eyes. He began to dance slowly, moving around her, his eyes never leaving hers. Her instinctive, instant attraction toward him was uncharacteristic of her yet completely undeniable.

Cyrus spoke casually and softly. "Just feel the music, and the motion of your body will take over. It's simple, although you are not familiar with this style. The music will become part of you, and soon you become the melody; you become the rhythm." He whispered seductively, as if they were alone. "Then it will be as though you are no longer here."

Cyrus drew her to him as if she was hypnotized, unable to control her will. She was reminded of the story her mother used to tell about when she first saw her father and had swooned, needing to support her body as her knees betrayed her and became weak.

Suddenly changing the tone, Cyrus pulled out a harmonica and joined Saaghi in playing a beautiful Iranian folk song, drawing Roxanna's attention deeper into him. From there, he switched to a faster dance style, smiling as he showed off. Roxanna smiled back, hoping Cyrus couldn't read her mind.

Realizing she had let her guard down, she looked around for Pary, afraid she might disappear from her life a second time. Roxanna's eyes found her standing in a corner, talking absently to a young couple, clearly distracted; her sad eyes focused on the dance floor, on Cyrus. Roxanna realized her intuition had been right. There was a history between the two.

Roxanna felt confused about how she should handle both Cyrus' attention and Pary's melancholy mood. Pary was very important in her life, and she couldn't afford to act on impulse. She needed Pary and even felt some kind of love for her. Their relationship was far too important for her to act on emotion and do something that might hurt her or drive her away. If what had happened between Pary and Cyrus was over, that was one thing, but she could tell by the look in Pary's eyes that, at least for her, it would never be over.

Roxanna's eyes scanned Saeed, who was still sitting at the same table, alone and still, his eyes staring blindly ahead, vacant, as if he was in a trance. He seemed lost in the middle of nowhere as if he didn't belong. An outcast.

A troubled, uneasy feeling came over Roxanna. She watched as Saeed calmly placed his hand flat on the table and stared at it. For him, nothing else existed. He stared with a detached expression as if it were something foreign, not a part of his body. Roxanna moved across the dance floor, trying not to take her eyes off him as she maneuvered closer.

Saeed puffed hard on his cigar. Then, without warning, he calmly jammed the cigar into the middle of his hand. Tears ran down his cheeks as his eyes closed and his mouth flew open, but he made no sound. He watched the smoke rise from his hand, spiraling upwards towards the hanging plants dangling from above.

The acrid odor of burning flesh found its way into his nostrils as Saaghi continued to play the violin and sing in her high-pitched voice, a strange accompaniment to this ghastly scene. Abraham, Saeed's good friend, walked up and stared in drunken amazement. He breathed in the smoke and burning flesh and promptly vomited all over Saeed's hand.

Saeed could no longer contain himself. His screams echoed through the restaurant sending chills through even the most oblivious patrons. Cyrus had been so engrossed in playing his harmonica that he had no idea what Saeed had done until he heard his blood-curdling screams. Everyone froze in place, their attention on Cyrus as he reached Saeed and forcefully snatched the cigar from his friend's hand. To their horror, Saeed rose and, without warning, lost his balance and crashed into a nearby mirror, shattering it and gashing his face.

Only Saaghi, drunk, spaceless, and still unaware of what was happening, continued on as before, playing a sad love song which would forever remain the eerie backdrop of the dramatic scene as it played itself out in the memories of those who would go on to retell the story. Her eyes, like curtains shielding her from the truth, remained blissfully closed.

Everyone else watched silently, without comment, as Saeed stumbled into the center of the restaurant, crashing into tables, and finally crumbled to his knees, his face and hands bleeding profusely, red tears streaming down his face. "You fool!" He yelled, pulling himself up from the floor, "This is not the way to change the country! Not by drinking, dancing, and doing drugs!"

Roxanna was shocked. The evening had deteriorated from joyful dancing, singing, and romance to blood, burnt flesh, and broken glass.

Saeed began to sing a revolutionary song in Farsi, drowning out the sad love ballad that Saaghi was still playing, singing, and dancing to. Roxanna stared at her in disbelief. How could she be so oblivious to what was happening around her?

The patrons were savvy enough to know it was just a matter of time before the Savak arrived and started arresting people. They quickly left the restaurant as Pary and Nader rushed over to help Cyrus drag Saeed outside.

Pary turned to Roxanna, "You are better off staying inside with Peter. We will take Saeed away before he gets arrested. I will come for you tomorrow." But before she could leave, Pary noticed Abdullah still wandering around drunk and lost. She rushed to him and helped him outside, leaving Roxanna alone once again.

Peter was sitting at his table, drunk and minding his own business, whispering the Rubaiyat to himself like nothing had happened, while a few uneasy waiters gathered awkwardly around. He tried to get up but was no longer able to stand. Unassisted, he fell on the table; Roxanna helped him up. He looked at Roxanna, wondering what her story was. He could see the tension that had taken over her entire body, and it gave him a warning. "A tourist, lost in the world of Persia, like many others. Like myself. She's just another lost soul." Peter responded in a melancholy voice, holding tight to the edge of his table. He began to recite from Omar Khayyam's Rubaiyat.

Having concluded his recitation to his satisfaction, he let go of the table and attempted to clap, winding up falling against a table and halfway into a chair as he looked around for Saaghi, but she was gone again. Then sadly, due to this disappearance, he turned toward Roxanna, "Well, I guess you're stuck with me. I apologize for the inconvenience, but don't worry, the night's still young. This is the beginning of the end. Let's go..."

It was past midnight before Peter managed to stand one last time and pronounce himself officially drunk. He signaled for Roxanna to follow him as he headed diagonally for the door.

*****

It was a quiet night on Jadeh Ghadime Shemiran Street ("Old Road off Shemiran") in the north part of Tehran. As if to show respect for his surroundings, Peter held onto Roxanna and tried very hard to walk as if he wasn't drunk but failed-miserably. The street was known to be one of the largest and most beautiful in Tehran, in some ways, a living memorial to Tehran's past. It had creeks running from north to south on both sides, with many beautiful, fragrant trees spaced equally between them on both sides of the street.

The north end of the street intersected at a side of Mount Damavand, which was grand, in and of itself. Peter loved the mountain, not only because the majestic, snowcapped peak was the highest in Iran but also because it was the highest volcano in all of Asia. Peter informed Roxanna that stories about it were well known in Persian, Zoroastrian, and Iranian writing and that he himself had memorialized it on many occasions.

In all the years Peter lived in Tehran, he had never owned a car. Besides the responsibility that went along with driving one, he found them annoyingly expensive. He much preferred strolling, stretching his legs, and letting the breeze touch his face. The breeze was medicinal, and he enjoyed every moment of the thirty-minute walk. The most enjoyable part was stopping to chat with the vendors he passed along the way. Every night, he encountered the same men, and if he missed a night, someone would always call or stop by the restaurant the next day to see if he was okay.

Perhaps his favorite of all was the young boy who sold shelled walnuts on the corner; his bright oil lamp always visible even though he was a few hundred yards from the restaurant. At fifteen years old, he was one-quarter Peter's age,–and his full name was Bolbol of Shiraz. Bolbol meant hummingbird, and Shiraz, the city that is known for being the land of poetry and flowers.

It puzzled Roxanna how they removed the hard shells from the walnuts without breaking the nut, but as hard as she tried to get him to tell, Bolbol said he was sworn to secrecy.

Bolbol of Shiraz earned his name because he had a wonderful voice and always sang to his customers. Every night, after leaving the cleaning up of his restaurant to the night shift, Peter would begin his walk home. It was his time to sober up and become a part of his surroundings, as opposed to just watching the world implode around him.

As he got closer to Bolbol of Shiraz, he would join in with whatever the young boy was already singing and dance. Bolbol would sing for hours while selling walnuts, and Peter was always happy to add to the entertainment by delighting his street audience with his skillful dance moves. That night, they got Roxanna to join the performance as well. He would then sit and eat walnuts, watching Bolbol mesmerize the crowds.

The boy had memorized a plethora of famous songs from a diverse group of Persian singers, including Googosh, a Persian legend. His other talents included imitating movie stars. One of his best imitations was of Mohammad Ali Fardeen, a well-known Iranian movie star and wrestling champion, who was infamous for his lip-syncing in his films. He was a great source of entertainment among the working class.

Bolbol's show would last for at least forty-five minutes each night and Peter, having to close up his own place first, was always his last customer. When Peter would finally feel sober enough to continue on his way, the boy would wrap up for the night, placing everything in his wooden cart and heading home, but never before Peter made an appearance.

Peter was a father figure to Bolbol, as his own father had been killed in an earthquake. After that, the boy had been forced to move to Tehran with his mother and two sisters. Now, as head of the household, he had to work late every night to help his family.

Peter knew that God had placed them together. Even with their 45 years age difference, they drew strength from each other. Bolbol would sell his walnuts at night and attend school in the day. Each night he would store his stuff at Peter's restaurant until the next day. On his way back from school, he would get the violin that was a gift from Peter and try to teach himself how to play before heading to work. Peter showed his appreciation by always having a bag of food for him to take home to his family.

Peter and Roxanna continued singing and dancing their way towards Ballaly, a middle-aged man selling barbecued corn, next to Bolbol, his face lit by a bright oil lamp. By the time Peter reached the man, he had a sweet piece of corn ready for him. Roxanna joined in, requesting hers without salt. She had developed a craving for the corn, the flavor and the aroma exciting her taste buds, as did most of the food in Tehran.

Nights always ended in a familiar and pleasantly predictable manner, but there was a subtle difference about this night. Roxanna noticed both Ballaly and Bolbol had small radios on their carts and were listening to the BBC Radio broadcast from London.

On BBC, the popular opinion was one that was critical of the Shah, publicly affirming and promoting their opposition to his rule. BBC had done a complete political reversal of its position; initially, the propaganda machine had supported him; now, it was condemning him. Britain's political bias towards Iran was fickle, clearly self-serving, and unfortunately, always came at the price of the lives and treasures of the Iranian people. For many, it was clear why BBC had changed its voice from being pro-Shah to calling for the Shah's downfall.

Their pragmatic political view included supporting a Theocratic government and the clergy if circumstances required such. The British opted to do exactly that, paying huge bribes covertly to undermine the Shah's regime. This campaign required the support of the Iranians, and to sway public opinion, all BBC broadcasts were filled with misinformation and self-serving propaganda.

*****

Chapter 7

The Birth of a New Incomprehensible Bond of Friendship with Your One-Time Enemy...

Before the morning light made an appearance on the horizon to announce one more Friday in Tehran, Roxanna was already in a taxi with Peter on another adventure, although what it was, Peter wouldn't tell her. Fridays were always a holiday in Iran, and people took advantage of their day off, giving Roxanna a new friend to explore Tehran with. She was crashing at Peter's place for the time being, especially since he had been a perfect gentleman and a great host.

Traveling through the empty streets, she studied the few city workers who were still up, sweeping the sidewalk debris into the small creek that ran alongside. As dawn began to shine its light on the new day, several people began to appear as if out of nowhere, headed in all directions.

Soon the taxi stopped in front of a small teahouse. "Just imagine getting up before dawn and getting some Kaleh Pacheh! Just imagine how that would taste." Not getting a response from Roxanna, Peter repeated himself with even more enthusiasm, "Kaleh Pacheh!" She was so focused on the taxi that she didn't even hear Peter's pronouncements. She had been preoccupied, studying the face of the taxi driver-to commit it to memory.

When the taxi finally left, Roxanna noted that despite the fact people were trying to get his attention, the driver made no attempt to have eye contact with her. She was thinking for certain that it was the same taxi she had ridden in before, the one that had been parked outside her motel room, the one with the rip. Questions flooded her brain. Who was following her? And why? What did they hope to accomplish? If it was the Savak, why didn't they just arrest her? What could she possibly have that they wanted?

These unanswered questions kept playing over in her mind, but she didn't feel that Peter was the right person to ask. Roxanna stared in the direction the taxi had gone long after it disappeared from sight, wondering if it was going to circle around and come back. She was brought out of her reverie by a loud commotion coming from inside the teahouse, and, looking inside, she saw that many of the customers were cheering for Peter.

His own coffee house was well known in the area, which made him very popular everywhere he went, and because Roxanna appeared to be with him, many were waving hello and gesturing for her to come inside. She stood in the doorway, cheering Peter on as he stood in the center of the group happily reading Omar Khayyam's poetry to everyone.

Cyrus approached from her blind side, surprising her with a flirtatious smile, and escorted her in. Peter stopped everything and waved for her to join him at his table, announcing, "She is here from America to try our traditional breakfast, Kaleh Pache!" As she approached, Cyrus pulled up a chair for her to sit before taking a spot right across from her.

When she realized Cyrus was sitting across the table, her heart skipped a beat. For the moment, Roxanna completely forgot the taxi, focusing solely on her weak knees and the butterflies in her stomach.

Oblivious to their attraction for each other, Peter followed his own agenda, pulling Roxanna's attention towards a dish that, unnoticed by her, had just been delivered to their table. She was jolted by what was staring back at her. Steam rose from the head of a partially cooked lamb displayed on a big tray. It had been cleaned and was grinning, teeth yellowed and stained, waiting to go back in the broth to swim with the other heads and hooves. She moved her eyes from the table to avoid looking at it, only to have them land on several more cooked sheep heads on the counter, ready to be devoured as steam rose up into the air.

Peter put an eyeball and some yellow brains on bread, added salt and lemon, and held it out towards Roxanna, as was proper in his adoptive country. The whole teahouse was silent, waiting to see what she was going to do. She took the bread, brains, and lamb's eyeballs from Peter and doubtfully, stuffed everything in her mouth to be polite— and perhaps, appear a little tough.

"Good! Don't worry, it's good for you, and now you haven't insulted them!" Peter blared out, a satisfied smirk on his face.

The place was filled with men; only two other women were there besides Roxanna. They all stood up, cheering the American woman for being such a good sport, but the fact that Roxanna had an eyeball rolling around inside her mouth made her oblivious to what was happening around her. She froze, unable to get her jaw, or any part of her mouth, to move. A blanket of silence hung over the room as Roxanna stood up and bolted from the table.

Dashing outside with lightning speed, she threw up in the nearby creek while everyone broke into uncontrollable laughter. Peter shouted, "Don't worry, folks, she's just purifying herself! It's an acquired taste! Give her time, and she will take all of you on!"

Outside by the small running creek, Roxanna was too sick to even think about being embarrassed. All she wanted to do was purge herself of the foreign food she had so futilely attempted to swallow. She was about to rinse her mouth in the stream when she noticed Cyrus coming her way with a jar of water. He slowly poured the water into Roxanna's hands, adding to the amusement of the onlookers. "You must learn to follow your own instincts and do what feels right."

Roxanna looked up, water dripping down her face, and stared at Cyrus, whose only reaction was a look of sympathy. Never in her life had she felt more embarrassed. "Thanks for your late warning…" Roxanna responded. Cyrus continued to make her at ease, "You know if these people ate a pork chop, they'd react just like you did. You have so much to experience, good and bad..."

In between gulps, Cyrus tried to bring Roxanna into the conversation and help her forget about the unpleasant experience of eating eyes. "What brought you to Iran? Not the Kaleh Pache?" Roxanna looked at him through the dripping water, wondering how much she should say.

"I am looking for a man."

Cyrus poured more water in her hands, "I'm a Man," he joked. He had been surprised and confused by her answer. He wanted to learn more but was afraid it would sound like he was prying. "You must really be a brave soul to travel alone."

Roxanna watched Cyrus for a few seconds, "Why? Do I need a bodyguard?"

Cyrus, playing her, spoke again, "It depends on where you are looking for him. Perhaps you'd like to start at the Bazaar! Then you need something harder to come by, a great bargainer."

"Unfortunately, I don't think this man can be bargained for." Roxanna was playing him and trying not to give out any clues as to her purpose for why she was in Iran, and Cyrus's culture was very clear: never get involved in another's business or ask questions about their life until they choose to open up themselves.

"I'm looking for my father." She continued. "I haven't seen him since I was a baby. I have no memory of him." Cyrus looked relieved as the word "father" slipped through Roxanna's lips. He sat on the curb and placed his feet in the water. A small smile appeared at the corners of his mouth, and at that moment, Roxanna knew he had feelings for her.

"You lost your father?" Cyrus asked softly.

"He left me and my mother in West Germany in 1952 to join Mohammad Mosaddegh, and I haven't seen him since. Are you actually curious, or are you just acting interested to get in my pants?"

Cyrus's cheeks turned rosebud red. He was not used to such boldness or such colorful language from a woman, but regaining his composure, he teased her back. "I am genuinely curious, but can I get a rain check on answering the second part?"

Peter approached and cut in, "Wash them down with some wine next time, and there you go!" She shook her head, amused, hoping he wouldn't push the offer any further. "Interesting life you have here. It's obvious why you never left."

Peter grinned. "No taxes, no credit cards, no stocks or bonds; just Kaleh Pache, Chello Kabob, wine, poetry, and pretty ladies. What else could a man ask for?"

Peter continued, "Do not chicken out! The day just started. The game will start in an hour."

*****

It was mid-morning, and the sky was clear and beautiful as a flock of stark, white pigeons flew information above the city of Saltanat Abad, northeast of Tehran. It had only been a few hours since she was introduced to Kaleh Pache, which she still couldn't believe was a traditional Iranian breakfast, and now, with full, heavy stomachs, the gang had surprised her by moving to another part of the city to play American softball. After all, they told her, it was Friday, and the entire country was off every Friday.

The pigeons landed in unison atop several swaying, tall trees that overlooked the dirt softball field, searching for food among the branches, unconcerned about the American and Iranian men and women playing softball below. It wasn't until the tattered ball slammed into a tree at the end of the field that they flew away.

Roxanna had jumped upward, sailing above the field as she reached for the ball but was unsuccessful, and it hit the tree with a thump, dropping dead on the ground. She picked it up and threw the ball toward third base without looking to see if anyone was there to catch it. By the time someone ran after it and picked it up, Cyrus was on second, and his teammate had already reached home, gloating like a twelve-year-old boy and throwing high-fives.

Little did they know that far away and hidden from view, Fred sat in his car taking pictures, first of Nader, then of Roxanna, and finally of Cyrus.

Three outs later, Roxanna walked up to bat as Peter provided a brief pointer to help her hit the ball. She looked around with a smile on her face, almost forgetting she was in Iran. Cyrus was guarding first base as Roxanna hit the ball; she ran with all her strength as it flew into the air. Peter cheered her on as she slid into first base, crashing into Cyrus, knocking them both to the ground. He had purposely let go of the ball so that he could have her at first base with him for a moment.

Realizing what Cyrus had done, the umpire called Roxanna out. Peter protested, kicking up dirt, reacting with such intensity that one would have thought that he was coaching the seventh game of the World Series in Yankee Stadium. Meanwhile, Cyrus sat on first, next to Roxanna, holding on to her. His eyes never leaving hers, ~~as~~ he said, "Do you know that beauty is one of God's greatest gifts? When something is beautiful, it should be admired. I admire you." Roxanna tried not to blush, but she could feel her face getting warm.

On the other side of the field, hidden from view, Fred snapped another photo of Cyrus and Roxanna.

*****

Chapter 8

When Your Most Trusted Friend Betrays You...

Roxanna had been wrong about Nader and Pary; they hadn't abandoned her. An uncle had died, and they had been forced to deal with some family matters, but once that was taken care of, they were back in her life, helping to find her father. Within days, both she and Nader had gone to a few different locations but, unfortunately, hadn't been able to find any information regarding his whereabouts. It had crossed her mind during their travels that most men on the south side of Tehran wore black cowboy hats, a sight that amused her.

She was sitting in a teahouse with Nader, talking about where they might go next, when a poorly dressed young man entered, obviously looking for Nader. When he was sure Nader saw him, he went back outside. Nader smiled and excused himself while he went outside to talk to his friend.

Although Roxanna found it curious that the young man didn't want to meet her, she enjoyed the time to herself, watching the patrons smoking out of colorful water pipes – hookahs that had elaborated decorations either painted on them or carved out of wood, while others smoked cigarettes.

A man pouring tea constantly made circles around the room, serving it in small cups with cubes of sugar. The patrons would toss the sugar into their mouths and hold it there, sipping the tea through it. When Roxanna was served fresh tea, she started to put her sugar cube in the cup but instead put it in her cheek and then sipped her tea.

She was having fun when she noticed an elderly man with stark white hair and a beard staring at her with a joyous smile. Fascinated with her, he forgot about his cigarette. The ashes had accumulated at the end and fell directly into his cup of tea. A moment later, he was about to take a sip when Roxanna gestured for him to look into his cup. He noticed the ashes and began to tease her by pretending to drink them.

Roxanna had hoped to be able to overhear Nader's conversation with the young man who had engaged him in what turned out to be a lengthy chat, but they were too far away from the door, so she decided to see how good she was at lip-reading. She was pretty sure she got the words "car" and "favor," but that was it.

The young man handed something to Nader, pointed outside towards an old Ford Grand Victoria, and then disappeared around the corner, all the time nervously glancing over his shoulder. Nader, too, seemed uncomfortably nervous. However, he returned with a smile on his face. "The young man heard you were looking for your father and has brought good news. But it came with a price."

Roxanna kept nodding. No problem! That was to be expected! Nader told her that he had said a man with Roxanna's last name used to have a shop in the bazaar and gave them an address, but he was uncertain if it was correct. Perhaps it was a distant relative. Roxanna had some slight recollection of hearing that her father's family used to have a shop at the bazaar; perhaps this was correct information!

Although Nader was delivering good news, his demeanor didn't reflect it. Something wasn't right. Roxanna asked Nader why he seemed so nervous all of a sudden. Nader explained to her that the Savak had ears and eyes everywhere; you could not trust anyone, and he didn't want their conversation overheard.

He continued by warning her she should not see or talk to her Embassy. The American Embassy had a lot of influence in the Savak, and they exchanged information. "They may help the Savak get to your father before you do." He explained. "If they do, your father will be arrested, and you will probably never see him. They may not like that you're searching for him, or they may just wish to keep you quiet. You are at risk of being arrested, or worse. Be extremely selective about whom you trust. Your life, as well as your father's, may very well depend on it. Keep information to yourself, unless you feel it is necessary to tell others and then only tell one of us." Nader looked straight into her eyes, making sure she understood how serious his words were. "Do you understand what I am saying?"

She nodded her head, "Yes, I understand…"

Nader still wasn't finished, "We are a country of favors. They are worth more than face value. He did us a favor, and now it is up to us to return it."

A few hours later, Roxanna was nervously driving the old Ford Grand Victoria through the streets of Tehran. The man had asked Nader and Roxanna to drop off the car at a friend's place in Tehran, as he had no one to help him do it. The thought of driving in Tehran had terrified Roxanna. She would have much preferred to pay cash for the favor, but if it meant she was closer to finding her father, she would do it. Nader was sympathetic, knowing that driving in Tehran was crazy, so he suggested they wait until past midnight when the streets were quiet.

Nader waved his hand out the window to get Roxanna's attention, gesturing for her to park next to the one-room traffic police station made from aluminum, with glass all around it, located on the corner of a three-way intersection. Generally, during the day when there was busy traffic, the officer on duty would be directing traffic, but now it was deserted.

Nader had told her to park behind the station that would be located just behind the officer who was sitting inside. She was to get out quickly and jump in Nader's car so they could drive away before they were asked to move it. She could see a young officer through the glass window with his back toward her, so she followed Nader's orders; she parked the car in a slot with three small parking spaces by the back office of the police station.

She got out and rushed across the street and got into Nader's car, he took off quickly.

"Thanks, thanks," Nader said. Roxanna couldn't help but notice that for someone who seemed pleased with her efforts, he was driving erratically, continually glancing in his rearview mirror. Without warning, he slammed on his brakes and looked back towards the police station with a pained expression on his face. Roxanna turned around and saw that a car had pulled in beside the one she had just dropped off. They watched as a man got out and walked inside, leaving a little girl about six years old in the car. Without explanation, Nader floored his car, stopping in front of a public phone booth.

He nervously searched his pockets for change while continually checking the time on his watch. Roxanna exited the car and walked to the phone booth, hoping to hear the conversation. If she had caused a problem, she wanted to help, but he wasn't talking to her at the moment, so she was at a loss. She watched the sweat as it dripped down Nader's face.

"No, no, no! Pick up the damn phone! Where the hell did she come from?" Nader was yelling into the phone, but Roxanna wasn't sure if anyone was on the other end. "Get the girl out of there! Hurry! What in the hell is she doing there this late? What are you waiting for, you idiot! Get her out—you're going to get blown up any second! Get out!"

Although Nader didn't see it, an old, black Mercedes was parked about a hundred yards away with a middle-aged clergyman sitting in the back, a young driver up front, and Saeed in the passenger's seat, his hand on a Colt, staring directly at Nader.

Horrified by the sight of the little girl, Nader started pounding on the phone booth as if he was locked inside, but he wasn't. His hand hit the wall so hard the glass shattered and cracked, causing shards to fly into the air, hitting Roxanna. Blood dripped from his hand, but he didn't seem to notice. Panicking, Nader started running towards the police station instead of away from it. Roxanna followed him in confusion. She had no idea what was about to happen, but she understood one thing, the little girl was in danger.

Nader was yelling and running toward the station with Roxanna a few yards behind. Roxanna's eyes locked with a little girl who had just exited the car. Within seconds, before Roxanna could react, the officer reached down and grabbed the little girl's hand. As soon as their fingers locked, a huge explosion tore through the entryway, violating the silence of the night and all that was right in the world.

The force of the explosion threw Roxanna backward, powerless, as she flew into the air and fell to the ground. The sound was so powerful that she felt her eardrums pulsate from the immense pressure as if they were going to blow out of her head. Debris was flying everywhere. The remains of the building and a huge part of the car crashed down from the sky, covering everything in its path, including Roxanna, who was closest to the station.

Stunned and terrified, Roxanna managed to crawl behind a large tree, grasping the palm fronds for support as her legs gave out beneath her. Nader, emotionally distraught and confused by the blast, was in absolute distress. Bloody from the force of the blast and the cuts he acquired when he smashed his fist into the hard earth, he rose and started looking around, frantically, for Roxanna.

Time was running out. People were already beginning to gather at the horrific scene. Nader knew he had to leave or risk being caught, but he couldn't find Roxanna. He was running around looking for her, not knowing that Saeed's car drove past him as it sped in the opposite direction from the explosion. He continued his search, but by now, Roxanna, hating him for what he had done, was determined to get away from him at all costs. Although she would never comprehend exactly what happened, she knew Nader was involved, and that he had lied to her and used her, making her an accomplice in the death of the little girl. If she could, she would kill him.

Anger and utter heartbreak boiled up inside her. The image of the beautiful, innocent child being blown apart like a rag doll was etched into her brain. She was ravaged with guilt, unable to wrap her head around the fact that she had been an unwilling participant in the murder of this innocent little girl. Her mind kept replaying the explosion in an endless loop. She turned down a dark alley and crouched low on the ground, hoping to catch her breath.

Police officers began arriving, and within minutes, they were scattered everywhere, followed by multiple fire trucks. She saw a plain-clothed policeman moving directly towards her and changed positions, squeezing herself between a large green car and the wall it was parked against. She had never felt so alone, so desperate, and so frightened. Her stomach was turned inside out, her body was heaving, and she was choking back tears, gasping to catch her breath.

Thoughts of being arrested by the police, or infamous Savak, were racing through her mind, terrifying her and making her feel as though her heart might explode any second. Stories Hussein had told her of torture and rape filled her head. Despite the fact Hussein had sent her to Iran to be used as a mule to transport weapons and bring chaos in order to destabilize the Shah's government, she had no idea she was being used. Her only clear thought was of her father. "Baba, I need you. Baba, where are you? I need your help."

A hand grabbed her arm, sending shock waves through her body. As far as she was concerned, it was worse than the Savak; Nader was trying to pull her towards him. She glared at him with a hatred she hadn't known to exist. He was the one she trusted most, and now, because of him, she had, unknowingly, helped to commit a horrendous crime... the murder of a little girl. It was inconceivable that she could have played a part in such a sinister affair, but there was no denying the fact that the child was dead, and she was a part of it. And now, all Roxanna wanted to do was get revenge for the little girl's death. Kill Nader. Place the blame where it belonged and punish him for the unspeakable crime.

She frantically clawed, bit, and finally jerked herself free from his hold. Nader looked like he had been holding a cat that just turned on him, planting its claws from all four paws in his face. His voice was urgent. "Come with me... I am not who you think I am... I am here to guard you, not to harm you... come with me, or we are both dead."

Roxanna crawled out from her hiding space and turned on him with rage, beating his chest with all the strength she had left. She had been used and betrayed. The feeling was vile; She wanted to run away from him, away from the guilt, the horror, the fear, the death, and destruction, but she would have to be smart to succeed; she went limp and feigned weakness until she could break away and lose herself in the crowd, heading in the opposite direction of the secret police. The mob that formed around the explosion provided a temporary escape route as she weaved in and out of the bystanders.

Nader was in shock when he realized he had let Roxanna slip away. He had no idea which way she went but continued his pursuit, hoping for a miracle. The police were everywhere by now, and Nader knew it was only a matter of time before he was spotted. The risk of being caught was simply too great, and he was forced to surrender his pursuit of Roxanna, who had retreated into the safety of the anonymity of the mob.

He had no idea that just a short way away, Roxanna was watching in horror as firetrucks made their way to the massacre, their loud sirens piercing her ears. She was limp and shaking, but at least she had freed herself from Nader's grasp. The car in front of the police station was still on fire and the police station, gutted; the charred body of the little girl seemed to be melted to the ground. Almost as if on cue, a taxi pulled up next to her. She jumped in, and it sped away.

The driver asked her where she was headed, but she said only that she needed to be as far away from the explosion as possible. The image of the little girl burning to death was all she could see etched, forever, in her mind.

Concerned by her unresponsiveness, the driver stopped his car near a phone booth and reached over and tapped Roxanna on the knee. Her eyes locked on the old man's white hair as he consoled her with what little English he knew.

"Everything is okay." He held his hand up to his ear like he was holding a telephone, "Phone, family . . ." Roxanna got out of the taxi and walked toward the phone, scrounging around the bottom of her purse for change. Realizing she needed help, the driver quickly gave her some change and put the receiver in her shaking hands, standing guard while she placed her call.

Finally, Peter's tired voice echoed through the wire. She could tell by the slow slur in his speech that he was drunk. "Allow . . . (hello)," he repeated several times. The old taxi driver encouraged Roxanna to answer. Finally, she whispered, "I need help, Peter! Please."

"Roxy? Is that you? Where are you?"

"I don't know . . . Somewhere horrible! I killed some people; I killed a little girl, Peter." The taxi driver took the phone from Roxanna and started talking to Peter in Farsi. Yes, he was very familiar with Peter's restaurant. Yes, he knew where Peter lived. He would get Roxanna there safely. No worries. The driver placed the receiver back on the phone and helped her into the taxi.

Roxanna sat in the back seat in silence as the driver pulled into a side street, making a hurried right turn. Immediately, two sets of blinding, flashing headlights went on in front of them. The unmarked cars had been invisible in the dark. The taxi driver realized he was being ambushed and tried to make a U-turn, but there wasn't enough room. Within seconds, armed men wearing strange clothing left their vehicles and surrounded the taxi, forcing the driver face down in the street.

A man dressed in solid, dark colors to match the night opened the back door and politely gestured to Roxanna to exit. Before she could react, he said, "Ma'am, you have to come with us..." Roxanna looked at her driver tearfully, but there was nothing he could do. She had gotten herself into something far deeper than she could have ever imagined, and there was no escape.

In fear of his life and hers, the driver motioned for her to do as they said. "Go... go... Just go with them. If not, they would kill us right here." Roxanna, visibly shaken, conceded, and was firmly escorted to one of the unmarked cars and forced inside. The taxi driver remained on the street, face down, long after the cars drove away.

*****

Later, Fred was at the Embassy showing images of the bombed-out police station to Dorian. He followed them with images he had taken of Cyrus, Nader, Roxanna, and Peter, finally pointing to an image of Hussein. "This is the boyfriend in LA who set her up to come here. Hussein Navab Safavi. He's an assistant professor at UCLA and one of the main members of the unit Shah group called Mujahidin. He sent her here to be used as a mule."

Dorian was not at all surprised. She knew who Hussein was, and if he was setting Roxanna up and using her, she was going to wind up in a world of trouble! She looked at Nader's image, "Nader? He is from Savak!" Dorian whispered. Fred put a question to Dorian, "Then why would he help her to bomb the police station?"

Dorian looked straight at Fred, "He's using the bombing to get into the underground movement to identify them… not good… Get me all the info you can on her father… we've got to find her." And doubtfully, she continued, "… and convince her to go back."

Fred shrugged, helplessly, "I already tried. She won't listen." Dorian looked through the pictures until she found Peter's. "She's too innocent." Then she picked up Peter's image and stared at it. Fred finally spoke up, "He's a strange one… a man with no passport… I've never seen him at the Embassy. He's loved by everyone; he's more Iranian than an Iranian."

"Her father, Assad… Find out who he is? What is he doing? Whom he is in touch with?" Dorian spoke up.

*****

Chapter 9

When You Give in To Your Enemy for the Goodness of Others…

It was one more calm and a quiet night in Tehran, with most of the city in a deep sleep. It was around two o'clock in the morning when Cyrus was awakened. He usually stayed at his own private hideaway, but lately, he had been staying at his mother's so she wouldn't be alone. Awakened by the phone ringing, Cyrus heard Peter's voice through the receiver yelling for him to get dressed.

The light was just beginning to edge itself over the horizon as Cyrus' Chevy Blazer sped down a curvy road, slicing through the outskirts of the city with Peter sitting beside him. They were headed for an abandoned house located in the city of Lavizan, which was used as a place to meet without intrusion, as very few knew of its location.

Upon their arrival, they exited the car and headed up to the abandoned house to see Pary's face, swollen, her eyes bloodshot from crying. Nader was standing not far behind. Peter tried to give her a hug to soothe her, but she pulled away and walked inside.

With Pary and Peter for support, Nader began to tell Cyrus what had happened to Roxanna. Cyrus listened intently, at first in silence, then with shock. He was furious when he heard Hussein had lied to Roxanna about her father. He had used Assad as a tool to manipulate Roxanna into working for them without her knowledge. And now, she had been kidnapped and very possibly murdered. It took all the control he had for Cyrus to keep from leaping across the room and beating Nader to death for being a part of this charade from the ground floor. Roxanna was as innocent as the little girl she unknowingly murdered, but Cyrus knew that Roxanna wouldn't see it that way; murder is murder. She would blame herself forever.

In Iran, nothing stood between two friends; you would give your life for each other. Your close friends would always protect and respect your family as if they were their own. Cyrus knew that if anything happened to him, Nader would have his back and look after his mother and sisters with the same love he would. Besides, Nader was his childhood friend and practically family. Nader's mother used to work for Cyrus's family from the time she was fourteen years old until she grew old and had to take care of her grandchildren. Nader had practically grown up with Cyrus and was kind of like family to him. So, Cyrus had to do what was right according to custom, not on what he felt. He was obligated to hold his temper. Still wrapped in a dirty piece of cloth, Nader nervously placed his injured hand where it could be seen. Dark red blood was visible all over the makeshift bandage. Cyrus had no sympathy.

The consensus was they had no idea who kidnapped Roxanna. They all stared at one another, waiting for someone to break the silence or come up with an idea …Frustrated and filled with regret, Pary whispered, "Getting her involved was a mistake. She is too innocent to be used..."

"She could have been picked up by the Savak. If she had been kidnapped by the opposition… she would be killed…" Cyrus had yet to complete his sentence when Saeed's voice echoed through the darkness, interrupting him, "I am wondering if our people are not as equal as of a murder pick American girl…?"

They all looked through a broken window into the dead of night to see Saeed appear from the darkness, climb up and sit on the edge of the broken window. For a long moment, all remained silent, surprised and confused by Saeed's appearance before them. Saeed continued evilly, "Besides, what is one American girl worth to you when her greedy government is stealing everything we have!? Even if she gets killed, her blood is not worth more than our people… Is it?" Then Saeed turned toward Nader and stared at him a moment before speaking directly to him… "The pig's devil! SAVAK has her! Ask our friend, who is one of Savak's dogs… Otherwise, why he is not arrested?"

Cyrus spoke up, "You've lost your mind…"

"No. I've found the truth. Something people like you have no concept of. After all, why would you go against the corrupt officials when it would be going against your own brother?"

Saeed was not done with his speech when Nader made an unexpected move and punched him so hard that he fell backward off the window edge, falling and landing underneath the window. Nader jumped out through the broken window and went after him angrily, punching him, "You! The murderer! Filthy communist … you switched the bomb! It was supposed to be a small blast to scare them! You lied to me…you killed a little Iranian girl and have the nerve to show your face…"

A craziness, a madness had taken over Nader's heart, mind, and soul, and if Cyrus had not moved in and held him back, he could have killed his one-time best friend, Saeed. They all watched as Saeed raised himself up and looked toward Nader through the blood that now covered his face and eyes, blurring his vision. He was so full of madness and hate for Nader by now that his voice could hardly be heard, "You will regret this…"

Before anyone could come to their senses and recover from what had just happened, Saeed slipped into the darkness. And after that, he was nowhere to be found. But something was clear to all. Saeed, the old best friend of Nader, was now his worst enemy.

As silence had captured the moment, and all were about to recover, suddenly, the loud sound of a fart interrupted their thoughts. All eyes turned toward the sound to see; Peter, so proud of farting, burping, and wobbling as he moved forward to claim his right to hold forth, "If I may interject; I must say, I think Roxanna has every right to kick all you guys in the balls, that is, if you have any left. On the other hand, I do think humanity should practice forgiveness, and therein lays the contradiction. I don't know what it is, exactly, but therein it lies. I've gotta take a leak. Hold on a second, don't move. I'll be right back."

Peter rushed to a broken window and, still holding the gun, unzipped his pants and began to whistle as he urinated out the window onto the city below! Peter continued, "Life is a battleground between truth and lies and humans are the victims of both. That is why so much corruption makes fast friends."

He swerved and used his hand to steady himself against the wall. He then began swearing at his own pee as it continued to interrupt him as he spoke, "May I have the floor and tell you guys who must do what…" He turned to Cyrus, "Like your brother… let's start with him…"

*****

On the northern mountainside of Tehran, a traditional, elaborate Persian wedding reception was taking place in one of the luxurious mansions. The bride and groom, both lavishly dressed, moved around the huge room, decorated with masses of colorful flowers and centerpiece bouquets, mingling delicate floral scents with the fragrance of delicious, exotic spices.

Cyrus pushed his way through the crowd of influential, well-dressed men and women, mostly government officials, rich guests, and a few uniformed officers, as if he was unaware of the nature of his surroundings. Some were engaged in intimate conversations while others danced to the music being played by a famous live band, as Googosh, the most famous artist/singer of the time, performed.

The serving staff circulated graciously among the guests with refreshments and trays of Persian delicacies. The house was decadent, opulent, gilded, and overdone. A giant chandelier with imported Swarovski crystals glistened and reflected soft light throughout the main living room. The floors were covered with large, expensive Persian rugs. Irreplaceable artwork covered the walls, and exotic plants of all kinds were strategically placed throughout the mansion.

A circular pond, edged in hand-painted mosaic tiles and filled with sky blue water and iridescent Koi imported from Japan, was centered in the large room where everyone was dancing and socializing. The water was vibrating, creating gentle ripples in sync with the music, and when guests gathered around the pond, orange, white and black Koi would rise to the top with gaping mouths, waiting to be fed appetizer crumbs.

Cyrus walked past a table covered with carefully prepared fruit, petit fours, various hors d'oeuvres, and several bowls of caviar without even stopping to look. He was there for a reason, and it wasn't to socialize. He started up a long-curved stairway, its balustrade made of delicately carved, exotic woods from the orient. At the entrance to the wide landing at the top of the stairway was an arched doorway framed by a beautiful, long velvet silk curtain where two young blondes stood, lighting opium pipes for guests.

As Cyrus passed through the arch, he asked a servant a question and was directed to an open the door to his left, where he was greeted by a haze of smoke and the distinct scent of opium. Inside, Hajji Mohammad Zadeh, a middle-aged man, was smoking opium with a couple of men and women. Surprised to see Cyrus, he cleared a place and gestured for him to sit. He offered Cyrus an opium pipe, not knowing he didn't smoke. Cyrus gently refused.

Hajji Mohammad Zadeh knew something very important must be bothering Cyrus, or else he wouldn't have come to him. Sensing that Cyrus was uncomfortable in the group, he rose and escorted him to another room as lavish as the first and shut the door behind them.

Hajji Mohammad Zadeh was very fond of the young man standing in front of him. He knew Cyrus' history, his conflict with his brother, who was a powerful government official. He also knew Cyrus was a free-spirited young man, always walking down his own path.

Hajji Mohammad Zadeh knew their beliefs and values were very different from one another and that Cyrus had contempt for those who lived lavishly, showing little concern for the condition of their own, needy people. Hajji respected Cyrus because of his honesty and his great sense of humor. He knew that Cyrus always had the option of going to his brother, Amir, for help to get what he needed, but was too proud. Cyrus knew that asking his brother for help meant he would have to give up something in return, and since nothing was free, his pride was usually the price. Hajji respected Cyrus for that. He looked at him and waited to hear what his purpose for interrupting his daughter's wedding was, knowing it must be important.

"I need your help." Cyrus's words brought a smile of satisfaction to Hajji's face.

"And as usual, you do not want your brother to know?" Cyrus handed him a fat envelope and nodded. Hajji did not have to look inside the envelope to know what was in it. He took a moment to put the envelope in a safe. "I am assuming you are paying for my services. I know that you could ask your brother. I suppose I may have to go to him for help, myself?" Cyrus nodded again, putting another smile on Hajji's face.

"Your brother is a good man. He is one of the few men that would not accept an envelope; he is honest and wishes the best for you. One day you will realize this, but it must be something of great concern for you to come to me."

"Very serious; otherwise, you know I would not be here."

*****

Chapter 10

Alone in a Brightly Lit, Stark, Interrogation Room, Fearing for Your Life...

It was a folding chair, hard and cold, without a cushion, designed to give backaches. The kind of chair that lets you know you're not going to get comfortable, so don't even bother to try. It was the kind of chair you saved for people you hated and wanted to go home early. Roxanna remembered sitting on one just like it one Thanksgiving at her aunt's house ...the one who hated children.

The dimly lit interrogation room was cold. It was more of a gray concrete cell. As soon as she entered, Roxanna could feel the coldness emanating from its porous blocks. It had the smell of a cave, spore-like and unhealthy. The walls were completely white and bare, broken up by one door and one mirror. Obviously, people were behind it, watching her. Roxanna stared into it, determined not to show any reaction. She wondered if she had been locked in.

Terrified beyond description, she wished that Hussein had never told her about the Savak. She would have much preferred to think things were already bad.

Time was at a standstill. Each minute, an eternity; she had no idea what she was waiting for or what would happen next. All she knew was she might never be able to tell her mother she had been right. But if things were as bad as she expected, her mother would know soon enough. There were two wooden chairs, a two-way mirror, and a similar cold table.

She sat in one chair and put her feet up on the other, and immediately removed them. No need to make things worse. There was a frantic commotion. She heard a language being spoken that she could not identify. Her body went numb. If their intention had been to frighten her, they were succeeding. Never had she known such terror.

Roxanna surprised herself. In the midst of this madness, she realized that her life could well depend on her keeping herself together. She was able to control her fear long enough to scan the room for secret cameras or devices, wondering if they were capturing her on film. Nothing seemed unusual, so she concentrated on the large mirror on the wall, trying to catch a glimpse of someone watching from the other side.

She flinched and turned quickly towards the metallic sound of the door opening. A man entered; one she hadn't seen before. He was of medium stature, in his thirties, with a face that was just plain mean. Cutthroat, vicious, "take no prisoners" mean. His forehead was furrowed, his eyes squinty and deep-set, as if he had been born a predator. Roxanna was surviving on pure adrenaline. Like a lion toying with its prey, he circled the chair, slowly ... twice, observing her. Roxanna sat, looking straight ahead, staring at the dingy wall. Finally, after several agonizing minutes, he acknowledged her presence, "Are you enjoying your stay in Iran?"

Roxanna knew she wasn't going to win this one. It was a leading question, designed to get her to say something she would regret.

She whispered, hoarsely, "Yes. At least, I was until I was kidnapped. What do you want with me?"

"Oh, not very much, perhaps a little honesty. Why did you come to Iran?"

Roxanna remained silent, going through different scenarios in her head. She had already made up her mind not to mention her father, Pary or Nader. Disclosing any information would put her friends at risk of being arrested or even killed. Finally, she decided on the path of least resistance. "I'm a tourist. I came to see the country."

The interrogator leaned forward. "Just to see the country?"

"Yes."

He took a passport out of his coat pocket and opened it. "Roxanna Fatemi. Fatemi is an Iranian name, is it not?

Roxanna was shocked. She was so good about knowing where her passport was at all times. "That's my passport! How did you get it? Do you always steal people's belongings?"

He smiled and waved her passport in front of her face. "Only from those that might belong to …or could help a terrorist group."

That was the moment Roxanna realized her captors were Savak. Someone once told her, when you don't know what to say, keep your mouth shut. It sounded like very good advice in this instance. "I'm an American citizen. I want to speak to my Embassy. I demand to have an attorney present! …That's all I have to say."

The interrogator smiled, amused, "Ms. Fatemi, you are in the custody of the Savak. Until we are through with you, this building is your Embassy, and I am your attorney. We need some information from you, and when we get it, we will let you go—of course, that is, if you are honest with us. We know you've been set up, but by whom? That is what we are looking for."

Before Roxanna had a chance to speak, the interrogator dropped a newspaper in her lap. Although she was unable to read it, the pictures of the police station burning, along with the photo of the two police officers and one of the little girls who had died, said it all. "Now, Ms. Fatemi, I need some answers—of course, it's up to you whether you want to make it easy on yourself... or not." The image of the little girl seized Roxanna by the throat; she could hardly breathe, let alone speak. Tears were blurring her eyes.

She knew that showing any reaction could imply that she was involved in some way or knew who was involved. She took a deep breath and tried to think of things that made her happy or laugh or at least calmed her, but she couldn't get the picture of the little girl out of her mind.

"Perhaps you are crying for the little girl you killed." Interrogation was an art, and he was the best, which was exactly why he had been called in to work with Roxanna. He was a firm believer that yelling rarely worked. Especially with women, they could tune out too easily. Moving slowly and confidently, like a puma with sharp teeth and long claws, he got within an inch of her face and whispered so softly that he could hardly hear himself.

"I want to know everything about your anti-government friends, the ones who got you into this mess…and then deserted you." Roxanna didn't move an eyelash. "Believe me, Miss Fatemi, sooner or later, you will want to join this conversation."

" I didn't kill anyone. You're mistaken. I'm an American, and in my country, people are innocent until proven guilty. I demand to speak with my Embassy and to have an attorney present."

The interrogator was starting to get mildly annoyed. It was rare for him to be assigned a woman, but when he did, it was always a challenge. Women were more "thought/family" oriented. He would have to try a different tack. "Are you aware that no one really cares where you are but your mother? And there's nothing she can do to save you halfway around the world?

"In fact, it's likely you've already put her on her deathbed from worry. No one is going to rescue you. You are in Iran, and that makes you guilty until, if and/or when, we decide otherwise. So, the only road to safety for you is to tell us whom you are working with. We need names."

He could see the blood draining from Roxanna's cheeks. It was time to go in for the kill. "We know about your boyfriend… Hussein. We know he sent you here as part of his political agenda. They were using you, do you understand? You were set up! You were their fall guy. Isn't that what you call it in your movies? You're going to take the bullet. Now … let me ask you this. How does it feel?"

Roxanna stared at the wall, her mother's voice playing over in her head, "You could be kidnapped, raped, killed, disappear without a trace." Then Hussein and Nader's words chimed in, reinforcing her mother's message: "You cannot trust anyone, do not talk to anyone."

She realized, or at least hoped, that as long as they did not get what they wanted from her, they would keep her alive. The fear of torture loomed heavily on her mind until finally, blood-curdling screams began to permeate the walls and, like trombones, drowned out everything else.

The interrogator pulled his chair up in front of her and sat down, getting in her face while trying to get a better sense of what she was made of. "Roxanna, where is your father?" She looked him in the eyes. "Dead, as far as I know. You're the intelligence agency. You would know better than me."

The interrogator was agitated by Roxanna's coolness and smart remarks, and under different circumstances, he would have shown her how it really worked in their country but knew he couldn't. He found it embarrassing that he was being observed while she mouthed off to him, and it infuriated him even further. He shoved his hands in his pockets and walked over to the mirror, staring at his reflection and then Roxanna's. She looked directly into the mirror with piercing eyes, "You are holding an innocent woman hostage. You must let me go. I know nothing. I am just a tourist."

The interrogator continued to stare at her reflection. "Perhaps you know more than you think you do. Or perhaps you have conveniently forgotten what you knew. Not to worry. We have ways to jog your memory." He left, leaving Roxanna to worry about what might come. Her gaze into the mirror remained steady.

On the other side of the mirror, two Savak officers watched Roxanna intently; one was Cyrus's brother, Amir. The interrogator tried to gloss over how bad it went, "She is not a good liar. If you let me, I can make her talk." Amir quietly and thoughtfully stared at her while the interrogator waited for a response. None came.

*****

Chapter 11

When You Are in a Car with Savak and Wondering, is it Your Turn to Die?

It was a beautiful, rainy afternoon in Tehran, nothing like L.A. A black Cadillac was traveling through the streets of Tehran on the north side. The street was lined with tall green trees whose branches glistened with moisture as droplets of rain gracefully splashed atop the leaves. Under different circumstances, Roxanna would have been fascinated by the beauty of the swiftly running creeks and the veil of flowering vines hanging over the walls.

Instead, she was wondering how long it takes to die. One of the men who had been watching from behind the two-way mirror was now sitting in the back seat, next to her, in silence. She heard the driver call him Amir. She had a sick feeling in her stomach, afraid she was being escorted to prison, or perhaps worse. Her eyes began to search the car, checking the locks, door handles, and a way to open the windows. There was no way out. Even if she could escape, where would she go? Or worse, how far could she get before she was shot? All she could do was sit and ...worry.

The fact that Amir was continuously writing something in a notebook while ignoring her didn't help matters. At one point, he sneezed and briefly turned his head to blow his nose, giving Roxanna just enough time to take a look at his notes but unfortunately, they were written in Farsi.

They had been riding around in silence for about thirty minutes. The few times Roxanna started to ask Amir a question, the driver cut her off, signaling her not to speak. Exactly fifteen minutes later, the car pulled up in front of a mansion more beautiful than any she had seen since her arrival in Iran; it stopped at the entrance, which was protected by two large, locked gates.

The old gardener, Ahamad Reza, came out of a guardhouse and, recognizing the car and driver, opened the gates. They passed through the tall seven-foot walls that surrounded the entire, beautiful estate to be welcomed by a kaleidoscope of lush colors; green grass and tall trees, gardens of blooming flowers, roses in every shade imaginable.

The rain began to stop pouring, silver raindrops danced upon the bendable leaves and flower petals; the smell of wetness was alive. There was a large water fountain where birds came to splash, numerous fruit trees planted in clusters, and quaint rock paths circulating through and around the estate. The experience was reminiscent of her first trip to Disneyland as a child, as magical as entering the gates to Sleeping Beauty's Castle.

The driver stopped long enough for Amir to smile and wave to the gardener, who she thought he called Ahmad Reza, before driving down a long driveway. A beautiful sable and black German Shepherd named Khally greeted them, running alongside the car and stopping by Amir's door, waiting for him to exit. As beautiful as the grounds and the mansion were, Roxanna had no intention of putting her trust in someone who didn't have the courtesy to say a word to her the entire trip. "I am not getting out of this car...I need to speak to my Embassy."

Finally, in a surprisingly calm and gentle voice, he addressed her, "Ms. Fatemi, be more careful in choosing your friends. You have been used. People are not always who they say they are. We are not the bad guys. Remember that." Roxanna gave him a confusing look.

Amir started to reach over the front seat for something when his driver handed him a large envelope. He got out and greeted Khally affectionately before starting up the granite stairs with the envelope under his arm. Roxanna couldn't imagine that this man lived in such a beautiful mansion, but it was strange that, instead of barking, the dog greeted him as if he was the master of the house, wagging her tail and jumping all over him.

Amir leaned down enough to see Roxanna inside. "Someone will be out to get you." Then she watched as Amir went up several stairs and entered the house while Khally bounced over to the car, expecting Roxanna to smother her with attention. Yousef, the driver, opened the door for Roxanna and introduced Khally, suggesting they sit near the gardens to play while he went about cleaning and polishing the black car, obviously part of his job description.

Finally! Roxanna found someone who would listen to her; Khally. Nothing Amir had done made any sense to her, she explained to the dog. Why had he brought her to such luxurious surroundings if she were on her way to prison? He had not invited her into the house, given her any instructions, or told her when he was coming back, or even let her know if she was free to go. Khally let out a whine as if she understood Roxanna's frustration.

"That's right! You understand, totally! Sit! Stay!" Roxanna nodded, "Does anyone talk here beside you?" She looked at Yousef, who was now busy cleaning the windows. He smiled at her softly.

Roxanna couldn't have been more shocked to see Pary open the front door of the huge mansion and come out, stopping at the top of the stairs. That was the moment the pieces of the puzzle all started to come together. What appeared to have been a series of random, incongruous events had actually been a well-orchestrated, vicious massacre. Looking at Pary and the men she surrounded herself with, Roxanna realized they were not Savak but the resistance. But then, who and what was Amir? She was now more confused than ever. What was the purpose of taking her hostage, terrifying her, and setting up that awful interrogation?

She was beginning to realize that she was being used, a pawn in this dreadful political nightmare. The intensity and destruction of the bombing and the death of the little girl were horrific enough! Now, these same people, people who Roxanna thought were her friends, just put her through hell again. These were the very people who Amir was warning her about. Pary and Nader! Traitors! But why was he in the house, and why had he brought her there?

Pary was afraid that if she approached Roxanna, she might try to run away, so she and Khally finally sat on the step by the car. Feelings of anger and betrayal welled up inside of Roxanna. She wanted to scream and beat Pary for being a part of the horrendous acts she had been drawn into. She could not rationalize how people who called her a friend could treat her in such an unspeakable way.

Pary knew she would have to speak first if there was any chance of forgiveness. "I am sorry. I am really sorry for what happened. None of it is your fault, and they shouldn't have involved you in their mess. That was why I did not come to pick you up at the motel in the first place. After I met you, I felt I had to protect you. I fought them over involving you, but it was too late. Maybe I did not fight hard enough, or I should have told you to walk away. I did not know about the bombing..."

Roxanna felt betrayed, and no matter how hard she tried, nothing Pary would say could change that, "Sometimes we become confused and unusual circumstances blur decision making. The difference between good and bad becomes hazy. Emotions, not logic, end up making decisions for you. I do not believe in violence. I am for a nonviolent struggle. If able, I would do anything to fix or change the things that have happened."

By now, Roxanna was out of the car, "What can you possibly do for a little girl who's dead? She could have been your little girl." Pary swallowed hard, "I'm afraid if you stay longer, you'll see much worse."

Amir yelling at someone in the house distracted them. Pary explained that Amir was Cyrus's brother and that the mansion belonged to their mother, Hajji Khanoum, one of the most highly respected women in Tehran. Roxanna asked why Amir would be yelling at their mother like that.

Pary shook her head, concerned. "No one yells at their mother here... he is yelling at Cyrus." Pary had known them all their lives and was familiar with their arguing, but it had never escalated like this before. Concerned, she quickly walked to the door, peering to see if she could help the situation. But the door was locked, and she could only pace around and yell, trying to get their attention. She could feel them both erupting like volcanoes. Suddenly the argument switched to English.

Amir blasted, "I've had it with you! You hear me! Next time I'll put you and your radical friends away, myself! For God's sake, you should have a wife, children, and a steady job! What's wrong with you?" Their voices could be heard clearly through the door as Amir continued, "When are you going to grow up? You're getting old. What if I can't protect you? I hope you didn't waste money on a bribe! That ruthless Hajji Mohammad Zadeh should be hanged. Sign the document, or I will put both of you away!"

Pary explained to Roxanna, "They are arguing in English so their mother cannot understand. They do not want her to know what the fight is about."

Roxanna suddenly felt safe, knowing that Cyrus was inside. She followed Pary to a tall, open window where they had a clear view inside the living room.

Inside the house, Hajji Khanoum entered the living room, holding a tray with tea and a few pastries. She yelled at her sons not to fight, and they followed her wish.

Seething with anger, Cyrus rested the document on the window ledge and scribbled his name and a date on the document Amir had forced in front of him. If it was not for their mother, Hajji Khanoum, he might have lost control.

Despite the fact that Hajji Khanoum had no idea what her sons were arguing about, she silenced them. It didn't matter what the subject was, it was her house, and there were rules. Speaking in Farsi, she reprimanded them both, "Amir, leave your brother alone! Now both of you stop! No more yelling in this house as long as I am alive and breathing."

Hajji Khanoum was smart enough to know they were speaking in English because they did not want her to understand. She set the tray down and looked around to offer tea to Pary, but she was not there. She handed tea to Amir, addressing him while nodding towards Cyrus, "You know he won't argue with his older brother!"

Then she handed tea to Cyrus. He placed it on the window ledge and looked up at his mother as she continued, this time speaking directly to him. "You need to open your eyes and wise up before it's too late. Maybe Amir knows something we don't! Nobody knows everything." Then she looked around, her eyes searching. "Where is Pary? See what you, two, have done? You upset her. She left without taking tea."

Amir placed the tea on the table and turned to their mother, speaking calmly in Farsi, "Hajji Khanoum, he is not a child anymore." He turned to Cyrus, switching to English, "Just remember the deal. God knows if you break this agreement, I will have you and everyone else arrested and put away, forever!"

He headed out, but not before throwing a last jab at Cyrus, "I'm hoping to see the day when I can look you in the eyes and yell, 'this is my brother, Doctor Cyrus. That day, you'll have a proud mother, a proud brother, and a proud family."

*****

Amir exits quickly and looks towards Roxana and Pary, both sitting with innocent stares as if they hadn't been trying to listen to every word peeking through the window. Amir spoke only to Pary, "Watch after her; she is our guest." Yousef immediately jumped out of the car opened the door for Amir, quickly driving out of the circular driveway of the estate. Cyrus walked out of the house as his car drove away and sat with Roxanna and Pary in silence, giving Khally the attention she was craving even though she was dripping wet.

The door opened like a floodgate, and Hajji Khanoum made her presence known. "What are you doing out here in the rain? Who is that pretty lady? Why don't you bring her inside? She might think we didn't want her in our house. Have you both gone crazy? Bring her inside. She walked towards Roxanna; with a kind smile, motioning to her, inviting her inside as she also turned to Pary, "Where are your manners? Come inside, pretty lady," she said to Roxana in Farsi, gesturing again for her to come inside once more.

Roxana could tell the elegant woman was extending a sincere invitation. Loving Hajji Khanoum instantly, she didn't know what to do. She turned to Cyrus and Pary, looking for a cue. Cyrus smiled as he played with his dog Khally, "She's the boss. I don't think you have any chance of leaving here until you go inside, and she feeds you until your stomach aches." She quickly stood up and followed Cyrus's mother inside as if she was her own.

Pary took Roxanna's hand, and they escorted her inside, "Turning her invitation down would be rude…and impossible. Her intentions are kind and compassionate. You are her guest." Roxanna gave Cyrus's Mother a warm smile and answered while Pary translated after her. The women entered the house, leaving Cyrus outside with Khally. He took his dog over to a small shed and began drying her off with some old towels. They both needed comfort from the storm that raged outside and the infuriating situation that festered from within.

Inside, Roxanna hesitated before sitting on the beautiful furniture, but Pary nodded that it was alright for her to do so. Hajji Khanoum immediately brought more tea, pastries, and fruit while two other ladies began serving them. Soon there was more than enough fruit and pastry and food for ten people. Roxanna found it impossible to believe that Cyrus had been raised in such opulent surroundings.

She was glad she hadn't known that he came from a family of such wealth when she met him, or she might have been too intimidated to talk to him. Hajji Khanoum wasn't at all like she might have expected when she first saw her. Although she had women helping her, she took her role as hostess very seriously and did most of the work herself.

She was so different from her friends' mothers, the Beverly Hills housewives Roxanna had come in contact with over the years, the ones who spent their mornings getting manicures, afternoons shopping on

Rodeo Drive, and dining at Chasen's. She used to wish to be just like them one day.

Of course, that ended when she got older, but still, that lifestyle never felt shallower than it did now, comparing it to this lovely, hospitable woman standing in front of her, offering her tea and pastries. Hajji Khanoum set a new standard for elegance.

Roxanna was starting to believe that connecting with others was necessary to survive in this fearful, dangerous, and unpredictable environment. After the horrible bombing at the police station, every event, regardless of its apparent importance, was viewed through the new set of eyes and ears that Roxanna had been forced to develop. She was grateful that, for the moment, Hajji Khanoum was giving her a reprieve from living in fear.

"You must not be worried about those two crazy sons of mine. They fight, but I know they love each other. You must eat. You are too skinny. You may get sick… who is going to marry you when you are so skinny… eat… eat…"

Knowing Roxanna didn't speak Farsi, she turned to Pary, "tell your friend she must eat more meat so she can gain some weight. Why don't you eat… eat… if you do not eat, she may feel she is not welcome… eat… so she would eat!" She called to the maid and asked her to add more meat to the stew, and then she turned to Pary, "You should tell her to come here to eat. She will stay for dinner. Is she sick?"

Pary laughed and tried to explain to her that in America, the women would kill to be skinny. Hajji Khanoum was sure that everyone in America had lost their minds. She thanked God that she was not in America.

Pary and Roxanna watched Cyrus and Khally through the window, playing in the rain as they sipped their tea. Like Cyrus, Pary spoke in English, so Hajji Khanoum would be unable to understand. "After you were kidnapped, Peter went to Cyrus for help, and he asked his brother to get you out. They made him sign a note that he would not do any writing or make any movies for a while… before they would release you to him…

that was what they were yelling about. Cyrus has never gotten involved with such a matter. Ever. He must think a lot of you..."

Roxanna knew Pary was right. She felt the deep connection whenever Cyrus looked at her, and she saw it in his eyes. It was immediate and undeniable. The two women stood beside each other, watching Cyrus, who was now playing with Khally in the drenching rain. Roxanna watched Parry while she looked at him. Her face seemed to soften. She knew, then, that Pary loved him as well.

Cyrus was not aware of Pary's feelings towards him. She had never revealed her love in any way. The pain of rejection would have been too much to bear. They had grown up together hiking, riding bikes, and horses. His thoughts about her were as his little sister, best friend, and confidant, not as a lover. It was Roxanna that had caught his attention in that way. She touched his heart.

*****

The next morning, the rain had finally subsided, and rays of golden sunlight sliced through a small opening in the white curtain of the guest room Hajji Khanoum had made up for her, illuminating Roxanna's face. In contrast to the freshness of a new day, Roxanna looked weak and tired and drained, like a lost dog in a rainstorm.

She had been exhausted after having gone through so many sleepless nights and had hoped to finally start putting the past behind her but found it impossible. Immediately upon awakening, the image of the little girl came rushing back into her head, and she sat up abruptly, her heart racing, her nerves on edge.

The previous night, when Roxanna was afraid her presence might be an intrusion, she politely attempted to leave, but Hajji Khanoum had stopped her. She told Pary to tell her they would be staying indefinitely and asked the maid to take her to a lovely guest room. Enjoying the challenge of being unable to speak directly to her guest, she cleverly let

Roxanna knows all the sheets were fresh, patting the bed and pantomimed sheets hanging on a clothesline, waving in the breeze, and being folded.

Cyrus and Pary watched, amused, allowing Hajji Khanoum total control over the situation, realizing that this was the safest place for her at the moment. Roxanna and Pary, who had been given the room next to her, sat up talking late into the night, bringing their voices down to a low pitch whenever Cyrus was the subject, aware that his room was on their left.

*****

The following day, sitting next to Cyrus driving through the streets of Tehran, Roxanna's mind drifted from one lovely, memorable experience she'd had with Cyrus to another. Her thoughts were brought to the present by the sudden breaking by Cyrus as he drove along the outskirts of Tehran, stopping at one of his favorite places by a stream to give Roxanna a closer look at the incredibly beautiful, crystal-clear water.

It was one of the most delightful afternoons she had ever spent, sitting with Cyrus, watching pupfish as they darted amongst the waves of seagrass, swaying gently in the current. From there, they picked up some food for a light dinner and continued driving until they turned onto an inconspicuous, private dirt road which led them over a small rustic bridge, just rickety enough to add an element of danger to the adventure.

Cyrus stopped the car behind a natural wall of trees and bushes hiding them from view and motioned for Roxanna to wait while he started removing piles of dead branches put there to block the pathway to a cottage. She watched as Cyrus disappeared down the path that led to wooden steps, warped from age and harsh weather. She waited for what felt like an eternity for Cyrus to call her to join him, but he never did.

Starting to get a little nervous, she followed the steps until, as if by magic, she found herself standing in front of a quaint, one-room cottage, surrounded by a wreath of wildflowers stretching to the river; a scene more beautiful than anything she'd ever seen in a painting by Claude Monet.

She knocked on the door, assuming Cyrus was already inside, but he appeared from behind, holding a sweet bouquet of wildflowers, a tapestry of fragrance, lingering seductively in the air. Roxanna blushed at his thoughtful and loving gesture. Once the delicate flowers were safely in Roxanna's care, he searched under rocks before he found what he was searching for. A key.

He dangled it playfully in the air and beckoned for Roxanna to follow as he opened the door. Cyrus had turned the abandoned cottage into a secret hideaway, a place for him, alone, to reconnect with his inner thoughts, to unwind and create. Roxanna looked around, intrigued, while Cyrus got the food from the car and searched for something that resembled a vase to put the wildflowers in. He decided an empty jar would have to do.

To Roxanna, the cottage was nothing short of magnificent in its sparseness. A small old, wooden desk with a typewriter held the central focus of the room. Against one wall was a metal icebox; the other, a bookcase reached from floor to ceiling. On the couch, a few blankets and a pillow sent a clear message that it was where Cyrus slept.

Roxanna was happy to note there was a small bathroom concealed from view by a white curtain. No shower and no electricity, just oil lamps and candles of all shapes and sizes. And underneath it all, a Persian rug pulled everything together and warmed the cottage, the necessities of life, and nothing more.

"This is my sanctuary, a place for me to meditate and find myself. I learn about who I am through my writing. I just feel. And that's when I hear voices. That's when the stories that need to be told come to me and tell themselves. This is where I read and study and learn about the world and the insanity that rules it. No one knows anything about the cottage but you, Pary, and Peter."

Roxanna looked around, cherishing the moment, feeling closer to Cyrus than she could have ever imagined. It was like a holy place, her silence acknowledging the importance of their surroundings. Cyrus lit several candles, which reflected in Roxanna's eyes, making them dance, "Why do you trust me enough to bring me here?"

Cyrus shrugged and smiled. "I don't know why, except that you're my guest, and you would have no reason to hurt me. And you're rather pretty ... and maybe a little crazy." Roxanna laughed at his boldness. Cyrus couldn't take his eyes off her.

"Are you laughing at 'rather pretty' or 'little crazy?'"

"Both. I can see why you love it here. It makes me feel ... safe. When I was a little girl, and we were in a crowd, my mother would always pick a place for me to wait if I ever got lost!"

Cyrus looked concerned. "Did you ever get lost?"

Roxanna nodded fearfully, reliving the moment. "We were at Disneyland, and she told me I was supposed to wait on the bridge to Sleeping Beauty's castle if I ever got lost! But she forgot what she told me and went to the carousel! Fortunately, when I wasn't there, she remembered she was in the wrong place! And I wasn't the one who got lost. She did!"

Cyrus stopped emptying the paper bags and looked directly into her eyes, "If we ever get separated, or you have an emergency, you know where the key is. Make your way here, and I will know where to find you. Both Cyrus and Roxanna could feel the strong attraction that was developing between them as, together, they set out a simple, lovely meal of Persian herbs and feta cheese, fresh and dried fruits, and exotic flatbreads.

Roxanna rinsed the dishes with water from the stream while Cyrus carried jars of candles outside and lit up the porch for them to sit in the cool air and take in the night. Sitting next to her, he held out a small flower, plucked gently from its sepal, and showed her how to suck out the sweetness. There was something about darkness, he said, that woke up the senses; honey was sweeter, more delicious, smells lingered, sounds of nature more meaningful. The body came alive.

After tuning in to their own senses for a while, listening to the sounds of the stream, the chirping of birds and insects, the rustling of leaves...Cyrus became serious. The senses, he told her, like the stream, were for cautious wading... they were an early warning system, sensing unknown danger. This time, when they sat in silence, they were more alert, listening for changes in sounds, birds and insects going silent, signifying someone's approach.

Were the sounds of the stream interrupted, suddenly less melodic? Louder? Someone wading? A boat? Footsteps? And then the howl of a lone wolf was heard, friend or not? Roxanna knew Cyrus was trying to prepare her for times when he might not be around... When she had only herself to depend on for survival.

Their talk was light-hearted at times and very intense at others, as they reviewed everything that had happened since that night when they first laid eyes on one another. Cyrus had a child-like wonder about him when he spoke about life and relationships, his dry wit often taking her by surprise. Sometimes when he spoke, it was difficult to determine whether he was joking with her or not, but she loved trying to figure it out, figure him out. He was a mystery that was slowly unraveling in front of her eyes, at the same time entwining their hearts, one moment at a time.

Roxanna's eyes traced Cyrus's figure in the stars as they talked. He was Orion, the supernatural hunter helping and protecting her. He was Leo, the lion who could not be killed by mortal weapons. When he had to walk to the stream to get water to warm over the fire, he told Roxanna exactly what he was doing so she wouldn't worry.

She followed him as far as the porch, studying his every move, noticing the lovely symmetry of his body, his ample shoulders, well-defined arms, and his strong legs, each muscle fighting against the fabric of his jeans. To Cyrus, she was simply the brightest star he had ever seen.

Back inside, Cyrus moved about his little nest in the woods with comfort, building a fire in the fireplace and making a rustic bed on the floor. Each cozy makeshift bed by the side of the small, stone fireplace. They were so close they could hold hands if wanted. The oil lamp was dead. Only the dance of the fire from the fireplace on the wall heated the room.

Roxanna wondered why Cyrus didn't attempt to kiss her or make love to her when everyone else was racing to. She thought maybe he wasn't attracted to her. Cyrus wanted desperately to touch her. But he was trying to follow a certain philosophy, one where women, children, and animals were innocent and not to be abused. Given the complexity of the situation, he was keeping his distance.

Cyrus spoke looking, directly into Roxana's eyes, "So you are here to find your father since we are both unemployed…why don't we do just that? Roxanna's thoughts of kissing Cyrus were tossed to the side as she was shocked by his words, staring back deeply.

*****

Chapter 12

Following an Unchartered Journey, in an Unknown Land called Persia...

Tehran was always famous for its lively bazaars, especially the lavish displays by gold vendors that enticed tourists to loosen their purse strings and walk away with treasures that could be passed down from one generation to another. The streets were a study in architecture; buildings with ornate carvings reflected the many influences of both the east and the West.

Along the streets were the artisans of ancient times, memorialized in stone and brick, stucco reliefs, tile murals, and fluted stone columns. Simply walking through the bazaar would capture the imagination, pulling one's senses back thousands of years. Almost the entire country's merchandise distribution system was set up at the bazaar and had not changed for centuries. The exquisite structures that surround the bazaar bear witness to their history.

Roxanna waited in a cramped corner in the gold bazaar, fascinated by the crowded mile-long conglomeration of shops glittering with riches, gold-laced bowls, statues, jewelry, bangles, ornamental trays, Persians tapestries, rugs, cloth, and fine teas and herbs. The Bazaar, which stretched several blocks, was covered on the ceiling with its original design, so shoppers didn't have to worry about the rain or sun as they strolled through.

Roxanna was awestruck and amazed at the total sensory overload she was experiencing. Each store had gold jewelry dripping from every corner. It hung from the walls and ceilings in excess as if it was raining gold. What amazed Roxanna the most was that none of the stores had security cameras or security of any kind, and clerks would regularly leave their booths unattended to prepare for prayer.

She was aware that people were approaching her to look at her unfamiliar type of beauty in admiration. They were a little shy, but some gestured a hello. This distraction from searching for her father was uplifting, a pleasant diversion from all that had happened since her arrival in Tehran. She could never have imagined such an intriguing place. As with everything in Iran, the gold Bazaar affected all the senses and had to be experienced and witnessed in person to be appreciated and understood.

On their drive, Cyrus had attempted to explain his disappearance a few nights earlier. He had gone to do some research on Roxanna's father through his connections. Nader was a great help, confirming that her father existed, but no one knew where he could be found. His knowledge of Roxanna's family, consisting of the fact that he used to be one of the biggest merchants in the old Bazaar, leads Cyrus and Roxanna to the jewelry Bazaar.

He wanted to ensure her safety from now on, and as far as he was concerned, she was only safe as long as she was with him and his family. To be sure nothing happened to her, Cyrus made the decision to continue to assist Roxanna's efforts in trying to locate her father, himself, insuring they would always be together.

But in a way ... without admitting it to himself, he was looking for a story for his next film as all writers and filmmakers do. He knew how important finding Assad was to her. Clearly, if that had not been true, she would have left Iran, especially considering the horrible events that had occurred.

Besides his genuine concern for Roxanna, Cyrus had developed very strong feelings for her. Not only was he moved by her kindness and physical as well as inner beauty, but he also found her intriguing and headstrong, a trait he was unfamiliar with in a woman, one which he found very refreshing...and attractive.

She was his window to a world unknown to him. Through her, he heard stories about her wonderful country, a land where so much was possible. It was a world he had only dreamed of, a place where he could live out his passions, writing, acting, and making movies without persecution and live out his Hollywood dream.

Cyrus had surprised her by informing her he would do whatever he could to assist her in finding her father and that Nader had given him a lead. Roxanna felt that if there was any hope, Cyrus would be the one who could do just that. What little she had learned about him had come from his mother and Pary, and it was all stellar though highly prejudiced, Roxanna guessed. Having learned that he had connections to both the government and the opposition and being loved by both sides, she had no reason not to be confident that he could succeed.

She had been attracted to him from the very beginning, but the more time they spent together, the deeper her feelings for him grew. He was a master of finding something positive in even the most tragic situations. She loved the fact that he was quite a prankster, always looking for a way to play a joke on someone to get a smile. He also had a very serious, intense side of his personality that made him feel solid, someone you could depend on in an emergency. They were qualities she considered necessary for survival in a country so full of tragedy.

The more time they spent together, the more she realized Cyrus possessed the rare and important attributes of a man with integrity and character, exactly what she wanted in a man.

When Cyrus finally returned from his playful interrogation of all the gold vendors, he had a huge smile on his face. Pointing to a stall, he informed Roxanna, "That place used to be your grandfather's, but after his death, and when your father was arrested, the store was sold. This happened a long time ago, and no one knows what became of his family."

Roxanna was hungry for any good news, and this was enough to quench her appetite. On one hand, she was ecstatic and, on the other, disheartened because it seemed like her father was so close but just out of reach. None of the information they had received so far had led her directly to him. They were nothing more than small crumbs, clues, leading them forward, but not to anything. Cyrus, on the other hand, seeing every clue as a challenge waiting to be met, took her hand and squeezed it enthusiastically.

Roxanna noticed something catch Cyrus's eye. From her point of view, it looked like he was staring at a stack of boxes, neatly balanced, one on top of another, swaying precariously, traveling through the Bazaar's traffic. But looking closer, she saw that, underneath it, all was an old man, doubled over from years of carrying heavy loads. "Come on! If someone might know something, it would be him! He is one of the oldest porters here."

Cyrus pulled her through the crowd towards the old man. As they approached, Roxanna could see that the boxes were actually strapped to his back. The weight was so heavy it caused the old man to almost bend completely in half, at a right angle from his waist, his face looking directly to the ground. Years of being forced into this unnatural posture had deformed him.

Roxanna felt tremendous sympathy for this broken man, forced to spend his life doing backbreaking work in order to feed his family. It gave her a better understanding of the discontent among many Iranians. This old man was a symbol of so many others who suffered great physical, emotional, and financial pain in the midst of the liquid gold, jewels, and rare objects that surrounded them.

Roxanna witnessed that there was a new system for transporting and distributing goods at the bazaar and that the porters no longer carried boxes on their backs, but Cyrus explained, some who were from the older generations, like the old man, were unable to adapt. The shop owners understood this and would give them their lighter boxes because of their loyalty to them.

The man stopped to unload. Cyrus approached and helped him unstrap the boxes. Even after he got out from under the weight, he was unable to stand upright, now, as suspected, permanently deformed by a grotesque curve starting from his neck and traveling halfway down his backbone. Still, Roxanna was able to distinguish a look of pleasure appearing on his face when he recognized that it was Cyrus who had helped him, almost as if he had been looking for him.

Roxanna was taken with the kindness Cyrus showed as he helped the old man to a table at the teahouse nearby. She was surprised when the tea arrived almost immediately, and Cyrus picked up a sugar cube and put it in the man's tea for him. And then she realized he was making it easier for the old man to drink. Unable to sit up straight, he forced his head back to sip the sweet, hot tea to keep it from spilling out of his mouth.

Her mother would have told her to avert her eyes as if that was supposed to be polite, but it felt more important to Roxanna to let him know that she accepted him the way he was, so she smiled at him pleasantly. She couldn't help but again think about how he was a metaphor for Iran and its people.

Roxanna sipped her tea from a lovely glass cup as she watched Cyrus go through all his rituals. He grabbed a sugar cube from the small, rounded plate under his teacup and placed it in his own mouth. Then he poured the tea into the small saucer underneath the cup and began to drink. Impressed, Roxanna smiled and copied him thinking that perhaps he had done it to cool the tea.

Cyrus smiled back at her and nodded towards the old man. Knowing immediately what he was thinking, she pulled Assad's latest photo out of her pocket and laid it in front of him. Cyrus, in turn, held it out to the old porter.

"Father, my name is Cyrus, and this is my friend Roxanna. She has traveled a very long distance to try to find her father, who she hasn't seen in many, many years. It is our hope that you would be kind enough to help us. We know that at one time, his family owned a shop right on the other side of the bazaar. His name is Assad. Our hope is that since you have been here for so long, you might know him."

The porter didn't hear a word that Cyrus said. He had more important things on his mind, like the young porter that was using a cart on wheels to transport boxes. It would be impossible for Cyrus to get his attention until he was sure the young man saw his disapproving look.

Finally, Cyrus reached in his pocket and took out some money that he tucked in the old man's pocket, hoping that might help. Insulted, the old man pushed the money back towards Cyrus. "The most honored things in life cannot be bought. My loyalty and advice are free or not at all." He said. Cyrus nodded, "Her grandfather was Hajji Fatemi. I am sure you must have heard of him."

A faint smile came across the porter's face as he took the picture in his hands and held it as if it might break. To him, the photo of young Assad with his father standing by their old store was truly a treasure that made him weak. Cyrus was certain the old Porter would have known Roxanna's grandfather, even if he didn't know Assad, and it frustrated him that he wasn't getting the information he was looking for. Roxanna, though, understood that it was hard for him to think, being in such pain.

Two hours later, Roxanna, Cyrus, and the old man were sitting with a few others, eating Abgoosht. She learned his name was Kal Ahmad and that he was an institution in himself, having worked in the gold bazaar for over 50 years. His stories were plentiful and entertaining, but he was yet to tell one they were waiting to hear.

Roxanna found the smells of turmeric and cinnamon almost too enticing to resist, but still, she was not willing to sample the dish until she knew exactly what was in it. Abgoosht was known as a working man's stew and was a combination of chickpeas and white beans, tomatoes, potatoes, onions, Persian lime, and lamb shank. Cyrus told her it was best when you smash it.

Roxanna made a funny face, assuming he was joking. He placed a little of everything in a bowl, drained the liquid off, "Now khoob mykoobemesh…", showing her that it meant mashing it up. He placed some of the concoction inside a piece of warm sangak bread and topped it with sliced onions, yogurt, fresh vegetables, and herbs. He took a bite and savored it, then held it out towards Roxanna. It was too tempting to resist. She took a bite and loved it, now completely convinced of her love for Persian food.

The crowded teahouse was entertained by Roxanna and her delighted reaction as she let the flavors roll around in her mouth. It was like watching someone eat their first cheeseburger and fries. The waiter came around and brought Roxanna some more tea and nabbat, bits of hard rock candy used in some restaurants instead of sugar cubes.

After two hours and some gentle, non-threatening coaxing from Cyrus, Kal Ahmad told them that after Assad had been arrested by the government, things were never the same for Hajji Fatemi. Later it was rumored that Assad had escaped from jail or had been let free and fled the country. He just disappeared, and the bottom line was, no one knew what happened to him.

After his disappearance, Assad's father never found peace. He knew that he and his family were being watched. Kal Ahmad continued, telling Roxanna that her grandfather had died of a broken heart after his favorite son, Assad, was arrested and jailed, then disappeared. Heartache ate away his soul when he realized that there was nothing, he could do to protect his son.

After his death, his youngest son, Akbaar, who later became a wrestling champ, decided to sell the store. He wasn't a businessman, and after being cheated out of a lot of money, he took his family and went back to their old farm. The old man told them that he used to go to Hajji Fatemi's house and deliver goods to the family. He thought the name was Ghamssar but would have to check for sure.

Roxanna noticed a smile on Cyrus's face and knew he must have heard some kind of good news. He put some money on the table to pay their bill and then thanked the porter many times, patting him on his bent and broken back before escorting Roxanna towards the door.

*****

Roxanna couldn't help but reflect upon the great spirit of this man she had not known, her grandfather. The long-standing love and loyalty that he must have felt for her father. Walking through the alley with Cyrus, she watched a woman near the entrance to the alley put her groceries on the ground to catch her breath while her two small children, ignoring her pleas to stay close, ran off to play.

A few more women and children gathered around a late-model black Cadillac where the young boy who had been handing out free meat stood, handing it out from the trunk. Roxanna caught a glimpse of the beautiful woman dressed all in black, sitting in the back seat of the sparkling Cadillac. She, too, was handing out packages of paper-wrapped sacrificed meat, a traditional event.

Whoever has any kind of wish or desires to be blessed by God or the holy messengers gives away meat to the poor. This tradition was brought about by Abraham, then Mohammad, to prevent the Arab tribes from killing their newborn daughters. Abraham and Mohammad changed the custom to have a sheep sacrificed instead of an infant girl.

Later, as times changed, traditions transformed again, and it became the practice of rich people to distribute sacrificed meat and food to the poor and those who lived in poorer neighborhoods. The meat or food carried a blessing from God or one of the holy messengers. Whoever ate it would be blessed.

During that time, it was common for rich women from the upper north side to drive to the south side and hand out sacrificed meat to the poor. The chauffeur, dressed in a black suit and tie, helped the woman distribute the meat along with pictures of the royal family.

The little boy held a package of meat out to Roxanna along with a photo of the royal family. Cyrus let the boy know that she did not need the meat, but the child insisted until, finally, she smiled softly and accepted the package.

Cyrus gently guided Roxanna to his car parked on the side, and soon, they were moving away from the scene. She thought about how different things were in Iran compared to Los Angeles. Such simple acts of kindness shown towards others less fortunate than themselves gave Roxanna the strength to continue her search for her father.

*****

Racing the sunset, Cyrus's car sped toward the flames from the Tehran Oil Refinery exhaust, flickering against a gloomy sky. Soon the flame was behind them. They were now headed for the village of Haykal. Kal Ahmad, the porter at the Bazaar, had given them enough information to guide them to her mother's relatives.

As they traveled towards their destination, Cyrus delighted Roxanna by sharing what he had learned. Kal Ahmad and Nader had a great amount of helpful information. Each story was a voyage of discovery, an adventure filled with intrigue and excitement. Like a hidden treasure, every word held a clue.

And like a puzzle, it was up to them to fit each piece together, creating a bigger picture. Roxanna didn't want Cyrus to ever stop. If she had her way, she would have had him translating all day and all night. For the first time in her life, she was learning about her family! Her relatives! She was ecstatic! Mostly, though, she was shocked that she was the center of all that was important to her father.

The words she had dreamed of her entire life were in the notebook being read to her by Cyrus. She hadn't been abandoned by her father! Assad's love was for Roxanna, and he was devoted to finding her. It described how he had been looking for his lost daughter all throughout his life, but that he couldn't get a visa to return to America. Roxanna cried endless tears.

*****

Chapter 13

Two Cultures Clash as Two Generations Face One Another over What is Done and Not Done ...

Deep bluish-green, iridescent hummingbirds were delightfully zipping through a grove of lush trees; the hum of their flapping wings joining the symphony of honeybees buzzing around the flowers blanketing the field. Sitting in the car in front of a roadside teahouse several hundred miles outside of Tehran, Roxanna was captivated by nature's concerto.

Her surroundings were a feast for the senses. Unlike teahouses in Tehran, where everyone was familiar with each other, this was more functional, a place where travelers would stop along the road to eat and rest before continuing on to their destination. The patrons were a melting pot of the varied ethnicities that make Iran so magnificent.

The countryside also had a very different atmosphere than Tehran, relaxed and much more at ease. Even the scent of the air was different, delicious. Food was being served and eaten very informally. It seemed to Roxanna that everyone was playful and joyous, and laughter and happiness were in abundance. Rich and poor sat side by side, bringing the tea-house alive.

Her thoughts drifted from the peaceful scene to images filled with wonder when her eyes caught Cyrus asking a waiter for directions. She smiled, studying his stature, his confidence, the way people looked at him with respect and admiration. She was thankful that Hajji Khanoum had put her in Cyrus' care. He planned their schedule every day, and it always revolved around her two favorite things: food and finding her father.

Cyrus had been diligently hunting for information through his connections from both the government and the opposition, only to hit one dead end after another. Still, he was a champion of her cause.

The fact that he was always respectful and didn't take advantage of their friendship made him all the more desirable to Roxanna. She wanted to know everything about Cyrus. What she knew of him was mostly from observation. It seemed he was born with a twinkle in his eye that grew even brighter because of his childlike sense of mischief. She knew he loved to laugh but, more importantly, loved to make others laugh. She loved that his life revolved around his passions and goals, motivated by his desire to change the world.

Their hunt for her father brought them to this teahouse and its owner, miles away from Tehran. Familiar with the surroundings and the routine of his regular customers, the owner appeared to be offering Cyrus some insight. He walked briskly out of the teahouse, followed by Cyrus, and pointed in the direction of a carriage, which was traveling on the dirt road.

Cyrus jumped in his car and started down the road, turning to Roxanna. "Your grandmother is somewhere on the other side of that hill." Roxanna could tell by his look that this wasn't another one of his jokes. She stared straight ahead in total disbelief, urging him to go faster as he raced down a small dirt road with switchback curves.

Further on, workers rested in the cool shade of a planet tree. Cyrus noticed Roxanna looking at them curiously, "It's traditional to take a brief nap after lunch. Most people do. It helps digest your food and recharges your body."

It had never occurred to Roxanna that either of her grandparents might still be alive, so the possibility of actually meeting her grandmother was terrifying. As Cyrus drove up the winding dirt road, Roxanna tried to imagine what the old woman would be like and wondered if she would be pleased that she had come. She was thinking and wishing that she might meet someone like Hajji Khanoum. Cyrus told her she would not be pleased and that she was a hermit with chin hairs, causing Roxanna to, accidentally on purpose, punch him in the thigh.

When Cyrus finally stopped the car at the top of the hill, their eyes fell upon a beautiful multi-colored farm, framed by a sunlit panorama brushed with shades of green and grey. It was springtime, and the farm was nothing short of a masterful painting highlighting a variety of fruit trees and farm animals as far as the eye could reach. The shrubbery and trees along the creek flourished in their environment and glowed with vibrant colors only good soil can create.

A young boy started running towards them, but when he realized they didn't look familiar, he turned and ran toward the house where a stoic older woman was sitting on the porch. Yelling toward her, "Guest coming! Guest coming!" Roxanna noticed the woman was resting on a red cushion atop a Persian rug. She had white hair and was smoking tobacco through a hookah.

Unsure of what their welcome might be, Cyrus pulled up directly in front of the house and waited, politely, for an invitation. When none came, they got out and stood by their car. Just then, a mature servant woman, Zahra, stepped out onto the porch and studied them curiously, leaving it up to the woman on the cushion to greet the unannounced guests.

"I'm guessing if we are at the right place, that she's your grandmother," Cyrus said to Roxanna in a soft whisper.

Goosebumps ran down her spine as she watched Zahra walk toward her, studying her face. "Her name is Roxanna...she came all the way from America to see her grandmother. She is Assad's daughter." Cyrus said in Farsi.

Zahra was unable to control her joyful emotions. She stretched out her arms and ran to Roxanna, pulling her into a powerful embrace as if she were a found princess. She kissed Roxanna many times, calling to the grandmother, "Dooayat mostajab sheh, Belakhareh omad."

"God answered your prayer. She finally came!" Zahra ran to the older woman and then back to Roxanna, taking her hand and pulling her along. Cyrus respected Roxanna's need to meet her grandmother without interference, so he stayed back, wanting to remain an observer, not a participant, for the time being.

Tears traveled down the wrinkles on the old woman's face. She was choking with mixed emotion as she reached out and opened her arms to embrace Roxanna. "Man, hech vaght nemymordam ta to rabebennam..."

"I refused to die without seeing you. Come give me a hug. You're beautiful. You don't have to tell me who you are. I know you are my beautiful granddaughter. Finally, you came to me from the other side of the world. Come! I am your grandmother," Cyrus laughed and began translating as he leaned against the edge of the porch.

Roxanna walked to the old woman and embraced her while she continued to speak Farsi, with Cyrus continuing to translate, "Tell her I'm crying because I am so happy, tell her not to feel sad." Roxanna could feel her grandmother's wet tears against her own skin as the old woman continued, "Let me look at you good. I've waited for a long, long time for this moment. You resemble your father so much."

There was much hugging and kissing going on as the culture requires when you see your loved one after a long time; to express your love as well as the physical touching of each other's hair, cheeks, and hearts. Not to mention Zahra's dancing! It was the language of love, the way a mother and baby would bond in the first weeks. Her grandmother reached her frail arms out towards Roxanna's face, softly touching her tears. There was so much joy between the three women that the world forgot Cyrus ever existed.

An older man, Mashty, holding on to his shovel, stood close by, staring right at Cyrus, never taking his eyes off him. Mashty was in charge, running the farm for Roxanna's grandmother. By the sour look on his face, he was obviously disgruntled with Cyrus but was choosing not to act on his suspicions so soon. Cyrus decided to ignore him.

*****

Chapter 14

When You Cross the Line Drawn and Challenge Your Own Culture, Hoping No One is Watching...

As the weeks passed, Roxanna became more and more disheartened. Despite all her connections, she had been unable to come up with any information regarding her father's whereabouts. She could only hope he was still alive. She was no closer to finding her father than she was when she left Tehran, but she had found a huge piece of the puzzle, her grandmother. The woman she descended from this made her happier than she had ever been in her life.

Roxanna enjoyed every aspect of farm life, from rising early to milk the cows, to planting vegetables, to driving a tractor. She especially loved being around Zahra, who had taught her how to milk the cows as well as bake bread, make yogurt and make traditional Persian foods. Roxanna fell in love with the flavorful spices: turmeric, saffron, and especially fresh mint and hot bread.

When her grandmother was invited to a wedding celebration near her farm, she insisted that Cyrus and Roxanna go with her and enjoy the festivities.

Roxanna was surprised to find out that the celebrations last almost twenty-four hours. She learned that a musician bellows out raunchy tunes while the groom is first taken to the public bathhouse by friends, dancing and singing on the way there and back. Of course, the bride gets to experience the same treatment. The bride is then dressed in bright, beautifully colored fabrics that drape over her body along with a soft, flowing veil that frames her face.

Friends and family walk with the bride to carry her "jahazyeh," her dowry, to her new home, which includes an abundance of household goods that the bride will need. People gather to watch as the bride and jahazyeh make their way down the street to the sound of beautiful traditional music. That night brings the main ceremony when everyone gathers at the groom's house. They celebrate throughout the evening until way past midnight with dinner, dancing, and music."

For Roxanna, the bridal ornament, which was adorned with colorful and cheerful fabrics, was exciting. She was especially fascinated by traditional music, which was played with traditional instruments, a large drum called "Dohol," and something similar to saxophone call "Saz." Grandmother searched her colorful traditional wardrobe for something appropriate for Roxanna to wear to the wedding reception. For Roxana, that looked right and was quoted by the parliament, especially when Cyrus got her to dance in a group with him and the other men while the groom was walking around the village and dancing in front of them, breaking the old-time tradition.

Mrs. Zahra joined Roxana so that she would not feel bitterly lonely and started dancing. Besides, it had won the admiration of all the ladies. But the older generations in the villages were very strict with their women. It was customary that only immediate family members were allowed near their women. Mashty was no exception in his thinking when now he watched Roxana and Zahra Mashty's wife had broken the spell for a moment. And this angered Mashty to madness.

Soon the opportunity arose for Mashty to let Cyrus know who was in charge when Mashty led one of the dances when they were taking the groom around the village to celebrate as custom required.

Several men of all ages were holding hands firmly and dancing following the lead man, who was Mashty, carried a wooden stick, and when someone tripped or made a mistake, the man gave him a gentle hit.

They were dancing in time to the Soz and Dohol. He immediately eyed Cyrus, who was at the end of the group. Mashty was dancing with a fury, grasping the stick with his fist and hitting Cyrus over and over, again. One thing was crystal clear; Mashty had no use for Cyrus and did not want him around.

He was in his seventies yet still functioned like a well-oiled machine. Still, he was no match for someone one-third his age. His challenge to Cyrus was wearisome, and Cyrus's frustration was fast approaching the tipping point. Considering Mashty's working position in the family, Cyrus felt he had overstepped his authority. Nevertheless, whatever he might do to stand up to Mashty needed to be discreet and calculated.

Cyrus smoothly broke away from the dancing group and began dancing with Roxanna. This deliberate move clearly enraged Mashty, who found this kind of brazen behavior completely unacceptable, even more so because he believed it had been done to humiliate him in front of an audience. The celebration lasted throughout the night and until an hour after midnight. The ceremony continued with guests sitting on the floor in a group, eating food and a traditional show.

*****

Every once in a while, Roxanna and Cyrus would sneak away to a secret spot they had found deep in the rocky hills which had become their private oasis, discussing what to do, to wait longer or continue on their journey? There was a small waterfall flowing into a clear river that glistened in the sun. Private and secluded, it was perfect for diving and disappearing under the water. Cyrus wore only his shorts, but Roxanna kept her dress on in case any villagers showed up, as it would not be proper for her to be wearing a bathing suit.

Cyrus was overwhelmed with the desire to touch her. He watched the way her dress clung, translucent, to her body as she waded out of the water, yearning to hold her and feel the warmth of her body next to his. The thin cotton fabric with small delicate blue flowers outlined her feminine curves as if the fabric was the canvas and she, herself, the work of art. He could see the gentle roundness of her taut belly, her breasts gracefully displayed, nipples straining against the fabric of her dress. A masterpiece, in his eyes, she was the personification of Claude Monet's Water Lily Pond, standing on the small bridge, looking down on him.

Cyrus was hypnotized by the scent of her body, the slight touch of her skin on his as she cupped his arm and took his hand, touching his fingers to her lips. All he wanted in the world was to feel her embrace, her lips touch his. Just as the moment was electric, and if he could have wished it, it would have gone on forever, his reverie was shattered by the sound of someone slipping on loose gravel, followed by the sound of rocks careening down a hill and splashing in the water. Cyrus didn't have to look up to know what caused the slide. He had a feeling they were being watched all along. He abruptly withdrew from Roxanna's gentle touch and stood defiantly towards the shadow of a crouching man in the distance. He knew it was Mashty, at least he hoped it was. As much as he disliked the man, there were worse options.

Exposed, Mashty stepped out into the open, hollering for them to follow as if God had sent him, personally, to fetch them. Before anyone could react, they were torn away by a younger boy yelling toward them, asking them to come back home.

When Cyrus and Roxanna were a few hundred yards from the house, they could see that several people had arrived in four or five cars and were gathered on the balcony looking their way. A tall, muscular man in his late fifties postponed entering the bathroom outside the house when he saw them approaching. When Roxanna noticed the man's priorities change so drastically upon their arrival, she knew something important was about to happen. Hesitating, she turned to Cyrus, "Is he my father?"

There was a stunned look on Cyrus's face when he finally got a good look at the man. It was a look of awe. He spoke to Roxanna in a hushed voice, "I don't think so. He is a world-famous wrestling champion. Our champions are much respected in Iran. They live very simply, and he is a good example of a great man."

Completely ignoring Cyrus, Zahra rushed toward Roxanna and seized her hand, pulling her up the stairs, past several guests, and into the house. Cyrus was too focused on the champ to even notice! All he cared about was waiting for the champ to exit the bathroom so he could have a chance to speak with him.

Inside the house, a group of women were sitting around her grandmother, all with tea in hand. A few men sat on the other side of the room, talking amongst themselves. When Roxanna entered, everyone rose, except for her grandmother, approaching her like excited puppies, all trying to see the beautiful Roxanna and lavish her with affectionate hugs and kisses.

Honored as she was by all the attention, Roxanna was focused on the front door. She was waiting for the man in the bathroom to join them, still hoping, by some miraculous gift, that he was her father. Careful not to insult the genuine kindness of these loving people, she gently disengaged herself from their embraces so that she could look for Cyrus, who entered after Akbaar.

Roxanna held her breath, frozen with fear, as Akbaar approached her and placed one hand on each of her shoulders. He had a formidable presence, much bigger and more muscular than she had imagined her father to be. He gently squeezed her, looked into her eyes for a moment, then bent over and kissed her forehead. Softly, speaking in broken English, he said, "So you are the daughter. Me, your uncle Akbaar."

"My uncle? Not my father?" She whispered hoarsely, trying to mask her disappointment.

A smile appeared on Akbaar's face, "Yes, your uncle." He sensed her sadness, and in an attempt to soften her failed expectations, he said, "Only a slight difference between uncle and father here. Uncle loves you ... father loves you ... the same."

She was taken away by Zahra, who took her hand and asked her to sit by her grandmother. When she sat down, her grandmother kissed her, stroked her head, and ruffled her hair. She was clearly proud of her and took every opportunity to show her off to the ladies. "This is my beautiful grandchild. She came all the way from the other side of the world, from America." Then she turned to Roxanna, "These are some of your relatives. They have come to meet you."

She was introduced to them slowly, so it was easier to remember their names. Each relative handed Roxanna a gift as they were introduced. Unable to contain his excitement, Akbaar began to translate, using his broken English. Soon, Roxanna's lap was covered with presents, each one handed to her, along with a kiss on each cheek. The women were all pointing to Roxanna and chatting in Farsi, talking at once and very fast, as if they were certain she understood every word.

"They're talking about your resemblance to your father," Akbaar interjects. "Especially his beautiful, soft brown eyes." Roxanna smiled at them, delighting in the reference to her father.

Wishing to be polite, Roxanna began to open her presents, but her grandmother looked at her with an odd expression that made her pause. Without a word, Zahra swiftly took the presents out of Roxanna's lap and carried them to another room for safekeeping. Akbaar leaned towards Roxanna and whispered, "It is considered poor manners here to open presents in front of everyone. Some gifts might be nicer than others, so we don't want to make anyone feel bad."

Roxanna's hand was touched by her grandmother, and when she turned, she saw her holding a strikingly beautiful old jewelry box encrusted with gold, turquoise, and other amazing Persian stones, which she held towards Roxanna. She accepted the gift graciously, tilting the box back and forth in awe, admiring the workmanship and how each stone had been placed to form delicate paisley patterns. The box itself was such an incredible gift that it never even occurred to Roxanna that there might be anything inside.

With great poise, her grandmother opened the exquisite jewelry box, lined inside with aged deep crimson velvet. Carefully, she lifted from it a pair of gold, deeply embossed earrings. She spoke in Farsi with Akbaar translating, "She says your name is inscribed on them, along with the date of your birth. They are for you." She then pulled out another pair, "And these are for your mother. She still considers your mother, her son's wife."

A flood of tears poured from Roxanna's eyes. She had never felt so loved and accepted. She leaned over and hugged and kissed her grandmother. Akbaar continued to translate her words, "She said all of the gold in the world won't bring back her youth and beauty, her old, lined face, it no longer serves her." He paused a moment, waiting for Grandmother to finish. He then handed the box back to Roxanna and quoted her grandmother exactly, "she said… You take the box now, my dear child. Jewelry is meant for the young and beautiful, for you."

Surprised, taken by what was happening, Roxanna reached inside the box and pulled out a gold necklace encrusted with precious gems, unlike anything she had ever seen. She then continued to hold and caress every last piece of gold, silver, and colorful stone jewelry left in the box, all treasured heirlooms, each one more exotic and breathtaking than the last.

When she reached the bottom of the box, she noticed some old, faded black and white photographs, obviously hidden away for safekeeping. Her eyes widened when she realized she was holding a picture taken at Assad and Linda's elaborate wedding.

"These are my parents! It was taken at their wedding!" Her hands flew to her face in disbelief. Another photo was of Assad with her uncle, Akbaar, and a third showed Assad with his Iranian wife and children. Roxanna was mesmerized but tried not to stare too long at her father's new family. Instead, she took the pictures and laid them side by side on a table, looking at them as if seeing her lost family, joined together for the first time.

"This is the latest picture of him," Akbaar said, pointing to one of Assad standing in front of a school, surrounded by a few teachers and a group of very young school children. "He doesn't like to have pictures taken of him."

Roxanna picked up the small picture of her father and studied it for a brief moment. Meanwhile, Cyrus seized the opportunity to examine the photos, discreetly slipping one in his pocket while Akbaar held Roxanna's attention, guiding her towards the small kitchen area.

When Roxanna had a moment with Akbaar away from the others, she pleaded with him to tell her more. Akbaar looked at her with gentle eyes, understanding her devastation, and tried to explain. Akbaar spoke in a soft voice and in broken English, so the rest would not understand their conversation. "Sooner or later, you will learn the truth about your father. You must be patient." What is happening is not only for your safety. It is for his." That was not an answer Roxanna was waiting for.

*****

Chapter 15

When You are Bored with Your Host's Customs and Culture...

It was early morning when the barn door opened and a beam of light pierced through the blackness, lighting up Cyrus, who was lying, unconscious, in a heap between two goats, a sheep, and several piles of fresh manure. Freezing water splashed directly into Cyrus's face, drenching him. Abruptly, he bolted upright, clutched his head, and gasped for air, damning no one but himself for his world-class hangover. He would take the blame for that, but who would stoop so low as to take advantage of a man in his sorry position by throwing ice water in his face?

He looked around for Roxanna but, not seeing her anywhere, he focused on revenge. A backlit figure looking an awful lot like Mashty stood in the doorway holding an empty bucket. Cyrus frowned; he had no choice but to back off. Mashty's eyes pierced clear through Cyrus, daring him to say just one word to him. Mashty disappeared.

Looking around in confusion, Cyrus wondered how he had ended up in the barn alone, but he wasn't about to give Mashty the satisfaction of knowing he had no memory of the previous evening. He had a throbbing headache, and as he massaged his temples, he felt a huge bump and something that felt like dry blood on his forehead. He looked at his hands and saw that blood had soaked into the lines formed by his veins and had dried a deep red-black color.

Holding on to his shovel, Mashty reentered, shoving the barn door wide open, spewing sunlight directly into Cyrus's face. The strong light was too much for Cyrus. Mashty threw Cyrus's small bag in his direction and gestured for him to leave.

As Cyrus stepped outside and took in some fresh air, the events from the night before came rushing back in a jumbled mess.

*****

Events started to return to Cyrus in bits and pieces…sneaking out of the house, being in the middle of a small garden underneath the canopy in front of Roxanna's Grandmother's house, hiding from everyone, enjoying the rain with Roxanna. The rain was pouring down, and where he was standing under the canopy was surrounded by fruit trees. Everyone was asleep. It was after midnight. Roxanna snatched the bottle from him and began to help him consume the contents.

Cyrus didn't usually drink, but when he did, it generally wasn't hard liquor. He was unsure of why he had decided to drink that night. A few days prior, when he visited the city, he decided to buy a bottle of wine but somehow ended up with a bottle of wine and a bottle of whiskey. He felt it wasn't his fault; it was a very persuasive Armenian/Iranian shop owner who talked him into it. In retrospect, he may not have needed much help. He was certainly looking to help Roxanna to escape from her overactive thoughts, the political dangers surrounding her father, and the uncertainty of the future.

Obviously, Roxanna was having the same thoughts about Cyrus, only she wasn't afraid to take the risk of getting caught. Or perhaps, she wasn't aware of the seriousness of Mashty's unhappiness with Cyrus or that he intended to keep her from being alone with Cyrus at all costs.

It wasn't long before they both felt the impact of the alcohol, especially since neither of them were experienced drinkers. Cyrus was unsteady on his feet, his arms taking up space as he spoke about the importance of life, and of course, telling his joke. The heat from the fire blazing through the moisture of the rain provided a delightful backdrop to their intimate soiree; their faces were aglow.

Cyrus began talking more loudly with each sip. Roxanna kept putting her finger to his lips, attempting to get him to lower his voice. Intoxicated beyond belief, he couldn't hold in his happiness a second longer. He began to imitate her. He tried putting his finger to her lips but kept missing. Roxanna playfully bit his finger as he tried, again, to touch her lips. They both began to giggle uncontrollably. Cyrus took his harmonica out of his pocket and began to play but Roxanna, worried about being heard, took it away.

"What's wrong with being silly or crazy? Why do we have to be so serious? It's all a joke, one big stupid joke, anyway." Cyrus looked up toward the sky as if he was speaking to the Almighty. "God? Why did you create women?" He listened for an answer, tilting his right ear toward the heavens.

Roxanna chuckled with amusement, "Probably just to bother men!"

Roxanna heard a door open and close from the direction of the barn. If someone was watching, she was being quite obvious about it. Still, Roxanna didn't want to create any problems with her new family. Cyrus had warned her they might ask him to leave if they caught them drinking together, and losing him wasn't worth the risk. With the nimbleness of a cat, she faded into the soggy night and, removing her shoes, slipped back into the house.

Cyrus, now heavily intoxicated, began looking around for her, drunkenly, unaware that she had left. He leaned his head out from under the canopy, feeling the cool downpour pelt his head and roll down his face. "Oh, I'm in love with her. God, why did you throw me into this hostile world with rules and regulations that are made by ignorant men with little life left in their bodies and no love in their hearts? All I want is love and affection."

He leaned further out and looked towards the sky, past the stars, "God, for once, say something! Can you hear me? Answer me— Answer me!" Cyrus inhaled, ready to continue his drunken rambling when a shovel appeared from out of the darkness and hit him square in the center of his forehead, with an angry voice, "I did…" He landed hard on the ground, rain pouring down on him. Just before he fell into unconsciousness, he whispered…

"Thank … you…" He even could not see Mashty was standing beside him, holding onto his shovel.

*****

In the bright light of morning, Cyrus still felt the impact of the shovel reverberating in his brain. As the events of the prior evening resurfaced, now, in the glare of the morning sun, Mashty was prodding him to leave. He was staring Cyrus down, ready to fight to the death if he dared to challenge him. Cyrus looked toward the house, questioning if Mashty was acting under the direction of Akbaar and Roxanna's grandmother, but the house was still. The only person he saw was Zahra, Mashty's wife, observing from the balcony.

Cyrus grabbed his bag and walked slowly to his car, stalling, trying to figure out a way to rectify the problem. He acknowledged that his actions had caused this terrible disaster, but if he had to leave, he was going to take Roxanna with him. He sat in his dusty Blazer for a long time, thinking about his options. What if Roxanna didn't want to go with him? What if she wanted to stay with her grandmother? He got out of his car and headed for the house, calling for Roxanna. At the very least, he would say goodbye.

Before he reached the steps, Mashty appeared with his weapon of choice, that damned shovel. There was no way he was letting Cyrus into the house. Zahra, who had been watching his every move, joined him with a weapon of her own, her harsh words. "You had better leave. Go… go…

you have embarrassed the family. Besides, there is nothing here for you! She is gone!" Cyrus was dumbfounded.

This news reverberated in Cyrus' ears, sending a surge of panic down his spine. "Gone where?" Cyrus asked urgently.

"They took her! Evil men!" Zahra shouted back in frustration. "They came in the middle of the night."

"I need to speak to Akbaar. Then I will leave. Tell him to come out." Cyrus yelled desperately.

Mashty looked at Cyrus with disgust, "He is gone too, fool. They took him as well. And now it is your turn! Go!"

Cyrus demanded to speak to Roxanna's grandmother! But just before the two could clash, the door to the second-floor balcony flew open, and Roxanna's grandmother appeared from behind the curtain where she had been watching. Cyrus pleaded, "Please! Grandmother! I really need to know who took her. She is in great danger! I need your help, please! Who took them?"

Roxanna's grandmother responded and was closing the curtain.

Cyrus was clearly panicked, "Who were they? Did you hear their names? Did they say where they were taking them? Please answer me. Any information is important. Don't you understand their lives may be in danger? Talk to me!" But she could say no more.

Afraid he was never going to leave, Zahra finally spoke up, "I was washing tea glasses and cleaning up when I saw headlights from a car move across the living room. I was the only one awake. At first, I was alarmed but thought it was perhaps a friend of Akbaar, paying a late-night visit... The car slowed to a crawl before reaching the side of the house. I heard the doors open and looked out. There were several men dressed in black shirts and trousers. They came right in without knocking and said they wanted to talk to Akbaar. Within a minute, they were gone with Akbaar and Roxanna. They disappeared into the rain." Zahra was fighting to hold back tears.

Hearing the sobering details of the late-night kidnapping, Cyrus grabbed his few belongings and headed out. They had made it clear that there was nothing more for him there. He jumped in his Blazer and left without so much as a goodbye or a wave from anyone, not even Roxanna's grandmother.

Zahra's words kept playing over in his head. Cyrus was overcome with guilt for drinking so much that he was incapacitated when Roxanna needed him the most. She and Akbaar had been kidnapped, either by the Savak or the guerrilla movement and whatever might happen to them from this point on was entirely his fault.

The Blazer sped through the narrow dirt road past two villagers who were sitting atop a small, barren hill, tending a herd of sheep. Cyrus sighed, envying them for their simpler life.

Obviously, these men were not shepherds! Cyrus slammed on his brakes and stopped, looking back, up the hill. The sheep had wandered off, and the men were hiding behind a rock, peering out in his direction, keeping track of his every move. Cyrus was now certain something was very wrong. The longer and faster he drove, the more he thought about Zahra's story. Why hadn't he been kidnapped, too?

*****

Chapter 16

Explorations of the Heart, of Old Iranian Cultures and Unexpected Tragedy...

The soft breeze of early spring blew the wildflowers and green foliage in one direction. As the wind would shift, the foliage shifted along with it, as if following the direction of a great orchestra conductor. The Blazer traveled along a quiet road as though the car was on automatic pilot. Cyrus's thoughts were on everything except the road in front of him. Nothing mattered but finding Roxanna. The underground movement might have wanted her because she knew too much and could break under enough pressure from Savak. The Savak could have taken her again to get more information. If there was a lesser of two evils, it would be Cyrus's wish for the latter. Still, the pieces weren't adding up. Why had he not been killed or kidnapped along with Roxanna and Akbaar?

Like the flowers, he was blowing in the wind, without direction. He knew he had to start contacting people, but who should he call first? His brother, Nader, Saeed, or perhaps Peter. He decided to let the birds flying in the distance decide. If one landed on the wires, he would call his brother, two, Nader...but none landed. He began to push the speed of the car to the max just because it was the one thing, he had any control over. His next priority was to find a phone. It wasn't until late afternoon that he arrived at a telephone company in a small town he had never heard of.

*****

The next day, Cyrus was sitting in another quiet roadside teahouse as promised, waiting for a friend and eating pastries sweetened with rose water. He rarely ate sweets but found himself devouring them as a distraction from the image embedded in his mind of Roxanna in the hands of her kidnappers. He watched several little birds flying back and forth from the tree branches to the small running creek near his table, wishing he could trade places. He was feeding them bits of his pastries, just as his mother loved to do.

Nader entered and could sense how unnerved Cyrus was even before he approached him. "Nature is cruel, but man is crueler."

Although Cyrus heard a voice, he didn't realize that it was Nader, standing behind him. The words continued to roll off Nader's tongue as he tried to rationalize life in one simple statement. "We cannot do a damn thing about it but simply try to live the best life we can."

At first, Cyrus was relieved to see his friend and impressed by the way he understood his feelings, but he snapped back to reality when he remembered that Pary had said she hadn't been or able to get a hold of Nader and that another friend, Maryam, was going to meet him. How did Nader know where he was?

Nader noticed a sense of distrust in Cyrus's eyes. "Maryam could not make it, so she called me to come and meet you. You don't know how sorry I am to have used Roxanna. We should have left her out of our struggle and especially out of the car bombing."

Nader continued his unwanted apology. "It was wrong, and I am doing everything I can to help find her. I should have listened to Pary and left her alone. I feel horrible! From now on, I will watch over her...which is what I was doing all along..." Nader's voice trailed off.

Cyrus had no patience for Nader or his apologies. He was interested in only one thing. Did he have any information on Roxanna?

Nader continued apologetically, "I spoke to Amir. The Savak does not have her. They have no knowledge or information about who took her." That was not what Cyrus wished to hear. "I have also talked to everyone I know in the underground organization, and they have no idea, either. I am concerned if Saeed abducted her and took her away. He has moved up in the organization very quietly and has formed his own gang. I tried to contact him repeatedly, but he is avoiding me and does not respond directly to me. Instead, he sends messages through Abdullah saying he will get back to me, but he never does." Abdullah was their common friend.

Cyrus was not surprised to hear this news. In retrospect, he questioned the wisdom of his trust in Saeed, but they had been friends for so long, he wanted to preserve that relationship if he could. He couldn't believe it was possible for someone to change so dramatically in such a short time. Cyrus knew that when people's thinking tended to be extreme, without checks and balances or neutral influences, they became radical in their ideology and difficult to reason with, only seeing things in black and white, with no gray area. The radical extremist knows no middle ground. Cyrus knew he needed Saeed's help, but Saeed had changed and could not be trusted. On that subject, he and Nader agreed.

Workers were looking at them from a distance and perhaps wishing to be like them— educated, intellectual city boys. Cyrus and Nader watched an old man sitting across the road selling watermelons and smoking his cheap cigarettes. He didn't know anything about politics. He just knew how to get up every morning, pray, go to work, sell watermelons, and go back home to his family. His happiness was simple—he just needed enough to care for his family, provide them with food and shelter and be sure he got into heaven when he died. Cyrus and Nader were both wishing they could trade places with the old man.

Nader finally broke his long silence. "It troubles me that every time I have seen you recently, it feels like it will be the last time. It makes me very sad. Cyrus, you are like my brother...so I want you to know, I never wished to harm Roxanna in any way...I came into her life to support and protect her...."

Hearing Nader's words just further irritated Cyrus. He stood up to leave but realizing Nader still might have some information on Roxanna, he changed his mind and nodded for him to continue.

"The Savak knew about her coming to Iran. Their intention was to use her. They set her up to try and find Assad by following her. Amir asked me to watch after her...and I failed... I work for Amir... but none of it matters... we need to find her before it is too late."

There was so much more that Nader wanted to tell Cyrus, but he didn't, out of fear for his life. During these times of strange alliances, Nader was actually an undercover agent working for Amir and for the Savak. And when Nader had provided reports on the activities of Saeed and his organization, he always altered details to the Savak in order to protect Saeed because of their long friendship. Now he was having second thoughts.

It didn't matter that Nader had changed in his beliefs; he was standing in quicksand and unable to get out. Saeed, in his narrow scope of thinking, was convinced that the change in Nader was simply the result of his attention being focused only on Roxanna and that he had fallen for her. He was sure that if he had not been arrested yet, it was because Nader was working with Savak. So, he had to be eliminated.

After an hour, Cyrus realized it was time to leave. They hugged goodbye tightly. There was an unspoken gut feeling that they might never see each other again, but it was overshadowed by the urgency to rescue Roxanna. Their plan was for Cyrus to return to the village and follow the lead he had about Roxanna's father while Nader headed back to Tehran in search of more clues as to Roxanna's whereabouts.

Taking his eyes off the road, Cyrus pulled the photo of Assad out of his pocket that he had taken from the jewelry box at Roxanna's grandmother's. Slowing, in an attempt to look closer, he could see that Assad was standing in front of a school with several other teachers and young children. The overall look of the students' clothing, as well as the building and background, led Cyrus to believe the school was clearly located in a village rather than a big city.

What Cyrus couldn't understand was what Assad—who had a doctorate in economics from one of the best schools in Germany—would be doing teaching grade school in a small village far to the south. The more information he was able to gather, the harder he studied the photograph. He could faintly make out the name of the school. It read "Bahaar. Spring." Cyrus smiled as he recalled Nader's words: "There are three schools with the same name in this area. One is more likely the one where Assad is teaching..."

The Blazer, which Cyrus now considered a dear friend, was traveling full speed toward the closest town. He had to find that school. Once he did that, he would find Assad and, hopefully, Roxanna.

*****

Chapter 17

When the Past and Present Meet Through the Arrival of an Unexpected Guest...

Two days later, Cyrus was aware of the sweat pooling on the back of his neck; the way it would reach its limit, pour down the small of his back to his jeans and then begin pooling again. He was parked above a graveyard in the scorching sun where he was able to observe a building on the far side of the headstones, unnoticed. The sign hanging over the main door read "Bahaar" in black. He studied the picture for comparison with what was in front of him and was pleased with the results. He had found the school's location by contacting the office of education of each city he passed through.

The school building and its surrounding trees and creek matched the photo in detail, although it appeared to be smaller than Cyrus imagined, with only six or seven classrooms.

The school bell's loud, prolonged buzz was so harsh it could have awakened the dead in the nearby graveyard. It was the sound he had been waiting to hear all afternoon. Cyrus watched closely as children, relieved that the school day was finally over, rushed out of their classrooms and began running around, in need of supervision.

Finally, a teacher, years older than the others, came out and accessed the situation. There was no question in Cyrus' mind. It was Assad, Roxanna's father. He calmly walked away from the school and headed toward a group of rambunctious students as he headed towards the village. The boys immediately calmed down as Assad passed, behaving politely out of respect for their teacher.

*****

A few days had passed, but Cyrus's routine remained the same; to find a way to keep an eye on Assad, hopefully, without being obvious. School was in progress. Assad was teaching and correcting papers in the classroom, although most of his attention was focused on watching Cyrus outside by the school playing a traditional sport with some locals. The game was Alak-Dolak. The sport was similar to baseball and softball, yet a bit more intense and several hundred years old; one could consider it the grandfather upon which baseball was created.

This game was very popular in the villages and was usually played after school or before sunset. The players would use a five-inch stick as their ball; this was the "Alack." A larger seven to ten-foot stick was used as a bat; this was the "Dolak." As in baseball, there were two teams. One team would hit the Alack, and the other team would scatter around to catch the Alack before it could hit the dirt. If they caught it, the batter would be out.

Each of the players who spread out to catch the Alack would carry a Dolack, and if they could not catch the Alack, they would throw their Dolack at the Alack. If the Dolack hit the Alack, the batter would still be out. They had three chances to get the batter out. The teams continued until all batters from the opposite team were out, and then they would exchange places. The biggest difference between Alack-Dolak and baseball is that the player does not have to stay at first, second, or third base, as there are no bases.

Running to catch the Alack, Cyrus's eyes caught Assad inside the classroom behind the window, looking out toward him, his shadowy figure clearly visible through the classroom window. Seeing Assad, he missed the Alack.

Cyrus didn't want to scare Assad away if he really was Roxanna's father, and he was fairly certain he was. By now, everyone in the village knew who Cyrus was. Cyrus believed that Assad was living in the small town under a false identity and if he suspected the government, or anyone else, might be closing in on him, he would quickly disappear and settle somewhere else with a new identity. That was Cyrus's biggest fear. He knew he would have to move very slowly so as not to alarm him.

So, to distract the people from his real intention and make Assad at ease, Cyrus pretended to be checking out the small village as a possible location for a film shoot. Only Assad and Cyrus knew about their game of cat and mouse going on between them. In a small village like Bahaar, in the middle of nowhere, everyone knew everyone, and all were frequently related. In what seemed like a matter of minutes, Cyrus was the biggest thing to happen to them. Not surprisingly, when students saw him, they started acting out and begging him to take their picture, hoping to impress him enough to be in his film.

Meanwhile, he was constantly phoning Nader, but there was no response from either him or Pary. And his mother had no idea where Nader or Pary was either.

*****

It was Friday, and the call to prayer issued forth from the ancient horn on the top of the mosque in an eerie, creepy, repetitive chant. The circular, sky blue pool was situated in front of the main entry door to the praying area and acted as a gathering place. Startled pigeons splashing in one of the small pools inside the mosque's yard flew away as children rushed toward them, giggling and laughing. The flying pigeons joined others as they flew off the mosque's dome. Cyrus sat on his bicycle, leaned against the tree, and watched some young boys play soccer on the dirt field right across from the mosque. He recognized one of the boys who was watching as one of Assad's students and paid him to let him know when Assad left the mosque.

Cyrus noticed an American car parked on the far side of the soccer field. A strange man was sitting inside, trying his best to hide his presence. He was too far away for Cyrus to be certain, but he had been in the village long enough to know when something didn't feel right. Just then, an argument broke out among the young boys, and Cyrus turned his attention away from the man and towards the scuffle. Some wanted to fight, and some others were trying to break up the fight. Over what, No one was sure.

Cyrus had been a soccer player in school and college and knew how to deal with young players when they started to get out of control. Cyrus reached into his pocket and pulled out his harmonica and began to play a folk song as he approached them. He began to play with one hand as he snuck their soccer ball away and completed a trick with the other hand. The boys were so surprised by Cyrus's actions they forgot about arguing or fighting. A few joined in and began singing along.

Soon, all of the kids joined in singing and having great fun, paying no attention to the angry voice of the clergyman that blared from the bullhorn, threatening to drown them out. The boys would not give up, and as Cyrus played louder, the boys sang louder … the natural merriment of the boys in sharp contrast with the harsh sounding Cleric.

It was common knowledge that some of the attendees in the mosque were trying their best to "buy heaven" for themselves by attending prayer. Others were begging for God's mercy to forgive their sins. Then, there were some who were pretending they were religious in an attempt to mislead the public for materialistic gains.

As far as the children were concerned, neither heaven nor the concept of materialism had any meaning to them. They were in the here and now, living for the moment. As one became tired or ran out of songs to sing, another boy would take over and keep the energy flowing.

Several new boys approached with drinks and candy and served them to Cyrus's audience. The crowd grew bigger, the boys' laughter more boisterous, and the singing and dancing reached a definite pinnacle. It was a joyous celebration in the midst of an uncertain life.

Inside the mosque's yard, background harmonica music was lost in the loud message of the mosque's bullhorn across from the soccer field. Muslims must wash their hands up to their elbows and their face before each prayer, and in addition, no jewelry or decorations should be on your body. The dictates of the religion demand one must also pray five times a day.

The prayers, known as Namaz, are done before sunrise, noon, before sunset, after sunset, and before twelve midnight. Muslims may combine two prayers in the noon and evening, which would prolong Assad's visits and allow for spiritual growth.

Assad exited the main mosque onto the yard. He put his shoes on and walked toward his bicycle. Just then, an old man left the mosque and happened to notice a new pair of shoes. Temptation got the best of him. As calmly as if they were his own, he put them on and started to walk away. Just as he was about to exit the yard, he paused in remorse.

He walked back to the row of shoes, placed the new shoes back where they were, and put his worn but well-earned old shoes on. Just as he let out a sigh of relief, he realized Assad had been observing him. The old man grinned sheepishly, "It's not worth going to hell just for a pair of new shoes." They both laughed.

At the outside of the mosque door, the young boy who Cyrus had paid to watch for Assad began to whistle to get his attention, but he was drowned out by the loud music and singing. He was getting angry and frustrated because he wanted to impress Cyrus so that he would remember him and put him in his movie. He began to whistle toward Cyrus with an over-exaggerated waving of the arms. When that didn't work, he raced toward Cyrus, whistling louder. Finally, Cyrus, who was playing and having fun with the children, noticed him.

The boy pointed toward the inside of the Mosque, out of breath. Just then, Assad appeared, walking his bicycle, exiting the Mosque. He looked around, searching for any sign of Cyrus, and when he didn't see him, he rode off.

Cyrus couldn't afford to miss the moment a second time! He handed his harmonica to one of the boys. "Now you're the leader. Play! Don't stop." The children continued singing to the cacophony of sounds produced by the harmonica as the boy attempted to play. Cyrus grabbed his bicycle and raced towards Assad.

Soon he noticed Assad in the distance. Cyrus made sure he stayed far enough from Assad. Nevertheless, Cyrus's concern for Roxanna outweighed every other emotion. He no longer cared if Assad knew he was following him. He could wait no longer. The time for confrontation had come. As for Assad, even without looking back, he had no doubt Cyrus was close behind. It was clear to both that their cat-and-mouse game was coming to a climax.

*****

It was late in the day when Cyrus finally caught sight of him. The sun was emitting one last surge of light before retiring for the night, spotlighting Assad as he glided along a quiet road on the outskirts of town. Afraid that Cyrus was still following, he pulled off onto an even smaller dirt road, barely wide enough for two people to pass, continuing along a fast-running creek lined on either side with massive, tall Senowbar trees. The trees were planted very close together and grew as tall as two to three-story buildings. He had picked the road because he knew the trees would offer shelter from prying eyes, and if necessary, he could ride between them and easily disappear in any direction.

Cyrus knew exactly what Assad was up to, so he took a shortcut, riding through a small path on neighboring farmland, pausing ahead of Assad to wait for him. When Assad saw Cyrus, he simply rode right past, ignoring him. Cyrus approached, on the other side, parallel to him.

Assad stopped abruptly by the creek and leaned his bike against a tree. Slowly and precisely, he walked to the edge and sat on the bank, dipping his hands into the creek, and splashing icy water on his face, cleansing himself as if he was preparing to pray. Cyrus leaned his bike against a tree and walked to the creek's edge directly opposite Assad. He sat on the bank and imitated Assad's every move. Both knew they had to talk. Both were afraid they would hear words that were not welcome. Assad stared at his reflection in a pool of water, amazed at how much he had aged.

"I'm looking for a man. His name is Assad. He used to live in West Germany. He left in 1952 to come to help Mossadegh and never went back, but he left a baby girl behind, who is now a very beautiful woman. Her name is Roxanna."

Cyrus took the pictures he took from Assad's mother's house out of his pocket and held one up for Assad to see, but he realized that he was too far away. He entered the stream and walked closer as if he was approaching a wild, wounded animal, afraid it would run away. Assad gazed at the photo quietly, without looking Cyrus in the eyes.

Cyrus took a deep breath and held it, fighting his frustration. "I believe you're the man in this picture. I took it from your mother's house. And that is how I found you." Cyrus pointed to baby Roxanna's image in the photo, "And this is you and baby Roxanna in West Germany." But Assad did not look. Instead, he rose, dusting the dirt from his pants, and pulled a handkerchief from his pocket to dry his hands.

Cyrus watched closely as nervousness crept into Assad's demeanor, "You're talking to the wrong man." His voice was quiet, dignified. He did not meet Cyrus's gaze. Instead, he turned and walked back to his bike and, holding the handlebars, walked away.

Cyrus began to walk in the creek, keeping parallel to Assad, "You must trust me. I'm here to help. I do not wish to hurt anyone. Your daughter has traveled halfway around the world to find you. She has put herself in serious danger. I would think that out of respect for her, you would want to see her, also."

Assad stopped and turned briefly to Cyrus. "Young man, I told you. I am not the man you seek. I'm Ahmad Rostamy. And as you know, I am a teacher. I have a wife and three children here in Iran, none in West Germany. In fact, I have never been out of the country. I was only in Tehran once, and I got lost." The lies rolled expertly off his tongue.

Cyrus continued making his way through the cold, clear water while addressing Assad. If it meant finding Roxanna, he was willing to play his game. "Listen, whoever you are, I am here to help her—not you, not me, and not the Savak and for sure not the underground movement. I know everything about you, whoever you are!

"Roxanna was kidnapped from her grandmother's house weeks ago, at midnight, and I have no clue who did it. We have to find her! The Savak and the underground movement both claim they don't know where she is, but it could have been either of them. She was used by the movement to place a bomb that killed a little girl. I helped get her released from the Savak before she disappeared from your mother's farm.

"She came here to find you. She risked her life for you! It's because of you this all happened!" Cyrus paused, afraid he had made a huge mistake, "I gave up everything I loved for your daughter. I'm wondering if you really are her father because if you were, you wouldn't be walking away now!"

Assad kept walking. Cyrus, soaking wet by now, crossed back over the creek to get his bike; after a few steps, he yelled back to Assad. "Akbaar also vanished. You must know where your own brother lives! Perhaps someone there knows something."

Assad stopped in his tracks but did not look back. He spoke sadly, with conviction, "Young man, I said you are talking to the wrong man."

Cyrus's frustration imploded. "You are right. Roxanna's father would give a damn!" He walked out of the creek, grabbed his bike, and rode away.

*****

Chapter 18

When Your Unexpected Guest Shatters the Wall between Past and Present...

The sound of the frogs let it be known who truly ruled the darkness, the music makers. What was their message? What could they have to say? Perhaps, if insects and amphibians could make such beautiful music together, what was wrong with man? Cyrus was lying on the bed, lost in thought, thinking of what was next. Even if the darkness just arrived, he wanted to fall into a deep sleep, but his eyes were so red that he could hardly close them.

He was so out of it that it took several knocks before he realized someone was gently knocking on the door. He was confused about who could be on the other side. He knew no one there. He got up and carefully opened the door. Seeing Assad standing in front of him, he was now more confused. "Are you ready to face the truth you are looking for?" It took Cyrus a long bit to understand what Assad was asking him.

*****

Hours passed from the time Assad surprised Cyrus at the motel. Cyrus was following Assad into the dark, slowly trying to place his feet securely on the uneven path as he walked. Cyrus's thoughts were fighting within his mind, going faster. The silence of the night, the sound of a soft night breeze, was all music to Cyrus' ears. Why had Assad decided to show up at his motel door at nighttime to bring him to this dark place that reeked of manure? What if it was a setup, and he was going to disappear? But Cyrus was not going to back off. He peered around every corner, making it a point to stay a few yards behind.

Although Cyrus had no idea how far they were going, by the pace at which Assad was forging ahead, it seemed to him that they had little time to get there. Cyrus continued to follow Assad, walking behind him, beside a wall covered with tree branches. He would have preferred to be anywhere but where he was, in the middle of nowhere on the quiet outskirts of town on the deepest, darkest of nights, without a moon or the soothing sound of crickets.

And it didn't help that Assad could see so well in the dark, almost as if blindfolded. It was clear to him that Assad had made this walk many, many times before. He did it without hesitation, whereas Cyrus, being overly cautious, was falling over things that weren't there. At one point, he tried to start a conversation, but Assad gestured for him to be quiet, and he kept his mouth shut after that. After about two hours of walking, Cyrus noticed they were approaching an area with heavy trees. A few lights glowed in the distance; they were about to enter a small town.

It was not much longer when Assad stopped inside a narrow alley at the doorway of a domed structure. The door was small and old, dwarfed by the size of the grand building. It was designed that way on purpose so that everyone from all walks of life, all shapes, and sizes, would be forced to bow in respect upon entering the sacred place. Cyrus looked up, reading a faded sign that was lighted by a small light above it, 'Zoorkhaneh Pahlevan.' Cyrus entered after Assad.

Inside the Zoorkhaneh, an old, stocky man sat alone in the box seat, playing ceremonial drums, or zarbs, and chanting at the Zoorkhaneh. It was a place where a traditional sport called Varzese-Bastani—meaning, ancient sport— was conducted, fusing elements of Persian culture with spirituality. Special equipment, wooden clubs called mil, and bow-shaped iron weights called Kabbadeh were used.

The performance was a combination of weightlifting, wrestling, and a form of exercise that looked like a form of dance and martial arts; it was quite interesting to watch. People who became champions at the Zoorkhaneh were always highly respected in their country.

It was a form of national pride for Iranians, and Cyrus was reminded that the sports champions had once defended their communities against the Arab invaders over a thousand years ago. Persian history had always shown Zurkhaneh as having a higher place in the struggle against Arab forces. All Zurkhaneh movements were based on combat movements.

It was a gathering place for Iran's freedom fighters against Arab invaders, and because of that, its entry doors were built very short. This was for the simple fact that if Arab soldiers were aware of their gatherings and attacked, only one person could enter at a time. It was a battle that had continuously waged since Islam was imposed on Iranians with spearheads and massacres. It was easy to fight one on one, but with Arabs outnumbering them, they have to even the playing field.

The stocky man inside the box who was playing and chanting, traditionally called a Morshed, was the most important member of the event, the name meaning "master who beats the drum," recites poetry and guides the rituals. As the Morshed chanted, the athletes, all barefoot, with powerful frames and clad leather shorts, came to their knees, began entering the naturally round ancient amphitheater, made simply and mostly from rock and stone.

The performers were separated from the audience by a wall around the stage, with the audience sitting above the wall, looking down. Besides local enthusiasts, several foreign tourists were watching the ancient Iranian ritual sport as well. As the chanting continued, the performers entered and stood around the stage next to the wall, each waiting to take his turn to perform in the center of the round stage.

Cyrus followed Assad to the top, where they found a place to stand further back, partially hidden behind a post where they would not be so easily seen. Cyrus watched Assad's eyes scan through the audience, searching for someone.

Assad was oblivious to the loud praying called by Morshed. He watched as his brother, Akbaar, the champ, with his large and powerful frames clad in leather shorts, entered, barefoot, and stood in the center of the sacred structure. The entire audience rose in respect and answered the prayer.

The sound of chanting erupted throughout the dome as the audience called a prayer in respect to Akbaar. A few performers around him began to go through their workouts and then, with all eyes on him, with great strength and power, Akbaar began to move the heavy clubs in rhythm with the drum, swinging one club back while holding the other club upright in front of him and then reversing the motions.

The weights were about four feet long, and his face would strain as he lifted them, with sheer strength, from shoulder to shoulder. In a similar manner, other men clad in leather shorts worn only by champions stood around the circle, performing a disciplined exercise-sport-cultural routine. Akbaar had brought Roxanna to the event and secretly observed her sitting in the front row, continually scanning the audience while he moved. Assad's eyes followed Akbaar's until he, too, found what he had been searching for, Roxanna.

Cyrus's eyes traveled from Assad to Roxanna and then back to Assad as he watched tears come to Assad's eyes as he stared at Roxanna, blocking out everything else in his life but that precious moment. It was as if the Zoorkhaneh and the people in it didn't even exist. He saw and heard nothing. All the things he had searched for and fought for the past twenty years, everything that he had given up his life for, paled in comparison to his daughter's beauty.

She had captured his soul and his heart just by existing. He continued to watch her, captivated. Although it was apparent, she was enthralled by her Uncle Akbaar, he could tell that she wasn't happy. She had been in search of her Baba, not an uncle. Hiding his weeping eyes from Cyrus, Assad walked away and exited the Zoorkhaneh.

Cyrus looked at Roxanna in disbelief. Even from the back, there could be no mistake. Every detail, every movement was a part of his memory; the way she shook her hair, cocked her head. It was her first time entering a "House of Strength," as it was called, and she was completely focused on Akbaar, performing his routines to the rhythm of the Morshed's goblet drum.

So many scenarios had played out in Cyrus' mind since Roxanna disappeared, but none had ended like this. She was safe and unharmed! He wanted to take her in his arms, but after what happened at her grandmother's, he vowed to keep his feelings hidden.

Unsure of what to do next, Cyrus followed Assad out, exiting into a dark alley where he inhaled a deep breath of fresh air followed by a long sigh of relief. Finally. She was safe. But where was Assad?

On nights with no moon, intuition takes over for what the eye cannot see. Cyrus chased his imagination towards the alley entrance until he caught up with Assad, invisible against the dark shadow of the wall. Still, he was there, just as Cyrus had pictured him, running away from Roxanna and his past. He stared at the old man's face, searching for answers. Assad chose to be silent but slowed his pace to allow Cyrus the courtesy of catching up.

After all, it was clear that Assad wanted Cyrus to follow him. Cyrus was a guest in Assad's hometown, so tradition and proper etiquette called for Assad to be his guide. But Cyrus wanted more than just an escort. He wanted answers. Quickening his step to match Assad's, he spun around and stopped in front of him, forcing Assad to lose his footing and fall against the wall. Cyrus waited for an explanation for his actions, but it never came. He was out of patience. "That's it? You came all this way to just look at her? That's it?"

Assad looked at him for a moment with tears in his eyes. "Young man, I thought by now you understood, the world is always more complicated than it appears." He attempted to walk away but stopped and turned, "Besides, it would be safer for her if she doesn't know who I am or that I exist. If God wants it, one day, I will hug her."

Their eyes met each other's, hoping that somebody would find the right words. Unwillingly, Assad walks away. Cyrus walks after him, "Do you believe what you say? Or are you a hypocrite?" Assad stops, gazing into the night confused. Cyrus continues, "This is your guilt talking... not you... you feel bad for her..."

Assad speaks up, his voice is filled with sadness, "Why shouldn't I? For years I brought pain and suffering upon my family, upon my wife and on her... I betrayed my families, and my people. I tried all my life to do things right... but every time it got worse; it did not hit me I committed these sins until I found she was here looking for me. Now, I don't know if I am doing the right thing or just bringing more suffering upon my family and the same people, I've fought all my life to protect."

By now, his voice is much deeper; he turns to Cyrus and stares a moment, "And now when I look at you, I see you are a mirror of my younger self, and I am frightened you will do the same to her that I did to her mother. I wish I knew what I know now, at your age. When you are young, you are passionate and feel pride in standing for the people, for what is right and what is wrong... you stand up for it... because you do not want to be ignorant... and I see you are worse than me... like a double edge sword ... passionate, and considerate of others.

You are a good man with a great soul. But you do not belong to yourself... you belong to your art ... you belong to your people more than yourself... we are the same... and during these struggles, somehow, we get distracted, and we hurt our loved ones..." By now, Assad was choking, "Please, she's suffered enough... I won't ask you to walk away from her. My only could wish is you do not hurt her..."

Cyrus watched Assad disappear into the darkness. Confused with his surroundings, he sat on a small bench, looking into the darkness where Assad vanished. The luminous sound of night crickets, chirping some sort of secret code, awakened Cyrus's inner consciousness. They echoed Assad's sentiment, to walk away from love with each rub of their legs.

"Sadness is a heavy weight to carry," Cyrus heard these words. Was it a message or just the voices in his head? He had never felt quite right since Mashty hit him in the forehead with that shovel. Cyrus noticed a man, Osta Ahmad, a few yards from him, collecting pieces of broken bottles on the sidewalk.

"Life has lots of ups and downs, good and bad moments, celebrations and funerals, life and death. It seems God..." he glanced to the sky and whispered, "I love you," then looked back at Cyrus. "As I was saying, God has put everything onto a scale to balance it." He looked up and began to speak to God again, "Thank you for giving me less sadness than happiness. Thank you for what you have taken away, which has made me stronger. I have my good health, and that is the best wealth you have gifted to me, my God." Then he turned to Cyrus again. "Yes, health is the best gift of God, I am sure of it."

Osta Ahmad continued his sweeping, leaving Cyrus and the crickets to ponder his augury. To Cyrus, it felt as if the old man had collected the bottles just to wash away his sadness as he rinsed them. He felt purged and enlightened.

He realized no matter how sad or difficult life could be, it was only temporary and that all pain and sadness is carried away in the end. A smile appeared on Cyrus's face. Before walking to Osta Ahmad, he reached inside his pocket, took a photo out, and began to write a note on the back. He walked up to Osta Ahmad, placing the photo in his hand. Osta Ahmad never looked at the photo; he was too busy listening to Cyrus as he pointed toward the Zoorkhaneh. With a look of great confidence, he entered the Zorkhaneh, leaving Cyrus waiting in the alley.

Inside, Akbaar was gripping a weight shaped like a huge bow in both his hands. He kissed it to show respect and then held it above his head, turning it, moving to the rhythm of the Morshed's drum.

Osta Ahmad had little trouble finding the beautiful American woman in the first row. As he moved towards her, people would rise and show him their respect. And once he reached Roxanna, a few people around her rose and offered their seats to him out of respect. He took the one beside Roxanna, and after exchanging polite smiles, she turned her attention back to Akbaar. Not to be outdone by perhaps the most famous athlete in the country, little, bent Osta Ahmad placed the photo that Cyrus had given him on her lap.

Roxanna was left speechless when she looked at the photo and read the note. She turned and looked at Osta Ahmad, "Who gave you this?"

"A young man outside." He answered. Just then, the audience rose and called a prayer in respect to Akbaar, giving Roxanna the opportunity to make her way to the exit. Akbaar watched in concern as Roxanna pushed her way through and disappeared.

Roxanna rushed out of the Zoorkhaneh, looking for Cyrus, but she couldn't see any sign of him. She raced to the end of the alley, tripping over the street cleaner's broom, before giving up. She sat on a bench with only a streetlight overcoming the darkness, acting as her beacon. If only she knew which way Cyrus went, she would follow, but it was futile to run off in all directions. It was better to sit under the streetlight, to wait, and to hope. He had come this far; he would surely take the final step.

It was not long before memories of their brief time together began to play on her mind. One of the most vivid was when she left her grandmother's house in the middle of the night without telling Cyrus. It was almost too painful to recall.

Sitting on the bench by the Zoorkhaneh, where Cyrus was sitting a few minutes ago, she carried on a conversation in her head just as if Cyrus was sitting beside her. She wanted to let him know what had happened to her that night in the rain, why she disappeared...

"I have to let you know I had no choice. Everything was out of my control... Later that night, after I left you in the rain, way after midnight, the next thing I knew, Zahra snuck in my room and started packing up all my things. She kept saying, 'You have to go. They are here to take you. You must be quiet. If you don't leave now, terrible things will happen. If you want to see your father, you must leave with Akbaar quietly, or you will never see your father...'

I drank so much wine with you... my world was spinning! I was so dizzy I had to hold on to Zahra, and she helped me down the stairs. It was still raining, and there was nothing but mud everywhere. The last thing I remember was Akbaar throwing me over his shoulders and carrying me to a car."

Roxanna's conversation was interrupted by Akbaar, standing in front of her still in his Zorkhaneh uniform, wearing a jacket, but still barefoot. It was apparent that he had ended his performance abruptly and rushed out in concern; he did not appear to be happy. Several other performers, still in their outfits, had followed, and the spectators seemed very interested to find out what was going on with the American guest. It was something Akbaar did not want.

Akbaar turned, noticing the scene he had created, and asked everyone to go back inside, assuring them all was okay. He didn't want to draw more attention to Roxanna. Out of respect for Akbaar, the spectators did as he wished. Akbaar sat beside Roxanna. She turned to him and handed him the photo Cyrus left for her. Akbaar looked at it and read what was written on it, not knowing what to say or how to react. "He lives about twenty minutes from here… are you going to take me to him?" It took Akbaar a long bit to reach and hold Roxanna's hand kindly and gently.

*****

Meanwhile, traveling through the darkness, Cyrus tried his best to find his way back to his motel. They had parted ways without any goodbyes, and he knew that was damaging. If broken, the trust he had built with Assad could have serious repercussions, especially in regard to Roxanna. But it was not easy for someone who was not familiar with the area. It took him hours or more to find his way. He knew he was by his motel when he heard the singing frogs.

He stood by the small pond listening to the frogs, confused, and lost as to what he had just witnessed. And why had Assad trusted him to reveal his identity to him? Even when he knew Cyrus's brother was one of the most powerful men in the Savak. It seemed he was talking to the singing frogs. But the answer did not come from the frogs, "Truth is not always present when a man is facing it…"

It was Assad, speaking as he appeared from into the darkness. The men looked at one another. Both had lots of questions to ask and intended to get answers. Cyrus realized Assad was waiting for him at his motel, so he could not wait any longer to seek an answer to what he was dying to know. "Why did you trust me?"

"Because I see the same man when I look into the mirror, a man about to walk a path that may bring regret to him years later, with a great cost and suffering which will come upon him and his family in these difficult times… and worst of all, he has nothing to show for it but guilt, shame, and regret..."

Assad paused, realizing Cyrus was having a hard time digesting his words. He continued choosing his words more wisely, "You question why those like us have nothing to show but pain, suffering, and regret. It is because we aren't in it for the money or powerful positions. We do it for the good of the land, for the people who just want to live peacefully upon it. And in the end, we may have achieved nothing. We know people are misled, uneducated, and some just opportunists who become traitors on a whim."

Assad walked closer and continued in a softer, steady tone, "and the saddest part of it all knowing all these facts, we still follow our hearts with no more will to back it up with, why am I still looking for these answers?"

It was not clear to Cyrus what Assad was referring to. He wanted more clarity. "I am confused. What are you trying to tell me?"

Assad thought for a long bit again before answering, "Maybe you have to look into the mirror and see clearer … come with me..."

Then Assad began to walk into the darkness. And Cyrus, again, had to decide regarding what to do - go after him or not. But there was no way Cyrus could refuse such a man like Assad. He came so far for this moment, and he was not going to back up or miss it.

*****

Chapter 19

When a man of experience risks his life to save loved ones...

It was a quiet night in the village with the moon shining above. Cyrus was sitting by a window in Assad's living room, watching Assad quietly playing his Tar, a traditional Iranian instrument. Cyrus had spent a few days with Assad; they still had not left the house. He was captured by Assad's personality and wisdom, wanting to learn more.

In the short time they had been together, both had been changed, their perspectives shifted. Cyrus thought he saw a faint twinkle in Assad's wife's eyes as if this was something he only did on rare, special occasions for the first time having a guest at her house; Cyrus was becoming more puzzled by this man as the evening progressed.

It was past midnight when Assad's three children sleepily appeared in the doorway, peeking in to see who their guest was. The youngest was a five-year-old girl who Cyrus imagined looked like Roxanna at that age. The eldest was fifteen, and the middle child, the only boy, was ten. None had ever heard Assad play the instrument before, and they stood there, entranced.

A change was occurring within Assad. A large part of him had been put to rest years ago to enable him to shut out the past. Being happy was a luxury someone in his position could not afford. Being happy meant letting one's guard down, and that was something he was incapable of doing. He had accepted this truth. But Cyrus's presence was slowly shattering the wall Assad had built between his present and past life. The ache of missing Roxanna and Linda had come back a thousand-fold and was ripping Assad's heart out. Playing his Tar after so long was the only thing he could do to help numb the pain.

Cyrus recalled what Assad told him when his eyes landed on a small mirror on the wall. Soon he was staring into the mirror, looking at himself. Assad's words began to play in his heart and soul as he was looking at Assad's image playing in the background, no longer seeing his own... "Because I see the same man when I look into the mirror, which is about to walk a path that may bring regret to him a year later, with a great cost and suffering which will come upon him and his family in these difficult times... and worst of all, has nothing to show for it but guilt, shame, and regret..."

Then it hit him, the realization of the life-altering sacrifices that Assad had brought on himself and had forced upon his family when he made the decision to put his country first. It hit him that Assad saw and was warning him that he was about to walk the same path that he did many years ago. It hit him that he was concerned he was going to do the same to Roxanna that Assad did to Linda, his American wife. Now, after all these years of sacrifice, did he have anything to show? Did he accomplish anything or help anyone?

Cyrus realized that his feelings for Roxanna were consuming him; he was so fond of her that all he thought about was marrying her and moving to America. He couldn't understand how this could be happening to him. He was in a quandary. Iran had always been his first love, his one, and only love. He had devoted his life to Iran, but in the end, he was feeling nothing but emptiness, loss, sorrow, and deep regret.

Even his feelings for his brother were becoming complicated. He understood that having a brother like Amir, with his politically sensitive position in the Savak, seemed envious to many, and it was true when he wandered into trouble or needed help, Amir was always there for him. But with the political climate changing so fast, Cyrus was starting to feel like an insect, pinned to a piece of cardboard in science class, constantly being scrutinized under a microscope.

Having a brother in the Savak was like being caught in a spider's web, having his hands and feet bound together, his vocal cords ripped out, and his eyes blinded. So, getting out of Iran, he thought, was his only hope. He dreamed of California. Hollywood! Bright lights! Big Dreams! And no bombs! And in the beginning, before he knew what she was made of, he saw Roxanna as his ticket out.

Just thinking about that now brought cold sweat of guilt into his heart and soul. Everything was different now. Dreams had given way to a deeper reality. Roxanna's life was in jeopardy, and danger was their constant companion. Hollywood was far from his mind. He had a new maturity and a new understanding of what it meant to love your country and to love a woman. The naivety of youth was gone. He was in love with Roxanna.

But at the same time, the idea of ever having to leave Roxanna the way Assad had left Linda distressed him, but it was something that they would have to face if he stayed with her. Committing one's life to a cause, an ideology, a country was always at the sacrifice of the more intimate commitment of marriage and family. He could either be married to his country or married to the woman he loved. It was an either/or proposition. They could not coexist.

Cyrus could not understand how he had let his feelings for Roxanna grow to the point that they were tearing him in all directions. He knew well what the consequences of marrying Roxana would be…at least for her. He would be offering her a life no different than Assad had given her mother … a life of heartbreak, loneliness, longing, and despair.

He knew in his heart if he truly loved Roxanna, the only way to save her would be to release her now before the repercussions would be too great. He was coming to the realization that love wasn't one emotion but all emotions playing out at different times in different situations. And that true love was more than putting Roxanna's feelings above his. It was to love enough to see beyond the present, into the future, and letting reality, not the heart, be one's true compass.

Cyrus became distracted from his thoughts by different sounds filling the night air outside; Neys (Flutes), dogs beginning to bark cutting through the quiet of the village. He looked out through the window into the darkness. He saw nothing tangible, but it was enough to give him a bad feeling. He sensed something move deeper into the trees. The sound of several dogs now barking and a wolf howling in the distance put Cyrus on alert.

Still, Assad continued his prayer with his eyes closed like he was not in this world. There was no doubt in Cyrus's mind that the wolves he feared were two-legged. A sudden feeling came over him as if he might have been the one to lead Savak right to Assad.

By now, Cyrus's eyes were only seeing Assad's old tar on the wall. His feelings were similar to what he thought Assad's to be. He began to hear the sound of the tar. As the sound of the tar played over in Cyrus's mind, the sound of a Neys flute rose louder and louder, echoed through the quiet village drifting inside the cottage, accompanying the tar in his head, overcoming the sound of Assad's praying.

Drawn to the balcony by the seductiveness of faint laughter and night music, Cyrus took the opportunity to peer into the darkness without alarming Assad. He was sure he could see someone lurking in the shadows, slowly approaching the swollen creek in front of Assad's cottage; one leap, and the man was on the other side. During his time there, Cyrus had learned that Reza, the principal of Assad's school, lived next door.

It took less than a second, and yet, there was no question in his mind; Cyrus saw a man jump off Reza's rooftop to a spot closer to Assad's cottage. Cyrus looked back with concern at Assad, who was still kneeling on a small rug, praying in peace. Something bad was about to happen, but before he could even consider a plan, a loud sound tore into the silence, resonating from inside the room where Assad was praying.

A coward would have hopped the balcony and disappeared, but Cyrus ran back inside to find himself staring down several armed men carrying American-made machine guns. Another kicked the front door with such force that it was left dangling by one small hinge. Two more rushed toward Cyrus, securing him with nothing more than the easiness in which they toyed with their weapons…The rest surrounded Assad, not wanted to risk hell by disturbing his prayer.

Now that they were contained, several armed Savak agents entered and took over, surrounding them both. Still, more agents rushed in to search the other rooms after each room had been secured. Cyrus, outnumbered and on his best behavior, was placed in handcuffs and asked to remain seated and silent. His eyes were only focused on Assad.

Hashem, the man in charge, prided himself in having great respect for the bravery and certain rituals. When he set eyes on Assad, who had remained unmoved by the sight of machine guns, he nodded to his men, signaling them to pull back. They relinquished their aggressive stance and waited for him to finish his prayer.

Assad placed his forehead on the prayer rock, his eyes closed. As he continued praying, he raised his head, "Allah oh Akbaar, Allah oh Akbaar." Assad lowered his forehead to the prayer rock again and continued praying, calmly, ignoring the commotion around him. "Allah oh Akbaar." Cyrus sat motionless alongside the armed men, watching Assad say his prayer.

While searching the house, the Savak intruders discovered Assad's frightened wife and children and gathered them up in a small corner of the main room where she embraced her children, protectively, as they cried in absolute fear. They were made even more inconsolable by a female Savak soldier, trying to calm them down.

Hashem noticed the tar and took it off the wall, carefully examining it as if he was a collector, then he placed it back gently and carefully. Several men emerged from the other rooms, their arms filled with stacks of books and anything else of value they could confiscate.

The female Savak agent, being unfamiliar with the ways of little girls, missed her chance to grab Assad's baby daughter as she broke from her mother's grip and ran to him, crying. She leaped into Assad's arms, finally breaking his prayer. The men shifted around nervously, holding their guns, watching what would unfold next. Assad finally acknowledged the men, calmly looking around the room, "She is just a small child, and I am just one old man. You aren't surrounding the Arab army."

Assad's wife hurried over and pried the little girl from her father's arms, then quickly gathered up the other children and disappeared into a small room, not wanting them to be traumatized any further. The female Savak guard, more comfortable with machine guns than little ones, made no motion to stop the children, but with a sense of authority, closed them in. Assad calmly got up and straightened himself out, looking as if he was about to give a speech. Everyone waited nervously, but none came. They politely handcuffed him.

As hard as Cyrus tried to catch Assad's attention, he refused to look his way. He was certain Assad would place the blame on him for his arrest. Cyrus was already working on a plan to get released from the Savak. He was hoping he could make a deal with his brother, although he knew things had changed between them. He realized his brother had deceived him and knowing that the first time was always the hardest, it meant Amir could no longer be trusted.

He realized Roxanna's capture and release by the Savak had been a way of setting her up. Amir knew one of two things would happen if they let her go; either she would find her father, or Assad would stop at nothing to find her. And for that, Amir was willing to deceive his own flesh and blood.

Cyrus could hear the loud moaning and sobbing of Assad's wife and children as he was marched outside by Savak guards. Cyrus looked up and saw Reza jump from one roof to the next, then down into the alley directly in front of him. It was just the distraction the guards were waiting for. They walked Cyrus away.

In outlying villages, small news was big news. Villagers emerged from their homes and gathered as close as they dared, near enough to Assad's cottage to see what was happening, but at a safe enough distance to be able to make themselves invisible if the police arrived. Just seeing Savak agents sent chills up their spines. Some ran, but most stayed at a safe distance, avoiding conflict, as they watched Assad being escorted out of his house in handcuffs, surrounded by several armed agents.

As word spread, people gathered on balconies, cars, and rooftops, squinting, and cupping their ears, each wanting to be the first to know. They held up oil lanterns to light the way, only to drop them and run if they felt they had drawn too much attention to themselves. An old woman stuck her face out of a neighboring window, filling the frame with glassy eyes, and hollered, "Are the Iraqis attacking again? What do they want this time?" Her face disappeared as quickly as it had appeared, and the window slammed shut.

Assad turned and looked at Reza, then to an old man who snuck a glance through his cracked door and said, "Don't hate them. They are just like us, Iranian—good Iranians. They are just doing what they have been told."

The guards continued walking Assad through the alleyway as the chanting of "Allah oh Akbaar" echoed through the village.

Meanwhile, Cyrus was escorted, at gunpoint, to the outer edge of the village where several vehicles were parked, far from Assad's but very close to where Cyrus had left his car. He recognized two of them as large vans designed to transport prisoners, equipped with metal rings attached to the seats for securing handcuffs and wide belts for restraining captives. Much to his chagrin, the guards walked Cyrus to the first van, secured him, and shut the door.

Almost immediately, a large black sedan pulled up with Amir inside. His brother had been waiting, inconspicuously, for the moment they would bring Cyrus to him. Little did Cyrus know that his brother had been there the entire time keeping him alive, and he had been doing the same for

Assad. Hashem opened the door to Cyrus's van, and Amir stepped up to the seat next to him. The van's door slammed shut behind him.

For several moments there was silence, each trying to formulate the words they wanted to speak without polluting them with overwhelming feelings of betrayal and confusion. Neither brother could comprehend how they had come to be so polarized in their beliefs. What had come between them was far greater than the usual philosophical and political differences generally expressed around dinner tables across the world. Their differences were born of events that had disrupted lives, destroyed families, changed history, and caused death.

Cyrus stared at his brother, unable to find words to express his feelings. He knew his brother was responsible for the sustained terrorist threats throughout Tehran. He knew that he, himself, had been used by the Savak— used by his own brother. All along, Amir had been manipulating him, knowing Cyrus would lead them to Assad.

"You used me—lied to me!" His bellow was filled with rage and pain.

" Isn't that what your friend did to Roxanna?" Amir asked calmly. "Use her and lie to her?" Amir tossed a flyer on Cyrus's lap, "When was the last time you heard from Nader? Nader was like your brother… he grew up with you. He practically lived at our house, remember? This is what your longtime friend, Saeed, did to him…"

Cyrus's eyes were fixed, in horror, on the flyer Amir had placed in front of him. It included several photos of Nader in flames. Amir's voice began to reverberate in Cyrus's brain, like the buzzing of a thousand Cicadas. He held his head in his hands and squeezed his eyes together, trying to rid himself of the sickening image threatening to destroy his will. He was no longer sure if he was screaming for himself or all humanity.

Unfazed by Cyrus's torment, Amir continued to describe the incident in detail. "Your friend set Nader up by asking to see him to make peace. They met at an abandoned barn in the south of Tehran. Nader arrived with Abdullah, who was in hiding, not facing the same way as Saeed. Soon Nader found out he was set up. Nader was just staring at Saeed and smiling, confused. Saeed's men sprayed Nader with gas.

"But it was your friend, Saeed, who lit the match and then held it under his own face, making him look like the devil. Nader's nervous smile faded away when Saeed threw the match at him. Saeed and Abdullah just stood there and watched their old friend go up in flames. He was burned alive. Abdullah was mad and confused as hell. As for Saeed, there was no remorse or sympathy in his eyes. He was cold as stone… then they blamed it on Savak…"

Cyrus was no longer able to restrain the avalanche of emotions that had been building up inside him since Roxanna's disappearance. Seeing images of Nader being burned alive pushed him into some alternative reality. It was almost as if he could feel himself morphing into some mythical wild beast only to be shot with a poisoned arrow. "So, was it not the Savak?!"

Amir's demeanor suddenly changed to anger and frustration as he watched tears fall from Cyrus's bulging eyes. He was not without patience, but he was running on empty. He could not believe how naive Cyrus could be. Slowly and deliberately, he leaned close to him and whispered, "This is what you do not understand. The same people you are supposedly helping or ignoring what harm they bring upon your country had FATFA on your head because of your playwriting. They want you dead.

"Anytime some kind of stupid uneducated radical who thinks by killing you would go to heaven would walk up to you and out bullets into your head or chest… do you know what would happen to Hajji Khanoum if this happen…? You see… You act like a ten-year-old who knows it all. Nader was like a brother to me, just as he was to you. Why would the Savak murder one of their own men? Nader was working for us, for me! Nader was assigned to protect Roxanna!"

His brother's words pummeled him as if a fistfight raged in his head. The more Amir spoke, the worse it got for both of them. Cyrus was caught completely off guard upon hearing Roxana's name as Amir continued. "From the minute Roxanna arrived in Iran, we were following her. We knew exactly where you were going and who you were looking for…"

Amir's words burned into Cyrus's thin skin, scarring him. He worshipped his brother, even though they disagreed on almost every serious issue. But no matter how heated their arguments could get, he had always known his brother meant good for him, and he would always be there for him. Wounded by his brother's sharp words, Cyrus looked down in silence and made no move to stop Amir from getting out of the car.

But Amir was not finished chastising his brother. In fact, he was just warming up. "At any rate, on Friday, you will leave for America. Your passport and visa have been taken care of." Amir hit the inside of the door with the side of his fist, emphasizing the fact that the subject was not open to discussion.

Hashed took it as a signal and opened the door before Amir had finished with Cyrus. Amir placed one foot on the ground before turning to his brother, staring Cyrus in the eyes, "I'm giving you one last chance, under one condition: you go to Mother and tell her that it's your decision to leave the country. I hope you've got enough sense to do what I say."

The two brothers challenged each other; their weapon of choice, silence. Who would speak first? What was the other thinking? What if neither broke the silence? In truth, as brothers who were not allowed to argue in front of their mother, they had faced silence, inexhaustibly, over the years.

Meanwhile, at the time Cyrus and Amir were testing their feelings, Assad, handcuffed, was being escorted through the village toward the vans, while villagers came out watching, some hiding in the dark. Assad, handcuffed, reached the other van. He stopped, and they exchanged looks, which lasted a long bit. Neither of the two men knew what to say or what they could say. A look and feeling of sorrow were on the faces of both men.

The door slammed shut, and the van took off. After that, the only thing Cyrus could feel was the movement of the car jogging his full bladder. He was afraid it was ready to burst. The metal rings cut into his body, reminding him he was no longer in control of his life.

The van took off. Assad and Amir watched the van drive off, taking Cyrus. Then one of the men opened the side door, shoving Assad in, face down on the floor. It was a brutal attempt to make Amir happy, but it had just the opposite effect. Furious, Amir immediately jumped on the guards, "Treat him with respect. Take his handcuffs off." When they were finished, Amir got in the car next to Assad.

The men locked eyes, like two animals sizing each other up; whoever blinked first, the weaker. Amir, having no reason to prove himself, broke his stance. Just before shutting the door, he turned to the guards, "He is Iranian, just like us. He is not the enemy, just very confused." Assad, now unrestrained, sat in the van at the mercy of Amir, who had chosen to sit across from him. The guards stepped far enough away to give them some privacy.

There was a long, long, long silence before Amir confronted Assad.

"Your daughter has come a long way to see you. It seems as though she will have to wait a bit longer." Assad sighed. It was always a relief to hear loved ones spoken of in the present tense. "Or she could be used against you, and maybe she will never see you. But, of course, that all depends on you and what you choose to do next. She is much better off if she has no information about you or knows where you are. She is young and inexperienced and unfamiliar with our culture ... you must be very careful your enemy would not use her against you and not to risk her life ... your friends have mercy on no one and nothing... I am sure if one day they do not like what you do and they know she is your daughter, they even may kill her ... This group of religious believers would not hesitate to sacrifice their own children to achieve wealth and status... it's definitely up to you, and your next choice will have a big impact on Roxanna's fate, but my advice is that no one should know or understand that Roxana is your daughter ..."

Assad was confused by Amir's words. Why was Amir sensitive to Roxanna? What did he want from her? Amir did not hesitate any longer and continued, "So, after we finish here, this van will disappear, and this conversation will never have taken place. As far as the world will know, you have escaped again."

Assad was debating whether Amir was playing one of the games the Secret Service played on people to scare them into agreeing to anything. Or, perhaps, he was speaking the truth. "Why are you risking your future, perhaps your life, to save me, to help me?"

Amir looked out to make sure the guards had stayed further away and then leaned in closer to Assad and whispered, "Because we both have good intentions for our country and our people. I cannot do anything more, but you may be able to do more in the future. Stop the madness that will come upon our country. Those clergies are not loyal to Islam or Iran... they turn against either to hold power... they will ruin Islam and Iran... but people like you are decent and may be able to help... and I am not even sure about that... I only hope..."

Amir got out and gestured to his guards to get back to work. He walked away, leaving Assad stunned. On that cold breezy night, Amir watched the van take off and rush through the dark night, taking Assad away.

The bright headlights of the van and several other cars, one being Amir's, cut through the alleys, lighting the mud houses as they moved deeper into the night. A few people appeared like moths in the path of the dancing lights, motivated by curiosity and the need for excitement.

As they began to caravan out of the village, they saw the dancing light of a lone car approaching from the opposite direction. They were forced to stop and wait for the cars to pass. It was Akbaar, with Roxanna next to him in the passenger seat. Once the last car passed them leaving the village, they were free to enter. Akbaar drove directly into the village and followed the narrow creek that bordered the town, running in front of Assad's cottage. Akbaar and Roxanna exchanged anxious looks as they stopped and began walking toward Assad's house, passing many agitated, vocal villagers. Akbaar knew then, the fears that had been playing out in his head had become a reality.

He decided to stay quiet, hoping that by some miracle, Assad was not the reason for all the commotion. But when they saw all the villagers gathered outside with oil lanterns, they braced for the worst. Next door, the old woman's face appeared in the small window, again, yelling, "Are those Iraqis gone?" Roxanna followed Akbaar to the cottage, both dismissing the old woman with a mere glance.

Once they were confident that the Savak had left, the villagers regained their composure, stepping in to begin repairing the damage, fixing the doors, boarding up the broken windows, and cleaning up the debris. Akbaar's immediate concern was for Assad's children. He found them with their mother, still cowering in a corner, covered with a blanket. It was as if the children had taken on the parenting role and were trying to console their mother.

Relief poured through them as they rushed to their uncle and jumped in his arms. He turned to Roxanna, who was standing in the doorway, concerned, and overcome with sadness but unsure of how to approach the children without frightening them. "These are your stepsisters and stepbrother," Akbaar announced, waving his arm proudly. Next, he pointed to Roxanna, "And this very special person is your stepsister from America, who came to see you. She loves you very much." Akbaar was wise and kind and knew that the best and only way to handle children was with love.

Roxanna's presence turned out to be a wonderful distraction from the trauma they had just witnessed. Tears welled in the children's eyes as they looked from their mother, who was still holding her knees tightly to her chest, to Roxanna. They were old enough to understand that something very serious was happening around them but too young to know just how much it could affect the rest of their lives.

Roxanna was about to kneel down to their level when the little girl broke away from Akbaar and walked to hug her. Both she and her sister rushed towards Roxanna, accidentally knocking her backward, winding up on top of her in a laughing, giggling heap. After a time, the boy, who appeared extremely shy, wiggled his way closer and pressed against her, wanting to feel her closeness but afraid to reach out and touch.

Roxanna's eyes filled with tears of joy when Akbaar introduced her to these amazing little children. They were a part of her, a part of her family. She felt their fear still emanating from them, but at the same time, she felt their warmth and love. Although they didn't quite understand the concept of stepsister, they were enthralled with this beautiful older sister who, to them, was like a princess.

Despite the tragic events that led up to their meeting, the moment couldn't have been more magical. The sound of the people talking as they were cleaning up the mess around them was lost in the excitement of Roxanna's arrival. She was a calming gift, a messenger of hope, hugging them and stroking their wonderful faces. She held them tightly in her arms, and all the fear and tension in the room subsided.

Sadness turned into a celebration, with a wave of women embracing Roxanna as the evening progressed. The night of terrifying fear was replaced with hugs, kisses, drinks, and food brought in by neighbors. Assad's friends and neighbors were stunned to learn the details of Assad's life in Germany and Roxanna. Everyone loved the story, and if that wasn't incredible enough, they were astonished to learn that their exceedingly quiet friend and neighbor had an American wife and daughter they knew nothing about.

Roxanna's eyes lit on her father's old tar, which Hashem had returned to its rightful place on the wall, and her tears began to flow. Remarkably, it had remained untouched, despite the destruction and chaos that threatened to destroy it. She had heard about the instrument from her mother but never seen one in person. She knew, then, that this was her father's home.

Once Roxanna was alone, she had time to study the tragic events as they unfolded, and as a result, a sinking feeling settled in the pit of her stomach. A profound awareness echoed in her head, enlightening her to the reality of the situation. She was the reason the government had located Assad. Her presence in Iran had brought attention to him, and the Savak had used her as a powerful tool to locate him. Both Assad and Akbaar were aware of the risk and danger Roxanna's presence created. It was as if she had thrown a snowball from the top of a snow-covered mountain. Once it begins its roll downward, the faster and bigger it grows until it becomes unstoppable, taking hold of everything in its path.

*****

Days passed, and the nights slipped away like silk between Roxanna's fingertips. Her stepsisters and stepbrother accepted her as if she was a treasured gift, making the transition into her new Iranian family flawless. The youngest child was so infatuated by her new sister that she would sit on Roxanna's lap and play with her hair for endless hours. Assad's wife tried to express her love and acceptance by teaching her how to cook Iranian dishes and by serving her several delicious kinds of food every day. Roxanna could not help but think of how young Assad's wife was and how different she was from her mother. Perhaps this woman's simplicity, her nonjudgmental warmth, and kindness was why her father never went back to the states. She didn't want to think about it.

Every day, at lunch and dinner, the neighbors would walk in with treats they had cooked, especially for Roxanna. Sometimes, three or four neighbors would appear on the doorstep at once, carrying fragrant bowls of Pomegranate Stews, eggplant and tomatoes, kebabs, and saffron rice puddings.

Staying with her extended family had enabled Roxanna to learn more about her father, who had been gone for a long while and was terribly missed by everyone. It didn't surprise her that he was known as a quiet intellectual who preferred writing and reading to sports and sensibility and simplicity to frivolity. She even understood more about the way he loved by the way he was loved by others. There was no blame. Love was accepting with no judgment and unconditional.

When he was gone, there was worry. He was missed but at no time was his absence questioned. She learned more about love from his family than she had learned in her lifetime. Her time with her father's family had been a joyous respite, but she knew it was only temporary. She had important things to do. Hajji Khanoum would be needing her, and the time to resume her search for her father was nearing. No one had heard from Akbaar since he had left, and it was very concerning.

When the day of leave-taking arrived, saying goodbye was extraordinarily difficult. Her stepmother, her little sisters and brother, and all the villagers formed a line to say goodbye. The children were kissing her and crying, their little hearts breaking at the thought of losing her. Roxanna got through the goodbyes by saying she would see them all again soon, and when she returned, she would bring their father with her. Her littlest sister was too young to know anything about being strong or hiding emotions. Lying on the floor, she held Roxanna's leg tight, wrapping both her little arms around her with a grip so firm that a neighboring woman had to use all her strength to pull her loose.

In the window next door, the old lady was not about to let the celebration go unnoticed. Her face appeared just as before, and she yelled, "Are the Iraqis back again?"

Roxanna broke into a smile. She knew she would miss that old woman and hearing that silly question. Assad's wife poured water behind her, explaining that it was a traditional custom that showed she was always welcomed back.

*****

Chapter 20

One by One, They Disappear...

Roxanna found herself back in Tehran thinking about her father every minute of every day. Several months passed. She had now assimilated into the role of a Persian woman living in Iran; the way she dressed, even the foods she bought at the grocery store were authentic. Memories of her time with her grandmother, Uncle Akbaar, and her new sisters and brother were all she had to keep her spirits up. Cyrus had disappeared without even saying goodbye, but as long as she had Hajji Khanoum, she would survive.

She was staying in Peter's large, second-floor apartment, which was located on the north side, at the end of a quaint cul-de-sac. A boy of fourteen who had become totally infatuated with Roxanna lived with his parents directly above. He was photographing Roxanna with his new camera at any opportunity he could find.

The owner, Farhad, and all the neighbors had welcomed her graciously and made it a point to keep an eye on her. Farhad's wife, Azaar, and his daughter, Farydeh, took every opportunity to learn English from Roxanna, even offering to pay her, but she loved doing it and insisted the money was not necessary; Akbaar and her grandmother had given her plenty of money to live comfortably for years to come. Cyrus had also left funds with his mother in case she needed it.

*****

It was one more calm night in Tehran. As usual, Peter was engaged in reading and discussing philosophy and poetry with the attendant. Pary sat with Roxanna in a quiet corner at Peter's restaurant. Both were overly happy from having several glasses of wine. They both stared at an image of Cyrus, surprised and concerned. They were looking at a picture of Hussein and his friend holding a machine gun, posing for him. They could see Cyrus was the only one who had no smile, only a look of concern on his face. Roxanna knew what she was looking at. She was familiar with the Yuma desert. Hussein had taken her there a few times. For a moment, Roxanna felt she was back in America in the desert with them.

The Yuma Desert was one of the most sparsely populated areas in the world and could be summed up in two words, sand dunes: not a particularly inviting place for a belated honeymoon.

Looking Cyrus directly in the eyes, Hussein released a weapon from its case and began to detail the specifications of his killing machine. The HK21 was German made in 1961. Its range was from 100 to 1200 meters, and it shot an 80 round drum magazine with roller delayed blowback. The more Hussein spoke, the heavier was Cyrus's heart. The world was upside down; his world was upside down. What the hell was he going to tell his Julia he was doing there?

Hussein walked away from Cyrus, firmly holding onto the machine gun. Looking around to be sure the others were out of danger; he aimed directly towards a sand dune and began shooting several rounds. First, the initial explosion of the gun was heard, followed by the sound of impact, finally resonating back to where they stood. Each bullet in the round had its own individual explosion, one following immediately after the other, hitting the sides of the dune, exploding it as if it was a small volcanic eruption.

Hussein was not the only one being trained on the killing machine. There were several other Iranians there; among them were Abdi and a young woman named Parisa, who Cyrus recalled from a meeting at

Hussein's apartment in Westwood. Hussein held his machine gun out to Cyrus, "You want to try it?" That was the last thing Cyrus wanted to hear. It was painful enough for him to watch; using it was out of the question. "I never touched it, and I never will."

Hussein teased his best friend, "It's good you're a black belt. But are you faster than a speeding bullet?" He passed the new machine gun to Abdi and Parisa, who took time to examine its parts with great care. Satisfied, Abdi looked through the scope, its gold belt feed dangling from the side like a trophy, then handed it to Hussein, who walked towards his target, finally getting the opportunity to test the weapon.

It was obvious to Cyrus that Hussein was about to impress him with his good aim. Had he lost his perspective? Good aim toward whom? Those with who you share blood? Cyrus wondered what in the hell was going on. Every time he had met with Hussein and his gang over the past two months, he had grown more concerned about Iran.

Hussein held the machine gun over his head. He was now speaking to all the men who had gathered in the desert, "Who is ready to take the first risk and go through American customs with a few of these?"

*****

It was just a few months later Cyrus was sitting on a large crate at Hussein's apartment in Westwood, near the UCLA campus, watching TV and waiting for Hussein to come out of the bathroom. Parisa was seated on the floor nearby, reading a newspaper. Abdi was preparing some food in the kitchen. Furniture was sparse; they were students with little money.

Some American government spokesmen appeared on the TV screen, "The United States has given a firm pledge to the establishment of human rights in Iran. We are supporting the Shah and believe he can lead Iran into progressive development that would benefit the people." Hussein's voice began yelling at the TV from the bathroom, "It's too late to save you fucking dogs! He's going down!"

The phone rang, interrupting both the TV and Hussein's rant. Parisa tried to answer it, but before she got there, Hussein rushed out of the bathroom with his pants around his legs, grabbed the phone, and rushed back inside to finish what he had started. Parisa turned the sound down on the television and headed to the bathroom door to listen. She had obviously done this before. Cyrus clearly heard Hussein's voice. "No problem, good news, brothers, good news indeed, more will follow. God be with you. See you in a short time."

Minutes later, Hussein walked out of the bathroom, zipping up his fly. He cheerfully hugged Parisa and then Abbdi. Parisa told him he should go wash his hands. Instead of a hug, Hussein gave Cyrus his usual persuasive speech. "The power of the people will bring the evil of the Shah tumbling down and out of the country." Without another word, Hussein whacked Cyrus on the shoulder and motioned for him to get up. He then began opening the box Cyrus had been sitting on to reveal several machine guns in various stages of assembly. He picked one up and held it in front of Cyrus, "That call was from Iran. They just passed four of these through customs. The hardest part is getting them. I want you to buy us more. You have the money and the Green Card."

Hussein did not wait for Cyrus to respond. Maybe he knew Cyrus's answer would be no, and that was not the answer he was going to take.

"And guess who helped to pass it through?" Hussein knew he had left Cyrus speechless, so he answered for him. "Yes. The CIA... you see, a few months ago, I was introduced to a lady who works at the American Embassy in Tehran. Her name was Soudabeh. We became friends, and through her, I met an American lady, Dorian... and yes, we had fun the entire night. Over time, trust was built between us, and consequently, she offered to help us pass the rifles into Iran. At first, I did not believe her, but when I saw the first batch pass through, I knew she was right. That tells me someone wants the Shah out."

Cyrus was so caught up in this one-sided conversation with Hussein that he hardly heard a car honking impatiently outside. Cyrus and Hussein looked out of a window to see a beautiful blonde sitting in the passenger side of Cyrus's car. It was Julia, waving for him to come. He really wanted to know more about the guns Hussein had hidden away inside his apartment, and more importantly, he wanted to learn more about Hussein's CIA connection regarding passing guns through Iranian customs, but he realized he had left Julia sitting in the car far longer than he had expected.

The idea that the CIA could be helping to send weapons to Iran was impossible for him to believe. Hussein was either a madman or a liar. But what if he was neither?

Cyrus was crying inside, his heart torn in two. Sending powerful guns into Iran to use against their own people was something he neither believed in nor understood. He could not reconcile any of it in his head. Under no circumstances could he justify killing. No matter how hard he tried, he could not block out Hussein's words from playing over in his head.

"Your people and your country will not forget you for what you are doing to bring freedom to them. The time is now. We need more guns. You have the money and the green card. You get them, we send them through. We will bring the evil Shah down."

Cyrus looked directly into Hussein's eyes and, for some reason, wanted to speak to him about Roxanna. But every time he tried, his thoughts were killed by some kind of unknown power or will, like he was afraid to bring the name Roxanna up. It was as if his entire soul and conscience were overtaken by sadness and fear, and uncertainty.

*****

It had been a long time since Cyrus had left but not as long as it felt to Roxanna. She occupied much of her time with visits to Hajji Khanoum, which were very important to all of them and became a routine part of their lives. In a sense, Hajji Khanoum had adopted Roxanna as one of her own children, and if she didn't show up at the same time each day, Hajji Khanoum would call everyone she knew until she found her. One evening Peter picked up the phone, and when he heard Hajji Khanoum's voice, he jokingly handed it immediately to Roxanna, knowing that Hajji Khanoum was not calling for him. She usually sounded relieved to have found her, but this time Roxanna noticed a feeling of urgency in her voice. She told her to come to her house right away.

Roxanna had grown to love her uncle as well and felt guilty that he was giving her so much money, knowing he was taking care of Assad's family as well, but he insisted, and she finally acquiesced. Such altruism was not common in America, and it was practically unknown to Roxanna. Their selflessness touched Roxanna deeply, and it was one of many beautiful aspects of Iran that she treasured and vowed to take as her own.

The taxi stopped in front of Hajji Khanoum's, where Ahmad Reza was waiting to open the gate and walk her to the house. Roxanna couldn't have been more surprised to have Hajji Khanoum greet her at the door with a large smile plastered across her wrinkled face. Roxanna had never seen the old woman smile unless Cyrus was around, and she got her hopes up. They had been together long enough, so they were beginning to understand each other without a translator.

She knew Roxanna was there to see if she could get any help from Amir regarding her father. She was told Cyrus's room was now her room. So, she had a room of her own there. And every time she walked into Cyrus' old room, his image was all over the wall, and she could not help but get lost in his memory, thinking, and guessing what he was doing in America … in Los Angeles, the city she had grown up.

But unknown to Roxanna, Cyrus was, in fact, lost in a world unknown to him. Undoubtedly, Los Angeles, where Cyrus was living now, was one of the best cities in the world to spend your life for many, with its blue skies, white sand beaches, and warm ocean breeze to nurture one's spiritual growth and Hollywood glamour and dreams. It seemed only Cyrus was blind to its attributes; the sound of crashing waves, suntanned students playing volleyball on the beach, and the carefree lifestyle perpetuated by endless summers.

To him, the city felt like a beam of blinding white light without a prism to bend it into a spectrum of colors, a stage without a play to give it depth and meaning. He was there in body, but his thoughts and his aching heart remained on the other side of the world, in his homeland of Iran. Even though there were things he enjoyed about American life, he felt as if he was in a vacuum, his thoughts filled with nostalgia for Iran and the rich life he had back home. It had been a life overflowing with substance, meaning, purpose, goals, and rewards. Los Angeles left him empty and cold. He missed the solid structure of productivity.

In Iran, Cyrus was not only a sports hero; he was also a movie star who was born into a rich and politically tied family and was living a life that most young men and women could only dream of. Yet, everything that was meaningful to him, everything that had given purpose to his life, had been stripped away. Why? Because he wasn't afraid to stand up for what he believed in. He was fighting for his people and a better Iran. He didn't take his life for granted, he knew he had been born into a lifestyle that afforded him the opportunity, and he truly wanted to use that opportunity to help the masses of less fortunate people in his country.

Then he watched his best friend and many others trying to destroy the land he loved. Cyrus knew that the way to change the future was not with guns and bloodshed but through knowledge and by educating people. He dedicated his life to trying to educate his people through his art, his writing, his poetry, and his filmmaking. But, unfortunately, especially the Clergies didn't agree with what Cyrus had to say, and his words and creative works put him in grave danger, forcing him to leave his homeland with nothing but his life. He had no friends.

Arriving in America, Cyrus was reunited with his old friend and classmate, Hussein, who, besides being an assistant professor at UCLA, was known as one of the leaders of the anti-group against the Shah. It had been in the car when Hussein picked him up from the Los Angeles airport when he asked him to join his anti-Shah group.

Traffic was unusually slow on the drive from LAX to Hussein's apartment near the campus in Westwood. Hussein used the extra time to sing a known revolutionary song to Cyrus, who would have preferred conversation. "Shahyed Jangal. Yaleh syahkal..." he sang, boldly. Cyrus didn't realize it until he arrived in the United States but meeting up with Hussein didn't help his situation.

Ironically, by making the decision to call his old friend, he wound up deeper into the movement in America than in Tehran. The whole point of leaving Iran was to stay alive so he could find a way to write and make his movies to educate people. If he was going to die anyway, he would die in his homeland, where now Roxanna was calling home.

Then there was always the voice of Hajji Khanoum, who would bring Roxanna to the present. She had no choice but to go to the kitchen with Hajji Khanoum, or she would bring the kitchen into her room, "Come in, my daughter, come in. He is here! You can talk to him. He looks mean, but he is a very nice man. Take advantage of this moment and ask him about your father. I already made him promise to help you. But first, you must eat something."

The minute Roxanna sat down at the kitchen table; the fighting would start. But it was a loving and kind fight, and it was always over Roxanna's small appetite. The scent of warm tea filled Roxanna's nostrils as Hajji Khanoum placed a drink called Sharbat on the table; many refills followed along with an array of endless snacks. Sharbat was a mixture of several fruit juices mixed with a sweet called zanjabil. Hajji Khanoum fussed over Roxanna, stuffing her with irresistible delicacies like all Persian mothers do.

No matter how hard Roxanna tried to get her to stop, it never worked. Hajji Khanoum would respond by calling for her helper, and more delicious foods would arrive from the kitchen, overwhelming her. Hajji Khanoum knew she had the upper hand and would win sooner or later, so she never gave up. Nothing tickled her more than to hear refusal after refusal and then… "Okay, just one more bite." If you were an outsider, you might think they were arguing. But, of course, it had always been an Iranian custom. Iranians believe that a guest is a "Gift of God" and that they must serve them to "a fullness." But even in Iran, where it is the custom, there is a fine line between showing love and friendship and harassment.

Roxanna was determined to force herself to eat a horse if it was a prerequisite to her meeting with Amir. And she felt like she had. She knew he was nearby because she could hear him talking on the phone in Cyrus's room. She was picturing him touching all of Cyrus's possessions out of spite. It was no secret that Cyrus was his mother's favorite and that she had insisted his room remain untouched ever since he got his own place.

Amir's voice steadily rose in volume, signaling to both women that something unpleasant was unfolding. Concerned, Hajji Khanoum opened the door to the bedroom and asked Amir to quiet down, or he would soon scare away their guest, but Amir was too angry and furious to even notice or acknowledge his mother's presence. Khally always knew when things weren't right and began to bark. Hajji Khanoum, who was not used to being ignored, knocked on the open door until she got Amir's attention. Realizing his mother and Roxanna were waiting, he yelled into the receiver before hanging up. "I am on my way. I will be there within half an hour."

Regardless of what was happening in the world or what chaos surrounded them, Hajji Khanoum was going to serve tea and food to everyone in her vicinity. No one, not even her son, had any choice in the matter. So, by the time Amir entered the living room, Hajji Khanoum had a cup of tea ready for him. He knew he had no choice but to take the tea and nodded, sending his regards to Roxanna.

"You must listen to her. If you help her, God will know and will help your brother. There!" Holding the cup, he tried to search for words to speak, but his thoughts were clearly somewhere else. His face was frozen, as if he was in a state of shock, a catatonic stupor. It was a look that sent shivers down Roxanna's spine. She had been told that Amir was an enigma of sorts, hardly ever showing emotion other than the occasional tiff with Cyrus, but this day, at this very moment, there was no doubt she could feel a sense of despair weighing him down.

Hajji Khanoum's lips snapped shut when she noticed tears welling up in Amir's eyes. The tray of food she was holding slipped from her hands and landed upside down on the Persian rug. Hajji Khanoum fell to her knees next to it, her face as pale as goat's milk. Attempting to control his emotions, Amir knelt down and pulled his trembling mother into his embrace.

"My son ... my Cyrus ... something has happened to him! That is why you are crying. What has happened to my son?" He sat down next to his mother, cradling her in his arms, just as she had done for so many others throughout her life. "Cyrus is in school in America, Hajji Khanoum. Nothing has happened to him."

"What is it, then?" Roxanna was afraid he was going to leave before saying more. "Something has happened in Abadan. The Cinema Rex movie theater was burned to the ground...with a full audience inside. Who could do such an inhumane act? Burning over three hundred people alive! What kind of human beings are these people? This is not opposition. This is murder!" Then he turns to Hajji Khanoum, "Please, Mother, I must go..." Slowly rising to his feet, Amir turned to Roxanna, "Please. Stay... She loves you. She is less worried for Cyrus when you are with her ... please." Then he left.

At a loss for words, Hajji Khanoum and Roxanna expressed the pain in their hearts through the sorrow in their eyes. There were too many emotions that had to be dealt with for Amir to stay any longer. He left, closing the door behind him. Roxanna sat by Hajji Khanoum, stroking her coarse, grey hair, fixing it into a knot. At least they knew that Cyrus was safe in America.

By now, Roxanna had figured out that BBC radio was the main source of information in Iran. She retrieved the radio and turned it on, now rubbing Hajji Khanoum's back and shoulders to comfort her. They listened in disbelief. "This is BBC in London, August 19, 1978. Today, there was another tragedy in Iran.

"In the city of Abadan, the Cinema Rex, a local movie theater, packed to capacity with families and children for an afternoon show, was burned to the ground. It is believed that the theater was set on fire intentionally. Authorities said all doors were closed and locked before it was set on fire, leaving no chance for escape. As of this report, there were no survivors."

August 19, 1978, the day the clergies planned and burned people in the Rex movie theater in the city of Abadan and blamed it on the Savak, was the day of judgment in Iran by Iranians. And for some reason, people trusted the murderers over the innocent, and from that day, people became blind, deaf, and mute. No matter what the Radio BBC would report, as far as the people were concerned, it was the truth.

The real truth was that a family movie, *The Deer's*, had been playing at the Cinema Rex when four opposition men to the Shah barred the doors and poured petrol everywhere. Not a single person escaped. By the time help finally arrived, it was too late. The entire theater was engulfed in flames, and over three hundred and fifty people had been burned alive…men, women, and children. Their screams were heard for blocks.

The clergy, headed by Ayatollah Khomeini, had blamed the Savak for this inhumane, ruthless, and brutal act. Khomeini blamed the Shah personally and called on the people to reject and disregard him as their leader and to demand that he leave Iran. That day, the theater fire was the topic of discussion on every street corner, and the blame was on Savak.

Roxanna felt even more nauseated as her eyes filled with tears. The truth now was whatever was constantly broadcast from BBC Radio in England, and the broadcast was so well-orchestrated, and the slaughter described in such detail that even Roxanna felt the Savak, the Iranian Secret Police, had committed this unspeakable atrocity and that it had been ordered by the Shah. Regardless of who was responsible, all those innocent people were murdered in the most horrific way, purely for political gain. It was more than Roxanna could bear. The only thing she could do was join Hajji Khanoum feeding the birds and watch them fly like they did not know what just had happened in Iran.

But one man was watching her from the second floor of the house located on the far right of Hajji Khanoum's, away from their view. He, Assad, her father, was standing behind a curtain, looking out through a small opening, watching his daughter with Hajji Khanoum, feeding the flying birds. The difference was he knew who the guilty one was.

He felt suffocated by the sight of birds flying freely, free from any anger, jealousy, or resentment. Watching Roxanna had become Assad's routine. Assad pushed the curtain a little further to see Roxana better. Unlike Hajji Khanoum and Roxanna, he knew that the clergy were behind the Rex cinema audience's burning and were directly responsible for the tragedy. Assad was very ashamed and depressed about such a barbaric act because he cooperated with them to gain power.

Of course, after he realized and witnessed such brutal crime the clergies committed, and also after several secret talks with the Amir, he had a change of heart, by now, having decided in his mind that he did not really intend to work with them, he decided to start and continue his activities with them because if there was a successful revolution and the Shah fell, he would try to prevent the clergies from coming to power. He knew that his anti-Shah friends were watching him like a hawk, and to guarantee their own chance to get a better position at the future government, they would do anything to push him away from Khomeini.

If they found out that Roxanna was his daughter and especially if they found out about his intentions, they would would use Roxanna against him, and there would be a big possibility even they would kill her. In fact, Assad himself did not know why he was involved in politics again. But now, he had become very friendly with Amir, and they were secretly in touch.

At the same time, Assad saw that his daughter had adapted to life in Iran with her mood and, like all Iranians, was in shock about the cinematic catastrophe, but nevertheless, she was still a foreigner among them. Roxanna did not know where the truth lay and from what source she should have received the right news. Cyrus was the only person she trusted. But he had now disappeared in the city of angels and seemed to show no importance to the events in Iran. Additionally, with Cyrus in America, she had no one to turn to. The consensus was that the Iranian people agreed with the BBC news station's assertion that it was the Savak. Who else would have committed such a horrendous act? The rest were adamant that the opposition had done to make this the Shah look like an evil and heartless man, not only in the eyes of his people but on a global scale.

Hajji Khanoum's voice grabbed Roxanna's attention, "These clergies are capable of committing any kind of sin; they did it; I am wondering where God is? How does he not see it?!" Roxanna glanced over and saw the sadness in her eyes as she left the living room.

At the time, the tragedy was so immense that the judgment of the people was clouded by a lack of knowledge. Unable to find contradicting accounts, most began to believe BBC News reports, despite the fact that the reports were based on false information. The truth had not yet been uncovered.

In the end, it was generally believed that the evil perpetrators were the Shah and the Savak, and as planned, people became enthralled with Khomeini, blindly trusting him without question, needing no evidence to support his claims against the Shah. After all, he was a man of God. His charismatic voice and personality resonated with the masses; he seemed to wake up even the dead. It became clear that a tragedy of this proportion, blamed on the Shah and the Savak, was the tipping point of the revolution. The well-orchestrated, vile act perpetrated on innocent victims was exactly what was needed to help topple the existing government.

It was as if changes started happening overnight. The radio became an even larger part of daily life. Even small children were glued to their radios, listening to BBC. No matter where Roxanna went, she saw people with one ear glued to the radio listening to foreigners, BBC describing what had just occurred or was about to occur in Iran. No one questioned how the BBC, so far from Iranian soil, could know the intimate details of this country before its people did.

*****

Chapter 21

Black Friday – The Turning Point of a Movement...

Sitting on the plane on his way to his beloved country, Cyrus still could not reconcile Hussein's actions in his mind. He was very troubled by what he considered weapons of death, being in the possession of his friends who, in turn, would arrange for their transport to Iran.

He closed his eyes and leaned his head back in his seat, sending a message that he didn't wish to be disturbed. His heart was racing. Hussein's words were flooding his head, but their impact and meaning were lost to him.

It wasn't long before Cyrus was breathing in the air of the land he loved so much. It was a moment he longed for but never dared to hope for. No one returned to Iran after leaving under conditions such as his. Why should he be different? His heart rejoiced the moment he set foot on Iranian soil. But it was a momentary celebration. It had only been a short time since he had left the country, but when he looked out of the taxi, nothing felt familiar. They were driving down the same streets of Tehran that just several months ago were joyous and beautiful, but now they were as cold and empty as his heart. What Cyrus had seen around Hussein had damaged his soul, but still, he could not believe his eyes. He sat in silence, trying to make sense out of the incomprehensible. The silence was starting to put the taxi driver on edge. He stared at Cyrus in the rearview mirror, trying to place him.

"Do I know you? You look like an actor."

Before returning, Cyrus had changed his looks in an effort to disguise his identity and was very uncomfortable with the taxi driver's questions. He was afraid he had not done enough. The worse thing that could happen would be for someone to recognize him and spread the word that he had returned. His life would be worth less than the tip he planned to leave the driver.

"Nobody. I am nobody. For sure, I am not an actor. But at the same time, aren't we all actors?"

Soon, the taxi driver was traveling through an exclusive residential area north of Tehran where the cheapest houses were more than he could make in a lifetime. He was very familiar with the area, but it didn't change the fact that he felt out of place and conspicuous every time he dropped someone off. Cyrus directed him to a dead-end alley one street over from his mother's and had him stop in the back of a huge mansion that took up half the block. The taxi driver stared into the rearview mirror, again, trying to place Cyrus.

"If you live here…for sure, you are somebody." The only response Cyrus could come up with was to give him a huge tip, hoping it would give him something to dwell on besides where he knew him from.

Once it was clear that Cyrus was returning to Tehran, his first priority was to find a place to hide where he wouldn't be recognized. Assad was able to help by finding a house that was perfectly located, directly across from Cyrus's family's house. The two upper storage rooms were provided to Assad by one of the rich merchants at the Tehran bazaar whose family had done business with Assad's family in the past.

Cyrus, dressed in clothes he normally wouldn't have been seen in, stood at the back entrance carrying a briefcase and a small, well-used suitcase. He was doing his best to hide his identity and thought a "businessman" look would be a good disguise since it was something he never aspired to be. Business and politics were too closely tied together in his eyes.

Assad opened the door, and Cyrus slipped in, unnoticed. Assad hugged Cyrus before leading him upstairs to a secret room that had been prepared for his stay. Other than light coming through a set of floral curtains, the room was small and dark with a simple mattress on the floor and a small refrigerator with a plate and a few eating utensils on top. The only bathroom was on the first floor.

The next morning Cyrus picked up the phone and dialed his mother's number. No matter what state the world was in, Hajji Khanoum would always be his first priority. He pulled the curtain just enough to peek out at her balcony. Finally, Hajji Khanoum's voice came on the line, and a sense of joy raced through his entire body! "It is me," Cyrus said.

"Cyrus? Cyrus? Is that you?" Roxanna and Ahmad Reza, the family helper, were relaxing with Hajji Khanoum in the upstairs sitting room when the call came in, but it wasn't until her hands began to shake and her eyes filled with tears of joy that they knew, for sure, it was Cyrus.

"Salam Hajji Khanoum..."

"They always say if you go to America, you never come back. When will you come back from America to see me?" Hajji Khanoum could hardly finish her words.

"Soon... Hajji Khanoum... soon. I have school here. Did you forget to feed the birds today? Look on the balcony. They are not there."

Hajji Khanoum carried the phone toward the glass doors to the balcony and looked out. She saw no birds. Not even the sparrows that would sneak the seed when bigger birds were not around. Warily, she opened the door to the balcony and looked around. "How did you know? How did you know my birds are not around?"

"Because I cannot hear them flying or singing to get your attention... to tell you they are hungry..."

Hajji Khanoum set the receiver down and stepped out onto her balcony. She grabbed a handful of birdseed from a jar and tossed it into the air. Immediately, a flock of birds flew towards her, squawking loudly.

Cyrus watched his mother with an ache in his heart. He wanted so much to let her know he was near, watching over her during these strange and uneasy times, but it was too dangerous, both for Cyrus and for her. He knew this was how he would always remember Hajji Khanoum, surrounded by her birds, caring for them just as she had always cared for her children. Cyrus's spirits lifted with Roxana's quick entrance onto the balcony. Her room used to be his. She delicately sauntered over and joined Hajji Khanoum feeding the birds.

Cyrus was startled by the sound of the door to his room opening. It was Assad, welcoming him with two cups of tea and a tray of pastries that he placed on top of the refrigerator. Cyrus waved for Assad to join him as he studied Roxanna's gentleness towards Hajji Khanoum as the women fed the birds. "Your daughter's heart is kind and filled with love. One day, perhaps, you will understand her need to share that love with you.

The two men, a generation between them, stood together in that cold and empty, dark and secret room, one watching the daughter he loved so much but could never hug and the other looking at his beloved mother, who thought her son had gone forever and was crying for him and praying to God to keep him safe. Though not a word was spoken between them, each had great respect for the other's pain. They were torn between and torn apart. It was a question of love. And her name was Iran.

They had been raised to be better human beings, to put the interest of their people ahead of themselves, to serve not one but all. They were willing to give up everything for the love of country, but little did they know they were entangled in a love triangle, the mistress, oil. In the end, nothing was to be gained, and everything was lost. Nothing was worth the sacrifice.

*****

The sun was rising over the top of Mount Damavand. Pary called to say she had a surprise for Roxanna and wanted to take her to meet someone special. As planned, Roxanna was sitting on a metal bench on a busy street in Tehran, waiting to be picked up, but Pary missed their agreed-upon time. It was late Friday. Roxanna was becoming concerned.

Friday was the day of rest, and most people would take advantage of it by taking the day off from work. It was the equivalent of Saturday and Sunday in America. The younger, more physically fit generation dubbed Friday 'Mountain Day' because they would typically join friends to go hiking in the fresh air. Mount Damavand on the north side of Tehran was the city's most popular destination, busiest in the early morning when it was cooler.

Roxanna used to go to Mount Damavand with Peter or Pary and Cyrus when he was around. To Roxanna, Mount Damavand was a beautiful imaginary land, a secret garden, where fairies and unicorns traveled about, dousing all they touched with magic; if such a place existed, it would be here.

The multi-colored trees and fragrant flowers enveloped a person, shutting out the bustling city as the sound of the river trickled into their ears. Born of melting snow and ice, the river flowed along the path and down the mountain, creating rainbow waterfalls and hidden pools to cleanse the soul; never resting, always nurturing the mountain and the gardens below.

As Roxanna waited for Pary, she recalled the earthy smells of her first hike up Mount Damavand, its winding path lifting her into the lush, moist mountain terrain. She recalled the river rushing from the top, each rock, twist, turn, an instrument of its own, playing a joyous song higher at its pinnacle, deeper at the base. Roxanna's soul was overwhelmed by nature's beauty and synergy. The place to display the latest fashion worn by the ladies and show off their good taste in style.

The walk started at the bottom, which was named the city of Darbband, and ended up on the top peak of Mount Damavand at a place called Pass Ghaleh. There was a large restaurant on the top, a special place to dine with friends, relax and look upon the graceful landscape that offered a respite from the pressures of Iranian life.

Still waiting on the street bench, Roxanna's tranquil thoughts of Mount Damavand were interrupted by the sound of loud, aggressive chanting. A noisy group of ten to fifteen boys, wearing white outfits spattered with blood-red dye, were running down the crowded sidewalk in her direction. Roxanna assumed they were teenagers and was shocked when she realized they appeared to be only about seven to twelve years old, wearing white, bloody shrouds.

They were chanting in harmony: "Death to the Shah! Death to the Shah!" People all around stopped what they were doing to watch the boys as they ran past, startling a policeman whose only response was to gape at them, dumbfounded.

Roxanna stared, aghast, at these young boys who could not possibly be fully aware of such political realities. What or who had prodded them into behaving in such a violent manner at such a young age? She always carries a small camera and thought perhaps she might chronicle some of the memorable moments she might witness. It seemed she completely forgot she was waiting for Pary.

She rose and followed the kids through the crowded street. Doing her best to get close enough to take photos, she began chasing the boys as they turned down a narrow alley, the policeman finally taking chase and on their heels. Hearing someone panting, she looked over her shoulder to find a second, heavyset policeman joining the chase.

Literally, from out of nowhere, a taxi came screeching into the alley with Pary in the back seat. She pushed open the door and yelled, "Get in the car, now!" Roxanna hesitated, wanting to take pictures of the boys scattering in all directions, followed by the policemen. Pary yelled again, "Get into the car!" This time, reaching out and almost knocking Roxanna down as she dragged her into the back seat with her. Roxanna caught her breath, both excited and astounded by what she had just witnessed, while the taxi sped off in the opposite direction.

A comfortable distance away, Roxanna felt comfortable commenting on what she had witnessed, "Those children have spirit." When Pary discreetly put a finger up to her lips to silence her, Roxanna realized that it might not have been the right thing to say. They were both relieved to see the driver was smiling. Roxanna realized why she was captivated by the boys.

They were too young to put together such a bold show alone, which meant someone was obviously behind the political parade. This was the kind of public display that was orchestrated by the opposition, knowing that young boys would have maximum impact on public consumption. The Clergy were smart. They understood the most effective way to use people to their advantage.

"Following the young mob was very risky. It is honorable to do something for the people, but it isn't smart to risk your safety for it; this isn't your war. You are here to find your father. Leave the struggle to others."

It was about 9am in Tehran as the taxi entered Jaleh Square and drove around looking for its destination. Aside from a few Army jeeps that were also driving around the square, everything was quiet. Pary got out first and motioned to Roxanna with her hand, directing her towards a small restaurant tucked neatly across the way. "Come with me. There is someone inside who is waiting for you." Filled with anticipation, Roxanna fought the wave of dizziness that had come over her by carefully putting one foot in front of the other so as not to lose her balance. She had no idea who was waiting in the cafe, but her gut told her it was her father.

Close enough now to see in the window, Roxanna observed a few people sitting at tables, engaged in conversation, and having tea. Although nothing seemed out of the ordinary, a feeling of uneasiness grabbed her, becoming an all-too-common emotion in Iran. An emptiness gnawed inside her for no reason, and she froze. Roxanna hovered near the old carved, wooden entry and looked deep into Pary's eyes. "Who's waiting for me? My father?"

There was a strange, hollow look in Pary's eyes. "The restaurant. Go into the restaurant. I'll wait for you."

The lights were dim. The cigarette smoke of attendants cast moving shadows, like puppets, along the smoke-stained, old grey plaster walls.

Roxanna's heart skipped a beat as she cautiously walked through the old wooden door. It was a small, cozy place, and as usual, BBC radio was on; patrons in rapt attention of every word spoken by the British newscaster. It was several weeks after the burning of the Rex Cinema in Abadan, and getting the latest news was the hot subject. People were so engrossed in the news reports that no one even glanced in her direction.

Roxanna looked around, her eyes still adjusting to the dim light. If she saw him, would she know? Would there be this unspoken awareness and recognition, a knowing, a transcendent bond? Standing in the middle of this small space, every sense was heightened. She could feel the slightest unevenness underneath her feet, the breeze through the door, smell the pungent scent of dried herbs, but she saw no one she recognized.

For sure, she saw no one who would have been her father's age. Her heart sank. As she turned to leave, her gaze fell upon a bearded, short-haired man with glasses. She could not mistake Cyrus, no matter how much he had changed his appearance.

Officially, only Pary and Peter knew that Cyrus had gotten married shortly after arriving in America, but in reality, all of their friends knew the truth. Everyone also knew that Cyrus and Roxanna were in love and that it made no sense for him to do something so drastic and out of character. Roxanna had heard the rumors and found them ridiculous, which was easy to do with Cyrus halfway around the world. But now that their hands were touching, she couldn't help herself...

She glanced down, looking for a ring on his finger, but there was none. Still, she knew. It was written in the way Cyrus diverted his eyes from hers. Roxanna had to control the intense sadness that threatened to overwhelm her. Her aching heart demanded a reason, an explanation. She wanted him to lie to her and say it wasn't true, but where would that leave them? What was done was done. They gazed at each other in silence, lost in a moment without past or future.

"The Imam is coming! Khomeini!" Someone continued to yell from another table, jolting them back to reality. Up to that moment, the name Khomeini meant little to Roxanna, but no longer. There was something about the way the man said it that made her realize the game had changed. She was compelled to take great care to look through the man's eyes and into his psyche as he headed out the door, onto the square. It seemed that just saying Khomeini aloud gave a person authority and power.

Still confused, she gently began to rub her fingers against Cyrus's fingers, wanting to know more. She wanted to take Cyrus back to America. She glanced down, looking for a ring on his finger, but there was none. Still, she knew. It was written in the way Cyrus diverted his eyes from hers. Roxanna had to control the intense sadness that threatened to overwhelm her. Her aching heart demanded a reason, an explanation. She wanted him to lie to her and say it wasn't true, but where would that leave them? What was done was done. They gazed at each other in silence, lost in a moment without past or future.

Her eyes followed Cyrus through the window outside, focusing on the obese man as he ran across the street, past Pary, waving his arms and pointing. At what, nobody knew. Pary had been leaning against a broken streetlight, staring towards Mount Damavand with a wistful look of longing that weighed heavily on her natural beauty. If there was a color to match her mood, it would be described as a dark shade of woeful melancholy.

By now, Roxanna had been more confused by the complexity of what she heard and also Pary's feelings lately. The loss of her brother had affected her greatly, but it was more than that. Pary's personality had started to change, at times sinking into unresponsive lows, even before his death. Roxanna sensed that she might be experiencing heartache, although she had never mentioned a man in her life.

Roxanna looked down at her hand, entwined in Cyrus's ,and it suddenly became clear. Pary was in love with Cyrus, and he knew nothing of it. If there was anything Roxanna knew about Pary, it was if she felt strongly about something, she never let it go. To a woman with Pary's fortitude, it didn't matter what she was fighting for; if she believed enough to fight, it was to the end. There was no compromise or substitution. So why would love to be any different?

Roxanna realized she was no different. She thought about her own love for Cyrus, realizing it was far more complicated than she had ever imagined love could be. When a heart falls for someone, it is done, and that is your love for life. Roxanna gazed into Cyrus's once again for a long time, lost in thought. Thinking, either the one you love feels the same… or not. Love happens in its own time and cannot be calculated, and often never repeated. Some are destined to love totally and completely, together forever, once in a lifetime. But what about those kept apart by destiny? Is their love any less perfect?

It was at that moment when Roxanna truly understood her friend and felt a strong sense of love for her. She knew Pary was standing under the sun, watching through the window, the man she loved as he longed for another woman. He was sitting with his best friend talking about his new love. Her heart ached, knowing he was now married to another woman in America. She wondered if he really gave his whole heart to Julia. Or did he rush into a relationship to avoid the pain and suffering of his complicated life here? Out of respect, Roxanna slipped her hand from Cyrus's and took a sip of tea. She wanted to trade places with Pary if just for a moment, caring enough to try and understand her friend's pain. How ironic it was…that their pain was so similar. They both loved someone they could never have.

As if she was watching a tragic play, Roxanna watched the events in her life as they were unfolding. Cyrus, the man Pary and herself loved with all their heart, shared his heart with an American woman, who, in her eyes and the eyes of her government, was an enemy to her, her country, and her people. Cyrus's love did not belong to Pary and never would; it was gifted to another. The only right thing to do was to honor their love and bring them together, if only for a brief moment, and that's what Pary did. Almost as if on cue, Pary turned away. Roxanna's heart broke for her.

Cyrus, too, had been watching Pary but with no clear understanding of her feelings. When she was out of sight, Roxanna reached out and took his hand, again, stroking it as if he could grant her three wishes. She would be happy with one. His heart sank when he noticed Roxanna looking at his hand. He knew exactly what she was looking for—a wedding ring. Their silence could not last forever. "I had to see you. I had to know you're all right."

Roxanna's head was reeling; her love had been betrayed. She reached deep inside her heart to put together the most important, gut-wrenching words she would ever say, "Do you love her?"

Cyrus was speechless. There were no words to paint a clear picture of his pain. His silence spoke volumes but not what was in his heart. "I do not know," he whispered, looking at his finger, where his wedding ring would have been if he had been wearing it.

"You do not know? Do you tell your wife you 'do not know 'when she asks you if you love her? When she whispers, 'I love you,' what do you say then?"

Cyrus had never seen Roxanna like this, and he wasn't quite sure how to handle the situation. He was caught off guard and felt sweaty and incredibly uncomfortable. It seemed it was hard for her to digest all she heard, or she was already overboard with the information she had received. He had not realized she already knew he was married, or he would have planned their meeting differently. He had been dealing with his situation the way most men dealt with matters of complicated love, by ignoring it.

Besides, how could he tell her he got married just to forget her love? To tell her he could not handle to see her father Assad tearfully asking him to walk away. And tell her perhaps Assad was right. He does not belong to one soul but, he belongs to the people. He couldn't mention that he was scared that he would do the same to her that Assad did to her mother. To tell her he is already full of shame and guilt, he even married his wife. He knew one thing was certain; anything he might say would only make things worse.

He looked anywhere but into Roxanna's eyes, her pain already radiating clear through his body. His eyes roamed the teahouse, searching for words, or better yet, a waiter, anyone to interrupt them ... but everyone was listening to BBC radio. He took a deep breath and decided to go with the truth, "I do not know how that happened. One day, I woke up, and I was married." Searching for words, Cyrus continued, "But I know I am going to be a good husband to her regardless of what or how it happened."

If he had thought for even a moment before opening his mouth, he would have realized, of all the things he could have said, none could have been worse. Telling the woman, he loved and who loved him with all her heart what a good husband he planned to be to his new bride was just about the least appropriate thing he could have come up with under the circumstances. But he had opened the floodgates and was determined to continue explaining until he drowned in his ill-chosen words.

"It was not my intention to leave Iran or either of you. My life was in danger. Most importantly, I visited your father, and I saw how his choices impacted you and your mother. I felt he did not want you to follow the path your mother did. It was then that I decided I could not risk putting you through the pain of life similar to your mother's. Having to decide between his love for you and his love for his country was the hardest decision of his life. But he never planned it that way. He told me he was denied a visa to the US and that he was dodging the Iranian government. Your father died when he left you and wasn't allowed to return. He died of a broken heart. It was then that I decided that I could not take this risk because it seems my life and destiny were not and are not my choice.

Cyrus looked down at his ring finger…trying so hard to explain the unexplainable. "I died when I left you… my heart will never know love again. So, to ask me if I know love is to ask what you are to me. Do not ask me to define 'wife.' The word alone puts me at a loss. The minute my feet touched the ground in the US, I went to your mother to tell her you were safe.

"What I saw was a woman as wasted as her life … waiting for a love that would never return. I pitied her. Should I pity you? You love like your mother for all eternity. And I live my life like your father, giving my last breath to my country. It was then that I realized if I truly loved you, I would leave my feelings toward you behind.

"I thought it was best for all of us. I had no country, no love, no direction. Roxanna, I was confused. I was mad at myself, mad at my brother, mad at my world and the circumstances thrown upon me. So, what did it matter what path I chose if it meant being without you?"

Roxanna was finally able to understand just a little of how the disaster had unfolded. She could tell that Cyrus had become a void, empty of words and feelings, a victim of circumstances of which he had no control. Slowly, he freed his hand from hers. It was time to say goodbye. Roxanna searched for words, "I know this much about you that you would have the decency to let her know where she stands."

Cyrus felt very uncomfortable talking about Julia. He had much more pressing issues that needed to be dealt with, like Roxanna's safety. He had an eerie feeling that something bad could happen at any time. "It is not safe to stay here with you too long…but I had to see you."

There were so many questions she wanted to ask, but Roxanna knew there was no purpose…the answers didn't matter. They wouldn't change a thing. But if she kept silent, she was afraid he would leave. "Why did you run away from us? From your mother and Amir? Why did you run away from me? Are you one of them?" Cyrus was crushed that Roxanna would ever think he would run away from anything, most of all, her. He sat back down to explain.

"I am not running from you or them. I am worried about their safety and yours."

Roxanna cut in, "I'm a part of this mess now, just like you and Pary and everybody else. You don't have to worry about me. I'm a big girl. I can take care of myself, thank you." Her words stunned him. He realized that the rumor of a revolution had gotten everyone riled up, and the energy was now flowing through Roxanna's blood. He had returned to Iran to convince Roxanna and his brother to leave Iran, but if this was truly the case, it would be impossible.

He also knew the people of his country were not aware of what their future held for them, that history was about to repeat itself. They knew nothing of what Cyrus witnessed in France. The only source of information they had was from the propaganda machine that passed their rumors on to Iran and the world through BBC Radio. Cyrus knew he needed time to convince Roxanna and Amir to leave Iran, but unfortunately, time was the one thing he did not have. Roxanna asked him one last question. It was a question that caught him completely off guard, "Why are you really here?"

Roxanna had changed in the months since he had last seen her. The difficult and tragic situations in Iran had made her more introspective, stronger, fiercer, more independent. He chose his words with care. "I am here to save your life . . . perhaps the people . . . my brother—he must leave the country before it is too late. Things are more complicated than I anticipated. I am worried for you. The stage is set for the Shah to leave."

Roxanna didn't understand what he was saying. Regardless of the inner turmoil in Iran, most believed the Shah was untouchable. "Things are changing rapidly. No one is certain who is behind it. Everyone is lying to everyone, and no one knows the truth. If I tell you about a single American lady from the CIA is removing the Shah from power and replacing him with Khomeini...you would say I was crazy." A flashing red light went off in Roxanna's head. She knew exactly who he was referring to! "Dorian MacGray…"

Although he had no idea how Roxanna knew Dorian, Cyrus felt excited and more comfortable sharing more information with her. "The CIA is doing the same to the Shah that they did to Mossadegh in 1952. Hundreds of terrorists are also arriving in Iran from Syria, Libya, and Palestine to lead this cause here. They would not have mercy on me or any other Iranians. They are not Iranian, they are Arabs, and Arabs traditionally hate us. Would they treat us fairly? Who is kidding who? What mind formed this sick joke?" It took everything Cyrus had to fight back his tears.

Cyrus looked out toward the square, checked his watch, and picked up his camera before turning his attention back to Roxanna. "I want you to speak with Amir. You might be able to reason with him. I could not. I phoned him and told him I was in America.

"Maybe you should visit your mother. Her heart is breaking."

"If my brother knows I am back in Iran, I will be arrested... I have watched her from a distance, as I have watched you many times," Cyrus replied.

It was then that Roxanna realized how deeply involved he was in this revolutionary chess game. She looked directly into his eyes, forcing him to answer. "What about my father? How can I see him?"

"Impossible. Very soon, the Shah will fall. Your father is one of the strong men behind the revolution. He might be the first president or secretary of the state of Iran after the revolution... the best is after the revolution succeeds, then it will be safe to see him... but until then your life is in danger ... these people who try to come to power are bloodthirsty people who think only of power and money and nothing else ... They do not have mercy on their mother or children ... for sure they will use you to get back to your father."

The thought that her father could go from being in the Shah's jail to possibly becoming president was mind-boggling to Roxanna. She could not have heard correctly. Cyrus was staring outside; his attention was diverted by a van that was passing by the restaurant. Roxanna's eyes followed his. They both watched as the van circled and stopped in front of a tall building near where Pary was waiting.

Several men wearing Army jackets, their hands hidden inside their pockets, suddenly rushed past Pary and disappeared into the adjoining building as the van sped off. There was something very strange and eerie happening out there. People were going about their lives as if it was any normal day while men were running around like they were playing war games.

Cyrus couldn't believe that he could be the only one who noticed the men in Army jackets with machine guns hidden underneath, running into buildings. Other than Cyrus and Roxanna, who were watching from the restaurant, only Pary stood in the square on high alert, staring in the direction of the men who had entered the building. She was sure they were speaking Arabic. Something horrible was about to happen.

Someone turned the sound on the radio up so the BBC report could be heard, clearly: "General Gholam Ali Oveisi, the new Prime Minister of Iran, announced a military curfew beginning at 6:00 AM. The Iranian Government has asked its people not to gather in Jaleh Square. The guards will retaliate if they do. People all across Tehran and the surrounding areas are ignoring the curfew and heading toward Jaleh Square..."

"You guys must get a taxi and leave now. It is about to become very dangerous here. I will be in touch with you later." Cyrus looked into Roxanna's eyes for a brief, intense moment before grabbing his camera and pushing himself away from the table. Roxanna's eyes chased him all the way to outside, where Pary was standing. She had a dark feeling that Cyrus knew what was going to happen and that he didn't want her to hear their conversation.

She ran until she caught up with them, "I'm not leaving! Whatever happens, I'm here to witness these historic events. This is my history as well!" Roxanna assumed they would shove her into a taxi but, instead, they looked at each other in silence and then let their eyes search the area for any unusual movements. Roxanna followed their eyes upward. She saw snipers crawling on the tops of buildings, positioning their guns, aiming directly into the square. She swallowed hard and whispered, "Are they government snipers?"

"No. No one knows where they've come from," He turned to Pary, "Take her away. Neither of you should be here..."

Pary flagged down the first taxi she could. Cyrus opened the door and motioned for them to get in, but Roxanna refused. It was too painful to say goodbye to the man she loved. Pary understood, allowing her time to say goodbye in her heart as she, too, was saying goodbye to Cyrus. They both wondered if they would ever see him again. Without looking back, Cyrus disappeared between two buildings, his thoughts no different than theirs.

Cyrus stood in the right place; his camera lens lined up with his eye. Looking for a suitable subject to take a picture of as he scanned the square. He noticed what looked like a rifle protruding from a small corner. He zoomed in on it quickly; it was pointed straight at the square. The camera lens went back and forth a little around the edge of the rooftop. He finally saw the face of a young, bearded man who was hiding behind something, adjusting his aim. Cyrus was sure he couldn't be alone and scanned the rooftops. He quickly noticed another shooter, realizing quickly that they were not of Iranian descent and confirming they did not appear to be government forces either.

Words that Hussein had said started returning to him, and, like pieces of a puzzle, they started falling into place. Hussein had told him a thousand Palestinians had secretly been brought into Iran with the specific goal of overthrowing the Shah. It was a backup plan just in case the Iranian forces didn't have the will or desire to do it themselves.

That very moment, Cyrus had an epiphany. He was helping the wrong people and fighting for the wrong cause. The idea of foreigners, mercenaries, entering his country with the sole objective of spilling Iranian blood was unconscionable and unacceptable. His anger was so intense that he found it almost impossible to calm down. He pushed his back against the side of the building with such force that he could feel the contour of each individual brick as it pressed into his body. He stayed there for a moment, breathing deep, knowing that giving in to his anger would not benefit his country and would likely get him killed.

Cyrus knew the reason foreign mercenaries were so effective was that they had no morals. There was no shared sympathy, compassion, or heart for those of a different culture or nationality. The Arabs, in particular, generally, had no mercy for the Iranians. After the army of Islam captured Iran, the tension between the two nations rose.

Cyrus stepped back from the building and looked up toward the rooftops, only to see more Arab snipers taking position and hiding like cowards, ready to rain terror on innocent people who were nothing to them but target practice.

Cyrus raised his camera to his eye, looking for the safest and best vantage point to document the events as they unfolded. His heart stopped when he saw Roxanna and Pary still in the square, their driver talking with someone and having a smoke. Cyrus waved to them, yelling for them to leave, but they were too far away to hear. He increased his waving until he got Pary's attention, and she finally waved back in acknowledgment. There was no mistaking the look of desperation on his face. Pary grabbed Roxanna's shoulder and pushed her towards the taxi. "Get in! You want to stay alive and see your father? Then get in."

The taxi driver and his friend were nervously watching an Army helicopter closing in on the square, its spotlight sending chills up their spines. Concerned, he threw his cigarette on the ground and jumped in the taxi, pointing skyward to show Roxanna and Pary what the hurry was.

Roxanna scanned the square one last time, hoping to get a glimpse of her beloved Cyrus, but all she could see were the long, dark shadows of the snipers, looking like elongated monsters. Before the taxi could exit the square, a caravan of Army vehicles entered, blocking all entrances, making it impossible for them to leave.

In the distance, the insane drone of loud, chanting voices, "Death to the Shah, long live Khomeini..." intensified as the mob grew dense, making its way towards the square. The thunder of helicopters hovering above the center of the square warned of impending doom. Voices, exploding through bullhorns, poured down like black rain. "Leave the square, do not enter the square!"

An angry mob squeezed towards them with great force from all sides, linking their arms together, forming a human barricade. Within minutes, their taxi was surrounded, but not before Pary and Roxanna escaped into the crowd. The more the news about the military curfew got out, the more people came. It was like a tragic Gustav Mahler symphony; the voices of all who swarmed the streets in protest began to utter tragic chords of protest, chanting, "Death to the Shah! Long live Khomeini. Khomeini is the leader . . . Death or freedom!" It was loud, angry, unruly, insane chanting, like a sick mantra. "Death to the Shah. Long live Khomeini!"

Roxanna gave up trying to find Cyrus in the hoard of protesters. She watched in shock as they ignored the warnings coming from the bullhorns above and continued to press dangerously close. The soldiers present at the square were no match for the dense, human wall of people being led by several clergymen who held the Quran, the Holy Book.

More soldiers rushed the square and started sealing it off, hollering, hopelessly, into the thick jungle of entwined bodies, "Martial law has been declared! Disperse! Disperse!" The soldiers had no training for such an event and were debating what to do as the loudspeaker from the Army helicopter continued to howl at the people, warning them to disperse.

Pary and Roxanna heard shots ring out so close they could sense the rushing bullets screeching past their ears. From the rooftops, snipers began firing their weapons indiscriminately into the crowd and at the soldiers, causing total confusion. Many soldiers, fearing for their lives, began shooting, blindly, into the masses. Others, seeing the snipers, returned fire.

The rest shot into the air, trying to scare the mob so they could look for safety. Within seconds, a simple protest turned into the worst possible scenario; chaos ensued, everyone frantically running in every direction, searching for protection against the bullets raining down upon them. No one knew who was shooting at whom.

As hard as they tried to stay together, Roxanna and Pary were torn in opposite directions as they attempted to make their way through the chaos onto a side street. Luckily, Roxanna got caught up in a group that was moving against the flow of the massive wave of protesters. By the time Pary reached Roxanna, it had taken everything she had to tug her down by a wall and shield her with her own body. She looked into Roxanna's eyes with the fierceness and sternness of a mother protecting her unruly child from harm. Realizing that Pary was risking her life for her was just another reason for Roxanna to love her.

Cyrus was looking and trying to reach them and help them to safety. He had seen Pary fighting her way towards Roxanna and was desperately fighting his way through the crowd to reach them, to protect them.

This incident was no different than so many others that had played themselves out in Iran. No one on either side of the violent altercation was prepared or trained for such unpredictable events. No one in a million years thought or believed such a horrendous incident would ever happen!

No one had considered that once this ugly political anger was unleashed that the devastation to the psyche of a nation that once was the beacon of light intellectually, artistically, and spiritually would be immeasurable. But it happened. And no one knew why.

The soldiers were nervous and agitated, in fear of their lives. Cyrus was certain that they had been instructed to avoid deadly force, but there was no formal flow of command to control the chaos. There were no superior officers to provide guidance, orders, or directions. It was a mob mentality, mass insanity, with everyone reacting in fear, shooting their firearms, and inflaming the riot to a deadly crescendo.

Their mission was to die and go to heaven. It was ironic that earlier in the day, Cyrus had read that the American government had refused to sell non-lethal weapons, tear gas, and rubber bullets to the Shah, which might have saved many lives. France, Germany, and England refused to sell non-lethal weapons to Iran as well. There was no explanation offered as to the reasoning behind this decision. There could only be one reason, Cyrus thought.

The distinct sound of gunfire, the sound of murder, the screams of horror, pain and dying, pierced the chanting. Snipers were shooting with absolute disregard for human life, directing the massive assault at anyone and everyone indiscriminately. The sparks emitted from rifles and handguns as they emptied their rounds lit up the square, briefly illuminating the destruction that lay in their path, the utter chaos. This was a rogue army, untrained in dealing with civil unrest or mob control. The fear and panic were palpable.

Cyrus continued to desperately push his way towards Roxanna and Pary as he scanned his surroundings to determine a safer path and vantage point from which to witness and document this ugly chapter in Iran's history. He saw a narrow path running parallel to the buildings, just behind the frenzied crowd, and looked around, mentally mapping his escape.

His eyes landed upon the face of a small, terrified boy who had gotten separated from his mother in the insanity of it all. Surely, she was frantic, having lost her child in this madness. One small child was no match for the violent behavior of the mob. He was bumped, trampled, tossed, and thrown like a rag doll as he screamed for help, tears streaming down his face.

Cyrus saw the anguished child and forced his way through the mob of people to reach him. But just as fast as he grabbed his faded yellow shirt, a tidal wave of people, pushing and shoving in all directions, carried him away. The child slipped from his fingers and was, once again, devoured by the crowd. Cyrus grabbed his camera and held it up to his eye, scanning the rooftops until he saw the sniper's rifle, still following the child. Desperately, he took off in the same direction, searching for the torn yellow shirt.

Roxanna and Pary had also been swept away by stampeding demonstrators and feared for their lives. It was everything they could do to keep from being trampled. They locked arms and held on tight, riding the wave of violence until they were slammed against the glass door of a small restaurant. Pary knocked and pleaded for someone to open the door, but it appeared to be empty. Finally, an old man with nothing left to lose peeked around the cash register and recognized Pary as a friend of Cyrus. Torn between what was right and what was best, he held his head in his hands and prayed. He decided if he was going to die, there was no better way than by trying to save these brave young women. Unfortunately, his wife did not agree.

Cyrus continued looking through his camera lens, focusing on people's legs as they were about the height of the small child, searching until he found a patch of yellow, a beacon in the sea of grey, blood red, and guts. He let the camera drop, unceremoniously, from around his neck, took a deep breath, and, leading with his right shoulder, slammed his entire body into the crowd, breaking a path through to the boy.

Roxanna and Pary had found sanctuary in an empty storefront where they were able to watch the massacre from a safe distance. Soldiers were circling the crowd, slowly tightening the boundaries in an attempt to reduce the mob to a manageable size in the square. Roxanna saw a small boy covered with blood and realized it was the child they had been trying to save. Her heart sank into the ground; this boy's life was just like Iran itself.

They were just about to leave the safety of the building to try and reach the child when they noticed Cyrus barreling through the crowd, hoping to catch him. They were relieved to know that he was still alive and even more relieved to know he was only seconds away from reaching the little boy. But it only took a second... No one saw where the shot came from. To Roxanna and Pary, it seemed as if the child just stumbled, falling into the tree-lined creek in front of the store.

A soldier reached down and pulled the bleeding boy up onto the sidewalk. Their eyes locked, the child silently begging for his life. It was as if everything was going in slow motion, almost as if, given a chance, Pary and Roxanna could change the events that were tragically playing out in front of their eyes.

Like a magnet, confusion and chaos blurred everything together, attracting the darkest part of humankind. It was as if death and pain became an acceptable price to pay, but for what? Distracted by the crowd, the soldier left the boy to suffer, torn apart and slowly dying, just like what they were doing to Iran.

Roxanna's eyes darted in all directions trying to determine if anyone else had their sites on the small boy. She saw two soldiers negotiating their way through the crowd and waited to be sure their attention was drawn away from the boy and towards the center of the square while praying for a window in which to get the child out of harm's way. But none came.

The intensity of fear for the child's safety hit Roxanna in the stomach, making her nauseous as she anticipated the worst. Her memory flashed back to the burning police station and the little girl and then back to the present; once more, they were at a crossroad, another grave error of judgment, another child's life hanging by a thread. If only a moment of clarity would overtake insanity and resurrect the damaged minds of the soldiers. Surely, they would hold steady and not fire at the child. They would let the boy go home, the victor, sanity. If only…

No longer able to support himself, the small boy collapsed, face down on the sidewalk, blood oozing from a huge hole torn in his back and through his chest and head. Blood-stained tears streamed down his face. Unable to move his outstretched arms, he stared into Roxanna's eyes and begged for help. She couldn't just let him die. She pushed the door open and threw herself over the child, placing her body over his, shielding him from any further madness. She would take the bullet. It was no less than what Pary had done for her.

The soldiers stood and stared at this crazed woman, immobile. Like deer caught in a headlight, their expressions remained frozen in the face of disaster. It was uncertain who had fired the bullet that hit the child, but it was clear to Roxanna and Pary that the soldiers didn't do it. The bullet had come from somewhere deep in the throng of faceless protesters. Everyone who stood in Jaleh Square shared equally.

The guilt of murder was theirs to own. It lay at their feet in the body of a dead child, riddled with bullet holes. It was a horrific scene; one Roxanna knew would remain forever in their memory. A shot was heard, and the innocent soldier who had been witnessing the event with Roxanna and Pary fell dead between them, shocking them both to the core.

Cyrus appeared from the crowd and fearlessly picked up the small child, draping his limp body across his arms like a rag doll. He carried him into the packed store and laid him down as everyone stepped back to clear an area for Roxanna and Pary to tend to him. The boy stared into Roxanna's eyes, his bloody hand resting on hers. His gentle touch was as cold as death, and Roxanna felt it to her bones. Cyrus raised his camera and began to document the event but was unable to continue when he realized the child would not survive. Roxanna lifted the boy's dirty blood-drenched hand to her cheek and kissed his tiny fingers, pressing them to her lips. There was nothing left to be done.

"Sleep, little man, sleep, you are being carried to God." Roxanna and Pary sat side by side the entire night, holding on to each other after carefully covering the body of the little boy in sacks, his shroud of death. When Roxanna finally looked around for Cyrus, she realized he has slipped back into the night. The voice of a BBC CORRESPONDENT cut through the silence. "This is BBC Radio London, reporting from Tehran. Thousands gathered in Tehran's Jaleh Square today for a religious demonstration. When orders to disperse were ignored, the military opened fire, killing and wounding dozens."

Someone began to sing a sad song, drowning out the BBC radio report. No one cared. They weren't interested in hearing anyone's misinterpretations of the massacre in Jaleh Square. They were there. They knew. A second voice joined in, and the singing grew melancholy and more poignant. The day was endless, and both Roxanna and Pary spent the long hours worrying about Cyrus. It was impossible for them to even think about leaving the safety of the store. There were still sporadic protesters in the streets, filled with rage, setting everything that hadn't been burned on fire. The night passed; the stench of hopelessness hung heavy in the air.

"This is BBC Radio London, reporting from Tehran. Iranians are already referring to the Jaleh Square massacre as Black Friday…"

They now understood the real tragedy of it all, the loss of innocent children who lived in a cold and empty state of fear, constantly aware of the sound of gunfire, of the unnatural gurgling sound that comes just before death. This dreadful, violent environment was becoming second nature, this horrific dance with its sounds of death, the nagging awareness of the surroundings, robbing them of their freedom. Of their childhood.

*****

Chapter 22

A Fire Destroys a Way of Life...

Sitting alone in Peter's restaurant, Roxanna couldn't help but smile. She had lost her appetite after Black Friday so decided on something light, Kashk Bademjan "Burani Eggplant," to eat with some famous Sangak bread. She loved eggplant, so it would make a perfect dinner. What she got was Beef Soltani Kabab, Walnut Pomegranate Stew, Sour Cherry rice, and Shirazi salad... And that was in addition to the Burani Eggplant dips that she originally ordered. In other words, a little taste of everything. Everyone had grown to love Roxanna, and she could tell who loved her the most by how much they force-fed her.

Roxanna was overwhelmed by everything she had witnessed since arriving in Iran. She couldn't get her mind off the tragedy at the Cinema Rex movie theater, the massacre that took place on Black Friday, Nader's death, or the sadness that now defined Pary. The images didn't come to her singularly, one event at a time, but superimposed, one body over another. The situation in Tehran was getting worse every day. All eyes and ears were on the TV and BBC, waiting to hear what Khomeini was saying. His audience was getting larger, his influence stronger, and his power over the country inevitable. As the situation worsened, many foreigners were now leaving Iran.

Off and on, there were riots in the streets, and people were protesting. What was the point of no return for her? For Roxanna, the point was crossed when Cyrus returned to Iran. Knowing he was back, somewhere in her corner of the world, she had no choice but to stay and see what the future held for her and the country she had grown to love. She told herself there was no such thing as shallow love. You were either in, over your head, or not at all. To turn her back and run now would make her a coward.

She hadn't heard from Cyrus since Black Friday, and without him, she found it almost impossible to continue her search for her father. The country had grown too violent, exploding before her eyes. Lost in thought when she was searching for answers to why or what happened to all those nice and kind people, she felt that a contagious virus had been sprayed into the air without anyone's knowledge. Everyone breathed it in, and no one was spared. Their minds and souls had been taken over by this evil force. This virus had erased logic and compassion and replaced them with hate, suspicion, and fear. When she returned to the present, visions of the nightmare lingered. She had been dreaming of Iran. It was hard for her to comprehend how such warm and loving people could become radicalized so quickly.

It was Hajji Khanoum that kept her feeling connected and safe. Surrounded by her love, feeding the birds, she knew she belonged, and for her, alone, she would stay in Iran. She knew that Hajji Khanoum needed her. They had something in common that they could share with no one else. Cyrus. Whenever Roxanna was away from her too long, she would get a call. Hajji Khanoum was either worried or concerned about something she had heard on BBC or heard from a neighbor, or a bad dream had come to her as a warning. Somehow Roxanna would manage to bring her peace and ease her mind.

Roxanna was full when a bowl of saffron rice pudding materialized in front of her. Stuffed beyond belief, she glared at it as if it was the enemy. At home, in Los Angeles, she would have simply ignored it. But something was happening to her in Iran. Her sweeter, more innocent, naive self had disappeared, and, in its place, she felt herself becoming a stronger, more responsible, more assertive woman.

She looked around, noticing these days Peter's restaurant was not crowded like before. It was empty, just a few people, apart from one table where Saaghi was sitting with friends, a few workers who had been cleaning up in the kitchen, and Roxanna, who was watching Peter drown himself in drink and sorrow. The phone was ringing, but no one seemed to care. It was clear to Roxanna that the situation in Iran was unnerving to him.

She thought of Cyrus and suspected that he had generally associated with people of many different beliefs, including believers of radical communism and Islam, to rightist, leftist, and moderates as well, but he did not appear to be influenced by any one of them. He had his own ideology, which included healthy living, serving humanity, and living in the moment. His apparent belief seemed to be that it was important to maintain balance, and without that, people would fall into an abyss of chaos.

It was close to midnight, and Peter, in his sad, drunken state, began singing an Omar Khayyam poem to Saaghi's violin. It was a sign for everyone in the restaurant, including the kitchen help, to join him for some late-night camaraderie while listening to BBC radio. Everyone knew that the Shah was very powerful. After all, he had the fifth strongest army in the world, and there was no match to the Shah's Army in the region. With this knowledge, it certainly begged the question. How could such a powerful man be in such a precarious situation? Even Saaghi's ear was listening to the radio over the soft tune she was playing.

"Iran is in turmoil. Most citizens have given up keeping any sort of regular work schedule. Their unified and primary goal seems to be to protest until the Shah is removed from power. Foreigners have begun leaving the country in droves."

Saaghi listened to the BBC, holding the violin in one hand while the bow sat on the strings without movement. She then began to play more loudly in an attempt to drown out the ugliness of the words coming through the radio. She was drunk and swaying back and forth to a violent rhythm, mesmerizing Peter and the others with her heart-wrenching violin solo.

Saaghi's intense, raw sensuality was left shattered by several Molotov cocktails as they came smashing through the small windows, their fuel droplets igniting, creating fireballs as flames shot across the room.

Thousands of glass chards flew through the restaurant, leaving no one untouched, some piercing skin, the rest glistening dangerously on tables and chairs.

In an instant fire, erupted on all sides, hot flames licking at Peter's mellow patrons, painfully drawing them back to reality. Panic ensued as everyone scrambled for the door, determined to get out before the entire place went up in flames.

One of Peter's workers rushed out the back door shouting, "Fire! Fire!" Grabbing a bucket of soapy water, he tried to extinguish the growing flames, but it made no difference. Roxanna immediately began backing up, away from the heat of the fire, only to notice Peter, drunk and in a stupor, still seated, staring into the flames. He took a sip of his drink and began to sing Omar Khayyam's Rubaiyat louder and louder.

Ignoring the fact that a large part of the restaurant was engulfed in flames, he got up and began dancing with the flames as if they were his Rumba partner. Roxanna screamed and ran to him. A few others joined her, grabbing Peter and dragging him away, still furiously quoting Omar Khayyam, almost daring the flames to touch him.

The first instinct of any musician is to protect his instrument like a beloved child. Saaghi's response was tempered, different. She made no move to leave, her silhouette backlit by a wall of orange flames, almost as if it was her destiny to burn with the restaurant. Her posture, seemingly melting in the heat, gave way to her true feelings. She was as tired of life as the old wood beams that secured the building and grounded it in place. She felt a strong heat nip at her hand.

Looking down, she saw that the fire had taken a corner of the violin. Still, she held on to it as the fire engulfed her treasured instrument and the hand that held it. In tears, she ran into the street, dropping the violin onto the pavement, its final insult. Her beloved violin, her expression of pain and pleasure, was gone, along with everything that had ever mattered in her life.

Saaghi finally realized her hand was on fire. And now, submerged in pain, she cried and screamed in agony for her hand and for her country, for the ancestors of Cyrus the great—for Persia. Horrified by the sight of this woman writhing in pain in the street, a man removed his jacket and wrapped it around her grotesque hand to put out the fire. His eyes began to burn, and his stomach turned from the billowing smoke and smell of burned flesh.

Knowing their relationship, the man managed to half drag Saaghi to Peter, where she dropped to the ground at his feet. He was still quoting Omar Khayyam as he wound his fingers around her hair and watched his restaurant crumble beneath the powerful flames; Flames fueled by his life, now in ashes.

He looked around at the hordes of people drawn to Peter's burning restaurant like moths, each blaming the other for the atrocity. It was as if the fire had ignited a small war. Dissenting groups screamed at each other, some in favor of the Shah and others against America.

Peter caught a glimpse of his young friend, Bolbol, running toward what remained of his restaurant. He was stopped in his tracks by the horrifying sight of orange and yellow flames leaping out of windows and doorframes. Looking around frantically, he found Peter and Saaghi sitting on the curb, having given up all hope. He had known nothing but tragedy in his life, but still, he was unprepared for his own reaction. They were more than friends; they had always treated him like family!

The fact that it was too late to make a difference didn't stop Bolbol from taking off his cowboy hat and scooping up water from the creek, throwing it onto the flames. He yelled for help, but by now, the burning restaurant was inconsequential in comparison to the personal, government, and religious battles the crowds were fighting in the streets.

Nothing more could be done. All that was left was to assess the damage and try to keep it from getting worse. A young woman was checking Saaghi's hand and wrapping it with a scarf. Peter was whispering Omar Khayyam to himself. Bolbol began to sing a song. Bolbol and Peter always sang songs in the night after the restaurant closed. It would be familiar to him, and Bolbol thought that perhaps it would help.

But this time was different; the song was sad. Tears were running down Bolbol's cheek, no happiness or smile. The two friends began to sing together, sitting on the curb as they watched the fire continue to rage. Roxanna was overcome with sadness but touched by the tear running down Bolbol's cheek.

Police and fire trucks arrived with their sirens blaring, followed by Pary, who showed up in a taxi. Astonished to see her friend's greatly loved kebab restaurant engulfed in flames, she told the driver to wait while she called to her friends. Relieved, Roxanna helped Pary put Peter inside and then began searching the crowd for Saaghi, but she was nowhere to be found.

The taxi pulled away with Pary and Roxanna in the back and Peter in the front, still yelling the Rubaiyat. Bolbol began to run after the taxi, singing and crying as his friend was being taken away. He ran after the taxi, singing as loud as he could, running until he fell and could run no more. He wanted to make sure Peter would never forget that he had been there for him with pain in his heart. He wanted Peter to hear his voice in his head, singing to him, forever. He felt as if his lungs would burst but continued to sing through heartbroken sobs long after Peter had disappeared.

Finally, without hope, he started to shuffle his way back to the end of the world. At least, that was what it felt like to a ten-year-old boy. An old street cleaner who had purposely been staying away from the disaster saw Bolbol and shuffled with him. "Nothing lasts forever, not your happiness or either your pain. It is just that we remember the pain and feel it more." And with that, the old man disappeared.

Bolbol was still whispering the song he always sang with Peter when he reached his walnut cart. "Where the hell were you?" The boy turned to see his other friend, the older man who sold barbecued ballal, corn, from a cart next to his, covered with blood and bruises. The old man was yelling at him, telling him that he should never leave his walnut cart! And that an angry young mob wanted to steal his walnuts.

The old man was in tears explaining that he had tried to stop them, but it was too late. He felt like he had failed. The young gang destroyed Bolbol's cart and his corn cart as well. They were the same kids that used to be so kind to him. He was watching as his walnuts were scattered all over. There was no more cart or light for him to continue his business. It was destroyed by sheer madness.

Bolbol didn't know what to do about the blood running down the old man's face, so he tried to help by picking up the corn that was now scattered everywhere. Realizing that the cart had been damaged beyond repair and there was nowhere to put the corn, he found the blanket that he kept for cold evenings and laid the old man's corn on that. But instead of trying to pick up the walnuts that were scattered everywhere, Bolbol kicked them violently. He didn't understand anything about the night except a feeling of anger was raging inside. He had never understood anger before. He had hit a milestone in his life.

Now the little boy and the older man, who as recently as yesterday had shared so much together, the songs and laughter and friendship, sat together as men, looking into the unknown future of their country, worried about what was to come next.

A grim look came over the boy's face. He was debating whether the way he had been raised was the right way to live. He had been raised with values, kindness, forgiveness, patience. But this night, he had met anger face on, and he let it in. He asked himself how it made him feel and was surprised by his answer, "Powerful."

Should he adopt the angry way of dealing with the events of the world as he was seeing everyone around him do? He wanted to know how such a calm person could survive in an angry world. He needed Peter. He would always know these things. The imaginary scale upon which Bolbol was weighing his good and bad thoughts was going up and down…

*****

Chapter 23

When Unexpected Violence and Anger Overpowers Peace and Takes Over the Nation...

Staying with Peter was extremely difficult for Roxanna after the fire had destroyed his restaurant. There were too many ghosts haunting him that he fought off with alcohol, taking in a little more ammunition each day. When she realized she had little or no control over his drinking, it became clear to her that his life in Iran would never return to the way it was or get any better, leaving him in limbo.

By remaining inebriated, he was able to block out the images that tormented his soul. Having no place to go, he no longer left his apartment, which meant he depended on Roxanna for all of his needs. But she still had Hajji Khanoum to care for, and it was becoming increasingly difficult to divide her time so that there was anything left for her.

And then, there was a curfew that was enforced by the government. She was starting to feel like a caged animal. After the burning of hundreds of people in the movie theater in Abadan, followed by the massacre in Jaleh Square, or Black Friday as it had been dubbed by BBC radio, martial law had been declared by the Army headed by General Gholam Ali Oveisi. Still, many ignored the martial law and gathered in the streets, shouting, "Down with the Shah" and "Down with the US." It was Ayatollah Khomeini who encouraged them not to follow the Army or the government's order.

He was whispering Omar Khayyam's Rubaiyat, which really began to irritate Roxanna. She was starting to feel like she knew it by heart. She had tried to convince him to leave Iran and go back to America, to his family, but that was not an option. He had become part of the culture. This was his home now, and he did not want to leave. Literally. He was very content to stay cloistered within the four walls of his apartment and be cared for by Roxanna.

Peter told her he came to Iran as a missionary and then got to know an Iranian poet, Saaghi, who introduced Peter to the magnificent writings of Omar Khayyam. This meeting had changed Peter's life, and he became a seeker. Soon, he became so obsessed with Omar Khayyam and the search for higher meaning that he pushed himself away from his work, from his church. Omar Khayyam had become his mentor, the most important pursuit in his life.

It had been such a long time since he had any contact with his wife and daughter that she finally went her own way, taking the little girl with her. It took Peter a week to notice. He had fallen in love with a mysterious water nymph, Saaghi, and she was the only thing in his life that was real. Of course, Peter lived in an altered state of consciousness, to begin with, so who was to say what was real? He devoted his life to watching her play the violin, sing a poetic verse, and move seductively in circles around him while he lay on a pillow on the floor, his head hanging off, attempting to follow her with his eyes without moving his head.

Not to be outdone, Peter became a wanderer, like Omar Khayyam. He began to seek his spiritual truth, to find himself, and get in touch with his inner being. Throughout history, Persian poets had gathered all across Iran in search of synergetic words to extol the virtues of their country. Peter met Cyrus at one such gathering of poets, and together, they shared their works and views on kabob, among other things. Cyrus's poetry was written in the style of Rumi and Omar Khayyam and with his great singing voice.

That's all Peter needed to hear. The two were destined to do great things together. They read and chanted poetry. But first, they would need a permanent place to meet so neither would get lost in his search for a higher power. Cyrus put up the money to open a cozy coffee house that became a gathering place for them as well as for other unconventional poets, storytellers, and artists to come and share their creativity.

Many years later, carrying her violin and a bag of cerussite twinned crystals, Saaghi strolled back into Peter's life without explanation. She wished to be called Devas, but only by Peter, and only when they were … alone. It seemed that she always had a way of appearing and disappearing, so Peter looked up her new name to see if he could find out where she would be disappearing next, just as he suspected, into nature and the woods.

Roxanna was very surprised when she heard that Saaghi had such a powerful emotional hold on Peter that she had changed his life forever. Roxanna wished that Saaghi could be with him now, as his emotional rock, but after losing her hand in the fire, she disappeared from his world forever. Peter was missing the sound of her violin, her voice, and her craziness, everything about her. Both Roxanna and Peter suspected that after losing her hand in the fire and no longer being able to play the violin, she may have ended her life, but neither spoke of it.

Peter took a swig from the wine bottle and attempted to stand on his feet. "We're all invisible men," It appeared Peter was perfecting his slur. Either that or Roxanna was developing an ear for his lack of pronunciation. Of course, he fell, this time hitting his head on the edge of the soft sofa arm. Roxanna reached out and took the bottle from Peter, which miraculously never hit the floor. She wiped his face and looked into his eyes. In them, she saw herself as the daughter Peter left behind. She was wondering if he ever thought about what kind of a woman his little girl might have grown into or if he had kept her frozen in his brain; a child because it was easier.

Roxanna knew why Peter's eyes were always looking toward the door because that's where Saaghi's face would appear a thousand times a day. Peter's smile would fade away when her face disappeared. One night, Roxanna finally had the courage to confront his demons for him, "You miss them! Don't you? Your wife? What about your daughter? Do you think they don't exist just because you erased them from your so-called life? Oh, noooo! They're out there! They exist! They hurt! They wonder why you abandoned them! They stare at a door every day, waiting for you to return!"

Peter suddenly remembered why he had kept silent for so long. He hated lectures. His silence irritated Roxanna to the core and caused her to break into tears. They both knew it was her relationship with her father that she was really talking about. She was the daughter whose father had left her. She was the one left feeling worthless and unloved from lack of recognition or even acknowledgment. She was the one who could not stop the bleeding from the tragic hole it had left in her life.

The absence of her father and her inability to express and receive his love had been the driving force behind her decision to come to Iran. Her need to fill that space in her, that part of her that was missing. She looked at Peter and summed it up, "Children need their fathers. You don't even know if your grandchildren are boys or girls! You don't even know if you have grandchildren. Do you even know if your daughter's alive?"

Peter took another gulp of wine before falling to the floor again... He was fishing for something in his pocket. Now, if he could only remember what it was ... His wallet! Thumbing through all his important papers, he finally found what he was looking for. Behind it, all was a faded and folded, dog-eared photograph. He slipped it out just long enough to take a mental picture of it and put it right back.

Roxanna knew exactly who was in the picture, and it gave her a small amount of satisfaction knowing that she had been able to reach him... At least Peter was starting to open that narrow mind of his far enough to let his wife and daughter in, at least for a moment. Attempting his best Led Zeppelin imitation, he started to sing... "There's a lady who knows, all that glitters is gold, and she's buying a stairway to Heaven."

Roxanna helped him off the floor, singing along. When they finished, he changed the mood, dancing as if he was performing some sort of childish skit in front of her. "Jack be nimble, Jack be quick, Jack is feeling a little sick. Jack jumped over the candlestick; let's hope his pants don't light up quick." Roxanna suddenly felt hopeful. After venting about how her father had abandoned her, she had felt like a torpedoed ship. But by doing so, she managed to raise Peter to a new and brighter level of consciousness. At least some level of consciousness.

It was late at night in Tehran, and the sounds of gunshots were building to a crescendo. The "music of the night," as Peter referred to the fighting, had become so commonplace it was hardly noticed. Aside from staying inside, it had little impact on their lives. Roxanna found it a little disconcerting how, after being exposed to violence and death for long, they were able to disassociate themselves from its horror.

Peter said "disconcerting" was not in his vocabulary and suggested she drink more wine. He added that "regression," however, was in his vocabulary, and it worked wonders on helping to escape reality. Roxanna and Peter decided to create a world of their own by becoming children again, decidedly, five-year-old. Peter continued dancing using his wine bottle as a partner.

As five-year-old often do, he tried to attempt a move far too advanced for his level of dexterity. With great finesse, he leaped into the air and soared over a low table. He missed and fell heavily. Roxanna grabbed the wine bottle before it hit the wall and helped him up.

Amused, she joined him in his childlike dance only to be interrupted by machine-gun fire shattering the window, sending shards of glass flying everywhere. Knowing that Peter's reflexes weren't the best at the moment, Roxanna pulled him to the floor, and like a typical five-year-old, covered their heads with a blanket, pretending to be invisible.

They positioned themselves comfortably on the floor and leaned against the sofa, giggling and wiggling, making sure the blanket still covered their heads. Roxanna's hand reached out from underneath and fished around until she was able to grab the wine bottle and bring it under the blanket with them. The bottle moved around in a ghostly manner as she took a long swing and passed it to Peter. And there they stayed, hunkered down in their homemade foxhole, hiding from the war raging outside.

There was a necessary silence between them. They had just exposed their deepest, most guarded secrets and were feeling vulnerable. Roxanna stared at the half-empty bottle of red wine as if it were to blame for her tears. Peter noticed and tried to comfort her, "Don't cry, little girl! There's more where that came from."

"I miss home, I miss my mother, and I miss bean burritos." Roxanna whimpered.

Peter took the bottle from her, took a swig, and leaned his head towards her. "I miss the Knicks, Earl the Pearl, and Clyde Frazier in the backcourt at Madison Square Garden—" Roxanna cut him off, "Hot Fudge Sundaes. Hot dogs—"

Peter began mimicking announcer Russ Hodges 'description of the 1951 home run, nicknamed "The Shot Heard Round the World." "Two outs at the bottom of the ninth. The winner goes to the World Series to face the Brooklyn Dodgers. Bobby Thompson steps in. Branca winds up! Throws, swings, and a hit—it's got distance! It's gone! The Giants win the Pennant! The Giants win the Pennant!"

Peter was good! He had Hodges down perfectly. "Go, Giants!" Roxanna cheered. The phone began to ring, but they were laughing too hard to care. Peter continued his announcing. "Oh, Lordie, what a shot! What a shot! Bobby Thompson homers with two outs in the bottom of the ninth; the game's over. The phone's ringing: it must be the president!"

Roxanna's hand reached out from under the blanket, searching for the phone, groping blindly, finally managing to cut herself on a sharp piece of glass. "Damn!" She crawled out from underneath long enough to grab the receiver and bring it back under the blanket. Getting back into character, she showed Peter her "owie" before she answered. "Hello?" Damn! It was her mother and that was the last thing she wanted.

Roxanna was hitting her head with the phone, chastising herself for answering. The timing was horrible but there was nothing she could do but listen while her mother threw questions out like BBs. Roxanna kept the phone under the blanket, covering the receiver so the sound of the fighting outside would be silenced, or at the very least, muffled. From the beginning, she was trying to find a reason to hang up. "Mom, it's hard to hear you. This is a terrible connection. Hold on, Mom . . ."

The fighting was getting worse, forcing Roxanna to slither along the floor with the phone in one hand until she was able to position herself under a table. She was yelling into the receiver, "What?! Gunfire? Don't be ridiculous! It's the TV. Why wouldn't I be safe? I'm watching TV with a friend! It is not dangerous! Oh, please, Mother! Don't believe everything you hear on the news. I miss you, too, mom."

In America, Linda was pacing around her living room like a caged puma, trying to get up enough nerve to ask the only question she cared about. "Roxanna? Don't hang up; I'm not through! Did you find him?"

Roxanna felt her throat start to constrict. Forcing back tears, she whispered, "Mom, not yet... but I'm going to find him and bring him back home. I promised I would bring him home."

"Be careful, Roxanna! It's so dangerous over there. The news makes me worried . . . please be careful. Are you okay for sure, my love? Are you safe?" Roxanna didn't want her mother to know she was crying, so she didn't respond. "Roxy? Are you okay?"

Roxanna had never been as patient with her mother as she was at that moment. "I figured something out since I've been here. Life's not fair. I thought you kept me away from dad because you were angry. I thought you were punishing me because you hated him for leaving us. But now I understand. You were protecting me. I love you, Mom."

Roxanna's words had been a long time coming. and just the sound of them brought tears to her mother's eyes. "But now I understand," were the sweetest words Linda had ever heard. "I've never been good at laying my emotions out for people to see. I've spent my life burying them. I didn't mean to hurt you. I'm sorry if I did . . . I love you, baby. Just come back, safely."

Choking back tears of her own, Roxanna hung up the phone. The sound of the gunfire was escalating, and she didn't want to answer any more of her mother's questions. Looking around, she was more than a little surprised to see that Peter had wandered out onto the balcony. He was still acting like a five-year-old. He knew better than to make himself a target!

Peter was looking up, watching his young friend with his camera. The boy was standing on the third-floor balcony, filming the barbaric battles taking place on the streets below. Peter's eye followed the boy's camera toward the alley to get an idea of what he was filming. There were several young men and women fighting their way through a narrow passageway, trying to escape a group of soldiers enforcing martial law.

Peter was suddenly distracted as a horrific scream came from overhead. Peter felt as if he got punched in the stomach, knowing in his heart what had happened. Looking up, his eyes followed the body of his young friend who was filming as he fell from the balcony, as it crashed directly underneath him. Blood splashed across the building and began to pool around his small body, but he did not let go of his camera. He was still holding it in his hand. The fighting continues without notice of the tragedy that had just taken place.

Peter rushed into the living room, yelling, "No! No!" as he blasted through the front door. The commotion was loud enough that it distracted Roxanna, who was still under the blanket, but when she looked around, the room was empty. Suddenly, Peter's landlord appeared from upstairs and ran in front of the wide-open door, and disappeared down the stairs. Totally confused, Roxanna ran onto the balcony and looked out to see Peter kneeling over his friend in the alley. The young boy was lying in a pool of blood, his camera held loosely in his hand.

Peter fought to get to his feet before staggering and falling backward, cursing the soldiers vehemently and calling them cowards for killing a child. Crawling, he reached out to touch the boy's hand that was still holding his most prized possession, his 8mm camera. The touch of the child's tiny hand, still covered with warm, sticky blood, sent shock waves of terror through Peter's entire being. Lying on his stomach next to the body of his young friend, he let out an anguished scream, beating his head into the ground, trying to wake from the horrible nightmare.

Farhad held up a white piece of material, its color the only protection between them and the bullets, while the boy's anguished father ran to help carry his child inside. In the fury of the moment, the boy's camera slipped from his grasp. Peter, still lying in the street, picked it up and held it in his hands, relieved, as if he intended to return it to the child.

The fighting was at its peak. Petrol bombs were being thrown from almost every house, exploding into fireballs all around him. In his drunken stupor, Peter had completely lost touch with reality. For all he knew, he was still at his restaurant, watching his life go up in flames. Roxanna yelled to Peter from the balcony, telling him to get back inside, but Peter either did not hear or did not care.

Despite the barrage of homemade bombs falling from the rooftop onto the alley, shooting flames in all directions, the soldiers fought back, using their jeeps for cover. They managed to start taking control of the streets, closing in on Peter, who lay in the center of the turmoil, indifferent to the danger he was in.

With great effort, he raised himself to his knees and stood. Slowly, he raised the boy's bloody camera to his eye and began to walk toward the battle zone. He filmed and recorded while yelling grief-stricken babble. The coldness of Sattar's blood upon his face sent a chilling cold through the soul of his bones. Peter was physically present, but his heart was so torn and tired it had no worries about the danger that surrounded him.

Peter stood, bullets and chaos all around him, "Look at me, you murderers. I am here in front of you! If you wish to shoot someone, shoot me, and leave these people alone! They are your blood. Shoot the American! Shoot the dumb American!"

No matter how loud she screamed, Roxanna wasn't getting through to Peter. In a panic, she gave up and disappeared from the balcony and started running down the stairs after him but was stopped at the front door by Farhad and his daughter, who were able to force her back inside and hold her there. Her screams and cries just brought unwanted attention as the approaching soldiers and fighters turned in her direction.

She was like a caged tigress, clawing to get out, "Please, somebody! Do something! They're going to kill him. Please!" In an attempt to make Roxanna understand that her actions were about to get them all killed, Farhad and his daughter moved close enough to the door so that each could take a turn looking through the broken glass plate. Roxanna caught a slanted image of Peter, begging to be shot, and she stopped fighting. Farhad was right. There was nothing more than anyone could do for him but die.

Although his legs were weak and unsteady, the raw urge for revenge, alone, made him a formidable adversary. Peter continued yelling and filming with great conviction, drawing dangerous attention to himself and further provoking the soldiers. Roxanna's heart was breaking, but she knew that even if she couldn't reach him, he was not alone out there. He was never alone.

Omar Khayyam was his rock. She could hear him chanting over and over, "...one day your soul will depart from your body, and you will be drawn behind the curtain between us, unknown...you don't know where you will be going . . . one day your soul . . ."

Reflections from the waning crescent moon played against the soldiers as they ran toward Peter. There were shooters on the rooftop aiming toward the soldiers at the alley. From surrounding homes, stray Molotov cocktails missed their mark and landed around Peter, erupting into scorching fireballs. The soldiers, fearing for their lives, shot at anyone or anything that moved and the fact that Peter was taunting them left no hope.

Being held back by Farhad and his daughter, Roxanna remained frozen at her spot by the door where she could observe Peter, unnoticed. She was aghast. There, in front of her, was Peter, walking calmly through the flying bullets and burning fire, still filming, without fear and impossible to distract. His heart was lost and broken, he was full of alcohol, and life as he knew it, had ceased to exist. His courage evolved from a man who had lost everything and everyone that he had loved. Bullets, fire, and death were of no consequence. He was ready to die.

The scene unfolding in front of her was more diabolical than Roxanna could have ever imagined when she watches. In the middle of the chaos, Peter stood tall, in spite of being intoxicated. He was hit first by a single bullet to his shoulder. The force of the impact turned his body completely around, causing him to stagger and stumble, losing his footing.

Desperate, they were determined to hold her down no matter how hard she fought to get to Peter. But Roxanna finally broke away from Farnaz and ran out and towards Peter, screaming towards the rooftops where bullets came flying from, begging them to stop. "For God's sake, stop it! He's an American!"

On the rooftop, a young, angry man stood among a few others, raising his weapon and yelling down at Roxanna grimly. "Where do you think this came from? America. You sold it to us. Bullets do not understand who's American or Iranian. Bullets only kill..."

He aimed his rifle towards the alley and fired as the rest joined him. The sound of gunfire echoed throughout the neighborhood as bullets began to hit around Roxanna. An officer dove towards Roxanna and pulled her down beside a VW bug parked over a small creek. "Get under the car!"

The officer took a bullet to save her life. Roxanna, horrified, realized he had been hit. She moved under the car and laid in the icy creek, watching Peter lying motionless only a few yards away, whispering, dying, "I sent my Soul through the invisible, my Soul returned to me and answered, I, myself, am Heaven and Hell..."

A few more Army jeeps arrived, entering the alley, heading towards where Roxanna was hiding. Chaos broke out. She watched hopelessly, in defiance. Peter gathered all his remaining strength and stood upright as the blood poured out of him, spilling between his fingers, still holding the camera. He turned slightly, in the direction of where Roxanna was hiding ... his eyes, lit solely by flames, searching for his friend. Hiding behind a car, with fire burning and closing in on her, Roxanna and the injured soldier continued to watch through a crack beneath the cars.

Peter's face was ghoulish in appearance, resembling some sort of death mask. In a flash, he was bombarded by bullets, his knees hitting the ground first. For one short second, his head rose toward the night sky, then his body fell forward. The only sound he heard was the soft music of Saaghi's violin playing in his head.

The only thing Peter could see was Saaghi walking toward him through the violence, playing their favorite song, like she was invisible. Peter's hand, now resting in a pool of blood beside his body, was still clutching the boy's camera; and from it came a familiar low humming sound, a repetitive soft drone that became the tragic music of the night. His eyes were looking directly at Roxanna, smiling, letting her know how happy he was.

Tears in her eyes, hopelessly, Roxanna watched. The red color of the scorching fire surrounding Peter caused him to shine like a burning sun. An Army truck pulled up, lighting Peter's mangled body with its headlights. The soldiers stepped outside of the truck, an officer walked up, gazing in disbelief.

There was nothing more than a camera in his grasp but no gun. They stared in horror, "He is foreign. He was filming?" Another whispered. "He must be American!" They all stared at Peter, each harboring his own complicated emotions. How could this riddled, bleeding body, lying motionless at his feet, make a sound? But it was.

It was likely that a few of the soldiers would have recognized Peter if the environment had not been so charged with fear or if there had been streetlights. But in the thick, black pitch of night, only faint lines and shadows could be seen through the darkness, making everyone a target.

Not yet dead, he was a messenger, softly whispering, gently chanting over and over, the words of Omar Khayyam. "I sent my Soul through the invisible, my Soul returned to me, and answered, I myself am Heaven and Hell," his words growing softer, more softly again, then no more. Silence. Peter was in Heaven.

Unable to take her eyes off Peter, Roxanna screamed as hard and loud she could, but her voice was held back within her soul, and could not reach out. She was begging through her tears, trying to say, "For God's sake, you can't do that to him! He is an American!" But she was the only one who could hear her own voice. She could only watch as they threw Peter's motionless body into the army truck.

The truck moved away, disappearing into the darkness, taking Peter's body away as the rain of Molotov Cocktails continued to fall from the rooftops. One landed on the hood of a jeep near Roxanna and exploded next to the VW Roxanna was hiding under, the VW catching fire.

The injured soldier watching her was shocked to see such a beautiful young woman daring to risk her life for a man so close to death. What emotion would cause a person to do something like that? He thought himself immune to feelings on any level, but her tears stung him. Although he couldn't understand her words, the agony and desperation in her voice had caught him off guard.

He had seen so much death – he, himself, was responsible for so much death – that watching the murder of Peter was the limit to what he could witness. He was not blind to the fact that his country of poetry and proud history had lost its way, had gone down a path paved with bullets, into darkness. And like so many others trapped in the disarray of extreme confusion, he was unsure of where the future of his beloved country was headed.

Ceremoniously, he took his gun in both hands and lifted it towards the sky. The fire against the dark metal reflected blood red, the shoulder strap draped low, around his wrists. He was faced with atrocities that he committed in the fervor of madness. He was wrapped in a web of international deceit that could not be undone, and just the realization of it devoured him. His eyes, at first riveted on his weapon above his head, slowly looked down, surveying the bloodstained square.

As if by black magic, the gibbous moon lit up every foreign object in the streets, turning the aftermath of the massacre into a macabre masterpiece of reflected light. With tormented soul, his shouts echoed in waves off the broken stone walls, then he slammed the gun to the ground with such force that it left an imprint; he held the barrel upright like a tombstone, marking the place of the dead, his sanity gone.

A rain of bullets and of Molotov Cocktails was still falling from the rooftops. Now the entire car Roxanna was hiding behind was on fire, and the fire was closing in on her.

Desperate for an escape route, Roxanna scanned every inch of the area until she saw a ray of light coming from a crack in a door. Looking closer, she noticed a young man waving frantically, trying to get their attention. It was clear that they had no choice but to take the risk if they wanted to stay alive.

Behind him, she saw two men, obviously not soldiers because of their jeans and tee shirts, holding machine guns, ready to cover them. They began shooting one magazine of bullets after another, signaling for her to run. The injured soldier holding his gun gestured to her to run, and he also began to cover her giving her a chance to reach the young stranger who was willing to risk his life for theirs.

He positioned his body to act as a shield. They could almost feel the bullets whizzing past them. Raising his gun, the young man attempted to buy them time, shooting rounds continuously into the air. When Roxanna got close enough, he darted out of his house and grabbed her, pulling her to safety, the boy just a second behind. She was safe inside. She looked back for the soldier to see he was lying down, dead.

Roxanna followed the young man as he raced up three flights of stairs to his apartment. These strange times forced young men to grow up quickly. Once safely inside, the first thing she heard was the familiar sound of BBC Radio playing in the background. Entering the living room, Roxanna smiled, relieved, at Mansour, a ten-year-old boy going on eighteen.

The man who had rescued her addressed Roxanna. "You are safe here; they would not come inside. They are Iranian soldiers just taking orders." He wanted her to feel safe; oddly enough, his name was Safe. Roxanna positioned himself on the floor away from the window.

Mansour stayed in the living room, but the rest headed up the stairs towards the balcony and rooftop loaded down with more Molotov cocktails and a variety of different weapons. A younger woman entered, carrying a blanket and dry clothing, and spoke directly at Roxanna. "You are American. Please do not worry. We don't have anything against you, but we do not like your government's support of the Shah. We will not harm you. We love the American people. You will spend the night here. Come with me before you catch a cold."

An older woman who appeared to be Mansour's Mother entered from the kitchen with fruits and tea on a tray and placed it in front of Roxanna with a smile, gesturing for her to eat. Then, unhappy because of the fighting, she turned to her daughter and asked her to serve Roxanna. She then began to clean the table but stopped to look at Khomeini's picture in a frame directly in the center of the table. She took the picture in her hand, looked at it, and quietly whispered a brief prayer to herself before placing it back on the side table, face down, next to a few other pictures.

The boy watched his mother's every move, then turned his gaze to Roxanna, watching them with sharp eyes. His senses were elevated, so when she tried to get Mansour to sleep, he resisted. She had played this game many times before and would not sleep until she was sure that all her children, and particularly her youngest boy, were tucked in safely within the protection of their walls, surrounded by love. Young Mansour waited for his mother to finally go to her own room before sneaking out and placing Khomeini's picture back on the main table, making sure it was visible.

Roxanna was taken aback by young Mansour's bold reaction. He was just ten years old, and yet he had formed such strong opinions as if he was mature enough to form political and philosophical ideologies of his own. It was likely that he was not even aware of who Khomeini was but was merely responding to what he had witnessed and the dogma he was continuously being exposed to. He watched the boy, acknowledging the power of propaganda, how it changed people and caused them to close their minds to such an extent that they saw only darkness.

It was disheartening to witness such young children cultivating so much hatred toward one another, the violent feelings growing like noxious weeds, poisoning the beautiful flower buds beneath them. Roxanna was reeling from the reality he was bearing witness to. The children, who had once been Iran's hope for the future, now the new benchmark of a misguided generation, had a lack of compassion, fostered mistrust, and misplaced their loyalties while becoming leaders shrouded in the cloak of self-promotion.

Roxanna watched silently, gagging from the effects of the nauseating irony playing out in front of her, like a tragic screenplay. In her eyes, the label on the blood-red Exxon can was the metaphor for the truth behind this revolution: money and power. Roxanna was more interested in observing and studying the juxtaposition of Khomeini's picture against the backdrop of this child making bombs.

The mere likeness of Khomeini with his black, piercing eyes residing in a house so filled with love and innocent people was like watching a wolf in sheep's clothing, grinning out from his den. The scene reminded him of something Cyrus's mother, Hajji Khanoum, once said when he was looking at Khomeini's image, her wisdom imprinted in his memory as if by a branding iron.

"Something about his eyes is frightening. I cannot trust his eyes." Her voice echoed, hauntingly, as if yelled into the side of a mountain of Damavand, returning to her in wave after wave. She quietly acknowledged to herself, I hear you Hajji Khanoum, I hear you.

Roxanna tried to stay awake. She thought she owed it to the people who were caught in the chaos that surrounded them, fighting and dying for Iran, to stay awake and listen to their cries.

As usual, BBC Radio was playing even if all were asleep, "This is BBC International, reporting on the most current activities within Iran. The situation in Iran is getting more unstable daily. The Army is scattered throughout the city, shooting innocent people with impunity." Upon hearing the broadcasters report, young Mansour raised his clenched fist into the air with fervor, his little face contorting as he shouted, "Baleh, Baleh," which was Yes, yes, in Farsi.

*****

Chapter 24

Conspiracy in France... Madness is Logic...

The days and nights were much longer these days in Tehran. The nights were not the same calm and peaceful ones they used to be. There was some kind of strange and nasty energy flowing through the air, making it hard to breathe. No one knew who a friend was or who was the enemy, who do you trust or not, was no different. It was a few nights after his death. Roxanna sat alone, confused, and lost as to what to do. She did not leave the house. Farhad, his wife, and their daughter took Roxanna in as they would their own, allowing her to stay in Peter's apartment as long as she wanted with no charge.

Knowing how close he was to Bolbol, she began to make trips shelling fresh walnuts, hoping to give him Peter's simple treasures. But after the tragic fire, he, too, had disappeared, as well as the corn man and so many others, leaving Roxanna feeling desperately alone and empty. But even though she was more at ease and comfort to stay at Hajji Khanoum's place, she thought and believed sooner, or later Cyrus would show up at Peter's house, and she would have a much better chance to see him.

She was not wrong, and just as she was lost, confused, and not knowing what to do, there was a knock on the door. It was the middle of the night; whom could it be this late? Hesitating, with concern and thinking it may be Pary, she walked to the door and opened it. She was stunned and happy to see that Cyrus was standing in the doorway. She was hugging and holding on to him in the door for a long bit.

Soon he was inside, and the door was shut. They had a lot to talk about. She knew Cyrus had gone again and heard this time he was in France. He was back right away after he heard about Peter. He was sitting on the floor, holding her hand kindly and gently. He was there to convince her there was time for her to leave Iran, and to do that, he opened up to tell her what was about to come about in Iran, telling her she should not be there…

*****

Sitting with Roxanna at late Peter's place, he continued the conversation, launching into his experiences over the last few weeks.

"A few weeks ago, Hussein called me in the middle of the night." He was in France. Hussein wanted Cyrus to come to France and said it was about his brother. Taking Hussein's advice, within forty-eight hours, he was sitting in the restaurant in the hotel Le Méridien in Paris with Hussein. Hussein's gathering was mostly at La Closerie des Lilas. This was where Sadegh Ghotbzadeh used to dine regularly. Seated at a corner table towards the rear, it was clear they were waiting for some kind of action to unfold.

Cyrus was still struggling with the web of lies he had told to his wife Julia to distract her from the real reason he had gone to Iran and Paris. It was much harder to get her to agree to stay home this time. She had been looking forward to a late honeymoon, and Paris was definitely a step up from the Yuma Desert. He had to promise he would bring her to Iran to meet his mother to get her to finally back down.

Hussein nodded towards a table on the far side of the restaurant. A very striking tall blonde, an American woman in her 40s, was dining with an Iranian man, Dr. Abraham Yazdi, and another middle-aged American man, on the other side of the restaurant several yards away. They were engaged in quiet conversation, and from their look and behavior, it was clear their conversation was very serious.

Hussein's voice played in the background. The American man was Ramsey Clark. "Ramsey Clark is one of the main members of the American negotiating team." The blond, "Her name is Dorian MacGray. She went to Iran when she was 16 years old as a CIA operative on The Fourth Principal Truman Administration, a project headed by a man named Warren.

"It was there she met Ayatollah Beheshti, who also was working there. He was wearing a suit and tie at the time. He was not clergy yet. That is the same place your brother, Amir, used to work and was one of the head guys. The rumor is that Beheshti and Dorian had an interest in one another, but he didn't let them pursue anything; he claimed it would be distracting. Your brother Amir was against their relationship and told her so.

"Later, Beheshti was assigned to become Clergy and was sent to Germany. Soon we know him as Ayatollah Beheshti. At the time, he was sent to Frankfurt to open a mosque to gather information from the opposition. However, many years later, they were reunited in Frankfurt – where they had an affair. The rumor is they have a daughter… who lives in the states now…"

Hussein took a sip from his drink and continued, "The man with her is our Iranian friend Dr. Abraham Yazdi. Yazdi lives in Texas with his American wife and children and is one of Khomeini's main advisors working directly with America."

They watched as Dorian, Dr. Yazdi, and Ramsey Clark rose and left the restaurant, disappearing into the elevator. Not long after, while Cyrus was trying to make sense of it all, another newcomer to the game arrived on the scene. An American man in an American Army uniform, Colonel Edward Thompson, entered the hotel carrying a hard-shelled small, black case. Hussein's voice echoed in Cyrus's ears. "He is also one of the main men among the American negotiating team. He always carries the same case. It holds the most sophisticated, secure communications equipment in the world. Americans here are in continuous communications with the White House through his safe and secure radio."

The case disappeared from Cyrus's view once Colonel Thompson stepped into the elevator, but its image was etched in his mind. Hussein had finally gotten Cyrus's attention, but being on the wrong side of the door, Cyrus was forced to imagine what was going on as the events were unfolding. In fact, Cyrus was right on target in his thinking. At that very moment, Colonel Edward Thompson was communicating on a secure line with Washington.

*****

It was midafternoon, and Cyrus had no interest in sightseeing. France had more romance than he wished to explore with a group of five men, including Hussein and Ghotbzadeh. Instead, he found himself sitting in a car with Hussein on one of the streets of Neauphle-le-Chateau, observing a large compound.

Cyrus observed a few French police cars driving around the exterior of the compound while at least three others continually circled the area on foot closest to the house. As usual, Cyrus reserved judgment and listened intently, "This is the house Khomeini will stay in when they move him to France. They have about 20 phone lines already activated. You, see? There are already French police guarding the house. Lots of activity going on. Iranian, American, French, English people going in and out."

Hussein nodded towards a few young men in their late twenties or early thirties who came out, searching the surroundings. Hussein pointed to one in particular who was a bit taller than the other two, wearing a green American Army jacket, "No matter what, you do not want to be around these people, especially the one in the green American Army jacket. He's, their hitman. He goes by Saeed but different than our friend. Whoever they need or want to be eliminated, he does the killing… He has been trained in Libya and Syria through Ghotbzadeh's connections. I met him at the camp, and I've had one conversation with him. It only lasted for a few minutes. He's mostly around Ghotbzadeh… but takes his orders from the clergy…"

A parade of buses approached, passing them and stopping by the compound. To Cyrus's surprise, about 300 Middle Eastern-looking men exited and entered the compound. It was clear that Hussein had done his homework, "These men just arrived from Libya and Syria to guard Khomeini. I trained with them a few months ago. Only four of them are Iranian. Dorian and Colonel Edward Thomson are on their way to Iraq to meet with Khomeini about convincing him to come here."

Cyrus turned to Hussein, questioning how it was that he knew all these details. It was as if Hussein had read his mind. "I have my connections... You play the game ... they want info from you... they have to give you something in return. It is an American soap opera. Everyone's juggling for position, playing games to secure their place in line as they climb to the top rung of the ladder, collecting information to blackmail one another, filming and taping one another secretly.

It's a jungle with everyone fighting to get his share of the kill. And in the end, they've forgotten what they were fighting for. As for me, I am working with Banisadr and Ghotbzadeh behind the scenes... I do not want anyone to know I exist here." Cyrus listened without interruption. "Just imagine. By now, Dorian and Colonel Thompson must have landed in Iraq to convince Khomeini it is safe to return to France. The rumor is Khomeini is having doubts about coming."

*****

Saddam Hussein's portraits were visible everywhere in the streets of Baghdad. Traveling through the city, Dorian and Colonel Thompson rode with a driver from the American Embassy. They were on the way to meet Ayatollah Khomeini.

By the time they reached their destination, Dorian had concluded it would be best to begin the meeting with the letter Khomeini had sent to President Carter. She knew that Khomeini wrote to Carter and wanted to assure Carter that he was a better choice than the Shah to protect American interests in Iran. He was ready to do whatever America wanted; sell oil cheaper than the Saudi's, kill all the communists, whatever they wanted as long as they dismantled the Iranian Army.

Dorian knew the letter was not the first time Khomeini had communicated with the United States. What Dorian did not understand was why Khomeini was so worried and scared about going to France when Washington and President Carter had given the green light to support him.

Now she was sitting face to face with Ayatollah Khomeini and Dr. Abraham Yazdi. Moments before, she had pulled a scarf out of her bag and covered her head in traditional Iranian style. The room was dimly lit, with simple and sparse furnishings that gave the impression no one had lived there in ages. Colonel Edward Thompson and Dorian, still wearing her scarf, sat on a musty, worn rug across from Dr. Yazdi. Khomeini stared at the floor, waiting for Dorian to speak, and when she did, it was in fluent Farsi. Khomeini kept his eyes down so as not to be distracted by her beauty.

"I am here to personally let you know President Carter has received your letter ... Among the requests you asked for was the dismantling of the Iranian Army... That can be done... But it seems you are still doubtful of our commitment... We are here to assure you that the U.S. and the West are committed to getting rid of the Shah. We are committed to protecting Iran and preventing the communists from taking over. We know Imam will be a great leader for the Islamic State of Iran.

"However, we were told Imam does not believe and trust that we are serious. That is why we came here, personally, to make it absolutely clear to you that the US and the West are committed to removing the Shah. We believe he doesn't have the people's interests in mind. He is sick and could die anytime. But we are more concerned that communists will take over. We cannot allow this to happen in Iran. We think Imam will be a great leader for the Islamic State. We have already coordinated your return to France and from there to Iran. The English and Germans are also with us. Colonel Thompson is coordinating every detail in Iran. He can share more info with Imam, so he won't be worried."

Colonel Thompson took over, speaking English and sometimes adding a few Farsi words to comfort them, with Dorian translating as necessary, "Yes. We have a few hundred men from Syria and Libya already in place in France to guard you. Dr. Yazdi has coordinated them. From there, they will move to Iran with you."

Khomeini raised his eyes for the first time, directing a question to Yazdi, "What about the Shah's army... what if they decide to defend him?" Before Dr. Yazdi had a chance to answer, Dorian spoke up, "Imam should not be worried. General Huyser is on his way to Iran to let the Shah know what the situation is and to convince him to leave peacefully. We also have our people in the Iranian Armed Forces. General Hussein Fardoust and General Abbas Gharabaghi are the ones who have everything under control.

"As you know, he is the head of Savak. He managed for the last several months to make sure the Savak hasn't reported the truth to the Shah. He has made sure the Shah is getting false information. However, we have a few backup plans if the Shah's Army resists... we have a plan to poison the Tehran drinking water... to create a 'chaos' ... we will provide you with the entire plan when you are in France... We just need to know if you are committed to following our advice. Dr. Yazdi, Ghotbzadeh, and Banisadr, and other people you trust are working closely with us."

Dorian pulled a paper out of her folder, holding on to it as she continued, "However we have one last demand that you must agree to before we will move forward. This is a list of officials and civilians who are to be executed after the Shah is gone to guarantee there will be no uprising or coup against you. Over 3,400 clergy and businessmen must be eliminated, all of which belong to the Shah's loyalists. This must be done to prevent chaos and backlash. We must be absolutely sure you agree with this."

Dorian placed the paper in front of Ayatollah Khomeini. The room fell silent as they waited for Khomeini to respond. He picked up the list and looked it over, glancing through the names. It was clear by his actions that he agreed. Khomeini finally looked at Dorian as if sending her a secret message and then to the others, unhappily. Dorian got the message and immediately motioned toward Colonel Thomson and Dr. Yazdi to exit, leaving her alone with him. Khomeini waited for the door to close before speaking. "President Carter will have my word. All will be killed. But I only trust you... I want to communicate only through you." Dorian nodded in agreement.

Ayatollah Khomeini studied Dorian's slightest move, trying to read her. Something very important was on his mind, and he wanted to be clear where she stood before he said anything. "Tell me something... why do I hear that America is using me to change the regime in Iran? Then they would have Ayatollah Beheshti take over..."

In her heart, Dorian knew Khomeini was right, but she needed to convince him otherwise. The plan absolutely was for Ayatollah Beheshti to eventually take over. Khomeini was nothing more than a steppingstone. Dorian chose her words carefully. "I promise you... that will not happen...as long as you honor your promise. Trust me."

*****

It was past midnight now, with only two lefts in the room, Khomeini, and Dr. Yazdi. It was dark, and Dr. Yazdi was having trouble reading names from the list. "Mohammad Kazem Shariatmadari and Ayatollah Mahmoud Taleghani...also are on this list..." Dr. Yazdi looked up toward Khomeini to get his response. It was as if Khomeini was picturing each face as the names were called off. He never looked at Dr. Ebrahim Yazdi's eyes, "What do you think? Should I trust the Americans?"

Dr. Yazdi didn't even have to think about it. "I don't see why not. They will help us to take overpower and afterward we can do what we want... Who are the Americans to tell us what to do and what not to do... especially now when American elections will be soon, and we can play Republicans against the Democrats ...I think Imam should come to France...Ghotbzadeh has managed to get 14 million dollars from Muammar Gaddafi to help us to finance the revolution... we must give it back to him after the revolution succeeds… and of course maybe a few favors…"

Khomeini wanted to make one thing clear before he made his final decision, "The list to be killed? Ayatollah Mahmoud Taleghani should not be killed. The rest is OK."

Shortly after the meeting, Khomeini, escorted by French security forces, sat on an Air France flight, on his way to Neauphle-le-Château, to take up residence at the house that had been prepared for him.

*****

Back in France, Cyrus and Hussein were enjoying a late dinner in their hotel, surrounded by soft, classical music. They were given a table in the back, away from other diners, at their request. In between bites, Hussein continued feeding Cyrus information, "You see… If the West didn't want to get rid of the Shah, France wouldn't give Khomeini a visa.

Also, they would restrict him from talking to the media. The entire world's media is focused on Khomeini. His message and tapes are distributed through Iran on a daily basis with RADIO BBC in London leading the propaganda, and all are managed by France, America, England, and Germany. That is why we all must get busy…"

Cyrus looked at him skeptically. "You mean join the US and the West to remove the Shah just so they can get cheaper oil? Doesn't that mean we are betraying our people?" Before Hussein had a chance to respond, Sadegh Ghotbzadeh's voice cut in, "That is one way of looking at it. However, it will be better than millions of our people dying…"

Cyrus turned to see Ghotbzadeh standing behind him, holding a drink. Hussein continued eating, but Cyrus had no appetite. Ghotbzadeh joined them, "Our intention is not to cheat or betray our people. It is to cause the least possible harm during the transition. Khomeini is only a puppet. He is being used to bring radicals into the streets and have them die for their Imam. Eventually, he will be replaced… perhaps by Ayatollah Beheshti."

Hussein interrupted, "We are all in this to be sure the clergy doesn't take over. That's what the West wants. That is the intention of the West. But we can't let that happen. If the clergy takes over, they will ruin the country."

Cyrus was becoming extremely impatient. "Why did you bring me here? What does any of this have to do with me? Or with my brother!"

Hussein and Ghotbzadeh exchange glances, neither wanting to be the first to respond, but they had no choice. Cyrus was waiting for an answer. Ghotbzadeh finally broke the silence, but not before taking a long sip of his drink. "You are here to save your brother's life and the lives of many others. And for that, you need our help, and we need yours."

Ghotbzadeh moved his drink aside and leaned closer to Cyrus placing a folded paper on the table in front of him. "This is a list of about 4,000 names of people who are going to be executed, starting the first day the revolution succeeds. The list was suggested by both the Americans and English, but the American's list is a bit longer. Today, after a meeting between Khomeini, Colonel Thompson, and Sanders from England, Khomeini approved all the names, but one... and that name is not your brother's. It is Ayatollah Mahmoud Taleghani who the English want dead. However, I can get your brother's name off the list if you go to Tehran and convince him to support Khomeini. We also know you have a good relationship with a few more high-ranking Army officers. If you choose, you may save their lives as well. If they join us."

Ghotbzadeh's eye caught Abraham Yazdi entering the restaurant, joking with Colonel Thompson and Sanders from England, as they were seated towards the front. Ghotbzadeh took a sip out of his glass and then turned to Hussein, frowning, "Do not trust this snake... he is the servant of the Americans... without their permission, he would not even drink a glass of water..."

The more he went on about Yazdi, the more frustrated he got. "Who got Gaddafi to put out 14 million to finance the revolution? Me. Who organized and trained the 300 bodyguards that came from Libya and Syria? Me..."

Of course, Ghotbzadeh was right; the most significant factor that changed the course of the 1979 revolution started with Lemond's article, written by Lemond's correspondent, who was Ghotbzadeh's friend and presented it to the France Secretary of State. And the reporter who wrote the article finally arranged a meeting between Ghotbzadeh and the French Foreign Minister, and it was there that Ghotbzadeh convinced him that the Shah should leave. The Secretary of State also persuaded the French President, Valéry Giscard d'Estaing, and he convinced President Carter.

Cyrus wanted to hear more about the folded paper he had in his pocket, but it was apparent that the discussion had ended, at least for the moment. It was at the point where nothing Ghotbzadeh was whining about was of any interest to Cyrus, and since he didn't want to listen to any more of his complaining and crying, he signed his tab and said good night.

Soon he found himself walking along the sidewalk in disbelief. Ghotbzadeh's voice kept playing in his mind, "The Shah's time is over. No one is sure if his Army will side with the people. If they don't, there will be mass murders that Khomeini approved. If things do not go their way, the opposition, led by the West, and Khomeini's people, plan to poison Tehran's drinking water in order to create chaos…

"Who do you think is controlling world politics? The people? No way! Or a few giant corporations? On the top are oil industries and military industries; the first one only knows how to burn and kill everything, and the second one only knows how to destroy whatever is left. We want to save as many lives as possible."

But it was something Hussein said that helped Cyrus make sense of the craziness surrounding him.

"Cyrus, you are like a brother to me… I wanted you here so you can witness and document the events to go down in history. That is more powerful than what we do. Soon full theaters will be set on fire in Iran, and massacres will take place in one of the squares in Tehran. And all by the Clergy, but it will be blamed on the Savak and the Shah… you must survive and witness and register the truth…"

It was the landlord, Farhad, and his wife who came up with fruit and pastry to check on Roxanna, breaking Cyrus away from what he was sharing with Roxanna. The problem was that the state of mind of both was not there. They were looking at them like they did not know them. Cyrus shared what he learned in France to convince her Iran was going to be in more turmoil and that it would not be safe for her and she must leave. But at that moment, Roxanna had just one task in mind, to find out what had happened to Peter and if he was dead, to find his body and send it back to the states… and she let Cyrus know about her feelings.

* * * * *

It was one more uncertain, rainy day in Tehran. Sitting in a taxi, spacey, in front of Hajji Khanoum's house gate, Roxanna was not even aware that the taxi stopped and was waiting for her to get out. "Madam, go…" The taxi driver let her out in the pouring rain. The gate was open, but she stayed outside during the downpour, observing Amir and Yousef having a conversation by the building. She approached the gate and noticed that inside the barn, Ahmad Reza, holding his smoke, watching Amir and Yousef also having what appeared to be a calm conversation, but not a particularly pleasant one.

She had seen enough to know something bigger was happening. She could see by Amir's expression, working further away at the yard, that he wasn't happy. Roxanna knew Amir never hung around when he came to visit Hajji Khanoum, and he never, ever got his hands dirty, but it looked like he had been planting rose bushes. She was sure something was troubling him. The conversation seemed to end abruptly when they realized Roxanna was watching.

Yousef acknowledged her with a concerned and unhappy look. He walked away from Amir and smiled as he joined Ahmad Reza and Roxanna, who was now inside the gate. Then Yousef left after saying goodbye to both. Amir, already drenched in the downpour, picked up a shovel and started digging a hole to plant another rose bush. It was as if he was determined to finish what he had started for his mother before he left, no matter how wet he got. He didn't have that much time to give her, so what was a little downpour?

At least the matter of planting the new rose bushes would be taken care of. It wasn't as if Ahmad Reza was above doing it. He would do anything for Hajji Khanoum. But it wasn't his place at the moment. Instead, he shrugged and took a drag on his cigarette. Roxanna thought it very strange that Yousef had left Amir alone. Perhaps Yousef was concerned about the current situation and had quit, although she wasn't sure a person could quit working for the Savak.

Finally, Roxanna calmly walked over to Amir, got on her knees next to him, and began to prepare the rose bush for the earth. With her hands in the rich black earth of Iran, she grabbed a fist full, felt it crumble between her fingers, and let it fall back down to the ground. She loved this earth just as Amir did, as Cyrus and her father did. She understood in her heart that nothing would keep Cyrus away from his Iran. She also knew they were words she would never say aloud for fear of setting herself up to be wrong.

At that moment, Amir's own words replayed in her memory, "This is a beautiful country. They intend to destroy it. It has already begun. The wheels of change are turning, rolling over, like a plow in the wheat fields, cutting down with razor-sharp blades, all that stood tall and proud and was Iran. I cannot live to see that happen. I will not live to see that happen."

She remembered the passion in his voice as he uttered those words, and she was very much afraid of the truth behind them. Ahmad Reza watched them both, down on their knees, their hands working in unison, making the hole deeper, digging a grave for Iran, as it was, as it had been and will never be, again.

Peter had read Khayyam poetry to her months ago. His words began to flow from her mouth, without control, as if he were directing her, "… each morn a thousand roses bring, but, where are the roses of yesterday?"

Just then, Hajji Khanoum appeared with a tray of pastries and waved for them to come in. Roxanna and Amir agreed that it was probably a fairly close interpretation of what was going on in her mind. They held out their hands to the rain as it poured down, rinsing the soil off. Hajji Khanoum held the door, waiting impatiently for them to enter, but when she saw how dirty they were, she decided they could sit on the porch.

Standing in the doorway, Hajji Khanoum proceeded to orchestrate the spontaneous meeting. "Help her. You know she has no one here. She is alone! Just like your brother in America. You help her; God will see it and help Cyrus. She is like my daughter; she is like your sister. Anything you want to do for me, do it for her. That is my wish. You have my prayers."

What Hajji Khanoum did not know was that Roxanna was there to ask Amir to leave the country. She was there to help Amir, not ask for help. A forced smile appeared on Amir's face as he unsuccessfully tried to hide his fears, not only for Cyrus but for all of them. Very respectfully, he turned to his mother. "I will Hajji Khanoum, I will . . ."

Hajji Khanoum set the tray down and motioned to Roxanna, "First eat some…eat... drink…then talk. It's not good to talk on an empty stomach." When she was confident Roxanna no longer needed to be prodded into eating, she exits but left the door ajar.

The silence between them was shattered by BBC Radio coming from Hajji Khanoum's living room. BBC was now the background noise that filled an entire country, saturating it with half-truths and misinformation. Amir had no faith in their self-promoting, agenda-driven broadcasts. If it weren't for his mother, he would have gone in and turned it off.

It took a moment for Roxanna to formulate her words. I have a message for you from Cyrus. He wants you to get out of the country as soon as you can. He says your life is in danger." Her message was nothing more than a confirmation of what Amir already knew but shared with no one. His posture was almost rigid, an indication to Roxanna that this was a very complex, smoldering conflict for everyone, and there would be no quick answers, responses, or solutions.

For the same reason, he stays less at his home and spends more time with his mother Hajji Khanoum. Amir had no wife or children and lived alone. He also had a room in Hajji Khanum's house where he rested when he came. Amir looked back towards Ahmad Reza, who was sitting just inside the barn, watching the dark, thunderous clouds, and listening to the rain.

For a quick moment, he secretly wondered what he could do to change places with Ahmad Reza. His was a straightforward life, his happiness stemming from his desire to make the garden beautiful and nurture the flowers to grow and thrive. Perhaps that's why he loved the rain. He knew the importance of it.

Amir prided himself in being the one in life who had something everyone else wanted, but suddenly, the tables were turned. Roxanna had something he wanted, and he wasn't quite sure how to go about getting it. Information.

"Cyrus? Is he back?"

Roxanna wasn't quite sure how to respond. It wasn't her nature to lie, but she had no choice. "I don't know. I got the message through a friend."

Amir thought a while before answering, "tell your friend to tell my brother that I was born here and I will die here. This is my land . . . my earth . . . my air. And I would not exchange it for anything or anywhere else, regardless of what could be offered to me."

Amir walked out into the rain, towards the rose garden, stopping by the rose bush he had just planted. Roxanna followed, watching tears fall down his face. They stood shoulder to shoulder, watching the roses of Khayyam being nourished as the skies opened wider and huge droplets washed over their faces. The salt of their tears mixed with rainwater and bathed the red petals.

*****

Chapter 25

When the Shadow of Death and Sadness moves the Light of Life Away from a Nation... and madness is Logic...

These days in Iran, no matter who you were with or where you were, sadness and the shadow of death were following you. BBC Radio blared from every corner of the country, and you had no choice but to listen to it. It was not long after the Rex Movie Theater and Black Friday incident that the Shah chose Shapour Bakhtiar as his new Prime Minister, hoping that this change in his administration would put a halt, at least temporarily, to the civil unrest. This was after the Shah fired and jailed Amir Abbas Hoveyda, who had been the Iranian Prime Minister for a decade.

Unfortunately, there was no stopping the changing tides. Mass demonstrations against the Shah had been taking place since August 1978. Widespread work stoppages by oil workers and the opposition had crippled the country's economy with the daily dose of violence, bloodshed, death, destruction, and mayhem.

The Shah finally came to terms with the fact that he was no longer able to hold onto his kingdom. The constant violence and destruction, which was not of his making, was so out of control it had to come to an end no matter what the cost. He could no longer allow his adversaries to make him the scapegoat, the reason that was given for so many innocent people being slaughtered.

Circumstances gave him two choices; hold onto his power, thus leading to the mass killing of his people, or leave Iran. Iran pumped through his veins; his home gave him life, but the thought of taking the advice of his army was just too much to bear; too much death would be on his hands. He chose to leave Iran for good, knowing the air he would breathe in the future would never be as sweet.

It was hard to imagine that people were shocked when the Shah was dethroned! He fled Iran, knowing what was coming; he was very cognizant of the tragic path upon which his country was being led. His failing, in the eyes of many, was the inability to communicate with his people. Upon them rained an oppression that would drain the soul from Iran.

The following months, years, and generations would see this new Iran travel down a path few expected. The Shah had fallen. The land he loved, the land of King Cyrus the Great, was doomed to retreat, moving backward, sinking into political quicksand.

Roxanna observed the people around her as they listened to the news of the Shah finally leaving to go into exile. Ironically, most Iranians were shocked as they watched him, with great ceremony, say goodbye to his general and his government staff, led by Prime Minister Shapour Bakhtiar at Mehrabad International Airport. It was the beginning of the end.

The Shah finally departed Iran but could not help the deep sadness that began to fill his body. Iran, he loved it so much, the good and the bad began to play in his tired mind. He was proud of how he reacted to the situation and of General Ali Neshat, the most loyal to him. He took an oath to honor and protect the Iranian land and his people when he entered the army. He remembered a phone call came to him from general Ali Neshat,

"Your highness… people are pulling your statue down… what should we do?"

There was a long pause until the Shah's voice echoed into the phone, "It is not important if they take my statue down. One day they will replace it with one made of gold..."

"Alahazrata, if you allow, I could resolve this coup, a few thousand will be killed, but we would save Iran."

The Shah quickly replied with ease in his voice, "I would not roll even if the blood of one Iranian is shed..."

There were more memories lingering around spilling from his heart. He recalled when Amir Abbas Hoveyda, who was the Iranian prime Minister for a long time during the Shah's ruling, came to The Shah and advised him, "Why are you messing with these MOBORHA (Blondes-Western/American)? They will bring you down, just give them something."

"If you are scared of them, quit your job," the Shah continued, "They exiled my father from his beloved land. I will not give them free oil. Our people come first."

Of course, the Shah went to war with the west and would not cheapen oil prices. When the west kept increasing the price of goods they were selling to Iran, his thought was that logically oil prices must be set by the price of other goods that were sold to Iran. Thus, he became the victim of being on the side of his people. There was no question in his mind that many problems existed in Iran through his ruling. But you cannot change people who had been controlled by foreign influences for centuries overnight.

Traitors to the Shah, General Hussein Fardoust and General Abbas Gharabaghi, who were first and second ranking officers of the entire armed forces, sided with the west, not their own people. They were pawns in the game the west always played when trying to bring down and assert control over an ally; use their own people.

*****

Of course, those who were so shocked and devastated by the Shah's departure did not know what was happening behind the scenes. They did not know that General Robert E. Huyser, United States Air Force, was in Iran to make sure the Shah would leave peacefully or that he had brought a message to the Shah which was not pleasant to him. Perhaps the Shah was saddened and outraged when for the first time, General Huyser met with the Shah after his meeting with all other Iranian generals to convince them and be sure they would not support the Shah.

At last, he came to visit the Shah to just deliver the bad news to him. The meeting with Robert E. Huyser, who came with American ambassador William H. Sullivan was the hardest for the Shah and the few of his generals who were present to come to peace with. The Shah was having a conversation with Robert E. Huyser and William H. Sullivan, American ambassador to Iran at the time, who kept looking at his watch.

"Why do you keep checking the time?" The Shah asked him. Sullivan politely but firmly responded, "Your Highness, the sooner you and your family leave the country, the more people you'll save." Sullivan waited, but the Shah didn't respond. He was in deep thought. For sure, he could not accept a foreign Ambassador and Air Force general standing in his people's castle, asking him to leave his homeland, the land he loved so much. Who is he to ask me to leave my country and why? What the American government did behind the scenes was completely different than what the public was witnessing.

He thought if the American government lies to its own people, why should he trust them? Remember, the only thing the American government and western industrial countries understood was getting cheap oil. They asked The Shah to attack Iraq and start the war, but The Shah refused to follow their wish. They wanted the Shah to sell them cheap oil, and that was something the Shah refused to do. He refused to give away the wealth of his people to stay in power.

By now, General Huyser and Sullivan were gone, and he was walking around with Amir while another of his generals was waiting for him to say something. But the Shah was in deep thought, remembering that he was told by his guest that, "Your highness, I know you love your country, and you do not want to turn it into another Lebanon. I know you love your country... you love your people, and you do not want to see millions of them killed, but things are already out of hand. If you do not leave, terrible plans will be put into motion. One being to poison the drinking water in Tehran, which will kill millions - with only you to blame..."

*****

The Shah's departure brought about celebrations that blanketed the streets of Iran as the news of the regime change erupted in the air, landing in every corner of Iran with great haste. Even Roxanna and Pary were in the street celebrating, and they did not know why.

Shortly after his departure from Iran, two French Boeing 200-747 planes simultaneously left terminal C at Charles de Gaulle Airport in Paris, headed to Iran. Unbeknownst to the public, there were four CIA agents, three British intelligence agents, MI6 agents, and eleven French Special Forces dispersed between the two flights. Two planes were most likely a diversion to throw any pursuers off. Khomeini was on board, in addition to his advisors, AbolHassan Banisadr, Sadegh Ghotbzadeh, and Ebrahim Yazdi. All precious cargo that also entailed a detail of surrounding U.S. air force, British air force, and French air force planes all making their way to Mehrabad Airport.

All of the extra security was to ensure their safety from the Royal Iranian air force that may feel inclined to take defensive action. There had also been U.S. military intelligence placed at all of Iran's air bases to foresee any issues and report on Khomeini's safety. All of these planes and fighter jets flew across Iran's border in violation of international law until the safe landing of Khomeini's plane took place at Mehrabad Airport in Tehran.

According to new laws, the free flow of information declassified hundreds of documents between the United States and Britain. All of these documents were previously completely classified. Yet all of the documents from the 1979 Iranian revolution were excluded from this release and classified for another 30 years. Why?

This is because the 1979 Iranian Revolution was nothing more than a performance. It was directed in London, produced by Washington D.C., financially backed by Jimmy Carter, French and German studios utilized, and sounds and effects contributed by BBC Radio in London. All that was needed were extras, supplied as the people of Iran.

It was not long after that when Khomeini returned from exile. Now Shapour Bakhtiar was in charge as Prime Ministers. Roxanna's father, Assad, and many of Khomeini's team were laying low and kind of went in hiding to be sure the army would not take sides, and they would be arrested. In fact, in the same month, Khomeini arrived in Tehran on Air France, February 1, 1979, and was proclaimed as the leader of the Iranian Revolution.

The streets were overflowing with people marching in celebration. And for sure, Pary and Roxanna were on the street observing it, and somehow, they became part of the celebration. BBC Radio announced that five million Iranians came out to catch a glimpse of Khomeini's motorcade as it headed to Beheshte Zahra Cemetery, where he held his arrival speech to show his respect to the many people killed during the revolution who were buried there.

Upon his return to Iran, Khomeini announced that the government of Shapour Bakhtiar was illegal. He also announced that Mehdi Bazargan was the new Prime Minister of Iran. Now Iran had two Prime Ministers; one was appointed by the Shah and one by Khomeini. And with that, the war of who was the legal Iranian Prime Minister had begun. What average people did not know was that almost all of the important meetings of Khomeini's people were conducted at Dorian's home at Darab Alley, north of Tehran, a region known as Quaternary Qanat (Ghanat). It was from there and Khomeini's place that the movement was being managed. This was something the average Iranian had no idea about it.

There was no gathering of any kind where there would not be a discussion about the Shah and Khomeini and how holy Khomeini was and how devilish the Shah was. And in the end, there were always disagreements or harsh arguments, or even fights. Yesterday, friends and family suddenly became your worst enemy.

Of course, Cyrus's family's house was no different. In fact, Hajji Khanoum, being the oldest, and Amir being the most powerful in the family, her house was always the gathering place for all relatives and friends to give respect. And now, with the situation deteriorating on a daily basis, friends and families had gathered to give respect and support to Hajji Khanoum and Amir. But this time was different.

Like every other house in Iran, political discussions among those attending were in progress - for and against the Shah, and few were too hot and passionate about Khomeini. That day among them was a young man named Javad, who was a Homafar. Javad was the grandson of Ahmad Reza, the older man who was with Hajji Khanoum's family for many years. He was there to show his respect to Hajji Khanoum.

Being at Homafar, just days before the uprising at the base, about 20 to 30 of Homafar visited Khomeini to announce their solidarity and shortly after there was chaos and revolt at the Homafar base and supposedly they joined Khomeini, and by Javad being there, so he was the center of attention, and some wanted to know what really had happened there.

Of course, breaking the backbone of the Shah's armed forces, they must create division between his armed forces. And that was planned when Khomeini was in France. they knew to bring the arm forces completely to the Khomeini's side, one of the divisions must fall and join, and they knew Homafar was the best choice. All Homafar were trained in America, in Texas or North Island New York. And CIA had a file on all of them and had recruited many of them, few also were kidnapped in New York and taken to Libya… and force and brainwash them to join.

To get more information, knowing Javad was on guard that night, a few turned to him and asked him to tell them what he saw and did.

Roxanna was attempting to have a conversation with her new friend, Javad, but found his responses very measured and brief, giving only short replies without any details. She wanted to know what had really occurred at the Homafar Military Base, and he was the only one who could tell her. A few others joined Roxanna, and they also wanted to know. He was there.

Then Pary arrived and joined the group. They all knew it would be worth the wait until he opened up.

Homafar was a special section of the Iranian Air Force that traveled to America for training. It was necessary for them to learn how to care for the F14, F15, and F16 fighter jets that Iran had purchased from the US. The incident at their base that Roxanna was waiting to hear more about was the turning point of the revolution. It spawned hope, confidence, and bravery among people throughout Iran, coming out onto the streets, fists raised in the air. This was significant because it was evidence that the military had turned its loyalty towards the people and away from the Shah's government.

Quite by chance, Roxanna and Pary had come across a member of the Homafar military, Javad, who was on base the entire night. In fact, from what little they had gleaned from Javad's clipped answers, he had been on guard duty and witnessed the entire incident. Roxanna and Pary suspected that he knew much more than what he was saying, and they would casually question him about what actually happened that night at the Homafar base.

They had heard the BBC news reports and also what Hussein had told Pary, which was confusing for Pary. Hussein told him that of the group who marched in front of Khomeini, only a few of them were ex-Homafar. The ones who were kidnapped and taken to Libyan camps, then they forced them to join through mental and physical torture and offering them three times more money they were making as Homafar, Some of the same men were personal guards to Khomeini when he was transferred to France.

Later, secretly, they brought them to Iran with other Syrian and Libyan missionaries who trained with them in Libyan military bases, with American army planning to contact other Homafar who their names were given to them. Soon about 20 Homafar visited Khomeini; most of them were brainwashed. The plan was to break the back of The Shah's armed forces and to do that, one of the divisions must be dismantled.

Hussein told Pary that everything was a setup. And now Pary was curious to know the truth. So, she was not going to leave Javad alone until he talked. What she really wanted to know was if Javad's story would match up with theirs. They suspected it wouldn't. They were hoping for clarity that could provide proof of the English manipulating events in Iran by directing misinformation and propaganda. If the English had been doing so, as Roxanna and Pary suspected, they would have influenced events that would have directly impacted the direction of the revolution.

But Javad did not open up until everyone left, and once Hajji Khanoum went to bed for the night, Pary and Roxanna would try to get him to talk about Homafar, but he continued to give answers, so cryptic that raised more questions than answers. This particular night, Javad ignored her questions opening up the way for his father to respond.

"I was on guard that night. My grandfather..." he points to the small cartage Ahmad Reza was staying, "... I received a phone call from my grandfather as he heard the report from BBC Radio; he asked me if I am alive, safe? I told him nothing is happening there. I do not know what you are talking about... then I stared at the BBC Radio and wanted to break it into pieces, but I did not." Javad scooped up more stew with his flatbread as he spoke.

Pary was shocked by Javad's boldness and tried to get him to continue, and so Javad began, with a long sigh that turned into a solid whisper. "If the Homafar had revolted against the Shah, and the National Guard was attacking our base, then why were none of us harmed, as we were gun to gun? We simply walked out. Why were we not arrested or killed as BBC Radio claims?"

Javad took a moment to gather his thoughts, as painful as they were, before continuing. "I was at my post. After my father's phone call, I turned my short-wave radio on to hear it for my own. I was very careful and stood by the window looking out. I did not want to get caught by our guard officer, listening to BBC Radio," and he went on to explain what had happened at the base...

"I walked to the window and looked out, still listening to the BBC Radio reporting,' The Homafar are being killed by the National Guard. Masses of people are on their way to help and to stop the massacre by the Shah's National Guard...'

"But I found the base quiet and all asleep in peace. There was no commotion as Radio BBC was reporting. Confused, I turned and stared at the small shortwave radio. I thought I did not hear it right because of the volume being too low. I had the volume low so no one could hear it outside the post room. But I did not hear it wrong. As I was thinking about why BBC Radio was reporting a lie, I turned back, looking outside at the base to be sure. It was then I noticed ... a man appeared from the dark and walked to one of the dormitory buildings. His face was covered. He opens the door and enters. I was wondering who he could be."

What Javad did not know was that the man was Shareef, one of Khomeini's Libyan bodyguards, who had been smuggled into the country. It seemed his assignment was to act out a script that they heard from the report that was broadcast on BBC news that same night. Before anything happened, BBC would report the event was currently happening, and that was the sign for them to start what they were going to do.

"I saw the lights come on inside the dormitory, followed by the sound of several gunshots. Hearing the gunshots, I ran out in confusion and saw a man run out of one of the dormitories and enter a different dormitory, yelling, 'The National Guard is attacking! They're killing us!' Then a few other men appeared from out of the dark and joined the man in yelling the same.

"By now, they reached me, and it looked like I was one of them. They approached another dormitory, opened the door, and yelled the same. Within a few minutes, all of Homafar rushed out and joined us. They were confused to see what was going on as I was. The same man was leading the gang, urging them on, 'The Guard did the shooting. We must retaliate! The guards are inside.' By then, there was chaos. Some of the men joined them, and others were totally confused about what to do next.

"But my eyes were on the man who started it all. He snuck away from the crowd he had rounded up and disappeared into the dark near where I was standing. I could tell he was getting his radio out, so I tried to get close so I could listen. He thought no one could hear him, so he pulled his radio out and spoke into it. 'The dance is on…' Right there, from his accent, I knew he was not Iranian, he was from the south, and for sure he was Arab.

"Then, through the radio, I heard a voice of an American man talking together with the voice of an American woman, 'Obtain all knives, at the Fridge. All knives are hot.'

"Baleh" the man responded, switching the Radio to BBC Radio. 'Homafar broke into the storage where all the rifles are stored. All are armed and ready to defend themselves from the Shah's Guard.' The man turned the radio off and placed it in his pocket before slipping into the darkness and joining the crowd.

"A middle-aged commander appeared, trying to calm the Homafar guards who had worked themselves up into hysteria, 'No guard is attacking! Get back inside!' But it was too late. They had developed a mob mentality and were frantic to figure out who the enemy was so they could attack."

Javad was totally confused and admitted that he had difficulty digesting the event as it unfolded. He was having trouble articulating what he had seen because he had no idea what was going on. Army helicopters began to fly above, and people who had heard of the attack on BBC were starting to arrive at the Base to rally for the cause. They faced the National Guards, who had been stationed outside to guard the base against attack.

"The National Guard surrounded the base and began firing warning shots to stop the masses of people from going inside the base. The crowd continued to grow.

"Right then, Shareef joined the crowd and began giving orders. 'We must arm and defend ourselves before the National Guard kills us. They are coming in!' A few others joined him in agreement, 'The guard had been responsible for the attack … The guard killed our friends… we have to quickly defend ourselves before we are all killed.'

"Our commander was ordering us to go back inside, 'The Guard is here to save you from the people. They are not shooting at you! Give up your rifles!' But our commander's voice was drowned out by the screaming voice of the crowd. 'We must arm ourselves to defend ourselves.'

"Several men, led by Shareef, disobeyed the orders. They hollered for all to follow, running to where the rifles were stored and broke the lock. Within a few short minutes, we all had loaded rifles in our hands. We believed the guard was attacking, and we were ready to defend.

"Out of nowhere, my friend Amir grabbed me to learn more. He had been sleeping in the same dormitory where the first guards were killed. He said that inside the dormitory, all the Homafar were sleeping in peace. A few of them were awakened when the light came on, and they noticed a man covering his face, standing by the door. The man began to shoot, killing the first few who were awakened before they were able to react. The man ran out, and suddenly the dormitory was filled with yells from alert Homafar, standing over the dead bodies."

And then Javad was quiet. Everything he had been trying to block out of his mind, to forget, was playing itself out in that room, raw and uncensored. It had been more than he could witness and was now, more than he could bear. Out of respect, no one pushed him to continue.

Javad listened as the others engaged in a conversation that reflected upon the major role BBC Radio played in fueling the revolution. BBC Radio echoed throughout every house in Iran, and because it had become such an integral, familiar, and trusted news source, people believed what they heard without question.

Roxanna recalled that BBC first announced the uprising at the Homafar base and encouraged people to go there to show support for the revolution. The sounds of the BBC report echoed, announcing that the National Guard had attacked the Homafar base and the men inside needed help, that a massacre was sure to ensue. It had never occurred to anyone, for that matter, that since BBC was in London, England, and was owned by the English, they were not likely the best source to detail events occurring thousands of miles away.

One would have concluded that they had been broadcasting directly from Iran as if they were the National Iranian Radio and had the best interests of the Iranian people in mind. Listening to the news, it sounded as if there was a reporter present at every location broadcasting the events as they unfolded. Now in retrospect, Roxanna was trying to deal with the creeping sensation of deceit crawling up her spine. If all of the reports were true, then why were the Homafar military trying to sneak out of the country? And why were some of the people questioning whether or not the National Guard had actually attacked them?

Javad whispered again, "Now looking back, I believe these men may have set the whole thing up, or at least were a part of it. Because right after, we could hear on BBC that the National Guard had attacked our base and that we were asking for the people's help or else we would be killed. How did they know so fast? Then our commander fainted—he fainted! It was so odd now looking back, but in all the confusion and chaos, none of us really had a moment to think."

Everyone in the room was listening in silence, intently focused on Javad, trying to see if they could really trust his words.

"And at this point, the National Guard was outside, and they had to deal with a mass of people coming from the outside toward them in addition to dealing with all of us Homafar creating chaos inside. Their mission was obviously not to harm the Homafar but to protect them from the people trying to come in and take over the base, which didn't seem to make sense as well. I don't think they really knew what to do.

"After a long standoff, they asked us to give up our rifles and immediately leave the base. Many protested, but a few agreed, and soon the rest followed. We all just walked out unharmed; not a single one of us was arrested. Now, all of a sudden, we were the people's heroes who had revolted against the Shah, and we didn't even know it!

"Many, including me, accepted the honor and enjoyed the attention from the people as we felt like heroes, which also was part of the game. I soon realized I was being vain and naive. It was all a chess game, and I, with the rest of the Homafar, were silly pawns."

Javad was quiet for a moment and then muttered, "Do you wonder who shot those Homafar men to death in their sleep? How did he get into the base and the dormitories? How did he leave without a single guard seeing him? And what benefit would the Shah or the National Guard achieve by doing this? I feel completely guilty and partly responsible for all of this mess, this big disaster we are all facing. About four hundred men missing from the base couldn't go unnoticed. I cannot just be a witness to all this injustice anymore, and I cannot prevent it from happening, so I must leave."

He stopped by the doorway and turned back, looking at his father and everyone in the restaurant for a long moment. "Do you really think the Homafar who marched in front of Khomeini were actual Homafar?"

He was stunned when Pary raised and, out of frustration, whispered, "Javad is right. They were not actual Homafar. They were fake." All eyes were suddenly on Pary... but that was all Javad had to say. Pary, who had been keeping a low profile up until then, spoke up, "It was all planned in France by an American team who was helping Khomeini at the time and had the help of Sargent Azar Brozyn, the second in command in the Iranian Air Force.

"How it happened was this... Khomeini and his team in France were advised by the Americans that they could not break the back of the Iranian Armed Forces. America knew they were loyal to the Shah and their people. They revealed to Khomeini and his people that Sargent Azar Brozyn, the second in command in the Iranian Air Force at the time, and Admiral Majidy, the second in command in the Iranian Navy, were working with America without the Shah's knowledge. This was confirmed when a Colonel named Goost sent a message to Khomeini and the Americans in Tofel Lo Shatv.

"The message said they should organize a march by Homafar in front of Khomeini on his return to Iran. So helping to organize the march, a few people like Reza Chaichi and Jamshid Naimi left France for Iran in an

American Army plane. They were under the supervision of Lieutenant-general Azar Brozyn and Admiral Majidi, with the help of Hajji Minyan. American, Colonel Thomson, got in touch with a few more Homafar whose names were given to him.

"Hajji Manyan had already ordered over four hundred Homafar uniforms and hats to be made in different sizes to be delivered to a man by the name of Khalil Ahmady. His sewing shop was located on Jaleh Avenue, close to region of Absrader, which is where my 'College of Dramatic Arts' is located. Then three hundred Libyan and Syrian militias who were guarding Ayatollah Khomeini entered Iran without the Shah knowing. These were the fake Homafar who had been dressed as Homafar to march in front of Khomeini. Only a few who were kidnapped in New York and brought to Libya and forced to join Khomeini's guards were real Homafar."

No one said a word; silence was the only response to something so heavy. Pary's words only confirmed what Javad was trying to get across. Relieved but still upset over what had happened, Javad strode out the door, his only wish, to be lost in the darkness.

Now everyone, including Javad, was staring at Pary in amazement, questioning how she knew all this information. Now Hussein was her source of information. Hussein's idea was no life was safe, so some of his friends must know about what he did so they could pass it out and use it against their compotator if they need it. If something happens to him.

*****

Chapter 26

Another struggle... When the Shadow of Misplaced Hope and Trust Moves the Light of Life Away from a Nation...

It was an unusually nice day in Tehran. Birds soared high above, riding the breeze like ocean waves, savoring the sun. Even descending into the unrest and turmoil below, their world seemed unchanged. Innocent to the ways of man, they sipped from ash-covered pools of blood-red liquid, the stench of which should have turned the thirstiest away, unaware of the dangers of living on the periphery, second-hand victims of man's inhumanity to man.

Iran was on the verge, echoing the final death knell of a fallen government, after what happened at the Homafar base, sounding when the military abandons its position and loyalty to the Shah's last prime minister, Shapour Bakhtiar. According to the BBC, the military had joined the people and announced that they would maintain neutral status. The Shah's last Prime Minister, Shapour Bakhtiar, went into hiding and fled the country to France in exile.

As always, The People had no idea what was going on behind the scenes. They didn't know that it was General Hussein Fardoust and

General Abbas Gharabaghi who changed the history of Iran by convincing other military leaders to stay neutral and, in effect, support Khomeini, which later resulted in all generals being executed immediately but General Hossein Fardoust and Abbas Gharabaghi were the only survivors.

Nor did they know that General Fardoust was a one-time classmate and most trusted friend and ally of the Shah and that he was the one who brought the Shah to his knees. The Shah did not know his friend was recruited by the English and then the CIA and Israeli intelligence MASAD agency, following orders and acting as their spy when at the same time he was head of the Iranian Secret Police, Savak, that was organized by the CIA.

They also didn't know that he was the one who orchestrated the plan for the Shah to be kept isolated from all current news pertaining to internal events unfolding behind the scenes so that they could keep the Shah in the dark. General Fardoust also used pencil so he could change reports and pass along false information.

And no one can blame the comment that the late Shah made, "We need 100 like William Shakespeare's to come and write the Hamlet then we may find out why Fardoust and Gharabaghi betrayed me and the people..."

People like Cyrus, who witnessed, firsthand, what was happening behind the scenes, were in shock as they surveyed Hussein's list of government buildings to be given up to the revolution. The revolutionary forces carefully planned the exact time each building or Army base was to be surrendered or go into retreat. Whoever was behind the plan was unknown to Cyrus and people like him.

It was as if someone had written a horrific play and it was being performed, live on stage, with BBC Radio from England announcing the events before they unfolded. It seemed BBC Radio was the only way to communicate, and it was giving the "go ahead" to people who were in place at each location to begin the actual takeover. But this was no play; this was all too real.

Almost overnight, Iran had a new interim government, headed by Dr. Mehdi Bazargan as Prime Minister. He was a longtime activist working against the Shah and had been a member of Mosaddegh's party who was ousted by the CIA when they had brought the Shah back in 1952. Khomeini asked Mr. Bazargan to organize his staff when he was still in France. Iran had indeed defined a new rule of law, establishing mandates in absentia for the first time from monarchy to a republic.

Celebrations caught on like wildfire; the flames of insanity were ignited by a government takeover with the same passion and irreverence that created, in part, its downfall.

For some, like Cyrus and his family, it was a painful time. They knew that because they had been close to the Shah just as Cyrus' brother had been, circumstances were about to become grave. Cyrus had tried his best to find a way to convince his brother, Amir, to leave Iran, but had been unsuccessful. Amir's mind was made up. He was born in Iran, and he would die in Iran. Under no circumstances would he leave his country, no matter what might be offered to him. Cyrus was very concerned for his brother's safety and willing to risk his own life to protect him, but he had no idea where to begin. Left with no other choice, he went to search for Assad to ask for his help protecting his brother and keeping him out of harm's way.

Cyrus also knew that there were people that had been placed on a "watch list," and he knew they would be executed. Hussein, who now was close to AbolHassan Banisadr, had access to much information that the average person did not have. Through him, Cyrus learned Saeed was now an important official in the new government, one of the men given the directive to take over for the old secret police, the Savak, now renamed Savanna.

Also, Assad had a direct relationship with Khomeini, and he was the one who coordinates the Bazaar to support Khomeini. Khomeini also trusted him very much and kept in touch with him secretly. But Assad was now more concerned about Roxanna's safety. He knew that the competition to gain power had begun between everyone around Khomeini, especially among the Clergies, and those are the ones, and they would not hesitate to use any weapon at their disposal to crush their rivals. Even kill their rivals or families.

For this reason, Assad knew that Roxanna's life is much more in danger now than before; he was sure if anyone became aware of the existence of Roxanna and that she was his daughter, surely Roxanna's life would now be in real danger. He knew this heartless community of religion and the clergy well, and he knew that they would not have mercy on their own mother to achieve their goals. So, he knew that now he had to be more careful that no one heard about the existence of Roxanna.

Assad knew very well that these days you could not trust your own eyes; he only trusted Cyrus and Amir, Hussein, and to some extent Dorian MacGray. Therefore, according to his suggestion and his own inner sense, he had to stay away from seeing Roxanna, and that was not easy. It was very difficult and painful to wait this long to see his daughter and have her be so close. But he was scared to see and hug her, and so he still refused to see Roxanna, to be sure of everything and her safety. Especially since he knew that he had secretly entered and worked against Khomeini and the religious people.

*****

Roxanna walked along the sidewalk in front of Tehran University. For more than a mile, mostly Dr. Ali Shariati and other writers who were, or at least were known to be, against the Shah covered the entire area with tables of books for sale. She entered the campus of the University of Tehran, fascinated by so many different groups of people arguing over ideology, each with their own opinion about what would be best for the future of Iran.

Almost the entire University was packed with young men and women who were sadly naive to the fact that their opinions and actions were of no value. Most were unaware that the carefully crafted plan for Iran's future had long ago been set in motion in secret, behind the shadows of closed doors by foreign countries and Khomeini's people that didn't have Iran's future in mind. Bad policy after bad policy followed, constantly undermining the economic progression of Iran. The students were victims of propaganda, sucked into a belief or movement that later they would regret.

Roxanna made her way through the throngs of people until she finally spotted Pary arguing with students and passing out flyers to reinforce her opinions. She smiled and handed Roxanna half her flyers as she continued her animated discussion. As Roxanna listened to the arguments, she found herself wanting to become engaged in some of the heated exchanges that were taking place. And such gatherings and discussions were the stories of every gathering in public places or homes in Iran. Roxanna noticed the familiar face of Hussein. She then forced her way into a larger group that Hussein was already participating in.

Roxanna was shocked to find Hussein in Iran! There was never a day when Roxanna was free from thoughts of the horrific events that occurred at the police station bombing or how Hussein had manipulated her into going to Iran for political reasons, she wasn't aware of. Her stomach turned inside out as the vision of the little girl, lying dead on the sidewalk, played over and over in her mind like an old movie reel.

It was a dreadful event that would haunt her the rest of her life. She held back tears and tried to bury the memory, at first rationalizing that Hussein felt he was doing the right thing by helping her get to Iran to find her father. But now that she was there, she realized she was nothing more than his pawn.

Roxanna was brought back to the moment by loud yelling. Hussein was arguing against the clergy's seizing control and power as he tried to educate the people regarding the dangers of a Theocratic government. His reasoning was based on the belief that political power should rest in the hands of individuals, not religious leaders and their dogmatic belief system. Knowing it was neither the time nor place to deal with Hussein, she forced herself to stay back and observe the heated debate from a distance.

But she could not help but watch Hussein closely, studying him, mentally comparing him to Cyrus, attempting to sort out her emotions. The main difference between the two was that Cyrus had no interest in engaging in group discussions or arguments, finding such dialogue a waste of energy. He was an independent thinker who always followed his instincts. His philosophy was if you belonged to any group, right or wrong, it was your responsibility to follow their ideology. And, being an independent thinker, Cyrus preferred to go it alone. Hussein, on the other hand, preferred to take a leadership role, seeking out followers, convincing the masses to come over to his way of thinking.

Pary had been watching Roxanna's reaction to Hussein's presence in Iran and was very aware that Roxanna's angry gaze was focused in his direction, a fact that caused her great concern. Pary and Hussein were of the same political mindset, each an integral part of a bigger picture. They worked together, determined to shift the thinking of those Iranians who were holding on to the belief that the Khomeini regime would be of benefit to them and their country. Pary feared if Roxanna felt a growing resentment towards Hussein, it would be difficult for them to manipulate her, ultimately making it 301difficult for them to move forward.

They were broken away from their thoughts, hearing a commotion outside of the school. They all rushed out, witnessing a protest by women against the hijab and the Islamic laws being imposed by Khomeini and the clergy. They were suddenly rushed and attacked by Islamic fanatics. Protestors rushed onto many buses trying to get away. And many began attacking the buses. To them, it was the beginning of a new Arab invasion, just in a different format, the control, and oppression still alive.

*****

Chapter 27

Friends Now Executioners...

Chaos and uncertainty spread throughout Iran. It wasn't long before the transition had taken place and Khomeini took power. People survived on a daily diet of international news, which was globally focused mainly on Iran and its reincarnation. The revolution was of interest to all countries; a textbook study of how to undermine the national spirit and bring a country to its breaking point, while self-anointed power brokers seized the reigns, watching everyone else throwing sticks. Iran had become national fodder. With each news segment broadcasting the death sentences handed down came a hubris that fed upon itself. Each newsfeed listed these tragic figures in greater numbers. A national apathy or acceptance or justification or a combination of each was the emotional opium most chose to digest.

Cyrus's family was no different. In fact, it was worse for them with Amir being on the side of the Shah and Cyrus in-between, both trying so hard to play peacemaker. Despite all the dissension and uncertainty in his life, Cyrus was happy, knowing that Roxanna spent most of her time at his mother's house. He knew that his mother had accepted Roxanna as part of the family and her presence there brought light into his mother's dark life, diverting her attention from the dangers her sons were facing.

Like every house in Iran after the fall, Hajji Khanoum's was a place for family and friends to congregate and try to make sense of the present while trying to predict the future of their beloved country. There would be lively discussions, bordering disagreements with everyone speaking at once, but when Hajji Khanoum entered the room carrying a tray of tea, all became quiet. The men always stood up upon her entrance as a show of respect.

Amir's future was of greatest concern to everyone, especially Hajji Khanoum and Cyrus. Amir was spending most of his days at Hajji Khanoum's house; his demeanor, one of quiet resolution. Because of the important position he held within the Shah's government, he was named on the list of enemies of the state but surprisingly, he made no attempt to lessen his presence in spite of the risk it imposed on him. He loved life but loved his country more and refused to leave Iran, walking the streets with his head held high, making no excuses for his life choices. He was a marked man. It was only a question of time before he was caught, his captors exercising their illegal right to persecute him.

For his part, Cyrus firmly believed that the new government was promoting the spying of friend on friend, the turning of family member against family member and that the open house policy enabled those with less than honorable intentions the opportunity to gather information to use against Amir. These friends and family became like observers approaching an accident on the highway; regardless of the horror, they could not help but stop and stare.

There was a bloodthirstiness, a morbid curiosity. Khomeini had ordered an edict that demanded everyone must report anything they had seen or heard in relation to friends, relatives, or neighbors as the will of God and as a moral and religious obligation. After that, everyone was at the extreme risk of exposure. These unsolicited visits were ultimately halted by Hajji Khanoum when Roxanna relayed Cyrus's concerns to her.

Roxanna would stay awake each night, waiting for Hajji Khanoum to fall asleep, reassuring her that all was well. She would sit by the fireplace holding a book, but her attention was on Hajji Khanoum as she walked through the house doing her everyday things. As the evening slid into darkness, Roxanna closed her book and stared into the fireplace.

She had decided to comfort Hajji Khanoum no matter what. Roxanna found comfort in the fact that Cyrus had said her father knew where she was and that he was not one of the zealots behind the wave of executions. Her last thought before she closed her eyes was to persuade Amir to leave before it was too late.

*****

Awakened by the sounds of weeping, Roxanna exits her room and found Hajji Khanoum back on her prayer rug in the living room. Taking her fragile body into her arms, Roxanna kissed her cheek and wiped her tears away. Her voice cracking with fear, the old woman whispered to Roxanna, telling her of the dream that forced her eyes open and made her fearful of closing them again, "I saw my dead mother cleaning a house, and I do not know whose house it was. I asked why she was cleaning some other person's house. She said, 'I am not cleaning other people's houses, this is Amir's home. I am getting Amir's house ready for him.' I woke up and could not sleep."

Hajji Khanoum was choking back tears as she continued. "I know Amir is in danger. They will kill him! They are going to kill my son, my baby. How can I live with that? His life will be taken, not by strangers on foreign ground but by our brothers from our common birthplace." She looked at Roxanna, her eyes pleading for a miracle. "Perhaps, you could make sense to him, appeal to him that we all need him and that he must protect himself. Convince him to go to America with you. Money is no concern."

She was weeping now, so powerfully, that the sobs were rising up from her stomach. Roxanna, tenderly and gently, wrapped one arm around her shoulders and held her tightly, guiding her towards the porch. "Let's go see if your children are awake to be fed?" Of course, Hajji Khanoum knew she was referring to the birds she was always feeding. She was hoping to awaken a sense of curiosity in Hajji Khanoum that would serve as a distraction.

The night had a deep, rich earthiness to it, rising like the smell of a warm muffin. They stood together in the dark, surrounded by twinkling. But no bird, even they were sleeping. Roxanna motioned skyward towards a thousand stars and told Hajji Khanoum they were waiting. Now the woman was thoroughly confused. "They are waiting?"

"Yes," Roxanna nodded, "the stars." Hajji Khanoum rarely had the chance to indulge in childlike anticipation and wasn't sure how to respond. "I am waiting, too." Roxanna smiled. "Now make a wish. With ten thousand wishing stars, at least one must be yours." Hajji Khanoum closed her eyes and wished for Amir's life to be spared. Roxanna did the same.

They stood for a long while finding peacefulness in a sky so far away it seemed impossible for man to do anything but look at it with reverence. Hajji Khanoum turned her eyes down towards the ground, almost as if she was hiding a secret. "I see one more star that is waiting for me."

Roxanna smiled. "Then make a wish."

"I wish to have you as my daughter-in-law." Roxanna realized that Hajji Khanoum knew nothing about Cyrus's marriage in America, which left her at a loss for words.

She realized she was being kept in the dark of all that was going on. She really wanted to sit and tell Hajji Khanoum about everything. Tell her that she was also madly in love with Cyrus, but he no longer belonged to her. She wanted her to know that she had come to terms with Cyrus's marriage but not with her feelings towards him. She would have thought that her love would have turned to hate, a woman scorned. In fact, she had wished for it as a way of getting revenge.

But when she realized her love went far beyond such childish pettiness, her feelings only grew deeper. Had she married Cyrus, it would have become some sort of self-fulfilling prophecy; her mother's heartache, passed down and lived again, this time witnessed through Roxanna's tears; history repeating itself instead of learning from it?

If Roxanna had said, "I love you." Cyrus would have said, "I love you more." But words to that effect had never touched their lips. To love too much is thinking too much. It can damage the heart. Would she ever have the chance, the nerve to ask Cyrus about his marriage? She wasn't sure she wanted to know the truth.

By now, Roxanna knew there was an irony about people like Cyrus, Pary, and Assad; they belonged to everyone and to no one. Love was what they lived for. And if it was worth living for, it was worth dying for, whether it be for a father, mother, brother, sister, lover, child, or as for them, a country. Theirs was an all-consuming love, given to many; like a puzzle, each piece a treasure of its own, becoming a part of something so much bigger, Iran.

Holding on to Hajji Khanoum's hand, she decided to make the old lady cheerful, so she only shared a little with her.

"I feel that I am your daughter-in-law, now." Roxanna kissed her forehead and helped her back into the living room, just as the phone begins to ring. Both women stopped and stared at the phone, wondering who could be calling past midnight. Hajji Khanoum reached for the receiver, "It must be my son, Cyrus." Holding on to the receiver Hajji Khanoum's voice echoed into the receiver with a smile on her face, "Cyrus... is this you?" But her smile faded, and she handed the receiver to Roxanna, "English... is for you..."

Roxanna grabbed the phone, "Hello...?" Then there was a silence ... it took Roxanna a few times, repeating, "Hello...?" Then, finally, a man's voice and an older man's voice were heard through the receiver, "May I speak with Amir...?" Roxanna knew from the accent he was Iranian, but what she did not know, the man on the other side of the phone was her father, Assad, asking to speak with Amir.

The slightest out-of-place sound, a car, footsteps, the rustle of tree branches scratching against a window, could signal Amir's death. And now a phone call, a faint dizziness that weakened every one's knees. It was after midnight, far too late for anyone to call.

Roxanna watched as Bebe, the helper lady, approached from one of the rooms and joined Hajji Khanoum as they were both staring at her waiting to find out who was on the other side of the phone. She placed the receiver beside the phone, "It is for Amir…" Hearing it was for Amir, Bebe headed upstairs to the room Amir was sleeping in. As she reached the top, she noticed Amir was in the doorway of his room waiting. "It is for you…" Then Bebe headed back downstairs and joined Hajji Khanoum and Roxanna, all lost in sorrow. Who could it be? Hajji Khanoum grabbed the receiver and quietly began to listen, then handed it to Roxanna.

It was not pleasant for Roxanna to hear or listen to other people's conversations in secret. Of course, the conversation was in English, and that was why Hajji Khanoum handed the receiver to Roxanna.

Assad spoke quietly, intentionally in broken English, so if Hajji Khanoum or anyone else was listening, they could not understand what was being said. Roxanna was the only one who understood the tenor of the conversation and the innuendos and did everything she could not let the women read the fear in her eyes and heart.

"They have just re-added your name to the fifteen hundred who are going to be arrested. You know you will be executed right after being arrested, with no trial? I tried and argued against your arrest, but they are bloodthirsty. I'm no longer certain that I can be of any help to you. There is no political structure, no chain of command, and no infrastructure. It is an army in total disarray, made up of power-hungry, violent men who act with impunity and feeling like they are God. Like animals that have had the taste of blood, they have an insatiable appetite for murder. They may come as soon as tomorrow night. Amir, if you wish to survive, you must leave right away."

"And what about my family?" Amir asked.

"You are the one who is in immediate danger to be killed… You must leave the country like so many of your friends. Perhaps your brother can help you to settle in America. You must go and go now, without delay … so there is less chance of a trail for the hungry dogs to follow. I may be able to help with your departure. Let me know…"

The last words Assad uttered before he hung up were, "I want you to know I'm very thankful for taking care of my daughter, Roxy." And then the phone went dead. Roxanna stood motionless when she heard the last word Assad said. She did not know what to do or say to Hajji Khanoum and Bebe, who were both staring at her. She was still holding the receiver. Bebe grabbed the receiver, listened, and then placed it on the cradle.

What neither of the three knew was Amir stood at the second-floor window looking out toward the window of where Assad always watched Roxanna. Assad was looking out through a small curtain opening across from the window Amir was standing in front of, looking out toward him. The two came a long way to get to the point of no return or success but disaster and hopelessness. Their hearts were as dark as night. Amir was gathering his thoughts, trying to consider the limited options he had available to him. His concern for his family was far greater than the fear of losing his own life. What would become of them? Would they also be at risk because of him? What of Cyrus? How would he cope, hearing about the death of his brother? And his beloved mother? He was her firstborn. His death would break her.

*****

In the living room, the women looked to Roxanna for translation. She knew the truth would kill Hajji Khanoum. She had no choice but to lie. She told the women the conversation was about some unfinished business of Amir's and that the man needed his guidance and assistance on something or other. A cold emptiness came over Hajji Khanoum as she watched Roxanna fumble through her lies. The old woman's eyes welled with tears, and she walked to her prayer rug, begging her God for Mercy for her son.

Watching Hajji Khanoum, Roxanna was lost in thought, thinking, the dramatic change that was being forced upon all Iranians was beyond troubling. It was the face of the darkest part of the human spirit. Amir was a man of great character. He lived by principles that defined him, and he would die by the same.

*****

The next day, Khally started barking outside. The barks grew louder and more frantic until Roxanna decided it would be a good idea to see if anything was amiss. It was. Two young men with short beards stood outside the gate near where Ahmad Reza had finished watering the garden and was now raking the yard, a cigarette hanging from his mouth. His apprehension was evident as he kept looking in their direction to determine if they had shifted their positions or had moved any closer. The men were doing their best to appear nonchalant, making them position all more obvious. It was clear that they were there for a reason, watching the house with great interest and a highly focused energy.

This felt uncomfortably familiar to Roxanna as she recalled the details of the dream Hajji Khanoum had shared. She watched Hajji Khanoum, pacing, moving restlessly from one room to the next, like a caged tiger. She was angry that she was a woman, an old woman, whose power and strength still rallied in her heart and mind but was not enough to overcome the frail body that betrayed her. Given a choice, she would have offered her life proudly, taking all the evil bullets the cowards would put into her if it would save her Cyrus and Amir.

As her limitations would allow her nothing more than prayer, she could be found on her knees offering her soul in exchange for the safety of her beloved sons. But prayer did nothing to quell the angry rage she felt inside. She was the matriarch of the family, powerful enough to head her household, raise her children, be the spiritual and moral leader to her community and survive a husband who was addicted to opium.

Yet all these accomplishments were insignificant if she could not meet this one monumental challenge of protecting her sons. The God-given decree to her as a mother was, at all costs, including the giving of her life, to protect her children. She was willing to do it, but how?

Hajji Khanoum stopped her anxious pacing and walked towards her balcony. She wished to breathe in Iran, its sweet and pungent scent so comforting in its familiarity and predictability. Even through eyes swollen from a river of tears, she could recognize serious trouble.

Hajji Khanoum stared fiercely at the chain of cars surrounding the gate. They were not friends. Friends did not gather outside like animals stalking their prey. Ahmad Reza stood by the gate, scanning them as well. He turned and looked at the house, relieved to see that Hajji Khanoum was on the balcony, finally aware of the seriousness of the situation.

Poised, she turned and entered the house before calling for Roxanna's help, "He is in his room. Go talk to him, please. Maybe you can get some sense into him. I did not know I raised such unreasonable and stubborn sons." But this was not about stubbornness. What Hajji Khanoum had done was raise her sons with character, morals, and the ability to discern good from evil.

These attributes of great men, of leaders, which she had instilled within her sons, would ultimately be the reason for their destruction. She had told Amir and Cyrus when they were children that man will fear, label, and attempt to destroy, that which they are incapable of understanding. "Go, Roxanna." Hajji Khanoum pleaded, "Go. Change his mind! Persuade him to walk away, so he may live on to do great things."

At Cyrus's request, Roxanna had already done everything she could to convince Amir to leave the country before it was too late. But it seemed the harder she tried to persuade him to go into hiding, the more he fought the idea. However, as Roxanna did not want to upset Hajji Khanoum further, she would make another attempt.

Amir had been spending most of his time at his childhood home instead of his own, opting to spend these important hours with his mother. It was just a matter of time before this imminent nightmare was to occur, and it was his wish that the last time his children would see him, their vision would not be one of him being disrespected, like an animal, chained and dragged away with no dignity, in front of their impressionable eyes.

Roxanna found Amir in his room, looking out of the window. Hoping to find him receptive to her idea of leaving the country, she entered carrying a tray with hot tea that Hajji Khanoum had prepared, the steam mixing with the spiced fragrance of the tea. She filled the glass teacup with the amber elixir and, as she had seen Hajji Khanoum do so many times, offered him a cube of sugar that he placed in his mouth to sip the tea through its sweetness.

A distant, unfamiliar noise shattered the sense of calm she had been trying to create. Amir expertly looked out the window without placing his body in harm's way. Ahmed Reza had disappeared, and one of the men who had been sitting in his car was now out walking around to check on things inside the gate. Amir knew they had come for him.

These men, the arm of the Imam's forces, had been lurking near the grounds like hungry cats trying to find sweet milk. Roxanna's original plan to try to reason with Amir had been sabotaged by their arrival. She no longer had the luxury of time. In an emotional burst that filled the brief moment left to her, she pleaded with Amir, "Please, you must leave! Amir, I beg you to leave! For me, your mother, brother, your children, and all that you can do to fix Iran once this insanity is over. You can be of no help to anyone if you are a martyr. We need you. Iran needs you. Come to your senses! There is no time left! Now! It must be now!" Roxanna was practically begging, just like an Iranian mother.

Amir began to speak with a resolution, a calmness, and peacefulness, as he stared not at Roxanna but outside, towards the gate. "I wish to see my enemy and look into their eyes, these zealous executioners. I have done nothing wrong. I will not run. I have served my people and country. The last moments of the story of my life will be lived with pride. That is what my children will remember of me. They will know that their father, in the face of the enemy, stood tall, that I mastered fear, not it of me.

"Our values, our beliefs, they define us as men and as a people; they are woven into the tapestries we make of our lives. Our values live beyond death to eternity. They are the tools that set the groundwork for all future generations. It will be our children and the children of our children's undeniable right to have learned from us and to believe in human dignity and be willing to pay the price to protect it. This is the legacy I leave the children of Iran, the children of the world.

"I am a son of Cyrus the Great, his blood is in me, and his courage is my birthright. Very few of us have the great gift of being able to choose a death of honor. I make that choice. Let my legacy be the benchmark that my children and the children of Iran use as the filter for decisions that they must make as they formulate our country's path into the future.

"One single man has the power to change the world by following his vision, but only if he is willing to walk without compromise. I will not turn or falter. I was born here, and I will die here. I cannot and will not breathe any other air than this air. This air keeps me alive and will be the last breath I take upon my death."

Amir turned back and looked at Roxanna for a long time in silence, almost as if he was trying to memorize the details of her noble face, an attempt to keep her with him in his final moments. But, it was more complex. He had a vision, a dream he wanted her to hear before time ran out. His words were profound. Roxanna felt obligated to memorize every word from his mouth as if she were a character in Ray Bradbury's prophetic book, Fahrenheit 451.

Amir turned directly towards her. His expression became pensive, he continued quietly, almost whispering, "You see, we were hurt, robbed, and destroyed and conquered throughout history by the Romans, the English, Russians, the Mongolians. But it was the Arab invasion in the thirteen-century which still today has left the deepest scar upon Iran that has yet to heal. In spite of our unfortunate defeats, we remain a country of intellectual curiosity, great writers, poets, and philosophers.

This is the heart of Iran; our greatness has been repressed by the power of others and the weaknesses of our own. And now, one more Arab invasion in its new format. That is where people like Cyrus become our army to register the history for the future… Tell him that."

Roxanna was left drained and speechless. She understood. And in spite of the difficulty in accepting the decision she knew he had made, she recognized that it was his decision to make.

Amir began to quote Socrates, "... I will not stoop to servility because I am in danger, and I do not regret the way that I have pleaded my case. I would rather die from my own defense than live by the acquittal of corrupt men. The difficulty is not so much to escape death; the real difficulty is to escape doing what is wrong."

Roxanna rose to leave, allowing Amir the space to find peace and honor through his selfless decision; he would remain in his homeland at whatever cost to his life. He needed time to accept the realization of what was to come, the separation between his physical form and his spiritual being. Roxanna was touched and frightened by what she had heard. "I know how hard this has to be for you, Amir. And I thank you for trusting me enough to take me into your confidence."

Amir hid his tears. "It is because I think you understood. You listen to my words, and without judgment, you can see into my eyes why this is the only right decision for me. In spite of the fact that you may disagree, I feel you comprehend the gravity of my decision and why I have chosen it. When you return to the US, tell our story. You were witness to the destruction caused by insane men. You have seen how a few misguided decisions can create a monster that cannot be stopped."

He paused to let his body absorb the pain evoked by such damning words. He could barely whisper. "Ask your people, 'What if we changed places? Would you wish the same for your children, for your brother, sister, your husband or wife...?' 'Tell them there are consequences to injustice. That is the lesson learned by past superpowers, ignorant and heartless destroyers of countries. History has shown that none last..."

Roxanna was stunned. The magnitude of Amir's words went far beyond anything she had ever imagined. She had become a part of something so much bigger than her search for her father. She had actually become her father in that she now had her own responsibility, like Assad, for exposing the fall of Iran by foreign countries in the name of greed, in the name of oil.

The future of Iran was laid at her feet as it had been laid before her father and Cyrus. She had been searching for her father but uncovered a truth so heartless, it was impossible to even grasp at moments. She was a part of a greater whole. There was nothing left to say. She hugged Amir, knowing that soon, he would be dead. "Thank you for what you did for my Baba..."

Amir looked out at the neighbor's window across the street. He had this uneasy feeling that someone was always watching. Perhaps he knew it was Assad. Without looking at Roxanna, he whispered, "I did it for our Iran..."

Roxanna headed toward the door and stopped, turning, "At least tell me, last night, the man who phoned you? Was he my father?"

Amir turned and looked at her for a long bit. "Your Baba..."

As Roxanna exited, Amir turned toward the window and looked out toward where Assad always watched them. He was not there. Distracted by Khally, who had begun to bark, he turned toward the gate seeing numerous cars and the same two men standing by the gate.

Khally had not warmed up to the uninvited guests who were continuously playing with the locks at the gate and barked loudly, attempting to breach the fence to attack these strangers with no good intention. Unlike Khally, Ahmad Reza chose to ignore the events over which he had no control over, but Khally's barking was a different story.

The gardener tossed the hand-rolled cigarette on the dirt and crushed it with the tip of his shoe before approaching the dog, trying to calm her. But Khally was crazed; she wanted no part of "surrender." She would make sure these men stayed off of her property.

Confused, Roxanna walked out onto the stairs overlooking the yard and the gate. Roxanna studied Amir, absolutely certain that she would never forget his words. He had gifted to her the wisdom of a man who had come to terms with life, death, and a vision of the future, in a small part because of his reflections on the footprint that would soon be left behind.

Roxanna noticed Pary enter the gate and approach her. Like Khally, she was determined to make her presence known to the cowards congregating out front.

The night before, after helping Hajji Khanoum to her bed Roxanna made many calls, trying to reach Pary. She wanted to share with her the vision Hajji Khanoum had seen in her dream. But more importantly, she wanted her to know about the call for Amir. She felt helpless and had hoped that perhaps Pary would be the one to get through to Amir or get a message through to Cyrus.

She was convinced that Cyrus needed to be brought up to date on the activities that had occurred during the night. She felt he should return immediately, and she knew the quickest way to get to him was through Pary. Pary would either know where he was or would know people who could find him, and that was why Pary came as soon as she got her message.

Pary approached Roxanna, who was now sitting on the stairs overlooking the garden overflowing with the beautiful flowers Amir had planted for his mother. She sat by her and then reached over and held her hand. Pary knew Roxanna was not happy and wanted to comfort her. Despite Khally's barking in the background, there was a brief silence between them, each touching the velvet texture of the delicate petals, lost in their own recollections of Amir.

Khally, soothed by their presence, came over and laid down between them, her eyes in constant motion, darting from the house to the intruders at the gate. Her second sense was warning her that something very bad was about to happen. The three just stared, in silence, not knowing what to say or talk about.

Roxanna, Pary, and even Khally were jolted by the sound of a gunshot. Paralyzed with fear, they looked towards the gate to see if the sound came from there. It was such an incredibly agonizing, primal scream that an entire flock of birds, nesting in a nearby tree, erupted like a geyser, flapping their wings simultaneously. Khally jumped up and ran around in circles, baring her teeth and barking furiously. Hajji Khanoum's loud, horrified, blood-curdling screams coming from the inside confirmed the direction of the gunfire. Roxanna watched as one of the men outside the gate grabbed the radio attached to his belt and began yelling into it.

Roxanna and Pary rushed inside, followed by Ahmad Reza coming from the gate.

*****

Rushing to help Hajji Khanoum, Pary and Roxanna ran right smack into Bebe, who was coming down the stairs, holding a rag to her mouth to keep from vomiting. She was groaning and wailing, making sounds that were meant to be words, but there were none for such a tragedy. All she could do was point towards Amir's room before collapsing on the floor.

Roxanna and Pary rushed inside Amir's bedroom in deference to each other. Pary went in first, stopping at the back of Amir's favorite recliner. Hajji Khanoum was kneeling down on the floor holding on to Amir's legs, covered with his blood, the blood of her firstborn son.

"Amir Joon, my love, my life, my dear boy, what have you done? Talk to me, I am your mother, talk to me, talk to me." Fueled by futile hopefulness, a contradiction understood only by madmen, she crawled on her knees and, using her old, frail hands to aid her failing eyesight, she reached beneath his blood-soaked clothes, searching his bare body for wounds, an entry point, a way to stop the bleeding.

Roxanna walked around the recliner, accidentally stumbling over Amir's gun before coming face to face with the unimaginable, the point of entry. Amir had shot himself in the head. Pary picked up Amir's gun, and she walked out onto the balcony holding Amir's gun dripping with thick, mahogany blood.

Khally knew from the strong smell of blood that a tragedy had occurred inside her master's house, and she was determined to get in to protect Hajji Khanoum. She ran in circles, barking and scratching, jumping up on the front door. When no one opened it, her bark grew louder, her demeanor more vicious, her whine more desperate.

Roxanna wanted to move Hajji Khanoum away from Amir's body, but the old woman remained where she was, still kneeling on the floor holding his leg to her chest, her cheek pressed against it. All Roxanna could do was put her own arms around her and hold her lovingly while Hajji Khanoum released the pain that was too much to bear. She wailed, in agony, again and again, "Khoda/Allah, why! Why have you let this happen?"

As Roxanna stroked Hajji Khanoum's hair, birds began to gather in the fruit trees just outside Amir's bedroom, singing. Roxanna had been trying to draw her attention away from Amir's body, but Hajji Khanoum wouldn't leave him. The birds gave her an idea. "I'm afraid they are calling for you to be fed..." Roxanna said, leaving the bedroom, walking gently onto the balcony, and began feeding the birds.

Realizing that Hajji Khanoum had taken the bait, she purposely tossed a handful of seeds straight down, over the edge of the balcony instead of up and into the air, the way it was normally done. Just as she had hoped, Hajji Khanoum joined her on the porch with a frown on her face, chanting, crying, and feeding the bird.

"That is not how to feed the birds." She took a handful of seeds and tossed them into the air, the seeds falling on the porch for the birds to flock to and fight over. She threw another handful over her head, and, again, they flocked to her, squawking, some sitting on her hand as she held more food out for them. "There. That is how it is done."

Even in the midst of all the tragedy, Roxanna couldn't help but feel a tinge of happiness watching this incredible, strong, nurturing woman that she had grown to love. She had been trying to distract Hajji Khanoum by making her understand that she had more children to care for than just Cyrus and Amir; the birds were her children as well, and they depended on her for survival. She wanted her to know that they all understood that she had done everything she could, as a loving mother, to save her son and that a man's love for his country was insurmountable.

Soon, Hajji Khanoum grew weak from exhaustion and slipped to the balcony floor. Roxanna slid down next to her and held her, rocking, crying, and singing to the birds. The flying birds circled them as if thanking them for their love. Neither Roxanna nor Hajji Khanoum had any idea that Assad was watching from behind the yellow curtain across the way. The phone rang, but everyone was still too overwhelmed and in shock to answer it. Roxanna pried herself away from Hajji Khanoum and hurried into the house while Bebe took her place on the balcony to comfort the old woman as best, she could.

Hajji Khanoum and Bebe felt the vibration of the front door slamming beneath them and moments later, saw Pary exit the house, walking with the determination of a fool towards the two men who had spent the past seven hours just sitting in their car, staring at Amir's bedroom. Like cowards, they hid behind hats and beards. Pary was almost marching now, holding Amir's gun, bathed in his blood and the blood of the revolution. Concerned, Ahmad Reza follows her to the gate.

Roxanna exits the house runs toward the gate, passing Ahmad Reza held Khally while she exits the gate. In a split second, she stopped, terrified, by the scene unfolding in front of her. Pary was shouting, fanatically, at the men in the car, pointing Amir's bloody gun in their faces.

"I have all day, and I have fought for this shit more than you! And I never hide my face! Cowards! Besides, if you are waiting to get to him, you are screwed. He was braver than me and you and your God-damn Khomeini. This gun is as bloodthirsty as I am! So, get the hell away before I shoot you, both. Leave the poor mother alone to grieve for her son." Pary looked them straight in the eye, daring them to make her pull the trigger. The driver was the first to avert his eyes.

Roxanna, realizing Pary had gone mad and was now completely unpredictable, rushed in to stop her from doing something irrational, almost getting run over by the men driving away. The car sped away and stopped by a car parked a few hundred yards away, with Saeed sitting inside, observing. "Boss, he killed himself…" It was the driver reporting to Saeed with Abdullah sitting beside him.

*****

Neighbors had heard the news and had begun rushing to Hajji Khanoum's side. Before long, the entire house was filled with friends and relatives. Roxanna watched with an aching heart as people cleaned Amir's body. It was a ritual completely unknown to her. There was a hint of camphor in the air as the women gently tended to him, cleansing him.

Hajji Khanoum stroked his mangled head and sang him a Persian lullaby, over and over, again. Finally, she began to sway, dizzy from exhaustion and devastation. Roxanna rushed to her side and held her tightly, securely. Her face wet with tears, her frail body trembling, the aged woman continued her loving, peaceful lullaby to her son one last time.

The ritual went on until there was nothing left but to say goodbye. The sight of her son being placed in his grave and covered with stones and wood, then dirt, was too much for Hajji Khanoum to bear. She lay on the ground, softly stroking the freshly turned earth, crying. It was the closest she would ever be to her son, again. It took the women several attempts before gently persuading Hajji Khanoum to leave her son's grave and return to the house. Finally, it was over, and Amir was left alone underneath the dirt, taking nothing with him but his pride and the love of his country.

Roxanna was the last to leave. She was waiting for someone, but he hadn't shown. Her eyes slowly surveyed the cemetery until she spotted Cyrus, far enough away to be unnoticed, sobbing. Even though he had attempted to hide his identity, Roxanna knew it was him. When he thought it was safe, he went to the grave and kneeled, laying his head on the fresh dirt.

Roxanna touched his shoulder, and he looked up at her, choking with guilt. How could it be that he was unable to save his brother's life? Roxanna wrapped him in her arms, his forehead resting against hers as she wiped away his tears.

*****

Chapter 28

A New Family...

Several months had passed since the revolution, and now, with Khomeini in power, things were changing rapidly. The clergy had confiscated almost every house belonging to officials of the former Shah. People's lives were destroyed, their possessions lost. Generations that had dedicated their lives to building foundations for their families watched in horror as everything was stripped from them in a matter of minutes; the most important was their freedom which they had sacrificed everything to gain.

One moment they were sitting in the comfort of their homes, surrounded by loved ones, enjoying the sense of peace that the physical and emotional treasures of life offered, giving thanks for the warmth and security that takes a lifetime to build, when, without notice, their lives were destroyed. Officials from the new regime swarmed down like killer bees and robbed them of every material possession and, by doing so, robbed them of their physical and emotional wealth as well. They were lucky to get out with their lives.

There was no system in place for such an unjust protocol; it was arbitrary. Property was seized at the whim of someone within the clergy. The most egregious abuse of power occurred after an execution. Transfer of property to ranking members within the clergy was immediate. It was referred to as "Islamic justice."

The complete blind eye to robbing the national treasures and the theft of personal property by the clergy created a shift of wealth, tilting it significantly towards those sympathetic to Islam and away from the secular population. There was a new class of wealth in Iran, the "nouveau riche," and the power that came with it was corrupt, evil, and intoxicating. The established families of wealth watched their fortunes, and their futures diminish as assets were stolen in the name of a corrupt theocracy.

People like Pary, Hussein, and Cyrus were altruistic and fighting for Iran and Iranian freedom; witnesses now to the gross abuse of power for personal gain, knowing that the shift of power and wealth would lead to the destruction of their beloved land. The new Iranian power brokers were looking to settle grudges, systematically targeting innocent people and accusing them of crimes that were manufactured by the clergy or their officials. Without explanation, they would be arrested and then jailed or executed.

After successfully taking an individual's liberty and, oftentimes, life, these ruthless men confiscated homes and the wealth of their victims, moving members of the new regime into these illegally seized properties. Sadly, many times the targeted victims were close friends with members of the new regime prior to the revolution. It was a time of distrust. Your best friend could be your worst enemy.

New positions of authority and power created within the new regime were given to selected people, and suddenly rules were reversed; employees became employers while the once-wealthy became subjected to the whims of newly empowered individuals unaccustomed to the lifestyle they were suddenly thrust into.

*****

Cyrus was distraught; he had his wife in America, but his heart was in Iran. He felt terribly guilty most of the time as he was torn between two completely different worlds, his love for his family in Iran and Roxanna and his family in America. They all needed him, yet he was not able to meet the needs of either. As a result, his marriage suffered, and he was at a loss as to what he should do. The irony of the situation he found himself in did not go unnoticed by either Cyrus or Roxanna. The fact that Cyrus's life reflected that of Roxanna's father gave her a window into understanding that what happened between her parents had nothing to do with her.

For the first time, she realized that the feelings of loss, rejection, and abandonment that had haunted her all her life were unfounded. Although she was a victim, she was a victim of circumstance more than rejection. What happened to her was merely a small part of something much greater, a tale of epic proportions. It was Linda and Assad's love story, a bigger-than-life, tragic love story, which was all the more heartbreaking because of where it left Roxanna, drowning in a cocktail of self-blame and mixed emotions.

It was a tragedy that Cyrus couldn't allow to repeat itself. The truth was that the strong connection and attraction that Cyrus and Roxanna felt for each other was no more or less vulnerable than the love each man had for his country. There were so many kinds of love, depths of love, so many reasons to love, and ways to deny its existence. Love could neither be defined nor denied.

Without love, life was without purpose, and Cyrus would die for it before he would compromise. Before Roxanna, love had been simple. But in the end, it was his inner compass - his upbringing and his loyalty to the institution of marriage that threw his life into turmoil. Cyrus found himself torn in a thousand directions.

At Cyrus's request, Roxanna was dedicating most of her time to watching over and caring for his mother. It was a welcome distraction for Hajji Khanoum, who had so many concerns and worries she didn't know where to begin her prayers. Now she was able to focus on the most important issues and concentrated on Roxanna and Cyrus. She would beg Roxanna almost every day to return to America as soon as possible, pleading with her to convince Cyrus to stay in Los Angeles with her and never return.

Roxanna knew Hajji Khanoum loved Cyrus with all her heart, and with Amir gone, she loved him all the more. For a mother to wish for her son to never come home, again, was the greatest sacrifice. Cyrus's safety was so much more important to her than her own happiness or even her life. Hajji Khanoum would have gladly sacrificed hers for Amir if it had been possible and would willingly sacrifice her life in the future to protect and ensure the rest of her family's safety.

Unfortunately, during these tumultuous times in Iran, no one could predict what would happen from one moment to another. The current state of affairs was so fluid, dramatic, and replete with fear and uncertainty that there was no place to find comfort or emotional peace of mind. Luckily, Bebe and Ahmad Reza and all the people who worked for Hajji Khanoum's family had stayed with her and supported her due to her position of great respect in the community. Their loyalty never wavered; they stood by her, as did all who knew of her honor, kindness, and love.

*****

While Hajji Khanoum rested on her cushion, Roxanna sat close to the window, thinking about all the possibilities that lay ahead, but mostly she thought about her father. She could not stop wondering why he hadn't tried to see her. It tore her apart to think that his new family was so important that she no longer mattered to him. Little did she know that just a few yards away, her father watched over her every day.

The truth was, without Cyrus, Roxanna was adrift at sea on a night without stars or wind to fill her sails. She knew her destination but had no heading. She had gone to Iran to find her father but had fallen into a forbidden love, the abyss of the Iranian culture, and the Revolution.

Bebe entered, carrying a tray with tea and Persian pastries, and put it down near Hajji Khanoum. The smells were exotic and enticing, just enough to bring Hajji Khanoum out of her reverie. Although she had servants to help, she always served her guests, filling their cups, herself. Her eyes were swollen and red, but Roxanna thought it best not to comment. There were no words to comfort Hajji Khanoum's broken heart. She had lost Amir forever, and now Cyrus had gone to America.

And even though her family would speak English when they wanted to protect her from the truth, she knew what that meant. That Cyrus, too, was gone, forever. There was nothing in this world that could lift Hajji Khanoum's heavy heart. They sipped their tea in silence. Earlier, Roxanna had phoned Pary and asked her to come over. She was concerned for Hajji Khanoum. She knew Pary was on her way to discuss what they could do to bring comfort to Hajji Khanoum. The poor old lady was not the same after Amir's death.

*****

In a vacant room across the way, a different story was unfolding. Cyrus was indeed back, watching over Hajji Khanoum from his secret hiding place. He longed to comfort his mother by letting her know he was close but knew he faced death if anyone found out he had returned. He was now working with Assad and Hussein to stop the Clergy from taking overpower in Iran. Forced to stay away from his mother and family; if something bad happened to him, his mother would never know and fall into a deep depression.

He was avoiding Roxanna as well; she wanted to be taken to her father. Her hopes of being reunited had not subsided yet. She also knew the opposition to her father would use her to discredit him. The fact she was from America could do enough damage on its own; neither of them would be safe.

Cyrus stood beneath the shower with his eyes closed, letting the hot water flow over his body, washing away the guilt that was gnawing at him. At least for a short while, he could feel cleansed. He knew when he got out of the shower, his feelings of guilt and inadequacy would return. It came from all sides, but mostly, it centered on leaving his mother alone after Amir had killed himself. But he had been given no choice. He was of little use to her now, but he would be of no use to her, dead.

Cyrus kept playing over the consequences of his actions in his mind. Like lying to his mother, she thought he was in America, but he was really just a few yards away. He knew how much Hajji Khanoum depended on him and longed for his visits. He missed her as well, but how could he show up unexpectedly when he was supposed to be in America? He had told her he was taking classes. If he returned so soon, she would know something was wrong, and it would put her in a worse state of mind than she already was.

Like lying to his American wife that he was in Iran and heavily involved in the politics that he was with a group who wanted to push Khomeini away from power, fighting on many grounds facing many superpowers who wanted him to have the power to guard their interest, which was cheap oil. The steam from his hot shower covered the mirror and clouded the bathroom. He closed his eyes and thought of Julia again as well, trying not to think of the consequences.

*****

Across the way and out of earshot, Khally's bark grew louder and more vicious. There was something about the man getting out of the car at Hajji Khanoum's that Khally didn't like, and she was determined to keep him from getting any closer. Roxanna went to the window and watched, horrified, as Ahmad Reza dragged Khally into the barn with him and shut the wooden door. They watched from above as the man pried the lock off the gate. Several cars entered and stopped along the side of Hajji Khanoum's driveway. Guards with machine guns jumped out and started storming the house, while others remained outside, guarding the perimeter.

An overweight clergyman emerged from one of the cars and watched as his men swarmed the mansion. The look of pleasure radiating from his face was more than Ahmad could tolerate. The barn door opened just enough for Khally to force her way out and charge him, barking viciously.

Like a true coward, the clergyman jumped back into his car, yelling for the guards to kill the dirty animal!

Several guards rushed toward the dog, drawing their rifles and waiting for a chance to pull the trigger, but she was too fast. The first one to reach Khally hit her over the head with his rifle, choosing to beat her to death rather than make it a quick, painless death. She fell back into a row of beautiful white tulips, bleeding heavily, staining the purity of the flowers with the violence of these insane, brutal men. Fighting desperately for her life, Khally managed to get back up and run away, but the guard chased her through the delicate tulips and continued to beat her with the butt of his gun any chance he would get.

The overweight clergyman let out a bloodthirsty scream, "Kill the stupid, filthy animal…" Then, satisfied that his officers would take care of the dog, he walked up the stairs and rushed into the house, as fast as his short, fat little legs would carry him.

Ahmad Reza had followed Khally but was unable to stop the barrage of cars entering the property. Concerned for Hajji Khanoum, he began to walk toward the building, doing as much as one man could do in such a situation, declaring his loyalty to the matriarch of the house.

Armed guards were running in all directions, surrounding the house like rats in a maze, chasing after a piece of cheese. Each was trying to see who could bite off the largest piece, becoming the victor. Roxanna was watching the events from the family room in horror, and although she couldn't see Khally, hearing her desperate cries coming from somewhere on the compound was almost too much to bear.

Roxanna still looked out, confused and doubtful as to what to do. She was interrupted by Bebe, who handed her an Islamic outfit and asked her to put it on right away, hoping to hide her identity as she was pointing to the outside and the guard. Bebe, seeing guard, thought Roxanna's life could be in danger, and she wanted to help her hide her identity.

*****

Across and behind Hajji Khanoum's house, Cyrus continued to let the hot water wash over him, enjoying the peaceful, cleansing feeling of the ritual, unaware of the catastrophe unfolding at Hajji Khanoum's. His mind was elsewhere, watching the clock, wanting to take advantage of every second of his precious time in the shower.

*****

Within minutes, the house was secured, and armed guards were looting like ravenous beasts. Ahmad Reza entered to see Bebe and Roxanna lying face down on the living room floor, guns pointed at their heads. The guards were more interested in Roxanna, who had darned the Islamic outfit, her eyes only visible to the men. They were surprised to see her in such dress at Hajji Khanoum's house.

But it was Hajji Khanoum who noticed the guard's interest in Roxanna and decided to take their attention away from her. Now the guards didn't know what to do with Hajji Khanoum. Most of them had known of her family status and respected her at some point in their lives. They weren't sure what to do when she refused to follow their orders, even when being delivered at gunpoint.

What under normal circumstances would have been devastating forced Hajji Khanoum to prioritize what held the greatest value to her. She would now be forced to bear witness to the theft of her home of fifty years. The house itself was less significant than the memories that were held within its walls. This was where her babies took their first steps. These walls contained so much; the joy of love, the sadness of death and loss, so many successes and failures, holidays, feasts prepared for family and friends, and most importantly, it was a haven of safety for those who entered her doors.

There were even a few hidden secrets that were entrusted to her sturdy, silent structure, and she knew that this was where they would remain. The incident that profoundly affected Hajji Khanoum the most was Amir's death. This home was the last place his eyes rested on, the place where his life tragically slipped away…the place where he chose to die. It was a shrine to his memory, the place where his soul left him.

The house was living history in its own right, passed down from generation to generation. Regardless of who stole the house from Hajji Khanoum, that powerful energy would remain within its walls, a power so incredibly personal, no robber would ever be able to reconcile, nor find peace within its structure. The house would know. This is the enemy.

Hajji Khanoum began to sing an old Persian lullaby that she had sung every night to her beloved sons, sounding almost like a prayer. She went to her prayer rug in the corner of her living room and continued singing it's comforting words to her enemies. She knelt down in the same place where she went to her knees three or more times, every day of her life. But this time was different and not just because it would be her last. The profound depth of her melancholy had made her question her God. Who was he? Where was his benevolence when she begged him to protect her son? To protect her human freedom? Still, her tradition, her familiarity with her God, and her connection to him would keep her on her knees as she had done for decades. She would ask for humility, and whatever, in his wisdom, was her fate, she would accept.

Hajji Khanoum knew that material possessions in this world meant nothing. As a young child, confused and devastated at the loss of her loving father, she remembered her mother's words. "I would give all, everything I possess, to have just one more day with my precious husband." She had always kept those powerful words close to her heart.

And now, on the precipice of losing all material objects, the home that held her memories, the land she nurtured and in return, had nurtured her, her riches, none of it mattered. It was love that couldn't be taken, robbed, stolen, or stripped from her by those who considered themselves to be men of God. The God she prayed to all her life three to five times a day, and it was love that would sustain her and her family into their future.

Although still on her praying rug, she scanned the rooms of her house in her mind, taking inventory of its contents, mentally caressing specific objects, things that she had owned for years that were gifted to her – a few small pictures her sons had painted for her in school, a special gold-painted tea set that was her grandmother's, tapestries that had been in the family for generations.

Then came a moment of clarity. None of these things were permanent, and therefore, they were unimportant. She would keep her soul; they could not take that from her. It was enough. She would have her soul to join her late mother, father, her husband, and her precious son, Amir. She was at peace with her God and would live with whatever the outcome was to be.

The fat clergyman finally decided and addressed the guards. "Let them go. They have only their clothes." Despite the clergyman's orders, no one moved too fast, afraid one of the trigger-happy guards might shoot them. Slowly, they helped each other off the floor and began to gather a few personal items of clothing. Hajji Khanoum, however, got up and stared at the clergy without moving.

Assuming she wished to bring her prayer rug, Bebe bent over to pick it up, but Hajji Khanoum gently touched her shoulder and whispered, "No. I have, at this moment, chosen to no longer pray. My God did not listen to this humble old woman, so perhaps he believes my words and prayers are of no meaning or value." Bebe touched the rug with her hand as if it were an old friend or a loved pet before leaving the praying rug behind.

Bebe rushed in from another room carrying some of Hajji Khanoum's personal belongings, such as clothes and hairbrushes. She showed them to the frail old woman, asking if there was anything else she needed, but was met with silence. Bebe looked at her, frustrated, "You must get your stuff, Hajji Khanoum. We need to leave." Hajji Khanoum looked around the house for a long moment. "I have no interest in any material things, which belong to this world anymore. They can have it all."

Her words were quiet and dignified, and she calmly walked out as she released her scarf and let her long white hair flow free in public for the first time in her life as her scarf fluttered to the floor. She walked out with the rest of her household following her, each carrying just a few objects in their hands which they hoped they could keep.

It took a long bit for the fat, overweight Clergy, and the rest to comprehend what she did. The fat Clergy yelled for her to put her scarf back on. A couple of the guards rushed in. One grabbed her scarf from the floor and rushed toward her. Bebe entered, fearfully, and grabbed the scarf away from the guard and placed it on Hajji Khanoum's head, holding it so it would not fall.

*****

Meanwhile, not aware of what was happening with his mother, Cyrus reluctantly turned off the shower and began to dry himself off. The peaceful calm that had come over him was suddenly marred by what he thought was Khally, barking and crying loudly, in severe pain, as if she had been hit by a car. He wrapped a towel around his waist and ran upstairs to see if he could get a glimpse of her from the window. He knew it wasn't Khally's usual bark. It was getting louder, interrupted by loud cries of pain.

He kept the light off so as not to draw attention to himself. Through the tiny crack between the yellow curtains, Cyrus could see no less than a dozen gunmen taking over his family's compound, two of which were chasing Khally through the flower beds, smashing his treasured dog with their guns.

Cyrus grabbed his clothes and ran straight out towards Hajji Khanoum's, racing barefoot and half-naked through the alley, down the street, and around the corner. Hearing Khally's cries, he ran as if his life depended on it as he was dressing on his way.

*****

Roxanna, Bebe, and Ahmad Reza followed Hajji Khanoum out of the building and helped her down the stairs just as three cars entered the gate and sped to the building, stopping by the stairs by Hajji Khanoum and Roxanna.

They could not believe their eyes when Yousef, Amir's driver of many years, got out of a car and opened the back door for Saeed, one of Cyrus' oldest and best friends, now bearded and wearing a green American Army jacket. They watched, seething but silent, as Saeed got out, ignoring Hajji Khanoum and the rest. He walked up the stairs and then stopped, turned, and looked at Roxanna.

He felt that it must be her, but for some reason, Saeed did not want to face Hajji Khanoum, knowing she was unhappy. He knew Haji Khanoum well and knew not to test her when she was angry; he would just end up embarrassed. He turned, feeling proud and victorious, and entered Hajji Khanoum's house with an air of superiority, as if it were his. But, still, he didn't have the nerve to look at Hajji Khanoum's eyes.

Leading from her house one last time, giving Hajji Khanoum a moment to stop to cherish her beautiful flower gardens and the roses her, Cyrus, and Amir had lovingly planted along the driveway. To say goodbye to a life, a lifetime, her entire world, was more than even she could bear. Her legs became weak, unable to support her frail body, and she swayed precariously, saved by Roxanna, who rushed in to support her before she collapsed.

The mood was solemn as they walked down the driveway past one of the family cars, its engine running, the guard waiting for permission to take it away. Once the order was given, Amir's cars, as well as two other family cars, were driven away, with total disregard of Hajji Khanoum's feelings. Roxanna was sickened by the vulgar callousness of the final act.

The guards couldn't even wait until they disappeared from view. She could not believe it was the same Iran from just a few months ago. She had developed such an understanding of the beauty, kindness, and love these people embodied, and now that image was shattered. Roxanna helped the old woman to the exit of the mansion, not understanding the full scope of the old woman's pain. She had worked hard for a lifetime, a devout Muslim who prayed regularly for the promises of health, justice, purity, compassion, and kindness.

Now in the name of Islam, Khomeini was drenching her country in blood and tears. She now doubted which Islam was true? What did Khomeini bring? How could God bring him and these corrupt mullahs into power to bring such heartache and destruction? She pulled on her chador, pulling it off her head; she had worn it her entire life. Her long white hair parted down the middle fell down her shoulders. Roxanna grabbed her more firmly as if guiding a lost child.

Hajji Khanoum walked straight forward, not taking another glance at her mansion that was full of lifetimes of memories. She left behind everything she had created everything she had lived for, and walked calmly onto the street, gripping Roxanna's hand firmly.

Just as it had the sick, cold, empty finality of a funeral procession. Khally was still running away from the guards who were chasing her, but her cry was weakened now. Behind them stood a house no longer Hajji Khanoum's, now a metaphoric coffin, filled with a lifetime of family treasures, a home, a lifestyle, and the memory of her son. They all watched the small fleet of cars, loaded with the spoils of war, turn down the street, and with it, everything that was once Hajji Khanoum's life was gone.

Roxanna, Bebe, and Ahmad Reza looked back at the house, thinking about the many memories they had all shared in this loving home. Hajji Khanoum, refusing to show weakness, stared straight ahead. Even the guards were shocked by the old woman's sense of pride and defiance in the face of such devastating loss. She had been stripped of her life and her loving son; any loss was incomparable to that, and yet she would not break. The housemaid took her hand to ease her pain, "Don't forget God is with good people. God would not leave you alone." Hajji Khanoum squeezed her hand tightly. "What God?"

No words of comfort existed. Ahmad Reza approached her quietly, "I am staying ... I know a few members in the clergy. I will go to them and get the house back." Ahmad Reza walks back to the house.

A few neighbors who had witnessed the unimaginable violence and the horrors that were happening at Hajji Khanoum's house came out to protect her, while others, afraid they would be next, watched from inside, peeking out from the corners of drawn drapes.

All were surprised, seeing Hajji Khanoum without a scarf for the first time. An older neighbor woman who had become fearless with age reached out to Hajji Khanoum while taking her small bag from Bebe, insisting she follow them to her house as she cursed the guards along the way. Perhaps due to her age, Haji Khanoum showed no resistance and followed her. Even when she looked at her dead in the eye, she hardly knew her, but her voice was pleasant and kind, "People are human, the need for each other becomes clear one its own. All you gain in a lifetime belongs to the earth, no? One day things come, and the next they go, you and I have our feet on the edges of our graves. We will go soon and won't be taking anything with us. Let's have a cup of tea together?"

Hajji Khanoum entered the older woman's home as the others quietly followed behind. Roxanna was the last to enter behind Bebe.

*****

Cyrus continued to run as fast as he could on a deserted street toward his mother's house barefoot. Although his legs were very tired and he was getting weak, the only thing he wasn't thinking about was stopping. Cyrus continued to run through the street towards Hajji Khanoum's, knowing that Khally's life depended on how fast his feet could carry him. There was only a block to go, but to Cyrus, it looked like a million miles. He ran, barefoot, past an old gardener, sitting on a motorbike, and considered asking him for a lift but decided against it. At the speed he was running, the motorbike would have only slowed him down.

*****

Like vultures after a kill, the overweight mullah joined his guards, rummaging disrespectfully through Hajji Khanoum's house, searching for any valuables that might have been left behind. The clergyman uncovered a few small pieces of valuable classical Persian art, framed in gold and carefully hidden in the back of a closet. His eyes darted around the house to determine if he was being watched. Deciding it was safe to carry on with his heist, he wrapped the artwork in one of Hajji Khanoum's scarves and tucked the pictures into an oversized pocket, a pocket that matched his oversized girth.

From the grand entrance, Yousef was able to watch, inconspicuously, as Saeed paraded around the living room like a peacock, surveying its bounty. Something had attracted Saeed's attention. In full view was a large, framed picture of Cyrus, Saeed, Nader, and Hussein, taken when they were in high school, together. Yousef knew that Saeed and Cyrus had been lifelong friends and wondered what his intentions were. He was surprised when Saeed broke both the glass and frame.

Carefully removing the picture, he folded it in half and placed it in his coat pocket, all the time looking around at what used to be his best friend's mother's house. As he walked into the entrance, he looked up the giant marble staircase to the balcony and grinned, "Home sweet home."

Upon hearing Saeed's remark, the overweight clergyman lashed back at him, "Haromet basheh, Saeed . . . You are taking a better house than I did, and it is fully furnished with antiques and treasures."

Yousef could not watch any longer. After he left Amir, he had remained with the Savak so he would not lose his pension. Only later did he find out Saeed requested him to be his driver after Saeed took over a high position. He was forced to remain with Saeed, or he would lose his pension from the government. The thought of what his future held for him was making him physically ill.

*****

As was custom in this particular neighborhood, the woman's house was very luxurious and richly decorated. Ornate Persian carpets flowed from room to room, highlighting Italian furniture. The walls were brought to life by rich wall coverings and expensive paintings while chandeliers hung from every ceiling, lighting the stage for the evening events.

The neighbor and her family were determined to do everything possible to let Hajji Khanoum know they loved and treasured her no matter what had occurred. They helped her to a gorgeous yet comfortable couch in the living room where she was to rest, surrounded by Bebe, neighbors, and Roxanna. She laid her head back and stared, blindly, into the distance while Roxanna stroked her hair and face, trying to comfort her and let her know she was surrounded by people who loved her.

One of the woman's helpers entered and began serving tea, but Hajji Khanoum was unable to even respond. This woman, who had lived her life as the matriarch of one of the most loved and highly respected families in Tehran, had lost everything. They could not begin to imagine her pain.

To Hajji Khanoum, the unspeakable had happened, and there was no longer a need for her to utter a sound. Her life had ended in tragedy, the curtain rising on Amir's death and the final act ending with Saeed's evil deeds. She had entered a self-imposed hell before death, created in her mind, imprisoned by her own body, held prisoner by her pain.

Roxanna felt sick to her stomach. The horror that she had just witnessed weighed heavily upon her, knowing that Hajji Khanoum's fate had been an unpredicted and unwanted outcome of the revolution she and her friends had ignited, and therefore, Hajji Khanoum's tragedy was in part, her fault. She and many of her colleagues had set up the political roll of the dice, never imagining that what she was now witnessing could have become even a remote possibility. Yet there it was, in all its horrific maleficence.

Roxanna overheard the neighbor's two sons talking in the kitchen, concerned maybe they were on the clergy's radar and would be the next target. Their father had been a sergeant in the Army and was now in hiding, making the house easier to acquire and therefore more desirable to men like Saeed.

Bebe surprised everyone with her uncharacteristic cursing as she watched what was happening at Hajji Khanoum's home from the window next door. After a brief moment of reflection, she concluded that this was indeed the worst and saddest day of her lifetime.

*****

Cyrus finally turned onto his street and ran through the front gate, ignoring the guard. His eyes searched for Khally, but the only trace of her he saw was a trail of blood leading towards the back of the compound. The loud sound of what could only have been the cries of a dying dog sent shivers down his back.

Ignoring the angry yells from the guards, Cyrus continued running to the aid of his lifelong companion, sweet Khally, who loved him unconditionally and trusted him and depended on him. By the time he stopped, he was staring down a dozen rifles pointed directly at him. Yousef, who up until now had remained silent, raised his hand, and yelled to the guards not to shoot.

From the balcony, Saeed watched one of his guards, mercilessly, beating the damn dog with the barrel of his gun. His eyes caught Cyrus, dodging guards as he ran toward poor Khally, lying motionless in a bed of blood-spattered, broken tulips. Several guards continued chasing him, shooting wildly into the air.

Next door, Roxanna was jolted by the sound of gunshots coming from the direction of Hajji Khanoum's, as if a bolt of lightning had pierced her body. Her immediate response was to open the front door, but she had been held back by the neighbor's desperate plea. Saeed's actions were so abhorrent, everyone was certain he had lost his mind and that there was a very real possibility he and his guards could start shooting, indiscriminately, at any moment. The plea fell on deaf ears. No matter how severe the warning, seeing Cyrus was all it took for Roxanna to push her way through the door and run to him. Bebe's heart urged her to follow, but she realized it was her place to stay behind to keep an eye on Hajji Khanoum.

By the time Cyrus reached his dog, it was too late. The guard had beaten her with such vicious intensity that there was no chance for her to survive. It was as if Khally was hanging on, waiting for Cyrus, and when she saw him, she took her last breath and lay still.

Enraged, Cyrus wrestled the guard to the ground, took the bloody rifle from his hand, and bashed him in the face with such force blood gushed out of his mouth and nose in rapid spurts. Cyrus reversed the rifle and aimed it at the guard's head, leaving him no choice but to beg for his life, slobbering blood through his broken teeth. Enraged, many guards immediately surrounded him, pointing their weapons at his head, creating a standoff.

Saeed approached from the house, and after taking a quick inventory of the out-of-control scenario in front of him, realized he would have to intercede. If he didn't, it was likely there would be several dead bodies in the middle of the yard of this elegant home, in this very respectable neighborhood, which Saeed reminded himself, was now his home and his neighborhood.

Clearly, that would not be good public relations for the new government; they were better skilled at handling these types of activities away from public view. Saeed thrust his hand in the air in a very authoritative manner and barked a few loud orders. The guards lowered their weapons but remained firmly in place, studying Cyrus, who was now engaged in a staring match with Saeed.

Meanwhile, Roxanna pushed through the gate, running toward Cyrus, as several more guards started shooting in her direction. Saeed yelled for the guards to stop just as she dove, head-first, into the bed of tulips near Cyrus's dog. The guards surrounded her; their guns pointed at multiple parts of her body.

Remembering the consequences of the last time she lost control, Roxanna grimaced in silence; her face pushed downward, being ground into the dirt by the foot of one of the guards. When he finally released her, she was able to pull herself up enough to wipe the blood off her face. It was Khally's blood, and it was everywhere.

Her eyes pleaded with Cyrus to hold back and not respond to the sheer adrenaline running through him without considering the life-threatening consequences to them all. After breaking the guard's rifle in half against the fence post in the yard, Cyrus's attention was directed toward Saeed. It took all the strength he had in him to resist the urge to beat him to death just as he had done to Khally. But seeing the woman who held his heart lying on the ground, several yards away, his fear for her safety stopped him from carrying out what would have been his final act.

Pary had warned Roxanna that Saeed had obtained a high position in what had been the Savak. And now that Saeed had managed to secure a position of authority within the organization, he had become a complete fanatic, which was why Roxanna had been willing to risk her life to calm Cyrus before he pushed Saeed too far.

Cyrus was suffering more pain than he ever thought possible. He kneeled down next to Khally and cried endless tears into her matted, bloody, open wounds. Beneath him, lying dead on the ground, was his joy, his laughter, his reason to come home at night. She was always waiting, greeting him with affection, making him feel needed and loved. She knew when he was hurting, even when he could hide it from others. She asked so little from him, and still, he let her down.

He hadn't heard her cries until it was too late. It was wrong to hurt and kill but to kill the innocent, whether it the elderly, a child, or an animal, that was pure evil. Tears streamed down his face as he picked Khally up and cradled her in his arms like a baby. Slowly, gently, in case there was a shallow breath still left in her, he headed toward the gate. The guards were on alert, waiting for instruction, but none came. Saeed, alone, blocked him. They stared into each other's eyes, daring one another to make the first move.

"Your brother was on the wrong side. You can still join the side of the truth, our path. God's way is the way, and you must understand that truth."

Cyrus stared at his dead dog and then at Saeed. "I see your truth! Did God ask you to beat this innocent animal to death? Did God have a private conversation with someone to inform them that they could rob and steal, and murder at will? This may be your God, but not the one I know. I do not know or understand such a God. My God is God of mercy. God of forgiveness..." Cyrus gazed, sadly, at the man who had once been his best friend. "Do you think this is the thirteenth century repeating itself, again? The Arabs are not invading us! We are inflicting this violence upon ourselves! We have witnessed this madness many times throughout our country's history. Why don't you see it? What in the world do you think you will accomplish with these insane tactics of death and destruction?" He drew a shaky breath. "Is this how you intend to win over the hearts and minds of our people?"

Saeed did not like Cyrus' answer, but he remembered that he was standing in front of his old friend, a friend who had helped him many times throughout his life, and because of that, he would temper his response. In the end, it was what his guards would think of him that mattered. He chose his words with caution. "She belongs to this house. I cannot let you take her." Cyrus stood his ground, cradling Khally's body in his arms. "She used to belong to this house... not anymore. She belongs to me and goes with me..."

Even though Saeed found the answer from Cyrus unacceptable and insulting, he also did not forget that one of his oldest friends was standing before him. Perhaps all the stood around them were unaware of their history, but Saeed and Cyrus knew. Saeed knew that if Cyrus spoke about the past, he had the power to embarrass him in front of all these men, ruining her current ambiance as a strong man of God.

Besides, Saeed was not stupid, and he was aware that Cyrus knew many people on the top and was afraid that if he went too far, the news of his migration and stealing would reach the higher authorities, and it would ruin everything he had made for himself, so he had to be cautious. Thus, he chose his words wisely as he replied to Cyrus, "She belongs to this house; I cannot let you take her."

Cyrus was not about to hand over his dog's body and stared into Saeed's eyes as he replied, "she used to belong to this house because it was her house, now she goes with me, her family..." It was a very tense moment, and anything could have happened. Unfortunately, neither of them was giving in.

Although Roxanna heard every word, she remained face down in the tulip bed, not wanting to add fuel to the confrontation. Cyrus was upset enough by the loss of his dear Khally without having to defend her from Saeed's wrath.

Cyrus ignored Saeed's request and began to walk, but Saeed stopped him continuing the quarrel, "I said I would not let you take her out of here!"

Pary's voice pierced the air, catching everyone's attention, "Just when it was possible, everything turned into a dark tragedy. Isn't it better that the poor miserable dead dog isn't more of a victim of this childish rage that's ravishing your own humanity?" All eyes were now fixated on Pary, who was walking onto the estate property with Abdullah.

From the corner of her eye, Roxanna recognized Pary, now dressed in traditional Islamic dress, rushing through the gate, her right hand hidden inside a deep pocket at her side. Ignoring the guards, she attempted to walk past them towards Roxanna, but they raised their guns and ordered her to halt. Although he had never seen her in Islamic dress, Abdullah, too, recognized Pary's distinct mannerisms and signaled for the guards to hold back.

Pary walked over and helped Roxanna out of the flowerbed while never losing her gaze on Saeed. She stared deeply into Saeed's cold, deceitful eyes, prepared to shoot him if he so much as spit. Saeed was aware that she had a handgun in her pocket, Saeed, having known her all her life knew she was also capable of anything. He stood still, meeting her gaze; Pary knew he had been fond of her for quite a while but hid his feelings once he found out how she felt about Cyrus. This fondness was allowing Pary to maneuver in ways others wouldn't get away with.

Pary walked to Cyrus and lovingly stroked poor Khally's lifeless body. She had been there the day Cyrus brought her home, and she loved her as well. She looked into Cyrus's eyes, hoping to diffuse the situation, "You must not take her away from her house. It is all she has ever known. She should be buried here under the trees, the cherry tree."

Cyrus looked at the cherry trees lining the ivy-covered wall, thinking about how Khally laid by his side in the sun while he planted them so many years ago. He glanced at Pary and gave a slight nod, knowing her idea was the best way to honor Khally. Saeed followed closely as they walked toward the trees, watching their every move with suspicion. Cyrus's heavy heart added even more weight to his overloaded arms as he gently placed his dog on the ground and began digging with his bare hands; his silence unsettling, a stark warning that deep inside, his body surged with raging thoughts. Khally, his best friend, murdered without cause; her death fueled by an urge to kill, by deeply rooted anger, and frustration born of a society on the brink of insanity.

Ahmed Reza, who was silent all this time, appeared with shovels, and they all began to prepare her final resting place, giving Cyrus time to stroke Khally's head, to feel her coarse fur on his hand one last time before she entered the earth; his tears dropping to the depths of the grave to be buried alongside the animal he loved.

Cyrus would later think of the profound sadness he was feeling, the act of preparing a burial site in his soil for his friend, as a metaphor for the new Iranian cultural disease. Iran had become a hot zone, and Cyrus had no sense of how the disease that engulfed his beloved country could be stopped.

Saeed, for reasons only known to him, grabbed the shovel from Ahmad Reza and began to dig. Still, on his knees, Cyrus reached out and grabbed the handle just above the metal, purple veins budging in his neck. Once again, they locked eyes. Cyrus would die with his dog before he would let Saeed pave his way to Heaven digging Khally's grave.

*****

The Iranian culture was built on ideals of trustworthiness and loyalty. Growing up, Cyrus and his friends were raised with the belief that a man would die for his friend, and yet, standing before him was Saeed, a murderer, and a traitor. It was incomprehensible. Cyrus hung his head in disbelief. Had someone else called him that, Cyrus would have defended Saeed to the death, but Cyrus had been both witness and victim to this barbaric behavior in real-time, literally watching as Saeed stripped his mother of her home, the home he had grown up in, leaving Hajji Khanoum in the streets to die of a broken heart.

Saeed had sold his soul to the devil, as did Faust in Goethe's classic story. Cyrus shifted his gaze to Roxanna's beautiful face, stained with Khally's blood, before lifting Khally and gently laying his fallen companion in her grave. Using nothing but his bare hands, he scooped the rich Iranian earth and scattered it over the dog's still body. As the last clump of dirt dropped from Cyrus's hands, the sky opened up, shedding tears of rain, crying for his loss, for all of their losses… and for those who lost their way, their vision, and saddest of all, their moral compass.

Pary took Cyrus's hand and held it in hers. Their business was done; nothing remained for him in this place. Buried along with his dog were the memories of his life and those of his family. Roxanna took Cyrus's other hand, and slowly, together, they walked out, hearing the sharp clang of the latch against the iron gate one final time.

*****

It was a mean, unforgiving storm leaving no apologies in its wake. The rain beat against the windshield of Cyrus's Mustang with angry determination, a constant reminder of Saeed's wrath. For the first time in his life, Cyrus drove with unbridled caution in consideration of his mother's frailness. Roxanna was by his side, her silent strength a comfort.

In the back, Pary and Bebe sat on either side of Hajji Khanoum, holding her hands tightly. Roxanna, too, was reaching back and touching Hajji Khanoum's leg, comforting her as her sorrow was immense. Cyrus was thankful that he hadn't told his mother about his wife in America. It would have destroyed all hope.

It was clear she loved Roxanna very much and felt she was strong enough to keep Cyrus out of harm's way, especially if she took him back to America, and that is all Hajji Khanoum could hope for at this stage of her life. She had felt there was something between her son and beautiful Roxanna but thought it curious they never spoke of a relationship in any romantic sense. Her heart ached for all she had no control over; a quiet anguish filled her body.

It had been decided that her daughter's house was the best place for Hajji Khanoum to stay until she was able to move back, as the surroundings were familiar to her. But Cyrus knew his mother would never see her home again. Her treasures, the photographs, her favorite fruit trees and rose gardens, the scents, and textures of home, were nothing but memories best forgotten, lest they punctuate the emptiness created by Saeed's inhumanity.

What Cyrus saw in the rearview mirror was more than a reflection of his mother. He saw her as the pillar she was; a woman of gentle confidence, the matriarch of her family. Her position of power and respect in the community was all she had known. She was a role model, teaching her children to be blind when it came to color, religious beliefs, and race, extolling upon them the belief that all people deserved respect equally.

When strangers arrived at her house, they were confused as to who the lady of the house was and who the caregivers of the estate were. She had saved marriages, brought people of opposing positions together, acted as a mediator when there were conflicts between families, she could be depended on for advice and wisdom as well as thoughtful understanding. She was the brightest star in the night sky, taken down in the evilest of ways, by a man Cyrus called ... friend.

Hajji Khanoum rested her head on the back seat, her eyes misty as tears slowly traveled down her beautiful face like dewdrops on a petal; each tiny line etched with the pain of disappointment, the thoughts of those who were now gone, dead, lost to her forever.

"God, I have no desire to live any longer," she spoke the words softly as if to release the agony stored in her heart. "I am ready to go. Take me." A gentle upward curve upon her lips spoke silently of an acceptance, a resolve. Piercing the silence, Hajji Khanoum uttered anxiously, "Do you see it? See the glow, the glowing image?" Pary and Roxanna followed the direction of her gaze but saw nothing.

Her body went limp, her head fell slowly forward, and her hands gently slipped away from their grasp. Pary yelled to Cyrus, "Stop the car!" Tears and horrified gasps came from the women, mixed together with profound sorrow. Their sweet matriarch was gone.

Cyrus hit the brakes so hard the car slid, hydroplaning off the rain-drenched road, coming to a stop in a field. There, in the back, between Bebe and Pary, was his mother's frail body, appearing more beautiful in death; her skin as pale as freshly fallen snow and on her lips, a sense of peacefulness.

Only Roxanna dared to look at Cyrus. He was fighting back the tears as he tried to accept the fact that the woman most dear to him in his life, the one who had given birth to him and raised him, loved him, and devoted her life to him, was gone forever.

Without saying a word, Cyrus got out of his car and walked into the woods, the harsh rain hitting him like sharp knives piercing him through his heart. He knew his mother had fallen into her last sleep and was now traveling to the place where souls rest for eternity, joining Amir and his father. His head was spinning with all she represented to him and what was lost to him upon her death.

His first thought was how she could comfort him like no other. Like a child, he would cradle his head in her lap as she ran her fingers through his black hair. That sense of unconditional love and warmth and security vanished with her last breath. Roxanna got out and stood in front of Cyrus, pulling him into her arms. Their embrace was urgent and tight, their cheeks touching, tears mixing together in the rain. Their world had grown smaller, and for the first time, they had only each other.

*****

Chapter 29

When Decisions for Your Future Are Made Behind Closed Doors and Without Your Knowledge, by Outsiders...

Life showed no signs of getting better after the revolution. The Iranian people were naive and hopeful with Khomeini in charge, but that was because they were unaware of what was really happening in their country. The General Assembly and especially the people of Iran didn't even know the truth ... that most of the decisions affecting their country were formed in Washington or England and were being fed to them long before the revolution. Nor did they know that those decision-makers were still in business behind the scenes, indirectly or directly, guiding the players to put those decisions in motion and force them upon Iranian people.

In 1979, one of the most damaging incidents for Iran in the eyes of the world was set into motion. A group of Iranian students supporting the Revolution stormed the U.S. Embassy in Tehran, taking more than 60 American diplomats' hostage for 444 days initiating what was to become known as the Iran hostage crisis. Every day massive protests were held in front of the Embassy, becoming nothing more than an embarrassment to the Iranian spirit.

Time after time, American hostages were blindfolded and put on display on the balcony of the Embassy with military soldiers holding machine guns to their heads. The macabre procession excited the masses of people who would gather in front of the Embassy, and they went crazy at this sight, not knowing they were only harming themselves and Iran. They had no knowledge or idea of the political games that were being played behind the scenes. They were innocent followers who believed that their Imam was powerful, holy, and so close to God that he could bring America to its knees. They called this "The Protest Against America."

Only a handful of people surrounding Khomeini at the highest level were aware of who was orchestrating the hostage crisis as the events played out behind the scenes. The rest of the country had no idea that the taking of the hostages was a scheme devised by outside interest to enforce and establish Khomeini's power in Iran and to force Prime Minister Mehdi Bazargan to resign. He had fallen out of grace because of his refusal to follow what the West and Khomeini had ordered him to do. He was a man of principle, determined to do what was best for Iran, not what was best for the West or for Khomeini's personal agenda.

The news broadcasted on TV and around the world was that the American Embassy had been captured by forces claiming to be followers of Imam Khomeini and his ideology and that Prime Minister Mehdi Bazargan was strongly against the aggressive act of capturing the Embassy and taking American diplomats' hostage. Khomeini didn't even know in the beginning that such an attempt was in progress. Bazargan publicly spoke against it, but Khomeini supported it.

Very few, if any, knew why the American Embassy was being taken over or that the American Embassy in Iran was in direct daily communication with the State Department and that they were giving them hourly reports. They informed Washington ahead of time that they were going to be taken hostage, but nothing was done by anyone in the United States Capital. The fact was, Washington or other forces wanted power struggles inside Iran; they found it necessary and needed that "stage" to bring Prime Minister Bazargan down from power for refusing to follow Khomeini's order – which was to execute over 2,000 people including politicians, judges, businessmen, and educators. But Bazargan believed the leftist led by Ayatollah Ali Khamenei must pull such act, to take overpower in Iran.

Assad and his friends agreed with Prime Minster Mehdi Bazargan and, as a result, were among those who were in opposition to the takeover of the American Embassy. Their opposition helped perpetuate the violence that Khomeini and his radical followers were practicing, creating an even bigger divide in their relationship, ending with the resignation of Prime Minister Mehdi Bazargan, exactly the goal the West had hoped to achieve.

Both the poor hostages and hostage-takers were suddenly surprised by the new direction the hostage story was taking. As to their fate, it was anyone's guess what the outcome would be. What they didn't know was, somewhere north of Tehran, in Gholhak on Darab Street, there was a small house where their future and the future of Iran as a country was being decided. They had no idea that every day and all night, people were coming and going from the unobtrusive house and that their fate would affect the state of the world.

They were uncertain about their future and their children's future. What they also did not know was that the decisions for how they would have to live or think or believe in the future were forming at Dorian's house and were dictated to the team by Dorian to the ones she had around her. She was so close and trusted by Khomeini that hardly anyone could challenge her. She was the eyes and ears of Khomeini.

And you never knew who the unsuspected or suspected visitor would be.

*****

Time was passing, and secret plans of dirty politicians were in the works with no concern for the Iranian people. It appeared the American hostage crisis was at a standstill. Nothing had been resolved; in fact, things were getting worse every day. Politics and the hostages were the main topics of conversation.

Washington and Ambassador Sullivan were determined, along with Ayatollah Beheshti, to take overpower from Khomeini as soon as possible. This was something Dorian was strongly against, but Washington ignored her recommendations. In order to keep Khomeini in control, Prime Minister Bazargan must be gone. He was not following what Khomeini, or the Americans wished to accomplish. He was strongly against the killing and executions. He was against the hijab and strongly against the taking of hostages and asked for them to be released right away.

But Khomeini had the last word, and many influenced him. Within a short time of coming to power, he was someone else completely. Even the people closest to him were not familiar with this knew savage-like character that came out of him. Power had blinded him, he had lost touch with reality, and he really believed he was the Imam. He had completely forgotten what he promised to do when he came to power, or what he had preached were all misleading lies.

In addition, whatever anyone wanted to do, they knew it must be approved by Khomeini. Therefore, they knew they had to get Dorian on their side. That was why Assad and Hussein were giving her a visit per Dorian's request. Dorian had a lot of respect for Assad. She knew he was not looking for a position, power, or wealth. He was an honest man; his main intention was to focus on the good of the Iranian people.

Many times, Dorian would seek Assad's opinion about policies or people. Dorian approached from the kitchen, sat on the couch sipping a drink, and glanced at Hussein, who was pacing impatiently. Assad sat calmly looking at her, "I know neither of you drink..." she turned to Hussein, "Stop pacing."

Hussein stops abruptly, pauses for a moment, then walks away toward the chair and sits unhappily. At this time, Hussein had distanced his relationship with Ghotbzadeh and knows he has to establish a stronger relationship with Banisadr.

Dorian turned to Assad, "The reason I asked you to come over is that you are the only one I can say will speak the truth, someone who is not looking for glory or position. I can trust you, and I want to know your thoughts. First, do we agree, Amir is a good man? His mother adopted your daughter Roxanna, I wish she would leave, but she is stubborn like you. And I... we owe you for helping us with the financial backing of the Bazar, so I take your word seriously about Banisadr as well, and I support him for the presidency.

The sound of the doorbell distracted them. Confused as to who it could be, Dorian glanced at the door, then quickly Hussein and Assad, "You guys go on the bedroom and close the door. "

As Hussein and Assad shut the door to the bedroom, Dorian crossed to the door. The doorbell echoed again, and extremely irritated by the intrusion, Dorian pushed the speaker button, "Who is it?"

Through the door's security system, a man's voice could be heard, "An old friend and colleague, Jeff." He sounded American. Dorian thought for a few seconds and then remembered where she knew him. He was an old friend and colleague from the CIA who she had not seen since he was let go years ago. The past memories played in Dorian's mind the moment she heard Jeff's voice. Intrigued as to the purpose of his unexpected visit, she opened the door.

He appeared middle-aged and slightly overweight, a revolting combination to a woman as picky about her men as Dorian. Accessing the situation, she peeked around him and saw a car parked in her driveway with a few Iranians sitting inside. The fact that they had driven Jeff to her house told her he was doing something of mutual interest with them. He didn't wait for an invitation, "Sorry to wake you up, but it's imperative that we talk. I am leaving tomorrow, and this is the only time I could approach you, alone."

A few minutes later Jeff, was sitting by the tall window overlooking the city of Tehran. Far into the distance, the flame from the oil refinery dances in the background, framing Jeff inside the flame. Dorian still debating in her mind, what was he doing in Tehran at such a precarious time? It must be something very important.

The rebels had taken over the American Embassy, and all Americans were hiding or escaping from Iran, yet it appeared Jeff was traveling with no problem. "It must be very important for you to show up in the middle of this crisis."

The fact that Dorian turned BBC London on in an attempt to muffle their voices didn't go by Jeff, who was hoping she was alone. Dorian brought Jeff into the kitchen to be as far from the room Assad and Hussein were hiding in, so their voices would not reach them, and poured a glass of water, waiting to hear his explanation.

I'll get right to the point. I am leaving Iran in four hours, so time is short. You know the takeover of the Embassy was staged to force Prime Minister Bazargan to resign. Khomeini's losing momentum and power because of his actions and wants him out. The man is a constant critic of Khomeini and disregards direct orders from him, more on that in a minute. Firing him would have its own consequences. It's better in the public eye if he resigns.

"Once that happens, Khomeini will appoint a new prime Minister that follows orders. Initially, the original plan was that after Bazargan resigned, the hostages would be useless and were to be released. However, there's been a change in plans. Are you going to offer me a glass of water?" Dorian was just about to take a sip but instead held her glass out to Jeff.

"The new deal is that Iran will hold the hostages until after the American election. Why? Because if Carter succeeds in freeing the hostages, it could get him reelected for a second term. Reagan's team wants the hostages kept here until after the election. That way, Americans will want to go with Reagan as president.

"With Reagan in, the Republicans regain power again. Our team is in again. By the way… this is Top Secret. The White House has no knowledge of the deal."

Dorian cut him off, "And what does Iran get?" Jeff grinned, "Good question. The American Government, under Reagan, will arm Iran against Saddam's attacks."

Dorian was more than a little surprised. She prided herself in knowing everything that was going on, "Saddam's attacks? What are you talking about?!"

"It's all part of the Pentagon's plan to start a war in the Middle East to destabilize the region. You know that. Why? So, organizations like OPEC can't monopolize oil any longer. By the time things get stabilized, no one will need their oil."

Dorian, concerned, looked towards the room Assad and Hussein were in. Jeff noticed her concern, moved closer, and continued with a much lower tone.

"Oh, you must have a guest? Listen closely here. We'll give Saddam the green light to attack Iran. And both sides need our help. We already took the liberty to inform Iran of Saddam's intentions, as well, and of promising to provide them with all the weapons, they need. We are then delivering the weapons to Israel, and they sell them to Iran for a good profit... everyone wins."

Thoughtful, Dorian recalled Washington and Ambassador Sullivan were determined, along with Ayatollah Beheshti, to take overpower from Khomeini as soon as possible. This was something Dorian was strongly against the idea, but Washington ignored her recommendations. Because she had kept her love affair relationship with Ayatollah Beheshti secret from all, including the CIA. No one knew she even has a daughter from Beheshti, who even Beheshti does not know. So, if he took power, she had to deal with him, and she hated the idea.

Dorian could see that Jeff was totally consumed by the thrill of the chase and that the excitement of it all was giving him new feelings of power and confidence. For the first time in his life, he had Dorian where he wanted her … on the edge of her seat, begging for more. He moved closer as if what he was going to say next was highly confidential.

"Iranians don't care for Carter or the Democratic ideology. You and I know Iran is not ready to be democratic. Carter made a huge mistake to get rid of the Shah! He would have been happy to get through his term. So! The reason I'm here is to find out if we're on the same team..."

Dorian's nod was hardly convincing, so he continued to work on her, "As you know, William H. Sullivan and the White House are setting the stage for Beheshti to take over from Khomeini. That is not going to happen! As long as Beheshti's alive, he can be used as a pawn which means it's just a matter of time before someone spills the beans about your longtime love affair with him.

"And then there's your daughter, Katrina, right? Your daughter in the States, by the way, how is she doing? Does she know her father is Ayatollah Beheshti?" Dorian wore her best poker face, not about to give away her true feelings, which were to kill him at that very moment. She was not happy to learn that Jeff knew about her daughter.

"We're confident you'll find a way to convince Khomeini to hold on to the hostages until after the Presidential election and at the same time convince him to eliminate Ayatollah Beheshti. We know the leftist who wants to get rid of him … but you are the key. That way, Khomeini can remain in power, and your love affair will be kept a secret forever. This is no time for error. It is good for us and good for America."

Jeff looked straight into her eyes and smiled, hopefully. There was still time for her to thank him for bringing her on board. There was no question in Dorian's mind. He was blackmailing her. It took everything she had not to reach down for her gun and blow his head off, but she knew he must be of use to someone, somewhere, so she restrained herself. Jeff placed the empty glass on the counter. As she headed for the front door, a fake smile appeared on her lips. "One thing I know, the hostages were taken by the leftist taking their order from the Russians..."

Jeff hesitated, trying to add urgency to his needs and awaken her desires, "Who cares who did it? We could use it to get what we want..."

Once again, Dorian, concerned, looked towards the room Assad and Hussein were in. She whispered, "I'll see you next time I'm in

Washington. But right now, we have to be sure the hostages remain safe." Deflated, Jeff was barely able to shuffle out the front door. No man had ever felt better about achieving his goals or worse about the way an evening ended.

Outside very few streetlights light up the area. Several cars are parked on both sides of the street with drivers sitting inside; it was sprinkling.

Dorian's front door opens. Lit by a lone streetlight, Jeff exits, satisfied, and walks in the rain to a car with a few Iranians' sitting inside waiting. He gets in, and the car takes off.

The car with Jeff in it drives, passing a car parked down the street where two men sit in the front, looking out.

*****

Inside, mad as hell, Dorian stood by the closed door. If what Jeff had been implying was true, America and the American people were of no consideration in this barbaric master plan. The only thing that was important was which political "party" was in power.

Dorian's house was calm and still, but Dorian was burning. Still standing by her closed-door confused, she noticed Assad and Hussein enter, looking more confused than her. There was dead silence throughout the room. Dorian sits silently as Hussein begins to pace. Assad looks out the window at the flames of the Iranian refinery burning in the distance, "Sometimes I wish we did not have this black gold called oil, how lucky we would be, it is becoming the weapon of destruction, pain, and suffering for our people."

Hussein's pacing was getting on Dorian's nerves. Hussein was concerned if Dorian would bring up Roxanna and reveal to Assad that it was Hussein who sent her to Iran; it was Hussein who put his daughter's life in danger. And now he was walking around working with Assad to help Banisadr become president. Hussein regretted what he had done, but it was too late to correct it no matter how hard he tried.

Dorian turned to him, "Stop pacing..." Hussein hesitantly stopped. Looking directly at the floor, she glanced at them for a long time and finally whispered, "Do you guys have any idea who the people are who made a deal and got paid to keep the hostages here?"

Hussein speaks up, "The rumor is Rafsanjani's people, and Moussavi Khoeiniha got paid 750 million from an Unknown Republican senator and a known American politician, in France, the deal is to hold the hostages until the American elections are over..."

Dorian and Assad still kept their eyes on Hussein, waiting for him to continue. He was silent, and Assad broke the silence, "And how do you know about this? Where did you get your info?" It took Hussein a bit, and a bit unwillingly, to speak again, "I heard it from a friend… he was not my friend; it just happened that I was there, and he was drunk and said he was one of the translators when they met. I do not know exactly who he is and have never seen him again." Hussein was quiet for a bit. Just before they were about to change the subject, Hussein whispered quickly, "He disappeared maybe killed, to silence him."

Dorian looked at him like she wanted to get up and kill him. She was more upset that a deal had been made without her knowing. She was also concerned about the hostages. She maintained her composure, raised up, and walked to the door, "It is too late… but let's make something clear between us. I believe you guys know that what you heard tonight stays here."

Then she turned to Assad, "I wish your daughter had a bit more of your understanding. She should just leave and make it easy for everyone."

There was dead silence for a long bit. Assad thought for a long moment about how to respond, "Perhaps she has more courage, understanding, and passion than I do…

*****

Now everyday people experienced the effect of the policy that Khomeini's government was making and imposed in Iranian politics were shown on a daily basis in Iran.

As another day of struggle and turmoil had begun in Tehran for many who did not believe in clergies and the entire country, each day brought increasing discord. The merciful God, the God of forgiveness that had been preached of before the revolution, no longer existed. The fanatic clergy and their followers were stretching their reach, gaining control of the country, to the chagrin of those who did not see it coming.

Many who were in support of Khomeini were now being hit with the unfortunate truth that they were facing a new enemy, making for extremely dangerous times. Unlike under the Shah's rule, one could not just simply write a letter of apology stating that one would change his political views. Those being arrested were guaranteed the strictest punishment. Death. One would be executed before he or she even realized they had been arrested.

According to the new regime, "Execution" was both the word and way of God, and when the name of God was used to justify an act, no one dared challenge it. When something was God's will, according to the clergy, no one had the courage to ask which God or how they had received such a message or why no one else had gotten this message from God. Any contention or questioning of Khomeini or any Clergy was construed as being against God and the revolution, and this meant automatic jail time, being lashed in public, or most likely, a death sentence. They were invincible.

For women, the traditional way for Muslims to dress was becoming a forced practice, a law that affected both Roxanna and Pary. This basic loss of freedom became a nightmare from which Iranian women were unable to wake. It was a violation more painful than the last Arab invasion, which brought centuries of unforgettable, relentless disaster and destruction.

People coveted both the personal and religious freedom they experienced during the Shah's reign. The Shah's father, who was the founder of the Pahlavi Dynasty, had done more for Iran in just a few years in power than any other regime had done during the past century. He took the veils off women's heads, and normal dress became the standard attire. Older Iranians considered covering oneself to be part of the tradition of "Hijab."

In truth, Hijab in Islam meant the discovery of yourself within your heart and control of your desire and will. This would achieve Jihad, which meant to revolt within yourself, to kill the evil in your mind and soul, and then you truly discover and love yourself and others. Achieving such an important feat is the path to an enlightened state and therefore reaching God or Allah. Thus, Jihad did not mean to revolt against another soul and killed it.

In fact, killing in Islam is prohibited. The Hijab did not mean that women should cover themselves from head to toe or else suffer harsh punishments. The Shah was trying to teach people that such customs of dressing came from Arabic countries because the climate was so hot that they had to protect themselves from the scorching sun.

After the Arab invasion, Iranians had been forced to accept Islam against their will. It was an act that was met with strong resistance by the Iranian people. They were given a choice between Ali, who Mohammad himself had chosen to follow him, or Omar, an Army leader who thrived on bloodshed and was considered a killer.

In an attempt to separate themselves from the Arabic traditional religious sect, they decided to take a path of peaceful resistance, choosing Ali, who would continue Mohammad's message of peace.

When Omar learned what was happening, he used force to take power away from Ali. By following Ali, the Iranian people created another branch of Islam and called it Shia, which is a much more moderate version of Islam. It was their way of separating themselves from Arabs who called themselves the Sunni. The goal of the Shia was to stop the Arabic blood bath at the time and allow freedom of religion to prevail. Later, Iranians created a branch of Islam called Sufism which was the religion of Rumi, Omar Khayyam, Hafiz, Saadi, Sanaai, and many other Iranian poets and philosophers.

A few months after the revolution, there was a natural resistance brewing against these newly imposed violations of liberty forced upon the people by the overly zealous new regime lead by Khomeini.

Educating the Iranian population became the newly accepted method of changing minds through handouts, fliers, and literature. Speeches were organized to be delivered wherever groups were forming. Newspapers and new publications began springing up everywhere. The assault against the people of Iran continued with impunity, and the clash of ideology continued to grow, creating an ever-increasing chasm of despair. Assassinations and abductions remained a daily reality in Iran as the entire nation spiraled out of control.

Pary stopped reading the article Roxanna wrote to be published at the small newspaper that Pary and her team had organized, which was growing daily in popularity.

It was clear that people like Roxanna, Pary, Hussein, and Cyrus were restless and unwilling to accept this continual devastation. They felt their presence was of the utmost importance during this strange and crucial time and devoted much of their time to the newspaper, their way of reaching the masses in hopes of influencing them.

Hussein was a contributor and a great help with both financial resources and information. At the time, Hussein was a close adviser to AbolHassan Banisadr, who was the top adviser to Khomeini and was also referred to as a son to Khomeini. It had been promised that he would be the first president of Iran.

Roxanna was helping Pary to run the paper. And now she wrote an article that surprised and shocked Pary. She was so into Iranian matters that it sometimes scared Pary. She really wanted to print the article, but she was thinking it was too risky for the paper and also for Roxanna if they find out who wrote it.

But she did not know how or maybe did not want to deliver the bad news to Roxanna. She was shocked to see how Roxanna understood and distinguished the Iranian societies and what was coming up on them. It was something that the majority of the people who were born and raised in Iran did not understand.

On this particular day, Roxanna, Pary, and several others were busily reviewing possible newspaper articles when the smell of ink got so heavy it was about to overpower them in the small, enclosed room. Despite the danger of being discovered, Pary was forced to open the window to allow some fresh air in. Sneaking a look from between the curtains, she noticed the car that had been parked across the street for days was still there and decided it was time to take a closer look.

Not wanting to be seen, she crept out the back door, through the alley, and headed toward the front of the building, approaching the car from behind, but before she could get close enough to get a good look, the car sped away. It was no longer a feeling. She knew, then, that they were being watched.

Later at the office, the staff continued the process of choosing new topics to write about while Pary looked over unpublished articles, trying to decide which one to use next, but her mind was elsewhere. Thinking about the car, she walked to the back door away from the office where Roxanna was making tea. She locked it as a safety precaution.

At the same moment, several men carrying large sticks barged through the front door, yelling threats as they began bashing the office with sticks and clubs. A familiar-looking fat clergyman entered brandishing a gun, followed by several bodyguards. Looking away from their view, Roxanna recognized him as the very same member of the clergy who led the takeover of Hajji Khanoum's house. To Roxanna's horror, the men began savagely beating the staff, violently grabbing people and bringing them to their knees before throwing them out the window.

Roxanna pushed Pary, who went for her handgun to shoot into an adjacent office, kicking the door shut behind them, hoping they had been able to make it in, unseen. Although Roxanna was becoming hardened by her time in Tehran, the violence towards their newspaper was focused directly towards them and, therefore, extremely terrifying. Not to mention she recognized the faces of the bodyguards as the vicious murderers who had killed Khally, a fact that sent cold chills up her spine.

Pary, on the other hand, was way beyond scared. She was outraged. Recognizing the faces of the madmen, she was certain that Saeed was behind the attack, and that enraged her even more. Just as Cyrus's mother, Hajji Khanoum, had been as close as family to Saeed, these innocent people were his neighbors, his friends, and his acquaintances. How could he turn against them, target them, in such a brutal manner? Using street gang mentality to achieve his goals was an abhorrent and unforgivable act. Pary drew her gun, preparing to reenter the larger office and stop the massacre, but Roxanna held her back.

Through the cracked door, Pary and Roxanna watched in anguish as attackers destroyed the office and beat their workers until, like Khally, they lay bloodied and motionless. A guard was kneeling on the back of a young girl, pushing her face into the concrete with one hand as he beat her with a wooden stick covered in blood.

Without warning, the back door of the office was kicked open, hitting the wall so hard that the glass window shattered, as if in slow motion, sending a cloud of shards spewing in all directions. Abdullah, followed by a few of his men, rushed in holding machine guns and began looking in each room, almost as if looking for someone in particular.

Seeing Pary, he stopped and ordered his men to help the others escape the massacre in the front office. He opened up the back door and reached for Pary, looking into her eyes. "Get away before it is too late." He had never forgotten that night at Peter's restaurant when Saeed burned his hand. It was Pary who had helped him out of the restaurant when everyone had forgotten about him. It was Pary who had kissed him in order to distract the policemen who had arrived. If he forgot everything else of importance in his life, he could never forget that kiss.

As Pary and Roxanna raced out of the printing shop and into the back alley, they passed a man stuffing a sandwich in his mouth, seemingly unaware of the massacre going on inside. Roxanna knew damn well that it was impossible for the man not to see the horrors taking place right before his eyes, and she was horrified by the thought that violence was becoming so commonplace in Iran that people were going about their lives ignoring it.

Suddenly, a bomb blast went off at the newspaper office and tiny particles of glass, like glistening slivers of ice, sliced through the air towards Roxanna and Pary. The smell of burning plastic permeated the air, gagging them. Victims poured out the back door, screaming in pain; around them, the color of blood, muted by a smoky haze. Terrified, the man stopped chewing and sprinted toward his car.

Pary grabbed Roxanna and pulled her along, making it to the man's car just in time to jump in the back seat before he drove away. The man looked behind him and, seeing two young women in his car, choked on his sandwich. They were the last thing he needed in his life at this point.

Hitting his brakes, he told them to get out. Pary wasn't in the mood to negotiate. She pulled out her gun and pointed it in his face, waving for him to get moving! He stepped on the gas, throwing Pary and Roxanna to the floor, where they remained hidden from view.

The last thing Pary saw as she slid below the seat was her ex-friend, Saeed, sitting in a car with that same fat clergyman who was always trailing him, watching the scene unfold with satisfaction. She felt sick.

Pary turned to Roxanna and looked at her for a long time. She was still thinking about the article she wrote. In fact, she still had it with her. Pary was thinking maybe she should share what he heard from her sources like Hussein regarding the American hostages. Little could they imagine that holding the hostage's captive for 444 days was about keeping the American people in the dark.

But no one knew if all that was said about the hostages was true or not. However, neither the Iranian people nor the American people had any idea that there was a deal made between Republicans and Khomeini's people to keep the hostages until the American elections, which resulted in President Robert Regan defeating President Carter.

As the hostage crisis continued, Tehran and Iran were saturated with unexpected and unexplained incidents, and no matter how hard citizens tried to stay neutral and avoid confrontations, they wound up involved. When the juggle for power was at its peak, and with Khomeini's support as promised, AbolHassan Banisadr would become Iranian's first president, Hussein, his foreign adviser.

As the presidency played out, the many groups conspiring behind the scenes, including the Mujahedin, teamed up with Banisadr to fight the clergy until the opportunity to attack arose. Ayatollah Beheshti, who was supposed to succeed Khomeini, was lying low, biding his time until the regime cracked.

During this same time, Dorian was secretly working against Washington to prevent Beheshti from taking over from Khomeini. What the General Assembly of the United Nations and the rest of the world didn't know was that America gave Saddam Hussein the green light to attack Iran while simultaneously informing Banisadr's administration about Iraq's intentions.

Or if they did know, they chose to be quiet and ignore it. The plan was for Saddam Hussein to destroy all Iranian planes and dismantle the Iranian Air Force. With war imminent between Iran and Iraq, America looked to profit by supplying weapons to both sides. It was also the intent of the United States to make sure that neither side dominated the vital oil region.

Meanwhile, in America, people were only fed stories dealing with the American Embassy's takeover by Iranian students. The fear-stricken masses leaned on Ronald Reagan to suppress their anxiety, and as a result, he was elected President of the United States. The hostages were released on the day of his inauguration. Now Reagan's administration was supposed to fill their side of the bargain they made with Khomeini in secret before becoming president.

But then if what Hussein told about the secret deal that Republicans made with Khomeini's people in France was true, to hold the hostages until after the American elections, and after Regan became the president of the United States defeating Carter, later continued to be a huge headache for the Reagan administration, because part of the deal was that the US sold weapons to Iran when Iraq attacked Iran. However, the House of

Representative was controlled by the Democrats, and they would not approve of arms sold to Iran.

So, they were forced to take different directions and forfeit their deal. And while in Iran, Khomeini and the mullahs shouted, "Death to America and Israel" and boasted against the destruction of Israel. The Reagan administration was secretly sent all these weapons to Israel from the United States, and Israel sold them to Iran at a higher price, and as planned, Israel would ship the weapons to Iran. But modifications were made in which part of the money from the weapons sales was used to fund the Contras, who were fighting against Nicaragua's socialist government. Israel also set its eyes on Khuzestan, a Palestinian population in southern Iran, as its new capital.

The result was the 1985-1987 Iran–Contra affair or Iran-Contra, also referred to as Iran gate, or Iran-Contra Affair, or the Iran–Contra scandal in (1985-1987), also known as the Iran Contra Gate scandal, for which Oliver North was imprisoned.

During the early stages of the war, Iran was winning and was about to take over Iraq. This was something America and the West went to great lengths to prevent because if that happened, Iran would seize control of the Persian Gulf, which was known as the heart of the world's economy and power. Therefore, America's goal was to defeat Iran at the time when Reagan's administration supplied Saddam Hussein with their best weapons to be used against Iranian and Kurdish enemies.

It was later known that Saddam Hussein dropped many commercial bombs on Iranian and the Kurdish people during the Reagan administration, killing many thousands of people, yet no one in the United States said a word about it or questioned Saddam Hussein about human rights.

Pary was still debating whether to share more with Roxanna or not. She was thinking she should not encourage her to get more deeply involved in a game that could put her life in more danger.

*****

Chapter 30

What at First Seemed Noble, Replaced with Sadness, Fear and Futility ...

Darkness had fallen over Tehran. An ominous night sky, filled with pregnant grey-black clouds waiting to drop their deluge, loomed above. And then, the rain began to fall in sheets, as if nature was determined to wash away the misery caused by the negative, destructive effects of the revolution. People suddenly faced with the magnitude of the harm that had been done to their beloved country were living their lives on the precipitous edge of hopelessness.

Pary and Roxanna were young enough to believe that rain could wash away anything, even the nauseating stench of thickening blood that seemed to follow them everywhere, bringing a country to its knees. For a moment, they felt pure and cleansed as they defied the elements, swinging their legs on the edge of a rooftop overlooking Tehran. They were mesmerized by raindrops, glistening like individual prisms, absorbing the city lights, magnifying their brilliance before splashing down, becoming part of something bigger, a puddle, stream, river, ocean. A metaphor for tears sheds; a country destroyed by the greed of others.

They were dressed in men's clothing. After the last attack on the printing office, they realized they could no longer go out without taking precautions. They found it easier to safely blend into the crowd as males and were surprised how quickly they were able to adapt to the male psyche, realizing that they were more male than female in their thinking on most levels. As they let the rain beat down on their faces, they reflected on the traumatic events that had brought them to this place. They filled the time with stories from their past. Each reached deep inside their heart to share words of wisdom gifted to them by their elders and parents.

Pary's mother, like most Iranian parents, wished for her children to grow up securely and have a loving family with children of their own. Unfortunately, these simple wishes became noble ideas, lost in a quagmire, caught up in the daily struggle to survive. Now living in Iran was like being caught in a spider's web, with its people, like insects caught in its maze, unable to free themselves from the sticky trap of intricately woven corruption. The realization of dreams for a brighter future, which included political, artistic, ideological, and economic freedom, would take continued vigilance not to be forgotten.

The demands of a country lost would require tremendous emotional and physical stamina from those who felt a duty in their hearts to fight for the greater good of Iran. Conquering the obstacles blocking the path to a country free from tyranny in the proud land of their ancestors was the altruistic dream. Nothing would be achieved without sacrifice. Thinking back to the first day she met Pary's mother, Roxanna was now in awe of the old woman, so full of wisdom and knowledge, the woman's words like buried treasure, unearthed only when spoken in a language familiar to each.

Both Roxanna and Pary had come to the realization that since the Revolution, Iran had actually stepped backward on issues such as human freedom, human rights, and economic stability. The thought that, instead of progress, they, in fact, had been part of a change that brought more sadness and hardship than previously existed was heartbreaking. Pary sat in circumspect, mentally replaying her recent history against the backdrop of a revolution that failed to achieve its goals. The revolution, which at first seemed noble and prosperous, had instead drained all happiness from the hearts of the Iranian people and replaced it with sadness, fear, and futility.

Most devastating for Pary, Roxanna, Cyrus, and Hussein, was the realization that their new enemy had once been a best friend. It was a terrifying feeling. The fact that Saeed was now working for the enemy had turned their world upside down. Pary and Roxanna realized that they, and their friends, could trust no one and were in imminent danger. With Saeed now holding a high position in the new Secret Police, it was only a matter of time before they were captured.

The government would continue its rampage against those who dared to challenge its authority, and the price to be paid was in lives. Theirs! Pary and Roxanna had no choice but to be constantly moving, hiding from everyone. Not even Cyrus knew where they were.

*****

For reasons unknown to them, they decided to visit Roxanna's grandmother; just maybe they could get a clue how to reach her father, Assad. They arrived, only to find out her grandmother had left the pain and suffering of this world; she was long gone to Heaven if one really exists. Now Mashty and Zahra were the only occupants of the farm, waiting to join the grandmother. The farm and the house, both, were like a dead soul without her grandmother.

Unfortunately, they had not heard from Akbaar and had no clue as to his whereabouts after they placed the grandmother in her lasting grave. Roxanna wished she had not taken the trip. Although they drove back to Tehran in silence, their heads were spinning, each buried in her own thoughts – a kaleidoscope of images conjured up like lightning, flashing in front of them.

For Roxanna, a teahouse, a car, a little girl, a bomb, glass shattering, blood, a dead child, interrogators, screaming, the Zoorkhaneh, Bolbol, sheep's eyes, Khally's body covered with blood as she was beaten to death. Hajji Khanoum dying in the car and finally Cyrus, sinking to his knees in the snow crying for everything he loved that was no more... A country lost.

Pary's thoughts were less like recollections and more phantasmic in nature. She couldn't shake images of Saeed growing claws and fangs, a monster killing everything surrounding him, eating his young. He had become a mythical bloodthirsty creature. She felt her sadness eating away at her...at everything she loved.

The image of Nader and Cyrus and even Roxanna, against the reality that everything they had fought for had been lost, was enough to push her back into politics with more commitment than ever, becoming more determined with each passing day to rewrite this political tragedy.

She knew it would never be her story, alone. It was so much bigger than herself than even Nader and Cyrus and Peter and Roxanna, but if one person could make a difference, she would do her part, setting an example, condemning the weak and ineffective.

She knew her commitment to her country was a death sentence, yet proudly forged ahead, willing to fight to her last breath if that was her fate. But she did not want to drag Roxanna into her struggle any longer. So, in order to follow her path, Pary knew that she must leave Roxanna or, even better, get her out of the country before she was murdered.

Roxanna had a price on her head, and it was just a matter of time before she was in the cross hairs. Pary had hated everyone for using Roxanna in the car bombing, but she hated herself even more for not stopping it. Now heavy with guilt, she was determined to get her out of this mess before she wound up dead.

What neither realized was that Roxanna's situation was far worse than they imagined because she no longer had a passport, and there was no longer an American Embassy for her to get a new passport. It had been taken over by the militias, and everyone around them was gone or dead. She was a prisoner.

*****

Roxanna and Pary were finally safely back in Tehran from her grandmother's farm. They had traveled only at night, covered in Islamic clothes to hide their identities; only their eyes visible beneath the layers of dyed cloth.

Roxanna was starting to flash back to her first night in Tehran when Nader picked her up at the airport and drove her through the city, its lights similar to other city lights, yet by day, it was a country unlike anywhere else in the world. The taxi was taking a similar route, turning down the same alley leading to Pary's mother's house.

Pary was the first to point out two undercover cars with several guards waiting, watching, and a few more guards on motorcycles. Pary immediately told the driver to continue and not to stop. They got out of the taxi a few blocks away and walked a block in the opposite direction before hailing another taxi and heading back towards Pary's mother's in still another direction.

They instructed the driver to enter the alley and stop by a friend's house in an effort to avoid getting noticed by the motorcycle police or guards of the clergy. But it was too late; a third motorcycle approached and stopped on the alley's entrance watching them with great interest. Roxanna paid the driver while Pary rang the doorbell hoping desperately, someone was home.

The alley was narrow, with little room for the taxi to pass, let alone turn around. The driver, getting increasingly nervous, brought even more attention to himself by attempting to back out the alley until he reached the street. The two motorcycle guards had a little problem passing the taxi, giving the driver no choice but to stop. The taxi driver opened his window, but the guards weren't interested in playing nice. "Who were those two women this late?" The guard demanded. "Where did you pick them up?" The second guard interrupted, "Where were they going?"

The taxi driver did his best to hide his fear. "I'm trying to make an honest living. They came from a funeral of a relative. Do they have to have permission from you guys?"

Speaking in unison, it was obvious the guards were not happy, "You keep your mouth shut! You want to go with us and never see your family again?" The driver immediately shut up. The guards paced back and forth, looking over their motorcycles, just waiting for him to open his mouth, but he didn't. Satisfied that they had terrorized him enough, they let him go. He drove away in silence, cursing himself for ever supporting the revolution.

The guards would have abused the driver longer, but they were more interested in finding out who the two women were and what they were up to. Again, almost in unison, the guards jumped on their motorcycles and headed towards where the women were waiting on the porch. Before they could get there, Sophia opened the door, looking at Pary, confused. Even after Pary unveiled her face a bit, it took Sophia a second to recognize Pary, and when she did, she hugged them both and brought them inside, and shut and locked the door.

The guards slowed to a stop and watched to see what was going to happen next. Someone inside walked directly towards the window and pulled the curtains closed. The alley was dim, lit only by three electric light bulbs spaced far apart, causing a silhouette effect on the curtain. The third guard approached, and they studied the window for movement, wondering if anyone was going to peek out, exposing their guilt, but the curtain remained still. What the guards couldn't see was the sweat dripping down the women's faces as they sat in silence, trying to imagine what the guards were thinking.

Finally, the women heard the sounds of the motorcycles starting up and leaving the alley. Not at all sure, they were gone for good; the three remained at the table and talked about mundane topics to keep their minds from wandering to the unimaginable. Sophie had been Pary's classmate and close friend in high school, but their lives took different paths when Sophie failed the test to get into university. From among over fifty thousand applicants, only ten thousand would have the chance to enter the university. Sophie was among the forty-thousand students who didn't score high enough. She didn't try for entrance the second year because she had gotten married. She now lived with her husband, Jalal.

Jalal, Sophie's husband, finally woke up and entered the living room, welcoming Pary and Roxanna with open arms and heart. Pary knew him as an easygoing, kind man who was very conservative and the last thing she wanted to do was jeopardize this wonderful family because of the political turmoil she was facing in her life. She had thought of him as uneducated and considered him part of the problem before the revolution but looking back on her involvement, and the way things turned out, a part of her envied his simplicity.

He wasn't concerned about politics or who ran the government as long as he was able to provide for his family and protect them. But Pary knew that even a man like Jalal could change and risk his life and his family when it came to a friend who needed help. Friendship in the Iranian culture has always been very important. One would give everything to help a friend in need, even one's own life. Jalal had seen the guards standing in front of the alley where Pary's house was situated, toward the middle, and knew it was impossible for her to enter. He knew the danger of helping but was willing to take the risk. It was required by their culture.

Still, it was extremely dangerous. Everyone had to temper their instincts and take each new step with measured caution that gave them ample time to formulate a plan. Dinner in Iran wasn't finished until ten or eleven at night, and after that, it was the custom to sit around and visit with family and friends. Therefore, it was after midnight before Jalal felt comfortable carrying out their plan. They quietly moved to the end of his backyard, hiding behind the safe cover provided by the trees.

Javad's yard reached almost to the back of the apartment building where Pary's family lived, which allowed him the opportunity of placing a ladder against the back wall of the building just tall enough to reach the second-floor window. Although it wasn't the window to Pary's apartment, she gingerly climbed the ladder and tapped very gently on the glass.

Through the weak light, Pary could see that it was Fardad, her drug-addicted friend, asleep in his bed on the floor. He usually stayed awake all night reading, and he would sleep most of the day. It frustrated her that for some unknown reason, he had fallen asleep with an open book lying on his chest. She knew if he was as drugged, as usual, he might not wake until morning, if ever. Pary usually tolerated Fardad, but this night, she wanted to throw him out the window.

Under normal circumstances, he was the perfect neighbor, always very quiet, minding his own business, and hardly speaking to anyone except those he felt comfortable with. He spent much of his time reading, was well educated, and had been a good student until he fell into the depths of drug addiction. He was from a wealthy and well-respected family, and in their eyes, he was becoming an embarrassment. Unable to solve the problem, they decided it would be best if he did not live with them.

His father, a wealthy merchant in the bazaar, had paid an entire year's rent in advance for Fardad's apartment to keep a roof over his head and, at the same time, hoping to keep his son hidden from sight. His family told their friends he had left the country and was living in America. Living in America was everyone's dream, so it was a very plausible story.

Fardad was in a drug-induced stupor, so when he continued to hear tapping on his window, he wasn't surprised to see a figure looking in at him, trying to get his attention. Over the years, he had seen wild animals, volcanoes, snarling three-headed women, mad dogs, and vipers, so this hallucination seemed quite tame. Deciding to ride out the experience, he closed his eyes and covered his head with a blanket, mumbling to himself, "Damn! One day I should become a man and stop the drugs. Tomorrow! Tomorrow! Someday…"

Pary was extremely concerned about drawing the attention of the neighbors in the middle of the night. If anyone noticed her yelling, they would think there was a break-in and would begin to YELL thief…thief… and that would alert the guards. She thought it best to continue to tap very softly, hoping she could irritate Fardad enough for him to want to check out where the noise was coming from.

Finally, he removed the covers from his head and started rocking back and forth in rhythm to some unwritten symphony playing in his head…but that bored him in no time. He decided, finally, to face his demons by sticking out his tongue and making faces at the figure outside the window. On closer inspection, he realized it was Pary who made no sense at all because he knew she couldn't fly.

But since things rarely made sense to Fardad, it seemed perfectly natural to unlatch the lock on the window and invite her in. She wanted to be absolutely sure he recognized her. Otherwise, he was very capable of yelling, "doozd," which meant thief, at which point it would alert the guards.

Pary was relieved that she was able to get his attention but horrified that her life depended on whether she could make Fardad, of all people, understand the severity of the situation.

Once both Pary and Roxanna made it inside and closed the window, he didn't let them down. "Since when did you learn to climb up people's walls?" He asked, having fallen completely in love.

"I promise, I'll teach you if you stay very quiet and just listen."

Three hours later, the drug had worn off, and Fardad was as normal as he was ever going to get. In complete alliance with the girls, he repeated over and over that it actually felt good, at long last, to be doing something other than smoking, drinking, and getting high. For the first time in years, he felt needed, vitally important, and heroic. It was a pivotal moment in his life. He grabbed some cheese and bread from the refrigerator, and they celebrated his new life behind the closed curtain, a thin veil of protection against the brutal forces that lay just beyond.

Pary was different than most females. She wasn't superficial; there was no sense of entitlement. And unlike most Iranian women, she carried her own weight and refused to be subservient to anyone. She was strong and fearless, a tigress…that was until it came to her family. Suddenly, being so close in proximity to her mother and caring less about letting Fardad see her weaker side, Pary became needy. She was desperate to see her and to be held in her nurturing arms, even for a brief moment.

They knew it was likely that Saeed had placed watchdogs both inside and outside the building, making it all but impossible for Pary to find a way to get in to see her family. It would require constant vigilance, with Fardad and Roxanna monitoring the balcony and the perimeter of the building to make sure she wasn't being watched.

The balcony extended along the entire second floor with the door to each room opening onto it, much like a hotel. Despite the fact that Fardad said no one had moved in or out in the past six months, they also knew he spent far too much of his life in an altered state and decided to err on the side of caution. They could not afford to trust anyone. The consequences for being caught would be disastrous.

It was half-past one before every light in every apartment had been turned off, and Fardad finally gave Pary a sign that everything was all clear. Once again dressed in an Islamic outfit, Pary crept out the door, followed by Roxanna. She cautiously walked to her mother's apartment several doors away, unlocked the door, and entered, surprised to find the children still awake on the floor and her mother sitting on the prayer rug talking to God. Tears begin to run down the beautiful old woman's face when she realized her daughter had finally come home.

Pary was filled with remorse, looking into her mother's eyes and seeing the pain she had put her through. The old woman still hadn't recovered from losing both her husband and Pary's older sister in a car accident, leaving her with two grandchildren and no income other than what Cyrus and his family were giving them, but there was no more help coming from them. Nader's death was the final blow. Pary felt sick about what she had done, fighting for her noble cause, putting her mother second.

When her mother continued to pray instead of going to the refrigerator and feeding them, she knew something was terribly wrong. Pary was distraught by the thought there was no food in the house. Given a choice, she wished she were dead. What had she done to the ones she loved most? How could she explain to this poor woman who was doing everything she could just to survive that it wasn't safe for anyone to know she was there? How could she explain why she was dressed in an Islamic outfit? She needn't have worried. Her mother already knew. Pary was her daughter; how could she not know?

Roxanna did her best to fade into the background, observing the interaction between mother and daughter while the two little children climbed on her lap and started playing with her hair. Concluding her prayers, Pary's Mother looked up with a loving look of sympathy and concern, waiting for her daughter to explain, but she never did. Instinct told her that her daughter was in some kind of trouble.

Pary attempted to divert her mother's attention by opening the refrigerator, only to have her worst fears materialize when she found it empty. Without saying a word, Roxanna dug inside the secret pocket in her jacket and placed almost all the money her grandmother, Hajji Khanoum, and her uncle had left for her on the prayer rug. Hugs, kisses, and tears expressed more feeling than any words. And soon, there was the time to say goodbye.

The mother and daughter well knew it could be the last time they would see one another. It seemed the children also felt it. They all were sitting on the corner watching, quiet, and with a deep sadness. A scene Pary, herself, hated to watch, asking herself, which was more important, her family or educating her people and fighting for the goodwill of her people? A question she never could answer. She was lost in between.

*****

Upon their return to Fardad's room, Pary surprised him by giving him a hug and a kiss on the cheek. He assumed it was for removing the ladder and putting it away, but even more, it was Pary's way of thanking him for the kindness he showed her family. Pary's mother had let her know that, even in his usual drug-induced stupor, Fardad had been helping them very much with food, and if it had not been for him, the children would have gone to bed with empty stomachs.

This was a side of Fardad that Pary had not been acquainted with. She had always thought of him as a rich, spoiled, lazy boy. She was happy to learn that he was deeper than he seemed and that sometimes we can all offer more than imagined if only given the chance to prove ourselves.

*****

Chapter 31

If This Wasn't a Time to Cry... There Was No Other...

Life became more perilous for Roxanna and Pary as the situation in Iran continued to spiral downward, out of control. Unlike most, Mehdi's outlook improved daily, being much happier with himself now that he was finally making a difference. He had developed self-respect as their watchdog, their own private security guard. Gaining entry and leaving the building was still challenging, but with Fardad's skillfully placed ladder, Roxanna and Pary were able to come and go late at night without being seen. They would use Sophie's backyard when they were sure her husband was not around, using Fardad as a messenger whenever they needed to communicate information.

This particular rainy night, Fardad entered his apartment very late. Pulling the curtain shut, he carefully looked through a small opening where the two panels met, giving Pary and Roxanna each a chance to look out. Fardad told them he had seen Abdullah knock on Pary's mother's house, and knowing Pary and Abdullah had been long-time friends, she invited him in.

Pary would have been more concerned had she opened up about her private activities to her mother, but she hadn't. She had been very careful to keep her political life secret, knowing that if her mother knew what was actually going on, it would pose a grave danger to her and her grandchildren.

Fardad's renewed sense of self-worth made him a loyal soldier to their cause, so Pary's first thought was to send him back out to do reconnaissance. He went willingly, at first walking past Pary's mother's, glancing casually in her window. He saw Abdullah sitting on a box, drinking tea while talking to Pary's mother, who, much to Fardad's dismay, had seen him pass by. Abdullah and Fardad knew each other, and Abdullah was happy to see Fardad. However, Fardad played dumb and walked away and quietly entered his place.

*****

Roxanna, Pary, and Fardad sat on the floor of his room in the dark, trying to figure out what Abdullah wanted from Pary's mother. The one thing they all agreed on was that he worked for Saeed and couldn't be trusted. A loud knock on the door sent a shock wave through Fardad's body, paralyzing him. Pary, however, jumped into action and grabbed her gun as Fardad shoved them both into a small storage area, separated from the rest of the room by a simple curtain.

Peeking out and finding Abdullah standing by his door in the rain, Fardad tried to calm down. He took a long, slow breath in an attempt to quiet his pounding heart and opened the door. But not before he put his hands in his pocket to hide the trembling.

"I have no place to go. Can I spend the night here? I will leave before dawn, I promise. I have no place to go." Abdullah entered without an invitation, afraid Fardad might shut the door on him.

"You're welcome," Fardad whispered unconvincingly.

"I will leave before dawn when the rain is lighter," Abdullah assured him. Fardad's entire place was one room with a small storage area. It was all the space he had to live, sleep, cook and entertain friends. Fardad put water in his tea pot and placed it on the fire for his unwelcomed guest, deciding to use the time to see if he could get any useful information from him. "I am not used to people being around me and hate politics... but you can stay here to get warm."

Abdullah could not wait to get in, "I must find Pary before Saeed finds me and kills me...Please tell me where she is if you know!" Abdullah's voice sounded different than Fardad remembered, and it only confirmed why he had alienated himself from them all.

"You look horrible. That is why I do not want to do anything with politics. That is why I do not know anything about her. Do you think I want Saeed to kill me?"

Fardad suddenly realized how important he had become to Pary and Roxanna. He was at the top of his game and found the sensation invigorating. Without drugs, his mind was clearer than it had been in years, and he wanted to test it to the limit. "What is bothering you, my friend? What could be so important to bring you out in the rain here? Abdullah looked at him in amazement. He had never seen Fardad when he wasn't drugged before.

The storage, where Roxanna and Pary were forced to hide, was so small, their bodies and feet were touching; Roxanna's head was resting on the wall; she looked at Pary holding her gun, resting her hand on her knee, peaking out through the small opening of the curtain, at Fardad and Abdullah inside the room. They found it almost impossible to remain frozen in such an awkward position, causing strain on every muscle, but they had no choice. And to make things even worse, Pary had stuck the gun back in the waist of her pants, and it was digging into her right side.

From what little they could see where the curtains met, Abdullah looked exhausted and run-down, and when he spoke, his voice was frail and weak. This was not the same Abdullah that Pary had grown up with. She had to remind herself, since the revolution, no one was who they once were. Thankfully, the rhythm of the rain hitting the rooftop was loud enough to cover any inadvertent sounds coming from the storage area.

Pary was able to move her eyes just far enough to the left to glance out the back window to try and see if Sophie was home. Any time Pary and Roxanna needed to leave the apartment, Pary would either turn the lights off and on or shine a flashlight in Sophie's window to communicate with her. Pary and Roxanna were in agreement that this was one of those times. If they didn't get out soon, their legs were going to start cramping, and it would be too painful to tolerate.

Turning the light on and off was not an option as it would have likely been seen by Abdullah. Pary adjusted her gun and then carefully took the flashlight out of her pocket, making sure not to drop it. She had only one chance to direct the beam at Sophie; more than that was just too risky. Roxanna watched the men, waiting for a time when Abdullah's back was to them so there would be less chance, he would see the light. Finally, she nodded. Pary turned the flashlight on and directed the beam at Sophie's apartment. They waited, but there was no response. They couldn't believe their bad luck.

Pary was getting extremely frustrated with Abdullah. If he was working for Saeed as they knew he was, he would have had a place to go on a night like this. Clearly, he had a motive for being in Fardad's living room, and she believed it was to get information from him. Pary was aware that Abdullah may have been playing the role of victim in an effort to secure Fardad's trust. She could only hope Fardad was smart enough not to be tricked into giving any information out.

They listened closely to Abdullah's whining, "I have done some bad things, Fardad. I'm going to hell. I thought I was doing the right thing, but I was brainwashed. As you know, Imam Khomeini's order called on us to turn anti-revolutionaries in. I believed that was the right thing to do. I turned in my own sister, but the guards raped her over and over, then they tortured her to death. Did the Imam do anything? No. Nothing! I thought I was doing it for Islam, for the good of the people. I was lost and confused. They raped her over and over! When my mother found out, she told me she wished to never see me again. She said I have carved a seat for myself in Hell. She is right. I am going to Hell."

Watching tears appear in Abdullah's eyes, Fardad was now feeling like a big man. He was important for the first time in his life. He had a man sitting in front of him confessing his sins. He understood that many were caught up in the hype of the revolution and the hope that it gave. He understood how it made men act in ways they normally wouldn't. Fardad didn't believe it was an act. He believed Abdullah was one of these men.

"Do you have some . . . I want to forget about my pain. I really need it . . . please. I cannot sleep; I am having nightmares, please, I beg you."

Abdullah's begging was accented by an abrasive whimper that was starting to get to Fardad. He watched as tears began to run down Abdullah's cheeks, wondering what he should do. This scenario was spiraling out of control, each second becoming more precarious. Pary and Roxanna were hoping he would not offer him any drugs. What if it was a setup, and they were looking for an excuse to arrest Fardad? The room would be overrun with Saeed's men in seconds.

There was still no response from Sophie, and unless she said it was okay to place the ladder on the back wall underneath Fardad's window, there was no means of escape. Pary heard Fardad offer Abdullah opium and looked through the curtain, ready to storm in and kill Abdullah before his actions brought the rest of the guards in to arrest them.

She heard Fardad's voice trying to control him, "Don't cry. Men should not cry. I don't want you to cry. Come on, my friend, I am nobody, but I never cry." Fardad smiled at the curtain, attempting to send a signal that they shouldn't worry. He had everything under control. That's all it took. Now Pary was twice as worried. If Fardad was going to start messing with drugs... anything could happen.

Fardad showed Abdullah how to make the opium pipe while he shared his own recent revelations about life, "I am in hell also, and have been for a long time. Every night I wish I was dead, but these days I don't . . . I feel I am awakened. I feel I am a man."

Hours passed, and they were both euphoric, high. Pary and Roxanna were still crammed into the storage room but had managed to make themselves relatively comfortable, knowing Abdullah was too drugged to notice them even if they walked right in front of him. Fardad continued with his mantra... "I said, don't cry. I told you, men do not cry. Just talk. Talk it out. It will help you to feel better. Talk even if I do not listen. Spill it out." Abdullah began to cry so hard he could hardly speak, "I may not be alive in a couple of days. I cannot carry my guilt with me. That is why I went to see her mother, to tell her what really happened to her son, Nader…but I could not do it. That is why I asked for Pary…I want to tell Pary before I die, but I may not have the chance to see her, either. Saeed will find and kill me."

Fardad smiled as if that was a good thing… "Just tell me, I will go to her mother and tell her, and who knows? Maybe I will see Pary someday and tell her, too. Tell me…"

Abdullah did some long, hard thinking before he spoke, "I killed my sister. I killed my best friend, Nader. I did not kill him, but I watched as they set him on fire. I took him there. I set him up, but I did not know Saeed had such a plan. I met him and took him to the south side. I told him Cyrus wanted to meet him, but it was a lie. We drove to the outskirts of town to an old warehouse and stopped. We got out and went inside to look for Cyrus, but instead, Saeed was hiding there with some of his men.

They came out, and before I could say anything or do anything, they sprayed Nader with gas, and Saeed lit the match, and I watched him! He was just staring at Saeed and smiling. Nader thought Saeed was joking or playing, and I thought the same. Saeed told me he just wanted to speak with him, but Saeed threw the match on him. Then Nader's smile faded away as he went up in flames. I watched a man who was my best friend, who had helped me many times, burn to death, looking straight into my eyes, and I did nothing.

On the way back, I asked Saeed, 'Nader was your best friend. How could you do such a horrific thing? What happened to you?' He stared directly into my eyes, like a sociopath, with no feelings, and said, 'He may have talked to the Savak, maybe already did, or maybe he was a dog of the Savak, or he would have been arrested by now.' There was no remorse or sympathy in his eyes. They were as cold as stone. It was Saeed's plan to blame his death on the Savak, to get more people to rise up against the Shah." Abdullah was sobbing, his words barely audible through his quivering lips.

Pary and Roxanna held each other's hands, squeezing them together, trying to deal with the heartache by sharing the pain. Tears rolled down their faces, but still, the story was so horrendous, Pary wasn't convinced of its truth. She didn't want to believe.

But Abdullah was far from finished. He had opened the floodgates; the wound that had been festering for so long was ripped open, and the agonizing truth flowed out of him with Fardad sitting there listening to his sins. "The next day, there were fliers everywhere, put out by Saeed, that said the Savak had arrested and burned Nader to death in the most horrific way. They considered him as one of the oppositions, and they said it was revenge for the bombing of the police station."

Fardad stared at Abdullah, riveted by the unlikely storyteller sitting in front of him who alternately divulged information and then beat himself up for his part in the horrifying acts. Finally repeating over and over, like a mantra, "I will go to Hell, I participated in many killings..."

Abdullah was strangled, and his voice was barely audible. He had to be patient for a while to find his center. His body was shaking. Roxanna held Pary tightly in her arms to comfort her. But there was no medicine that could work on Pary at that time. The suffering of the two was common. Pary had tried her best not to shed tears, but she could not hold back her tears anymore; her silent tears now covered her face. Everyone was still waiting for Abdullah to continue, but it seemed his long silence signaled the end of the line. His throat was blocked; sadness and emotion-filled his mouth. The wound that had grown in his soul and body for a long time had exploded, and now pus, blood, suffering, and hatred had taken over his whole being.

Fardad stared at Abdullah, imagining that he was sitting at the foot of an incredibly famous and different storyteller. Abdullah kept repeating, "I will go to hell ... I killed a lot of people, for the sake of Islam ... I thought I was doing this for Islam ... I made a mistake ... I want to die." Fardad was heartbroken for him and wanted to tell him not to cry; men do not cry. But he stopped himself; that had nothing to do with being a real man.

He had been involved in the massacre and atrocities of his people; he had wounded the history of the country. If it was not time to cry now, then it never was. Fardad could only prescribe more opium to endure the pain and resentment. It was the only drug he was familiar with at the time; it was the only way Abdullah could escape his guilt, "You need ... I have no more," Fardad muttered softly.

By now, Abdullah's words were cluttered and incomprehensible, slurred together. He was gasping for breath as tears fell in torrents down his face. "I thought I was doing it for Islam . . . doing it for the truth... I was wrong . . . I want to die." Fardad could only think to offer more drugs, as that was what was familiar to him. It was the only way he knew to escape. He knew well the thoughts that could haunt a man's mind, and his sympathy for Abdullah was enormous, "You need as much as you can get, my friend."

Fardad truly felt sorry for him and was just getting ready to, once again, say, "Friend, don't cry. I said men don't cry." But then realized that this was a time to cry, being a man or not was irrelevant, mass murder was an atrocity, a scar upon the history of his country, carved and paved in blood.

"I am not a man. I am weak; my mind was given to enemies of my people. They filled my head with lies. Made me believe I was an extension of the hand of Allah. If I was a man, I would have killed those who raped my sister, the one who raped her. After a few months, I was able to get her out of harm's way. It was too late. She had gone mad from the constant and brutal raping of her body and spirit. Nothing was left of her. She was an empty shell. When I approached her, she stared at me as if she didn't recognize who I was, then spit in my face. I did nothing to protect her. In her eyes, I was no better than the abusers.

And the words those mad men used to justify their actions, 'You are a virgin, God only protects virgins from death, so we have to rape you, so you are no longer a virgin and you then, are not protected under Islamic law. It is because you deserve to die.' That is what they said. The next morning, she hung herself. I was there to find her. I pulled her body down."

Fardad leaned back in a trance, staring at a small hole in the wall as a refuge, wishing he could crawl into it. Pary and Roxanna held each other for support as they attempted to digest the gruesome details. The next words that left Abdullah's mouth were quiet, "This is living in Hell. Sorry, I am. But I will not die quietly! I will not die until I look into Saeed's eyes and spit upon his face as I stand over his dead body."

For a brief moment, a hush sat heavily in the air, like the scent of rotting onions and potatoes. The sound of rain overtook the silence, pouring down in sheets outside. Echoing from the rooftop, it was like a contrasting movement in a nightmare symphony, juxtaposed against the melodic dancing of rain drops; exquisite music drowning out the vocal composition of what they just heard, the orchestra bringing them back into the present and out of the nightmare Abdullah had just exposed.

Roxanna felt as if she was on a stage, an actor in a strange and violent play of which there seemed no end. It was way past midnight, and they were all exhausted, unable to keep their eyes open a second longer. Drifting into an edgy sleep, they hoped to erase the horrific images Abdullah's words had created in their minds.

*****

The rain subsided, and light was now beaming in from the small window, letting them know it was morning. Pary and Roxanna had been in their self-imposed prison so long their bodies were locked in pain, but once they were able to straighten their legs and move, they carefully assessed the situation. They were angry with themselves for not taking turns sleeping throughout the night so they could monitor events in their very fluid environment.

When they peeked through the curtain, they saw that Abdullah was missing, and Fardad was standing at the window looking out. Then Fardad grabbed his sword and walked out. Quietly and carefully, they went to the window and peeked out through the outside curtain. They saw Abdullah standing on the top of the stairs, staring into the yard below. Pary's mother and her sister's children were standing on the balcony, also watching the confrontation.

An old man was sitting by a small fountain in the courtyard, looking down at the gravel below his feet; his head hung low as if he had suffered a great shame. The man's wife had collapsed, surrounded by their sparse belongings, all she had left of her life; items more precious to her than antiques or treasures. She cried for mercy and begged to be allowed to remain in her home.

Holding on to his last shred of pride, her husband stood his ground, "This is living in hell. Sorry, I am... but I will not die." Pary and Roxanna watched what appeared to be their pompous, oversized landlord as he continued to throw their possessions on the ground, evicting the elderly couple. What he lacked in compassion, he made up for in arrogance, wallowing in his role as a bully. Roxanna noticed that he wore a collarless shirt similar to the attire that the clergy wore.

The tenants were already trying their best to conduct their daily activities, washing clothes, dishes and beating rugs while the landlord was evicting their beloved neighbors. Of course, one or two of the tenants seemed to know what the landlord's intent was; they knew that he was going to evict everyone eventually and knock it down to rebuild it. Life was hard enough, and they were hoping to get through the incident unscathed.

Just then, a man entered the yard from the alley, herding several sheep into a courtyard, something that had never been done, and now they had to worry about being displaced by smelly sheep. The landlord's intention to evict this family had become crystal clear. Chaos ensued. A few men approached him on behalf of the elderly couple only to be cursed and slapped by the beast of a man. Others, less brave but not without compassion, took their aggressions out on the sheep, pushing them out of the gated courtyard as fast as their gangling owner moved them in.

The old woman threw herself at the feet of the landlord and grabbed hold of his leg, "Please. We are old, our son is dead, and we have nowhere to go. Just a little more time so we can get money." The landlord began kicking her, but the more he kicked, the greater her hold on him became. Finally, he kicked the old woman so hard she flew sideways into the air and landed on the edge of the pond, her head spurting blood. Enraged, her husband grabbed a frying pan from their scattered belongings and slammed it into the landlord's head. The landlord's helper joined the fray, and together, they beat the couple without remorse.

The whole time Fardad watched the drama unfold from the top of the stairs. One of the few items he took with him when his family asked him to leave was a very old, ornate Persian sword that his father had given him for his 18th birthday, his pride and joy. Fardad would spend hours polishing the blade, keeping it sharp enough to slice paper, otherwise, hanging it on the wall, dormant.

Unexpected to all, including himself, he raised his sword waiving it in the air, descending down the stairs as the sun reflected off its shiny blade. He began to dance in the courtyard around the people as he cried for revenge. But before he could reach the landlord, he was interrupted by a boy poking his head inside the courtyard and yelling, "Sacrificed meat! Free meat!"

Fardad was confused for a moment when he heard the voices of young people yelling inside. He stopped with his sword, still holding it in the air. It took him a while to realize what the young boys meant and that they were letting people know free meet was being given away out on the main street. Fardad watched, annoyed, as most of the tenants sprinted after the boy. Even Pary's Mother ran to get some of the free meat, leaving the old couple to fend for themselves, causing Fardad to speak up in disgust, "Anytime you want to do something good, the damn stomach stops you."

He dropped his sword and walked out. Victorious, the landlord told the skinny man to put his sheep inside the old couple's room. The fact that the landlord had lost his audience only made him madder. He and his helper continued to violently attack the old man, hoping to win them back.

Inside the room, behind the curtain, crazed and distraught, Pary was about to give up her position of anonymity to come to the aid of the old couple when they watch Abdullah reached out and grabbed the landlord from behind. His eyes red with rage, he then grabbed the landlord's hand and slammed it over his knee, breaking it. The landlord screamed in pain as Abdullah continued his assault, flipping the coward into the fountain.

The helper rushed toward Abdullah, but Fardad's sword appeared in the air, and with a quick and lightning movement, the hand carrying the club tore off, and blood erupted from his hand. The club fell from his hand as he felt Fardad's sword touching his throat, ready to slice through. Sheep were running around bleating and crying. Abdullah looked first at the old man and then towards the bloody sword, "Nature takes its course and gives every man his turn. This is yours, and you may never get another chance."

The old man took the sword from Fardad and stood on the edge of the fountain, looking down into the landlord's eyes. He delicately raised the sword above his head, intending to pierce the landlord's heart, just as the man had done to them. Looking down at his intended victim, he hesitated for a split second before returning the sword to Abdullah and whispering, "I had no luck in this world. I don't want to jeopardize my chance for the next one. I shall not seize the opportunity to avenge evil with evil... I forgive him, but I cannot talk for God..."

The old man placed the bloody sword on the edge of the pool and walked to his wife and began to gather his belongings. Realizing the old man could have killed him, staring, paralyzed, and in disbelief. He raised his eyes to the sky and thanked Allah for sparing his life, only to see his good fortune end. Abdullah was staring down at him with one foot raised and a look of hatred mixed with anger on his face.

He watched Abdullah's foot grow larger as it slowly moved closer to his face. Finally, Abdullah placed his foot on the landlord's chest and pushed him under the water, holding him there just long enough to terrify but not kill him. When he surfaced, Abdullah pointed his gun barrel in the water and fired, giving the man a long moment to realize his bad karma. The fountain filled with blood, turning the water a smoky red.

Everything had changed with Abdullah's bullet; they knew very well that when they heard the sound of the bullet if Saeed's people did not act, other policemen would respond. But Saeed's mercenaries were the main danger for them, "My friend, you have to run, you have to hide, why did you shoot him?"

Abdullah came to his senses when he heard Fardad's voice and turned to him. He saw out of Fardad's window as he turned his gaze and saw Pary and Roxanna behind the window. After seeing Pray, Abdullah did not hesitate and hurried to Fardad's rooms.

Fardad, who was not very happy with his decision, protested as he walked towards his room, "Are you crazy or on drugs? You must run from the cage, not enter it and stand waiting to be killed!"

Inside Fardad's room, Pary and Abdullah's eyes were locked, both with guns in hand. Fardad entered and stared at the two for a while, then turned to Abdullah, "Well, my good friend, you just signed our death certificate, I am not scared of dying, but anytime they will storm in and will take us all, I am worried if in the jail would not find my medicine, and die… I am wondering if you are such an expert shooter, then why not just shoot and kill me out there."

Fardad's voice brought Pary to her senses, and within in a split second, she realized she had no choice but to trust Abdullah and take him with them other than to leave him at the mercy of Saeed. They had to leave as soon as possible. Roxanna and Pary dragged him back behind the curtain. Abdullah, in his desire to right his wrongs by coming to the aid of the elderly couple, had done exactly what Pary had been trying to prevent; bring the enemy to their doorstep. Pary knew they had minutes, possibly only seconds, to escape before Saeed and his men surrounded the building. Exiting through the courtyard was too risky. It would be filled with people; morbid curiosity befriends even the faint of heart when there's a dead body to be gawked at. It would take just one set of eyes seeing them leave the building to confirm their presence to Saeed, putting Pary's mother and the children in harm's way.

There was only one option, the ladder. They were fortunate that, hearing the gunshot, Sophie had already placed the ladder underneath Fardad's window. Roxanna went first, then Pary. Last down, Abdullah laid the ladder on its side so as not to arouse suspicion. Sophie was waiting for them at the back door. Fardad entered and watched them leave. He stayed behind, deciding to lose himself to drugs. Anything else would have created suspicion.

The courtyard was crawling with Saeed's men breaking down doors, entering each room, and terrifying innocent families. The less the people knew, the bigger their lies; anything to send the guards off in another direction. This raid was being carried out on Saeed's orders, fueled by the desire to capture Pary and Roxanna. Saeed had saved Pary's mother's apartment for himself, his desire to flush out Pary and Roxanna becoming an insane obsession.

Finding the apartment empty, Saeed's men ripped the room to pieces, tearing even the furniture to shreds. Her neighbor ran down to the courtyard and told Pary's mother of the invasion, warning her to stay away. Dropping the free lamb meat, she grabbed her frightened grandchildren and held them close, protecting them as best she could from the chaos. Still, upon leaving, Saeed saw her standing by Fardad's and had his men surround them. Like her daughter, Pary's mother was not one to shy away from a confrontation, especially if it involved protecting her grandchildren.

Although it was shocking and very surprising for her to witness the monster Saeed had become, she stood her ground. Thankfully, it was a moment that passed quickly. Saeed had so disassociated himself with his past life and loyalties, he acted as if he didn't know Pary's mother when looking directly at her. How could this be possible, she wondered? He had grown up with her children as if he was part of her family! After ransacking her place and finding nothing, he looked at her with disgust. She was of no use to him, so he continued on.

A few minutes later, Saeed entered Fardad's room, which had been completely pilfered around him as he lay unconscious on his couch. Furniture had been tossed upside down, pillows ripped, and feathers strewn everywhere, glass broken in shards all over the floor. Saeed kicked the addict, but he didn't move. He pulled him off the couch and watched as he rolled on the floor, unconscious and completely unaware of the turmoil surrounding him.

He had two choices; throw away all his opium or eat it. He did not have time to smoke, so he had to eat them, causing him to pass out and possibly die. Saeed pulled the curtain to the side and looked out the back door toward Jalal and Sophie's house. He hardly noticed the ladder lying on the ground. Fardad's voice could be heard crying out in the background, "I killed the bastard. I have done something right . . . finally." Saeed had better things to do than to watch Fardad all afternoon, but he found the addict's banter entertaining.

"See what this damn opium has done to you? You even are a killer now. They still will not believe you. You are not a man." Fardad went back and forth between chastising himself and defending his own feelings, "I am a man! I have proven it."

*****

With Sophie's help, Abdullah covered himself just like Pary and Roxanna from head to toe in Islamic Hijab, hiding his identity as much as possible from the guards. They exited the house with Abdullah and entered the alley like cats on the prowl with light feet, carefully hugging the wall and walking its perimeter towards the alley entrance. Heading for the busy street, they could hear the same young boy run past them shouting, "Sacrificed meat! Free meat!"

People rushed out of their houses towards a late-model black Mercedes parked in front of the alley allowing the three to move among the group of people, doing their best to blend in. A woman dressed in Islamic fashion, wearing black gloves, sat inside the car, handing meat out along with Khomeini's photo. People were fighting to get the meat, a confirmation that so many were suffering economically, unable to purchase meat or other staple food items so soon under the Islamic government.

Roxanna was startled when a hand reached out and touched her. She looked down at a poor-looking little girl, holding out a small piece of lamb in one hand and the photo of Khomeini in the other. "Do you want the picture or the meat?" She did not wait for Roxanna's answer. She handed Roxanna the photo of Khomeini and ran away, keeping the meat.

Pary grabbed Roxanna's arm and pulled her along, knowing Saeed's men were still searching for them. They looked at Abdullah with mixed feelings as his presence was awkward; he did not know how to behave like a woman. He was starting to feel like a liability. Pary, more than Roxanna, was convinced that regardless of his claim of no longer having any loyalty towards Saeed, they would be better off without him. She saw a taxi approaching, and without waiting for it to stop, she pushed Roxanna in and jumped in after her, yelling to the driver. "Burro! Go!" The taxi sped away, leaving Abdullah standing in the street, waving his arms in desperation.

Several streets away, the taxi became further immersed in the heavy Tehran traffic. It was madness, the driver yelling at someone else for his own mistake. It seemed everyone was on edge, seeking revenge. The taxi stopped at a busy intersection, but before the driver had a chance to ask where they wanted to go, the light turned green, and he started to move with the traffic. In an instant, Pary jumped out of the car and slammed the door, disappearing into the crowd. Roxanna attempted to follow her, but it was too dangerous. The driver yelled, "Shut the door! Shut the door!"

Zigzagging to avoid an accident, the driver slammed on the brakes and stalled in the middle of the next intersection, giving Roxanna enough time to jump out. She ran as fast and as frantically as she could, searching for Pary in every face until she finally caught up with her, "Why are you trying to get rid of me?" Pary was distraught and running out of time, "You must leave. Being with me means risking your life, and that is the last thing I want. Leave!" Pary wove her way through the crowded street with Roxanna following after her, shouting, "Leave and go where? I have no place to go. I only have you."

"Go back home. Back to America! Your father will get in contact with you. Go back home and come back when it's safe." Feeling helpless, Roxanna screamed in despair as she worked her way through the crowd, "I can't go home! I don't have a passport! The Savak never returned it to me. I can't even get a hotel without a passport! And the American Embassy closed down! I have nowhere to go, and I have no one else. Just you—" Pary stopped short and cut her off, "No, Roxanna, this is not your struggle. Get out before it is too late. Go to your grandmother's place, Akbaar will find and help you. Swedish Embassy, go."

"This is my struggle! I'm just as much a part of this as my father is—and as you are..."

"Why don't you understand? Being with me is like being with a time bomb! Your life is not safe. Please go away and don't follow me."

With no taxi in sight, Pary jumped into a random car as it passed by. Roxanna watched, horrified, as her friend disappeared into a maze of traffic, leaving her with no way to survive. She had no direction, no one to turn to, no place to stay, and no way to leave the country without a passport. Never had she felt so alone or more terrified.

*****

Chapter 32

When You Are Imprisoned by Your Own Convictions...

The taxi stopped a few hundred yards from the Swedish Embassy. Roxanna, sitting in the back, noticed several Revolutionary Guards standing around, on the lookout. After the takeover of the American Embassy, The Swedish Embassy at the time was taking care of American citizens in Iran. Roxanna had hoped to make her way inside, but the driver warned her that the minute she got out of the taxi, she would be swarmed by the guards and arrested. It wasn't worth the risk.

A short time later, the taxi stopped in front of a bookstore called "Kamran" in the north of Tehran, the street called Vozara. Kamran was Cyrus's friend, and Cyrus had introduced them all because of their similar beliefs. Roxanna stayed in the taxi, watching the store and its surroundings for a while, making sure all was as it appeared; quiet. Seeing nothing suspicious, she paid the driver, crossed the street, and looked in, but the stores appeared to be empty.

Disappointed, she remained at the entrance, whispering Kamran's name, ready to run if she had to. A tall, hefty man with a beard and mustache came out from the back and looked at her, trying to figure out who she was. Roxanna had never seen him around the store before, and her first reaction was to run, but she had nowhere to go, so she waited to hear him out. "Wait here." She could hear him talking softly on the phone. When he returned, she was gone. He looked outside, but she was had disappeared.

*****

The rain was falling. The night was wet and sad. Roxanna sat motionless among stacks of trash in a quiet alley, not visible to the public eye. She could not get any help from Kamran; she was told he was out of town due to a family issue. Everything is dead silent around her. She sits leaning on a cold wall. Suddenly she hears a voice; "You are addicted, too? Shame on both of us, you see, I wasn't always like this ... too many sudden changes, like I do not know our people anymore. Too much violence... it may help not to feel the violence..."

Roxanna found the voice she heard was coming from behind a stack of boxes. A skinny, young drug addict in his 30's is holding a piece of bread towards a white cat.

The sky opened up, and it began to rain harder. Roxanna's voice could be heard over the man reacting to the rain. He grabbed a few boxes and covered himself, trying to keep the cat dry.

Roxanna stared into the rainy dark night; she had almost forgotten her previous life, memories so old they were fading to black and white. Even thoughts of her mother were fading, like an old photograph. Her heart bled for Nader and Peter, ached for Pary, cried for her father, and longed for Cyrus. Still, Roxanna felt as though she had been reborn, gaining life from the ashes of those lost, like the Phoenix. She was Iran and its people.

This particular night she reflected upon her grandmother, longing for her, feeling cheated of her love. If she was being selfish, so be it. Unlike the lonely childhood that had left Roxanna needy and insecure, her grandmother had given her a taste of what it was like to be part of a loving family, including Akbaar and the children. She cherished the warmth and security, the sense of peace that had come with being surrounded by people you loved and who loved you back.

She had become addicted...to love. Only to be scarred again by her grandmother's death, so final, so cold and incomplete, stripped of goodbyes. The pain of being unable to tell her grandmother how much her love had meant to her, of being forced to whisper her goodbyes, kneeling over her grandmother's grave, was unfathomable.

It seemed that with each loss came less sleep and more time to think about what Roxanna wished never to have imagined. One by one, all of Roxanna's hopes slowly dwindled away as the people she had grown to love disappeared. Both Cyrus and Pary felt that, for those who were fighting for true justice and freedom, the real fighting had just begun.

It was a way of survival much harsher than before, living life underground. The Shah was gone, Iran in turmoil. The precipice had been reached. There was nowhere to go. And the rules had changed. It was merely a question of time before the walls came tumbling down around and atop them all. Staying alive was the primary goal encompassing everyone's mind.

Life in Tehran was dangerous for everyone, but Americans who remained in the country put themselves at extreme risk. In order to survive, Roxanna had gone into total isolation, having no contact with anyone. Her only hope had been Cyrus, and she wasn't even sure he was still in Iran. Living in the shadow of Saeed's men was her greatest concern. She knew he was obsessed with her and that they had orders to find and arrest her, perhaps even kill her. She was lucky to slip through his fingers once. She was the one that got away. He would not let that happen again.

Rain slammed the city, relentlessly lulling its occupants into a deep sleep. Roxanna, feeling like a caged animal, took it as an opportunity to slip out into the night to stretch her muscles and perhaps even search for Pary. She welcomed the rain, its pounding wetness cloaking her like wet seal skin. Her heart began to pound when she noticed a Revolutionary Guard car passing by. He made a U-turn and stopped in front of the alley. Pulling his personal raincoat over his shoulders, he exited the car and peered through the alley, shining his flashlight, taking all the time in the world to look for anything unusual. Disappointed, he got back in his car and left.

Collapsing under an overhang in the alley, alongside the bookstore, she could feel herself succumbing to feelings of despair and defeat. Scanning the surroundings to be sure the guards were gone, her eyes landed on a public telephone booth being lashed by rainfall. She blew hot air into her cupped hands to try and warm them; her eyes were fixed on the telephone booth. She was lost in deep thought. Subconsciously, she was searching her pockets for a phone number; she was thinking that the only hope she had left was…Dorian MacGray. Still, her eyes did not leave the public phone booth, standing alone, being lit by the dim streetlight.

A few minutes later, fearful of being noticed at any time, she saw no other choice but to take the risk. She sat inside the phone booth so as not to be visible and held on to the receiver as if it were her lifeline. Every drop of rain falling and punishing the phone booth was frightening to Roxanna.

"Hello?" Dorian's voice sounded groggy.

"You said to call if I was ever in trouble. Well, I'm in a world of shit right now." Dorian knew immediately who it was. She told Roxanna she was probably safe where she was for at least an hour and to watch for her black four-door sedan. She was on her way.

Although the rain was relentless, to Dorian, it was just another minor annoyance in her already complicated life. Pressing ahead, she drove through the streets of Tehran like her father was Chief of Police. She was untouchable, and she knew it. When she got to where Roxanna was supposed to be, she saw no sign of her. She pulled off onto a side alley and stopped, accessing the situation.

When she felt it was safe to continue and flashed her lights three times. Nothing. She flashed them again. Finally, Roxanna appeared from a pile of empty boxes and trashed pulled her drenched body into the car.

The silence was broken only by the pounding rain. It was obvious to Dorian that what she had been trying to avoid had already happened. Her efforts to get Fred to find a way to send Roxanna back to the States before she became an innocent victim had failed. The "kid" was still in Tehran being used as a pawn, a puppet, a shill, a scapegoat, whatever her political friends needed her for.

She had come a long way since they first met, from American tourist to being on the most dangerous list a person could be on in Iran. The new Iranian secret police, Savanna's hit list. Dorian didn't pressure her for information. When you're drowning, it doesn't matter who threw you overboard. What matters is keeping your head above water, and that's what she was there for, to be Roxanna's lifeline. First things first, "Do you have your passport?"

"Savak never returned it. And now there is no Embassy to get me a new one."

When there was no response from Dorian, Roxanna looked over and realized her attention had been diverted to something in her rearview mirror. She looked behind to see flashing red lights pressing down on them, punctuated by four sets of headlights being turned on in unison. The effect through the rain was dramatic enough to send Roxanna into a panic. Dorian, on the other hand, looked like she was studying a chess board, plotting her next move. As tricky as it must have been, the Revolutionary Guard's jeep and several of his other cars had been traveling without lights.

The first car passed the jeep, sped up in front of them, and slowed, forcing Dorian to come to a complete stop. A second car passed the jeep and pulled up alongside Dorian, blocking her in. Two young guards wearing beards approached the car in the rain, their machine guns pointed at Roxanna while the other two, one of whom was middle-aged, approached with their guns pointed directly at Dorian's window. She rolled down her window, poker-faced, not wanting to give away her hand.

The middle-aged guard, who was wearing green American Army jackets and feeling like kings, spit on the side of the road before speaking. He knew the younger guards were watching him and wanted to give them their first "How To" lesson in intimidation. He let his actions speak for him. Go slow, let the person in the car sweat. Make him nervous. Terrify him. Let him dredge up every reason why the guards stopped him. Then wait for him to blurt out his defense. That way, you find out what he's guilty of.

It might have worked most of the time, but not this time. It was an all too familiar game to Dorian, something she had thought to the man's boss. She was willing to sit there all night and let the guards stand in the rain. After what felt like an eternity, the older guard realized he would have to resort to Plan B. He sized Roxanna and Pary up and decided they were American. In that case, he would bully them in Farsi, "American? Running away…?"

Dorian calmly smiled and spoke up, "Yes, we are American..."

The guard cut her off, "Yes!? American from an American Embassy, hiding…" He grabbed the door handle, but it was locked. Knowing his guards were watching, he reached in the open window and unlocked the door. "Get out!"

Dorian continued the conversation in Farsi, "I'm going to reach in my glove compartment. You're not going to shoot me, are you?" At which point, all of the guards pointed their guns at her, just waiting for the opportunity. The older guard waved his hand to call off his troops and nodded for her to continue.

Dorian removed an envelope and took a piece of paper out of it. "Maybe you should look at this…" The guard reached for the letter, but Dorian pulled it further away from him. He tried to grab it a second time, and once again, she pulled it away from him. "You do not want me to bring my hand out, so the rain washes your Imam Khomeini's seal. Besides, he personally told me not to give it to anyone. He said, if you have any questions, follow me to Imam's place. I know how to get there. Do you want to follow me?"

The fact that she was speaking in Farsi had caught the attention of the others waiting on the sidelines. They moved in, standing guard with their machine guns. Another older guard, his ego larger than Mountain Damavand, had reached his limit. "Dirty murderers! Americans? Running to hide?!" By then, the middle-aged guard had noticed a seal on the letter and tried to regain control of the situation. The older guard asked Dorian her name before studying the letter to be sure that it was Khomeini's seal.

Satisfied, his demeanor changed, and he became extremely accommodating, waving to the guards that all was well. "Let them pass! Let them pass! They are American, but they have Imam Khomeini's permission with his personal seal. They are one of us." The guards jumped to attention, opening the way for Dorian to leave.

"Madam. Do you wish for us to escort you to your place?" Dorian shook her head and waved a polite 'thank you' to the guards as she continued her journey. Roxanna sat motionless, holding her breath, until the flashing red lights, dancing in the rain, discontinued their threat. It took at least another minute before she was able to get the nerve up to ask the question haunting her. "What was that all about? Who are you?!"

Dorian was busy thinking about other things and didn't even hear Roxanna's question. Something was bothering her, and she was trying to unravel the dynamics of the situation before it turned into a serious problem. She had been trained by the CIA, she was the best, and she knew it. There was no situation she couldn't handle. And even if she couldn't control it, she was trained to control herself at all times.

Yet when it came to dealing with Roxanna, she found herself overcome with deep, conflicting emotions every time they had any type of interaction. She found herself acting unprofessionally on all levels, and it frightened her. She had learned the hard way that there was no quicker way to turn an ordinary situation into a potentially dangerous one, but she couldn't help herself. She noticed Dorian watching her closely with a smile, loving the thrill of it. Roxanna intrigued, could not help but to speak her mind. "Who are you?!"

Dorian looked at her, debating how to answer, "You ever hear a man talk about a woman and say, 'You can't live with 'em, and you can't live without 'em'? That's me. I'm the woman no man can live with.... or without. However, you'll be safe with me. Until I find a way to get you out of Iran." Dorian's car disappeared into the night.

She laid out some towels and clothes for Roxanna and left her to unwind while she looked for something to make for dinner. Roxanna let the steaming hot water glide over her body as she took a long shower but finding herself too weak and exhausted to stand for long, she lowered herself into a sitting position and tucked her knees up into her chest. She watched the water draining into the hole, feeling as though it represented the story of her life.

Everything she had worked for, fought for, longed for, down the drain. What a waste. She felt broken and old. Ashamed. She had never failed at anything in her life, but it wasn't until she went to Iran that she realized she had never attempted to do anything in her life, so it was easy not to fail. She reflected on her childhood, living with her mother and going to school.

At the time, she had no idea how spoiled she was or what a sense of entitlement she had. She had never known how easy she had it. How quick she had been to judge her mother, her father, without walking in their shoes. She was ashamed of who she had been and hoped to continue on a new path of enlightenment.

Roxanna slipped into an old pair of Dorian's jeans and a top before making her grand entrance into the kitchen. Dorian couldn't help but smile at the way her clothes didn't quite fit her. Still, the jeans worked, and the two sat down together to share a simple Iranian dinner of Kabab and rice which, to Roxanna, was incredibly delicious. After being in Iran so long, foods that had started out as new and intimidating now felt like comfort food. "We have to get you back to the States as soon as possible," Dorian said.

Roxanna looked at her helplessly, "But Savak never gave my passport back..."

Dorian waved her hand, unconcerned. "They'd arrest you at the airport as soon as you handed them an American passport!" She thought for a minute, we'll get you a new passport through the Canadian Embassy."

A worried look came over Roxanna, "It seems you are the only chance I have to help me to see my father. At last!"

This was a question Dorian did not want to hear from Roxanna, so she had to be honest with her, "He's the last person you want to have contact with. He has more Savak enemies than ever before. I guess we already talked about this… You'd be endangering your life and his. If the Revolutionary Guards get their hands on you, forget your father! You'll never see anybody again! When the time comes for you to leave, you must leave Iran as soon as possible. End of story."

*****

Chapter 33

When You Share More Than a History Together...

Time was passing, and secret plans by dirty politicians were much hotter than ever, and still no concern for the Iranian people and well-being. American hostage crisis still was the hot subject and yet had not been resolved.

Politics and, specifically, juggling and struggle over taking power were in its pick. Unanswered almost daily assassination and their verbal insults were the food and headline of all papers. And still, one street in the north of Tehran was the most interest of all who were looking to get their chance to be Khomeini's interest and that he likes them.

Streetlights about fifty yards apart brightened certain sections along Darab Street, where Dorian's house was located. Cars lined both sides in the darker sections only, taking up every available parking space, signaling something was going on in the area. Although no one knew it, the most important resident in the area was Dorian.

Her place was where the most high-powered, influential meetings in the country were held, meetings that could change the future of Iran, the world. This evening the traffic going in and out of her house was unusually heavy, and although the participants did their best to be inconspicuous, it was hardly a secret that she had a lot of people coming and going.

Tucked into the darkness, Ayatollah Beheshti sat in the back of a car, hunched down, concealing himself from view. He was peering out the window, looking toward Dorian's house, very unhappy. But theirs was not the only car observing what was going on at Dorian's. About one hundred yards away, Hussein and a friend were watching everyone entering and leaving.

Across from Dorian's, more observers were camped out, indefinitely, in apartments on the second floor, over-looking her place. In one, American and Iranian CIA agents remained on high alert, accessing every move with night vision cameras and weapons, ready to eliminate any threat to Dorian or their mission.

It was close to 2 A.M. when the front door to Dorian's house opened, and people began to slip out quietly, if not unnoticed. Among them were Rafsanjani, Dr. Mostafa Chamran, Ghotbzadeh, an Iranian lady, Soudabeh, followed by a few more. They all walked to their cars in silence, got in, and let their drivers take them to their final destinations.

Soon, the street was clear except for one man, Ayatollah Beheshti, who remained hunched over and motionless in his car, observing every detail up until Dorian disappeared inside her house. He gestured for his driver to make a U-turn and stop in front of Dorian's.

*****

Inside, Dorian took the last sip of her wine and placed it in the sink with the other glasses. She'd deal with the mess in the morning. She was tired, emotionally, and mentally drained, and heading for bed. The sound of the doorbell felt like a gunshot. She considered not answering it but knowing it had to be someone who had been at the meeting, she opened the door and found herself face to face with the last person on earth she wished to see, Ayatollah Beheshti. He was not pleased. It was his belief that he was slated to replace Khomeini as the leader of Iran, and Dorian was to be working beneath him, so why was she having meetings with the most powerful people in the world without him? He felt betrayed.

"I guess I am the only one who is not welcome here any longer..."

Dorian knew he was right, but under the circumstances, chose to ignore the comment. She headed away from Roxanna's bedroom, knowing he would follow. She wanted to take him the furthest she could from the bedroom Roxanna was asleep in. She did not want Roxanna to hear their conversations. She already had a deal with Roxanna that when she has a meeting, she should stay away and told her she does not want anyone to know she exists or lives there. They both knew that was the best and much suffered for her.

Most of all, Dorian did not want Roxanna to know what was going on between Beheshti and Dorian. It was common knowledge that they had been involved many years earlier, but the extent of their relationship was never openly talked about. It had been at least fifteen years, and as far as Dorian was concerned, everything about him was "past history."

Their separation had caused just the opposite effect on Beheshti, who became more obsessed with Dorian every minute of every day. The passage of time had only worked to deepen his love for her, yet she no longer treated him like a lover. He was just one more Iranian politician she had to deal with.

"How is it that recently I am left out of your meetings when you and I know I am the one who is going to take over from the old dog, stupid, Khomeini? Is your ambassador Sullivan playing games with me? I met him three days ago before he left for the States." In an effort to distract him, Dorian adjusted her skirt just enough as she sat on a stool in the kitchen and smiled innocently as Beheshti continued,

"We spoke of how Khomeini must leave for Qom... and Sullivan is right, Khomeini is really starting to believe he is an Imam!" He waited for Dorian to respond, but she said nothing, so he continued, "Is something else going on? Why am I in the dark?"

It was Dorian's job to prepare for the unexpected, but lately, she'd been slipping, and she was really angry with herself for not assuming he'd be watching her place. Since when did he think he could spy on her? How dare he? She'd deal with that later, but for now, she had to figure out a way to keep the truth from him without causing suspicion.

Dorian knew she must keep Beheshti hopeful and, more importantly, in the dark. She knew she was the only one who could keep this deal together because she had the full trust and confidence of Khomeini, even more than his own son. She also knew that whether she went along with what Jeff asked or not, they would still stick with the deal, and that worried her. The lives of the American hostages would be in danger, and she felt she would be responsible if something went wrong.

It was believed that if Beheshti succeeded Khomeini, he would not stick to the deal that some of the Republicans made with Khomeini's people and Khomeini as well; to hold the hostages until after the presidential election which Carter and Reagan were competing in. This could place the hostage's life in more danger, especially since Khomeini's followers had control over the hostages. Her assignment was to trick him into believing he was going to take over from Khomeini as leader of Iran until it was time for them to make their move. As quick as Dorian stood, Beheshti sat down. He had known her too long; they had been too close; he wasn't falling for her tricks. "Why is it that you are having meetings with Mujahedin and other snakes like Rafsanjani, Ghotbzadeh, and others, and I am the one in the dark?!"

She gave him one of her looks before attempting to end his visit, "This is not the time to question loyalty or doubt one another... we're all on the same team. It's late, and I'm tired." It was obvious by the way Beheshti had settled into the couch, sipping from Dorian's wine glass, that he wasn't going anywhere. Dorian resorted to smiling seductively as she spoke, "You must keep your cool, or we all lose. It's normal after any revolution for parties to juggle for the position, but who wins? The one who keeps his cool. Do you understand? If Sullivan said you are going to take over ... then you will."

Dorian's smile brought back so many memories, not all of them good. Beheshti suddenly came to the realization that their thirty-year relationship, starting with their affair, had been based on lies that he either went along with, told, or ignored. He knew Dorian for what she was, a CIA operative. Suddenly, he calmed down, realizing that he, at least, knew who he was dealing with, and that was more than most people could say.

Two could play this game. He would let her think she had won him over. Well, she had, but only for a moment. Whether she realized it or not, she had offered a challenge, and he was about to accept. He wanted her more at that moment than ever before. Beheshti well knew that having Dorian by his side meant he would take over the power from Khomeini for sure.

The burning he felt inside only worked to inspire his creativity. He moved toward her with soft words and smooth moves. "Okay, okay. You are right. We go back a long way… After all, soon or later, everything will settle, and the old, stupid dog, Khomeini, will resign in Qom… and I will take over. Of course, you will move your office from Khomeini's headquarters to mine… and … when the time comes, you should resign from the CIA and move here…"

Dorian realized she had created a monster. All she wanted him to do was shut up and leave before she killed him in her own kitchen.

Neither had so much as mentioned their affair. They had danced around it as if it was some kind of a priceless commodity to be bartered with, traded, or, if necessary, used for revenge.

Dorian was allowing herself to reflect on her past, another dangerous move on her part. Her relationship with Beheshti had been wrong from the beginning, but Dorian was a teenager in a foreign country, without parents or family. She belonged to the CIA, but no one had bothered to explain the consequence to her. Compared to the big picture, accepting the advances of an older man seemed like nothing to a young girl who had no idea the power a woman could have over a man.

At the time, it was all too exciting not to experience everything that came her way. She had no idea the compromising position she would leave herself in. It simply wasn't done, but she did it anyway. And in her case, it was too late to rectify.

As she got older, she realized that she had been manipulated into something that, at the time, when she was young, felt right and good, but later, when she accidentally got pregnant from Beheshti, it turned out to be a confusing time. The decision of whether to keep the baby or have an abortion was the hardest decision she had to make.

Finally, she realized she could not kill the baby inside her and decided not to have an abortion. Now she has to care for her daughter. After her pregnancy, she went back to the states until her baby was born. She kept the father a secret. Most of all, she did not want Beheshti to learn about their daughter.

She never told the CIA she was dating Beheshti. Nor did she report his many wrongdoings because she was worried that the CIA would dig into his life and uncover their affair.

Beheshti assumed by Dorian's sudden eye movement that he was winning her over to his way of thinking, "When I take over… you can have whatever you want. Iran will belong to you. It will be just like it was… We had fun… right?" He took her hand, but she pulled back, repulsed. Damn! What was wrong with her? She has spent her life-giving Oscar-worthy performances! Why now? Why couldn't she hide her feelings from him? Because of their affair, once you've had a child together, it's hard to play games. You want to go for the jugular. The middle ground is an awfully thin line, all that separates love and hate.

Dorian spoke with anger guiding her words, "Let's get something straight… what happened between us many years ago was wrong. No one knows about it, and I want it to stay that way."

Beheshti knew he had to keep Dorian on his side, and it was his belief that the best way to ensure her loyalty was by using their love affair as a weapon. He was fully prepared for games. In this case, his weapon of choice was simple but effective, one man commonly used on women, the almighty dollar. He reached into his pocket and pulled out an envelope, holding it out to her with a fake smile, but she just stood there, glaring.

In a sudden move, he grabbed her hand and placed the envelope in her palm. "Five million American dollars. Of course, when I am in charge for good... you will have whatever, you desire." Still holding on to her hand, he pulled her to his body. It was a move he quickly regretted.

Like white-hot coals bursting into flames, his boldness fanned the angry fires raging deep inside her. She was a lioness enjoying the thrill of the hunt, preparing to go in for the kill. Looking at him as if he was beneath her, she laughed in his face, "You think you can buy me? What do you think I am!"

Suddenly Dorian remembered about Roxanna, and she was concerned she may awaken and heard them; her head turns toward the room where Roxanna was sleeping and stares at the door a bit, then turns to him, lowering her voice, losing her temper...deeper, more threatening, "Do you think your daughter is only worth five million dollars? Get out of my sight! Now! Get out!"

Beheshti was rendered powerless by her sharp words. "We have... a daughter!?" The second she whispered those words, she regretted it. Not even her daughter knew the truth. Overcome with anger, Dorian had accidentally played her trump card. "What happened between us was wrong. I broke the oath I took. This dies in here. No one will be able to save you if you try to use this against me...not even God! Not even your God."

Dorian showed him to the door. "Do not drop by here unexpectedly again. There are eyes everywhere, and the last thing we need is for anyone to see you leaving my house." Beheshti wasn't to be dismissed that easily. He hadn't given up hope that she might let him spend the night, especially now that he knew they had more than a history together; they had a child.

He whispered, "How old is she?" Ignoring him, Dorian tried to keep her temper. It had already gotten her into enough trouble. "Go. If Sullivan said you are going to take over ... then you will." Beheshti shut the door and disappeared into the night, not knowing what to believe. Beheshti realized he should not push this any longer. He felt Dorian was getting mad and that the right move was for him to leave for now. He exited the door, and Dorian shut the door behind him.

Dorian went to the kitchen, lost in the moment, got a drink, and leaned against the kitchen counter, closing her eyes, lost in thought.

"She has the right to know who her father is… and it's his right to get to know her…"

Dorian was at a bit of a loss. It took a moment to collect her thoughts, to realized she was so mad and out of it that she didn't notice Roxanna has left her bedroom and walks to her and leans against the kitchen counter next to her. She could not help it any longer and keep it secret any longer. She felt she wanted to talk and get it off her chest and release herself. Filled with emotion, she whispers, "You're not much older than Katrina. You're so much alike. Headstrong. Incorrigible! Determined! Frustrating! Both of you have Iranian fathers… And you blame your mothers for keeping them away from you, for not having them around to watch you grow up. You both have fathers who are wasting their lives in politics… going nowhere. Achieving nothing. Both are so lost in their own Goddamn… idealistic holy ideologies… that they never see the truth. But your father, he is the decent one." Those were the first words Roxanna had heard anyone say about her father. She knew then, he was alive and that one day she would meet him.

"You know … I can replace kings of countries, create wars between two nations… make peace … but sometimes it is so hard to have a simple talk with your own child. To share your experience with her… to let her know when you were young, you were tricked, manipulated into being swallowed up in an alternative world that at the time was so giant and idealistic you were swept away by it. And before you realize it, you're so deep in a pile of shit that you are about to suffocate from the smell, but still, it's like quicksand pulling you down. It's almost impossible to get your feet out. And even if you do, the smell never goes away, the guilt never leaves your heart." She paused; Roxanna watched her, choking in emotion and tears as Dorian continued.

"You want her to know what has happened to you, so she doesn't walk the same path… but… before you open your mouth, the door slams in your face, and it seems you're talking to a wall…"

Roxanna reached out and touched Dorian's hand. "You've told me. Perhaps someday I can tell her for you."

Realizing she had shown far too much emotion, Dorian changed the subject, "You've already been here way too long. Tomorrow, I'll pick up your passport. Whatever you heard tonight, understand that it's bigger than you or me or Iran. There's nothing left to do but hope the foundation of this country is strong enough to survive the flames it's going up in.

*****

Chapter 34

Lost Everything You Have Known, with No Place to Go, in the Middle of a Revolution... with the Entire Revolutionary Execution Guard looking for you...

It was a foggy and cold late afternoon in Tehran. The sky was pregnant with rain that would begin its deluge soon enough. Dorian stopped her car a few hundred yards from the Canadian Embassy, doing her best not to attract the attention of the Revolutionary Guards on the hunt for Americans attempting to escape the country. Because of the closing of the American Embassy in Iran, the Canadian Embassy, Swedish Embassy, and a few others were taking care of American citizens who were trying to leave.

Roxanna hesitated as if she was about to jump into an ice-cold mountain lake before getting up the nerve to get out of Dorian's car. Before she even had a chance to try and lose herself in the crowd, two guards approached Dorian and waved her on, leaving Roxanna helplessly alone. Just then, several guards rushed a couple and roughed them up as they were going to arrest them.

A fight broke out, and more and more guards rushed in. Now they were arresting whoever they could get hold of. She peered through the crowd, letting people push and pull her in all directions like a rag doll, watching the dynamics of the situation. It was clear that demonstration was in progress. She was almost sure she would be swarmed by the guards and arrested if she tried to move any closer to the Embassy.

Dorian's words echoed in her head. "You will be putting your father's life at risk as well as your own if you get caught. Your father has more enemies now than before." The situation at the time in Iran was so uncertain that even Dorian, with such closeness to Khomeini, was not sure she could save her. Sometimes Khomeini would know about the event way after it happened. She made her way back to where Dorian had dropped her off, hoping she had been circling the block for her but found nothing.

She felt the eyes of the guards watching, burning into her back. She quickly began a conversation with a young family passing by the Embassy, pretending she was with them, and together, they walked away from the tense scene unfolding in front of them.

Eyeing a taxi in the distance, Roxanna flagged it down, surprising the woman and children she had joined by giving them hugs before leaving as if she had known them all their lives. Her quick thinking was just enough to say to the guards, she wasn't a threat, giving her time to jump in the taxi and get away.

The skies had opened up, releasing a freezing rain as they traveled the desolate roads on the outskirts of Tehran. The driver, thankful for the fare, drove cautiously, concerned about his precious cargo, a young American woman wearing Islamic attire, traveling alone after the Revolution. The windows steamed up inside the taxi, causing the driver to stop and wipe them down on at least two occasions.

When they finally arrived at the market they had been searching for, he grew even more concerned for her welfare. The small structure was dark and closed for the night. "This is where you wish me to let you out? I think there is a mistake."

Even though nothing looked familiar through the fog and pelting rain, she knew she was close and told him to continue on a little further. To her relief, she recognized the familiar sound of wooden slats vibrating as the taxi bounced over a bridge. She told herself, "Yes, behind those trees, there's a river, and there's a cottage." She asked the driver to stop. He got as close as he could to the side and stopped. "So, this is where you wish me to drop you off?"

Roxanna hesitated, realizing she had made a terrible mistake. She was giving away her hiding place, and no one, not even a taxi driver, could be trusted. Anyone could be watching her, relaying information to someone else. She forced herself to sound relieved as if she suddenly realized her mistake before speaking. "No. Not here. I remember now. It was behind the general store! That is where they live. Further up… please…"

The taxi took off, and several hundred yards further stopped in front of the General store. Roxanna assured the driver she had friends living in the back that would let her in. She paid him and waved goodbye, slipping into the alley behind the general store where she planned to remain until the threat of spying eyes disappeared.

Although she was dripping wet and on the verge of tears, a sensation came over her she hadn't felt since her arrival in Iran. Hunger. She had gone an entire day without anyone trying to force her to eat and found herself missing Hajji Khanoum's gentle forcefulness around the dining table. Knowing she wouldn't be able to buy food until morning, she did something that, normally, she would have considered unimaginable.

Once she was sure the taxi driver was headed back to the city and no longer a threat, she tucked her chin into her chest and began to force her way through the driving rain towards the cottage, each drop bitter cold and unrelenting. She leaned into the headwind to keep from getting pushed down to the ground. Soon fear became her biggest enemy, questioning her judgment, sending chills up her spine, telling her she had wandered off in the wrong direction.

Still, she forced herself to continue on using nothing but instinct. After all, the taxi driver had already taken her to the bridge, so she knew it was there, she just had to find it on her own. Thankfully, through the rain and fog, her eyes caught the dim shadow of what appeared to be the bridge, transcending the river.

As she was crossing, a loud boom billowed down from the sky, causing her to flinch and lose her footing, falling from the rickety bridge into the raging water. Shaken to the core, she grabbed some branches to steady herself as she crossed through the rushing water. The loud boom was followed by a crack of lightning that lit up the sky with such intensity, for a brief moment, it was as bright as day. It was then she saw a wall of mud slick water raging from the hill in her direction.

Holding on to anything she could to keep from being blown away, Roxanna managed to pull herself out of the water and fight her way through the brush to the cottage. The ground was blanketed in branches and wet leaves, making it impossible to use anything but prayer to find Cyrus's key. It had been hard enough for him to find the key during the day, but at night, in a torrential downpour, it was almost impossible.

If it weren't for the night sky letting out with another loud crack, followed by a white, electric flash, Roxanna might never have found the key. Holding on to the wooden sides of the cottage to keep from being blown away, she tried to look inside to be sure it was safe but soon gave up. Her entire body was shaking from the cold, and it was all she could do to unlock the door, the wind slamming it shut behind her.

Knowing her life depended on the choices she would make during the next few hours, Roxanna visualized Cyrus and followed his footsteps as if they were there, together. She remembered how he had started their fire and repeated his actions, finding the smallest twigs in the log basket and building from there. Just as he had done, she counted her matches before striking them. There were a few, but no room for error. She searched for some old papers and twisted them together to make tiny logs, sticking them in between the twigs. A short time later, she had a commendable fire burning in the small fireplace and held her hands close to the flames, trying to get them to stop shaking. Finally feeling like she was going to survive, she removed her wet clothes and covered herself with an old cloth blanket, naked underneath.

*****

The endless storm turned the dark, foreboding days into night, the slow monotonous, passage of time taking its toll on Roxanna. The cottage that had been Cyrus's secret place before becoming their hideaway was now just small and dark, like a prison cell. He had told her to go there if she was ever in trouble. He said he would find her there, but what if he didn't know she was in trouble? It seemed she wasn't on his mind. She thought the place was safe during the Shah's time, but these days no place could be called safe for sure. During the endless hours in their secret cottage, Roxanna came to the realization that her presence in Iran was taking her father, Cyrus, and Pary away from fighting for their personal beliefs and from their primary goal, which was to guide Iran to a better place after the Revolution. She knew there was only one reason Cyrus hadn't come for her. Like her father, he had put his country first. Her thoughts drifted to her mother, and for the first time, she began to understand her pain. Her eyes caught a shadow of a man outside, on the other side of the river; he was looking into the cottage from the other side of the window. Her vision was blurry, and she was out of any energy to move or do anything to get to safety. Hopeless, she closed her eyes in sadness and left her fate in the hands of God…

*****

Chapter 35

Sad Old Jokes about Clergy; Trouble was on the Way...

The most tragic and old joke in Iran had become very much popular, again: 'If you take off every turban from the Clergy's heads, you can see "English Agent" written underneath it.' It was becoming increasingly clear to the people that such clergy in Iran was a creation of the English government in an effort to control Iranian politics.

In fact, many of the top clergy members were being paid, and paid very well, by the English government, during the last 150 years, who would call upon them when they needed a clergy member to cause chaos in Iran. Khomeini was one of the clergies who was supported by the English. History showed that the clergies in Iran are supported and are influenced by English intelligence. In fact, it is a joke that underneath the turban of all clergy, there is a flag of England.

And in the case of Khomeini, it was no different. And due to their interest, the fact that they had to act and saved Khomeini's life during the Shah's time. When he was supposed to be killed. But the English intelligence asked Ayatollah Mohammad Kazem Shariatmadari, one of the most influential Clergy at the time, to interfere. He personally visited the Shah and asked him not to execute Khomeini. So, he was sent to exile in

Iraq. And what Khomeini did in return to the man who saved his life, the first person who was put out of business was Ayatollah Mohammad Kazem Shariatmadari, and later Khomeini's government secretly and quietly killed him.

It was obvious to people like Assad, Cyrus, and Roxanna that the clergy saw themselves as the sole authorities, the only ones to guide society. There was no room for individual expression or freethinking. He and many of his friends had arrived at the conclusion that the clergies, as before, considered the people sheep and easily manipulated.

Assad could not tolerate when they were hearing that Khomeini was being fed lies and false information and asked to see Khomeini, but for the first time, was denied access. He knew exactly who was feeding him the lies necessary for all the juggling being done to obtain power, Dorian MacGray, but there was nothing anyone could do about it.

They all knew she had full influence over Khomeini, and therefore, no one wanted to get on her bad side. Assad, on the other hand, had no intention of meeting with her or negotiating with her on any level, believing that all decisions about Iran must be made by Iranians without influence by other countries.

Assad and men like him were concerned about the direction of Iran after the revolution and hoped to guide their people towards the freedom of a secular society and government. He also knew it was not the direction that America and the West wanted for Iran as a secular government would never follow their suggestions, firmly believing that Iranian interests came first.

America and the West knew a secular government would never consent to the execution of the more than four thousand people that they wanted killed. It was only Khomeini and the clergy who could use the Sharia law. And under such law, which was man-made by the same clergy with the influence of the English, the purpose being to rewrite the Islamic law, they were able to use it to their own advantage.

Assad reflected back to the time Khomeini moved to France and shook his head in disbelief. Andrew, an American official, had said, "Khomeini will eventually be hailed as a saint." And William Sullivan, Carter's Iranian ambassador at the time, said, "Khomeini is a Gandhi-like figure." Even James Bill proclaimed on February 12, 1979, that "Khomeini was not a mad Mojahed, but a man of impeccable integrity and honesty."

Roxanna wondered if the American officials even knew what they were saying, if they were actually clueless, or if the policy at the time was to sell Khomeini to the Iranian people with the objective of bringing down the Shah and his government.

*****

On one of the quiet days in Tehran, a meeting of the Islamic Republican party with over 350 in attendance was in progress. Among them were Assad, his friend Mohammad, and an older clergyman, sitting together, unhappily listening to the proceedings as the men argued, loudly. A few others were dressed in suits and ties, while the rest were clergymen. Imam Khomeini's ideology was popular, and Assad, in particular, couldn't tolerate hearing what they were discussing.

Assad's eyes roamed the room, pausing on Ayatollah Beheshti, who was one of the most influential figures in, and a main orchestrator of the revolution. Behind the scenes, he was more powerful than Khomeini and refused to pay attention to Khomeini's orders. The plan had been for him to take over after the Shah. Assad and Beheshti had a long history together, and he considered him a friend and confidant.

He, himself, had considered the idea of putting his support behind Beheshti with the objective of pushing Khomeini out of power. The two men had worked endlessly to put all these elements together, and now, looking around the room, they realized they were about to lose all the work they had done to a bunch of opportunists looking to get paid.

Assad reflected on a past filled with hard work and suffering and how his dedication to his country had affected those he loved and that loved him. He had given up everything, his entire life, just to bring a democratic government to Iran, a government that would not be influenced or commanded by another foreign power. What he didn't know until too late was that as long as oil, that black gold, filled Iran's belly, such a task would be impossible.

But as cliché as it sounded, they couldn't give up hope, not now, not after they had come so far and sacrificed so much. And now Assad, who had completely tuned out to the meeting, stared at his friend Ayatollah Beheshti, recalling their last conversation when they were at Khomeini's place.

Assad was lost in thought and stared at Beheshti like this, as if silently talking and remembering the past with him, remembering when they were sitting in a large room in the presence of Khomeini. Khomeini was sitting on a red and black mattress, and next to him was an American woman in an Islamic hijab named Dorian MacGray. Several people were sitting inside, and many outsides were waiting to see Khomeini. Of course, everyone knew that Dorian was Khomeini's eyes and ears.

Everyone knew she whispered things in Khomeini's ear, advice that Khomeini would most likely follow. Assad knew everything about the relationship between Dorian and Beheshti, and recently Beheshti had confessed to him that he had a daughter with Dorian; both now regretted the conversation. Because now both were doomed. He has sympathy for Beheshti, though, because he had witnessed and understood from conversations that over the years, Dorian had used him to advance her goals, and she had made Khomeini her instrument. It was not a secret to them that Khomeini had to go along with Dorian and their goals in the first place. Otherwise, he could not have remained in power and strengthened his foothold.

At that moment, Assad understood how deeply involved MacGray was in Iranian politics. He was in shock, realizing how easily trust could be misplaced. Beheshti continued, 'Love, most of the time will turn to hate, or maybe there was no love at all. Maybe we were using one another. She used me, and now she has made Khomeini her puppet. Khomeini is stupid; he really believes this was his revolution. This Yazdi and a man named Bruce Lange from the Embassy are responsible for taking the hostages.

Finally, Assad was brought back to the moment, at the revolutionary consul meeting, as an object hits his chest, he looks down it was an apple that was thrown by one of the clergies at his collies but missed him and hits Assad. He looked up and listened to the clergy yelling, "Islam comes first, who are the people, what does Iran means nothing when it comes to Islam… we revolt that Islam rules, not people… we revolt for Islam not for people or Iran."

The apple throwing and the Clergy's comment caused Assad to lose his patience with the men at the meeting and began to speak out, "How can you force all these people to believe what you believe? By killing them? This is not what Islam is about! These executions must stop. We are hurting Islam. This is what the English thought for you! This is what the West wants us to do! This is what the enemy of Islam wants us to do! The enemy of Iran wants us to follow?" But he was unceremoniously cut off by more clergy yelling, his words deemed blasphemous. He headed for the door in frustration as a few others, including a man wearing a suit and Mohammad, followed after him.

A stout clergyman rose and yelled, rushing toward Assad to attack him and accuse him of being against the Imam. "How dare you say such things? Maybe we cannot force ignorant adults like you to understand Islam, but we can teach and train their children, show them the light."

Assad would not be silenced, stopped, and turns. "Religion is a personal relationship with God for each and must be separated from nationality, politics, and especially, state. We cannot forget we are here to create rules and procedures that will govern this country. We are a very diverse group of people—Christians, Zoroastrians, Buddhists, Bahia, Jews, and Muslims— what you say the people who do not believe in Islam they do not belong to here?" Though he spoke firmly and clearly, his words fell on deaf ears.

Now few more clergies tossed objects they could get a hold of toward Assad. Assad tried his best to dodge the incoming items toward him and loses his balance. Without hesitation, the clergyman took the opportunity to deal a second, more lethal blow to Assad. "Don't you know we know who you are? You are an American agent… we know you have an

American wife... you and your American master will take your wishes to Hell..."

Assad could feel the blood drain from his face as he went pale. The words he had feared most in life had been spit out without any warning. The most important people in the world to him, Linda and Roxanna, the people he spent his life protecting by keeping them hidden from harm, had suddenly been publicly exposed. The clergy had known all along who he was and how to bring him to his knees. All they had needed to carry out their mission was Roxanna, and by coming to Iran, she played right into their hands, making herself, and more importantly, Assad, prime targets.

Helpless, Assad couldn't handle being any part of "the cause" anymore. He no longer wanted any part of the mess it had become. He stared at the door as Mohammad walked out and considered leaving along with him but was distracted by Hussein, who entered, looking around. Hussein found Assad standing a few rows away, watching him. It seems he was lost. Hussein gestured to him to move out immediately as he approached Assad. He could see the worried concern in Hussein's look and behavior.

Mohammad joined them. As they headed towards the rear exit, his eyes caught Akbaar Hashemi Rafsanjani leaving as well. Everyone knew he was one of the most powerful figures in Iran at the time and watched closely as he left.

With a worried look, Hussein grabbed onto Assad and tried to get him out as soon as possible. Assad was worried about whether something had happened to Roxanna. But he did not want to question Hussein with Mohammad was present. At the time, you could not trust anyone, not even your best friend.

But what Assad did not know was that Dorian had contacted Hussein and informed him of Roxana's disappearance and informed him that she had never been to the embassy and wanted to know if he or Cyrus had any information on her whereabouts. When they found out that Assad was in the party meeting, he was very upset, and Dorian immediately sent Hussein to take Assad out of the meeting. Hussein had his wire on him.

Assad couldn't figure out why he seemed worried and, in a hurry, to get him out of the building. Coincidentally, just a few hours later, Cyrus returned to Iran and was with Hussein.

Hussein, Assad, and his friend Mohmmad exited the building, heading toward a car parked further away from the building. Cyrus was waiting for them by the car. Cyrus had shaved the beard that he had had for many years and was wearing western clothing. This was to show he was not following the new trend by wearing a beard and a sloppy collarless shirt, and absolutely no ties, to pretend you were a true follower of Islam and the revolution.

As hoped, they were almost unrecognizable. Cyrus had been watching every move that was going on outside the Headquarters and was now on high alert. He opened the door for Assad while Hussein, looking frantically towards the Republican Party Headquarters, then toward Cyrus, attempted to fill him in. But it was not the right time.

As Cyrus got in with Assad and Mohammad, their car took off with Assad in the back. Hussein raced towards his car, then hesitated looked back toward the building a moment, questioning Dorian's warning, trying to determine if what she had said could have any validity to it. It was a hesitation he would never forget.

The entire Islamic Republican Party exploded; the power of the blast knocked Hussein several yards from his car while at the same time ripping his clothes and skin to shreds. He stumbled and fell to the ground, covered in blood; in front of him, the remains of the Republican Party Headquarters, being swallowed up in flames.

The car Cyrus and Assad were riding in stopped as they heard the explosion. They got out and looked back to see the building was gone. It was then that Assad realized why Hussein was so nervous and worried. He realized Hussein had just saved his life. Cyrus got them back in the car, and the car took off and disappeared into the distance. As Hussein rose up in confusion and pain, he got in his car and drove away.

A few streets away, Cyrus, Mohammad, and Assad were feeling their own repercussions from the explosion. The sound of the blast ripped holes in their hearts. Cyrus shook the image of the dead and dying men in the Islamic Republican Headquarters party and tried to concentrate on what was important. He had Assad next to him, but what about Roxanna?

Hussein told him she had disappeared and was in great danger. He was devastated. He knew there was only one place to look, but would she go there? Was he too late? Had she gone there and left? She was willful and headstrong, and he didn't put anything past her. Cyrus shook his head, remembering the day in his youth when Saeed had dared him to jump, bareback, on a wild horse. The horse had been easier to tame than Roxanna.

He had been spending much of his time these days with Assad trying to persuade him to see his daughter, but the old man always refused, saying it would be too dangerous. He had not wanted anyone to know about Roxanna being in Tehran or that he even had a daughter. He didn't trust the leadership or the direction that the revolution had taken the country and was afraid if he was seen with Roxanna, he could be putting her life in serious danger. Still, he knew where she was at all times and went to great extents to keep her out of reach of Saeed and his Secret Police.

Cyrus began to understand Assad's caution and concern, realizing, for the first time, that his reluctance to see his daughter was based not on selfishness but on love.

Bright red lights and sirens started zeroing in on them as police and fire trucks shot past, heading toward the Islamic Republican Party disaster. The streets were filled with people wearing shell-shocked expressions, trying to find out the details. Cyrus's driver turned on the radio and searched until he found a broadcaster talking about the terrible explosion and loss of life. It was an early, superficial report of facts without substance.

Mohammad could not be quiet any longer. "It's a strange time, and nobody trusts anybody. Today you're their friend, tomorrow the enemy. Bloodshed for power." Although Cyrus could hear them talking, his attention was on the motorcycle with two men on it, waiting at the light next to them. The man on the back was wearing a large overcoat that appeared to be covering something pretty big. It was rumored that men on motorcycles were carrying out assassinations.

Unaware of the possible danger, the others continued their conversation; the eldest clergy member finally breaking his silence, "I clearly see the revolution taking the worst possible course, one which will simply result in another dictatorship and more pain and suffering for our people... I sometimes wonder who is in charge or if we even had a revolution."

He continued, unable to make sense of it anything. "An American lady who is everywhere, issuing orders, and all are scared of her?! I am confused. Who really created the revolution? Us or... who? Does anyone know? Who is this American lady who is everywhere, and all are afraid of her and follow her directions? Even Khomeini!?" He waited for an answer, but none came, so he continued, "Some unknown forces behind the scenes are running the show. Therefore, we are not a factor?"

Assad nodded sadly, "Therefore, I no longer wish to be responsible. I leave it to those younger souls who are angrier."

Assad continues, his voice filled with sadness, "Do we ever learn that with guns and terror, anyone can rule the country? Sadly, such a brutal approach will end in abuse, corruption, and a dictatorship. And eventually, it will result in another revolt by the people. The losers are always the same people you are fighting to protect and make their lives better. This country doesn't need any more bloodshed."

For the first time in his life, Assad was thinking about death and wondering if he had waited too long to fulfill the dreams, he had set aside so many years ago, "Maybe it's time for us to call it quits and spend time with our children." Cyrus heard the statement and understood that Assad finally wished to meet Roxanna.

In a split second, the motorcycle sped up, paralleling them within inches of their car. Just as Cyrus had feared, the man on the back pulled a machine gun from his coat and fired at their car. While the driver swerved in an attempt to keep them from becoming an easy target, Cyrus shoved

Assad to the floor and threw his body over him, protecting him from gunfire.

The driver's guard made a vain attempt to return gunfire but, as he was sitting on the wrong side of the car, he found himself no match for the motorcycle. In an effort to bring a quick end to the chase, the man on the back of the motorcycle aimed for the driver, the bullet hitting him in the head, causing the Ford to careen out of control and crash into a tree.

Shaken and bloody, Cyrus managed to pull himself out of the mangled car and quickly survey the damage, which was much worse than he had suspected. It was so bad, in fact, he could do nothing but access the situation in total horror. Mohammad and the older clergyman were dead, the driver was dead and the guard, badly injured. Assad was lying on the floor in the back seat, blood seeping through his shirt, but alive. Cyrus realized he must have gotten hit during that single moment he left him vulnerable, trying to steer the car away from the tree.

Onlookers were already beginning to gather, offering what they could to help, lifting Assad from the car and moved him gently away from the accident. Cyrus then asked the bystanders to stay and help the others, knowing he had to get Assad away before the police arrived. He feared the assassins could still be around, perhaps hiding among the people. It was not safe for them to stay around, and he knew he must take Assad away to safety.

People were rushing to the car, shouting their support, for or against, what had just happened. A mob mentality began to emerge as people surrounded the car and pulled the bodies of the older clergyman, Mohammad, and the driver into the street, shouting, "Death to the West! Death to America!" And "Praise Khomeini."

Cyrus covered Assad with his coat to hide his blood-soaked shirt as they calmly cut through the chanting crowd. They passed several groups of people that were busy fighting and arguing politics, but Cyrus hardly noticed. He was observing the Revolutionary Guard, moving in their direction. After three failed attempts, he managed to hail a cab and carefully helped Assad inside, but his relief was short-lived.

The taxi was almost immediately forced to stop to avoid hitting the people who were rushing toward the scene of the assassination. Cyrus's eyes caught a little boy watching, terrified, as two dissenting groups broke out fighting near the taxi. Although it made him sad to see the child's face, it was just the distraction Cyrus had been looking for. But soon as the taxi drove away, he could no longer see the little boy.

The taxi passed a large mosque called Hosseinieh Ershad, with its light blue dome. Assad and Cyrus were both familiar with the mosque, which had been built across from his house when Cyrus was in high school. It had become the central gathering for the opposition, which was one of the reasons Cyrus's family moved away from the area.

*****

And finally, the taxi reached a hospital and stopped. Cyrus and the driver help Assad inside, and once inside, they were met by a team of medical professionals who rushed to help. Assad was placed on a gurney and wheeled to the operating room, Cyrus holding onto his friend's hand the entire time. Assad closed his eyes, happy to surrender to unconsciousness, as the work of saving his life had begun.

*****

Chapter 36

A Path to Heaven from A Trail of Blood...

The north side of Tehran, where all the wealthy people lived, had become the epicenter for all undercover deals and meetings. But these rich dealmakers were all newcomers to the neighborhood who took over other people's property by force. And now, gradually, the intellectuals who had been behind this revolution were waking up to the harsh reality of what they created, while at the same time, smaller new power groups, mostly clergy, were enjoying the wave to the fullest, instilled with feelings of being Godlike and untouchable.

As time passed, people like Assad, who were involved with the revolution for 50 years, and Cyrus, who had been involved for a shorter time, were getting more frustrated and disappointed by what was happening; another was the dissolution between Hussein and his friend. It was after midnight when Hussein approached the familiar door and rang the bell, but no one answered.

Uncomfortable, he looked around, wondering if he was being watched. A light came on in a window on the second floor of the building across the street, a shadow, someone hiding behind a curtain, and then the sound of the door opening behind him and Dorian standing in her nightgown, tired and unreceptive. She turned and walked inside, saying nothing as he followed. There was something about his look she didn't like.

Rather than sit on the couch where he might try and slink closer, she casually walked behind a counter area where she stored some trays ... and a gun, waiting to hear what he could possibly have to say that couldn't wait until morning. Ordinarily, she would have blasted any man for dropping in unexpectedly at such a late hour, but something in his eyes told her to act with caution; things weren't normal. It was a crazy look, enough to put her on guard up but also assume she needed to hear what he had to say.

"It just hit me... if I have the power to choose what is right or wrong for others... like deciding it is all right to taking innocent lives to enforce what I believe is right – then later I realize that I was lied to and that I was wrong to do what I did, then what are the consequences? Like robbing the museums, which I thought we were doing to guard the artworks against the Shah's people so they would not export them out... but in fact, we were the robbers, not the Shah." Hussein was having trouble hiding the deep emotional impact these events had inflicted on him. "We robbed the same people we're fighting for, robbing them out of ... how much? Perhaps four hundred million dollars and killing nine innocent workers to hide your tracks! Then we mask it in the name of Islam. Blame it on the Queen. It is all false! How can we simply lie in the name of religions... under the name of Islam... how can we criminalize the same things we perpetrate? I must question, what justifies what we did or what we are doing?"

Dorian well knew Hussein was referring to the robbery of the Iranian artifacts and jewels from the Iranian Museum of art, which had been orchestrated by Dorian and Colonel William Baker. It was clear, she did not like the tone and directions Hussein was going. She was tired and bored and really annoyed. Is this what he had come for, to give her some "Holier than Thou" speech? She had to cut him off, otherwise, he might continue spewing out his moral conscience all night. She reminded herself that she had her own speech for just such an occasion.

"You may forget in the world of politics, injustices don't exist. We do not judge guilt or innocence. All that matters are succeeding at any cost. So, if you have any questions regarding your art effects and jewels." She pointed to Khomeini's image inside a colorful frame displayed on the table. "Go and ask your Imam why he approved the robbery and the killings. He is the one making a path to heaven from a trail of blood. Not me … not you… and for sure not Islam… only him, he is 'the people,' and he is Islam now…he is your Imam…"

Unable to control his feelings any longer, tears started streaming down Hussein's face. His emotions had always been his Achilles heel, his weakness. Although he tried to control them, he had a

tendency to get so emotional that logic and balance escaped him. It was the reason he wasn't in the CIA, and Dorian was.

"He is not my Goddamn Imam. He is yours… manufactured by you and the English to do your dirty work. You used him just like you used me and Mujahideen and others. To get what you want. You told me the artwork would be kept in Iran in a safe place, but where is all that precious art now? In Libya! Murmur Gaddafi is enjoying our wealth. The wealth that could be spent for these poor people.

"You used me to set you up with the Mujahideen and other groups to eliminate a few people, that is what you said, a few people who were not right for the people's cause, not to blow up about 300 innocent people!" He walked to the door, then stopped and turned. "You didn't even have mercy for the father of your own child! Did you!?"

He moved closer into her space, a scary, angry look on his reddened face, "Blowing up 300 people? Deceiving Iranian people and your boss and the CIA? You even betrayed your own people! You don't even care about bringing hardship to your own people who were taken hostage by you, not by Iranian people… They were kept hostage to make your political party win. If all you care about is that the Republicans win your election… then how could you ever possibly give a damn about how many Iranian lives could be lost?"

Dorian was sorry she had let him in, but now that she had, there was nothing else to do but glance behind the counter to be sure she was within reach of her gun. It was there, but it would take a lot for her to use it. Unfortunately, she still needed Hussein. He was her connection to the group called Mujahideen, who were guerrilla fighters in Islamic countries, and more importantly, he was very close to Abol Hassan Banisadr, who was like a son to Khomeini, and therefore a key player.

She always looked at every situation from every angle, manipulating events to her best political advantage. Her confrontation with Hussein was no different. For the moment, he was of more use to her alive than dead. But that could change.

"You have no idea what I give a damn about because you know nothing. You are an outsider, ignorant of facts, judging what's going on behind closed doors without the knowledge of what's happening inside that room. Life is never as it appears. It's not up to me to explain what goes on between my country and yours. But understand this, as far as the Beheshti goes, I did Iranians a favor by getting rid of him."

Hussein's face flushed red with anger. "You did my people, my country, a favor!?" Dorian placed her hand on her gun and kept it there. If she needed to point it, she would, but the last thing she wanted to do was pull the trigger and alert her neighbors of a problem. To her Iranian neighbors, she was just a quiet American lady who loved Iran and her people so much she refused to leave after the revolution, a fact that made them love and respect her all the more.

The sound of a gunshot would have them coming to her aid in a matter of seconds, something she couldn't afford to let happen. They were honored to have her as a friend and under no circumstances could have imagined or believed she was the brains, the mastermind, and voice of Khomeini and Iran.

The fact that she occasionally had men over late at night was her personal business, the occasional traffic helping to disguise the two CIA teams of mixed Iranian and American agents, placed on the second floor across the street, on twenty-four-hour watch. She knew about both teams and was in constant communication, but still, she didn't want to have to count on them in a life-or-death situation. For the moment, she would try her best to rationalize with Hussein.

"Yes, Beheshti was supposed to replace the Shah. But Washington didn't know anything about him or the plan! They didn't know he was in bed with the left! With the Russians! I didn't tell the CIA because I couldn't. He would have made Iran another Lebanon. I didn't want such a thing to happen! I love this country! I love the Iranian people! Iranians are the most decent people I know."

Dorian meant every word, but Hussein wasn't buying it. He had known her long enough to know she was a manipulator and a game player. And even if she was telling the truth, he had heard enough. "The people are capable of choosing their own destiny. They do not need you or me as guardian."

Dorian could feel her blood pressure rise, "Which people? The people who rush to the streets and yell for Mossadegh today and then cheer for the Shah the next day? Or the ones who cheer and give their lives for Khomeini, believing he is their Imam, believing he would guide them to heaven? Only God knows who they'll cheer for next! How about the people who sell out their country just for the chance to go to America, or people like you who are so radical, so rigid in your tunnel vision, that you can't see the big picture, anymore!?"

Enraged, Dorian swept her hand across the counter, sending glasses and dishes flying everywhere. "Understand this! People deserve what they get! Rights aren't handed to people; they are earned. People must demand their rights, and they must demand them together if they ever hope to make change. So, if you really mean to help your people, educate them about what's going on! Give them real knowledge. Keep them informed!

"Otherwise, you've got a country of sheep! Leaders make change, not followers!" Dorian noticed that there was still a pen on the counter, and she took a swipe at that, too. "And don't you dare pull that stupid radical innocent "guilt" game on me! I should feel guilty? How many people have you killed? You're no better than me. In fact, you are worth..."

It was Hussein's turn to listen. "You intellectuals! Always wanting the goodness of the people to prevail! Look in the mirror! See yourself for what you really are! You, who blamed the uneducated, average Joe for betraying Mosaddegh in 1952, for the Shah! And then, in 1979, it was you, you again, who supported Khomeini by turning your back on the Shah! And yet you stand there and blame everything on the CIA!? Didn't you join us, the CIA, to get rid of the Shah?

"How dare you?! It's you who need to educate your people so Islam, or any other religious or political ideology that could be used for that matter can't keep turning their lives into chaos. You think you're the only country that can't find balance? Read books, Mr. Intellectual! The basic beliefs of all religions are similar. It's when ungodly, greedy, and dishonest leaders get a holier than thou attitude ... that's when corruption and lies bury religion and destroy its very foundation."

Finally grabbing the gun, "You intellectuals, you know so much you end up not knowing shit! Recall your own history! The great Iranian race, the formidable, gallant, and fair Cyrus the Great! Take a long look at who you were and who you are now after Islam bombarded the Persian Empire. Have you ever really believed that giving power to the clergy would be the best plan for Iran's future? Because if you did, you're dumber than I thought!

"Eventually, the clergy will bring so much hardship on the people that they'll lose hope! And you know what they'll do then? They'll put their faith in Islam to save them. Why? Because under Islamic law, they allegedly have a heavenly life and, therefore, will go to heaven! And when that fairy tale doesn't come true, maybe finally, they'll stop believing in false promises that have lasted a century! That's when Islam will lose its influence!

"Then, and only then, can you highfalutin intellectuals step in with a solid foundation of knowledge and hopefully, an actual democracy. When that happens, it will be the beginning of a proud Persian Empire, once again based on a foundation of respect and love. And yet you, with your big brains and lion heart, can't see how you've become the evil you deplore. But you have no place there because you would not live to see it..."

Hussein could not take his eyes off Dorian's gun as she waved her hands around, gesturing with it, fighting her instinct to stick it in his mouth and pull the trigger. She was madder than mad. "Don't you look at me like you're some wide-eyed innocent! I'm not into your Goddamn games! You better go and look at your face in a mirror and ask yourself, who allowed you to deceive an innocent girl like Roxanna and send her here and risk her life just for your dirty political purposes?

"Do you see you have no value for even innocent girls like her? Do you know that she has been missing for some time and no one knows where she is? Is she alive or dead? Then you consider yourself human? People like you should be ashamed of themselves ...! You see, you're guiltier than I could ever be, and the fact that you're blind to it makes you all the more dangerous."

Dorian was making more sense than Hussein wanted to give her credit for. He realized he had been pursuing a radical ideology and a way of attacking matters that weren't of his mindset, becoming a follower, one of those sheep Dorian had been referring to. He suddenly hated her for shoving reality in his face, destroying everything he believed in. Even if she was only half right, he was all wrong. There was nothing further to say.

No longer paying attention to the gun, Hussein shook his head and opened the door. He would leave, but not before he got the last word in, "You are sick."

"And you are dead!" Dorian whispered. She already had her hand on the phone, knowing it was about to ring. "I am okay... just some idiot friend who has his head screwed on backward..."

Outside, the team from across the street had closed in on high alert, rifles pointed on Hussein as he exited, just waiting to take him out.

*****

The hour was late, past midnight. Tehran was settling in for the night as BBC News continuously broadcasted in regard to the bombing at the

Islamic Republican Party headquarters and how many people were killed. Unable to unwind from the latest news and from his fiasco with Dorian, Hussein drove straight to the hospital clinic to check on Assad. He hadn't heard from anyone since he was admitted and was gravely concerned for his welfare.

Hussein entered the hospital and walked down the halls, slowly overcome with the sickening hospital smells that was permeating the corridor. By the time he reached the end, he was gagging from the acrid smells of urine, feces, disinfectant, and blood.

When he finally found Assad, he was asleep on the bed. Hussein couldn't understand why he had been left alone, unguarded, and wondering what happened to Cyrus. Concerned, he pulled his gun from under his green Army overcoat and quietly opened the bathroom door to find Cyrus on the toilet, sound asleep. It appeared that the clinic had taken pity on him and rebandaged his arm along with Assad's wounds.

After a night of terror, Hussein was thankful that he had walked into such an amusing situation. He was in need of a good laugh, and finding Cyrus passed out from exhaustion on the toilet with his pants around his ankles was just what he needed to help him refocus. Still holding his gun, he kneeled down, leaned against the wall by Cyrus, watching him for a little bit to wake up.

But he could not help no longer to stop his thoughts to recall his past sad memories, he could not hold back any longer to begins to hear his own voice echoing in his heart and mind, recalling his past, soon his silent voice now was whispering out, breaking his silent cry within to whisper and cry out, not knowing if he was talking to himself or Cyrus.

"No matter how hard I tried all through the life... to do the right thing... somehow everything turns to nothing... but pain..." Hearing Hussein's voice, Cyrus opened his eyes, startled, with a confused look on his face that had been well worth seeing and listening to Hussein speaking in a hushed voice, seething with frustration.

"At least in the past, they would give you a chance to change your political views. Then you stayed in jail unless you have killed someone.

But now they kill you first, then they question your guilt or innocence. They charge the poor mourner they used to murder … execute… their loved one and released their body to them… I blame myself."

A deep sorrow came over Cyrus. He knew Hussein was sincere in his actions and, like himself and so many others, had sacrificed everything for democracy in Iran. Cyrus had been a witness when the Shah sent Hussein's father to America to try to get Hussein to leave the Communist Party and join his government. Hussein was even offered a ministry and permission to marry the woman he loved, the daughter of the head of the guard of Javidan, General Ali Neshat.

Her name was Shirin, and Hussein had met her at UCLA when they were both students. When she returned to Tehran, her father did not permit her to return to America, and after she lost hope that Hussein would not change his radical ideology, she left him for good, and soon she married one of the Iranian officers. It was after her marriage that Hussein had begun to date Roxanna.

Although Cyrus hadn't met Roxanna while the two were dating in Los Angeles, he knew Hussein had found someone on the rebound and that it wasn't serious. When Hussein realized that Roxanna's father was Assad and that she was willing to go to Iran to find him, she suddenly became more … attractive.

Cyrus could see by the expression on Hussein's face that he was sinking into the depths of depression and regret of his past. He could feel his friend free-falling into a deep crevasse and was hoping that, by letting him open up to him, it would bring him back to the present and relieve his guilt or at least reduce it and encourage him to talk more and more.

Cyrus's strategy worked, and Hussein slowly, softly began to pour out a world of pain he had been holding in, "I feel guilty… I did some bad toward my people… I let the bitch use me… she used me to rob our country… You must know about her… Dorian. She was the brains behind the theft of all the Iranian Jewels and Museum artifacts from the Golestan Palace and Iranian Museum of Art at Ferdowsi Avenue in Tehran.

"And it was done with Khomeini's knowledge and approval. All was accomplished with Colonel Edward Baker leading the operation and Colonel Tavakoli from the Iranian army as the inside man to provide the team with Army vehicles, soldiers, and permits to travel through Tehran's streets. At the time, Shapour Bakhtiar was still the Prime Minister, and martial law was still enforced. The training was ongoing long before I got involved…

"Colonel Tavakoli and Dorian talked to me and convinced me to join and help. He provided the Army trucks, jeeps, soldiers, and weapons to be used. I do not know what his take was or why… It was early morning; we began from the Gholhak area, traveling toward the Museum. Several civilians were dressed in Iranian Army uniforms. Rafsanjani was one of the main architects of the robbery… Dorian misleads me to believe it was to safeguard the artifacts; a caravan of about four Iranian Army trucks was following a few Army jeeps.

"Life was going on as usual, with no knowledge that an American team to rob the country's jewels was traveling through streets of Tehran passing people who were yelling, 'Death to America.' Our caravan moved through Old Shemiran Avenue and then through the streets of Tehran going south… I was looking out, wearing an Iranian officer uniform, and I was so proud I am saving their wealth… their jewels, so they would not be stolen by the Shah or his people. Few other unmarked cars are following.

"We finally reached Ferdowsi Street. The trucks reached the Museum of Art and stopped in front. Suddenly about 100 Iranian soldiers exit them, making up several teams, running to cut off all traffic in all directions. Soon soldiers were scattered all around and, in the front, guarding the building.

"I was wearing a fake Iranian Officer uniform… and an American was wearing an Iranian Army officer uniform as we walked up to the museum door. We entered after other soldiers, some fake and some real, were already inside securing the inside of the museum. When I entered, I saw armed men scattered through the museum, holding all workers at gunpoint.

"A few guards who realized the robbery was in progress attempted to stop them. They reached for their guns, but they were shot dead and left bleeding on the floor. But I still thought we were saving the jewelry for our people... I watched the fake soldiers shoot their AK-47's in the air, yelling to the guards to cooperate or they would be killed.

"The museum guards and employees followed orders, and the survivors were laid on the floor, their mouths covered, hands and feet tied. I could see they were worried about their lives, looking at the dead bodies lying beside them. Colonel Baker and a few other Americans were present. Colonel Baker was running the show.

"I knew Dorian was on her way to the museum. It wasn't long before she entered. We were in the office, looking down from above. She stopped and scanned several Americans and Iranians who were busy boxing the artifacts. Several boxes were already packed. She came upstairs and entered the museum's main office on the second floor. I believe later, over eighteen boxes were transferred to unknown locations.

"Later, all museum employees, the dead and the ones still living were transferred to a safe house in Narmak area. They were guarded by Jaffar Shafizadeh and his team, also Abu Sharif. How interesting that suddenly your worst enemies become your best friend and ally. Abu Sharif was one of the most wanted international terrorists by the CIA, and suddenly, he was flown to France and became a trusted ally and the head of Khomeini's security guards in France."

Choking back tears, he could hardly continue, "Later I heard Rafsanjani and Dorian decided to kill all guards to cover their robbery... As you know, the nine dead workers of the museum killed in the robbery were buried at the Behesth-e Zahra Cemetery. The next day, Khomeini lied to the people of Iran and called them the First Martyrs of the Revolution. He told our people they were killed by the Shah's Army."

Hussein finished by whispering, "The recent incident at Mehrabad Airport, the shootout between Mohammad Montazeri, who was known as Ringo, was when he took the stolen artifacts, about eighteen boxes, through the Mehrabad Airport and transferred them to Libya. The artifacts were transferred to Libya to pay off about fifteen million dollars Gaddafi loaned to Khomeini via Sadegh Ghotbzadeh to spend on a supposed revolution. And God knows what happened to the rest… There was a rumor that the rest was transferred to America by President Carter's brother, who was Mummer Gaddafi's financial adviser at the time."

Hussein finally finished by whispering, "… and as you know the fifty BBC Radio stations began their propaganda yelling, "Today, the Museum of Art was robbed by the Shah's Armed Forces who took every artifact, by order of Princess Farah Pahlavi known as Farah Diba, the wife of The Shah…'"

Cyrus finally moved and sat across from Hussein on the floor. Hussein stared blankly at Cyrus for a long bit. He reached out and held Hussein's hand to comfort him. It was Cyrus's intention to make an effort to help ease his friend's pain and to help his best friend to understand that he was not to blame for what happened; that he, like so many others, had been victimized and manipulated.

Cyrus's companion did not stop talking, with tears running down his cheeks. What Cyrus did not know was that Hussein's mind was traveling to his past, recalling all the painful memories of the past as he was reliving the horrible beatings from his father when he was young and also in his teenage age.

A YOUNG HUSSEIN grips the back of a chair while his father beats him in front of his two tearful younger brothers. His father's hand comes down hard and fast, lashing Hussein with a belt over and over. Shaking and angry, Hussein glares at his father defiantly. Although tears are welling in his eyes, he doesn't give him the satisfaction of crying.

But his younger brother Homan and later his stepbrother Hesam who were watching, were crying for him. Hussein faded sound was hitting Cyrus so painfully in his heart as he was whispering through his tears. "Ever since I was a kid … the harder I tried to please my father and take the blame to save my brother from being punished, the worse it was. You try all your life to be helpful and educate your people, but they don't want to listen, and then, in the end, you realize you hurt the same people you were trying to help."

Now Cyrus was holding onto Hussein's hand to just maybe ease his pain.

The longer they talked they realized they had reached the same conclusions. Regret and revenge walked hand in hand, and there was no place for either during these precarious times. The past was history; they were all about change, born in the here and now. It was only the present that mattered. But Hussein was not done. He had to confess or talk through his pain, "I betrayed my people and my country," he muttered off.

"It's an Arab invasion in modern times..."

The two, by hearing Assad's unexpected voice, subconsciously turned and looked towards where Assad's voice came from. Cyrus had followed Hussein into Assad's room, wondering what the future would bring. Hussein looked at Assad as he slept, "See how far you have come? In the eyes of your old friends, you who were the soul and spirit of the Revolution are now their worst enemy. They want you dead; they see you as a threat to their power."

Cyrus turned to Hussein, "We have to move him to a safe place right away, regardless of his condition." Forgetting about Cyrus's injury, Hussein placed his hand on his shoulder, making him wince, "I have already arranged it with Akbaar. I will take him to the city of Brojerd by train. We have a family house in the middle of nowhere where he will be safe. You must find Roxanna, and when I get back, I will contact you and give you the location where to find him."

*****

Chapter 37

Hidden in a Place So Secret, No One Will Find You but Death...

Tehran was under attack by pouring rain and lightning. It seemed even nature's wrath showed no mercy or compassion for the Iranian people. And that was not a good sign for Roxanna, who had spent the past week huddled in front of the fireplace in the cottage, shivering out of control and burning up with fever.

Although she could no longer open her eyes or focus on her surroundings, she was faintly aware that she had thrown everything possible, including Cyrus's precious books, into the fireplace over the past few days to keep from freezing to death. The thought of it was devastating, but she had no choice and hoped Cyrus would understand.

She had even tried to burn a few wet pieces of wood she found outside; she disregarded the fact that they were soaked and unusable. She was desperate. All they did was fill the cottage with a cloud of heavy, choking smoke and alerted people outside that someone was hiding inside.

Roxanna was delirious, fading in and out of consciousness. No longer waiting for Cyrus to find her, she waited for death to take her. It was clear no one knew where she was, and no one would be looking for her. Resolved to the fact she was dying, the sound of loud pounding on the door meant nothing to her. She had opened the door too many times the past few days, only to be greeted by hurricane-force weather to do it again.

But the pounding continued, getting louder and more desperate, each bang weaving itself into Roxanna's terrifying hallucinations. Howling, hungry wolves were shaking and turning the handle on the front door; still, more were pounding on the window closest to where she was lying, their furry bodies distorted by rain streaking down the glass. Then a boom, a crack, and a flash of lightning turning the wolves into shapeshifters, half man/half animal, terrifying her even more.

Roxanna pulled the blankets closer to her and crawled to the corner, making her body as small as possible by hugging her knees to her chest while all the time was praying for help. Next, the sound of glass shattering… and everything went black. She did not even see or know Cyrus was by her side.

*****

There was a fine line between panic and sensibility, and Cyrus found himself balanced somewhere in-between. Afraid to move her too soon, he stayed by Roxanna's side, destroying cabinets to burn for warmth, endlessly wiping her forehead with towels, touching her hair, and whispering softly to her, "You are not going to die on me. You will stay alive; can you hear me? You are going to stay alive; you will…"

As no darkness and hard suffering time would not last forever, finally she opened her eyes, but this time there was no darkness or coldness or shaking worried about dying, everything was white and warm, her weakened eyes scanned through the hospital room and stopped on her angle sitting on the chair fallen asleep by her side, holding to her hand to be sure she feels secure and warm. She did not want to take her eyes off Cyrus, who had passed out after he brought her to the hospital to save her life.

Only he mattered; it was unimportant where they were; only that he was with her. The soft touch of her hands stroking his arm woke him from his sleep. They were lost in each other's eyes. Time did not exist; it stood still and they in its stillness. And finally, the first words her ears heard was, "Are you ready to see your father at last?"

A word she was waiting for years to hear. And no matter if she was still weak and was going in and out of consciousness, his words still lighted her soul and heart. She looks into his eyes as she opened and closed her eyes until her eyes could not stay close no matter how bad she was seeking or out. She only could hear Cyrus's voice whispering into her heart and soul, "Are you ready to see your father at last?" With the sound of Cyrus's harmonica to complete the heart-felt song.

*****

Chapter 38

Willing to Do Anything to Protect Friends. Even Kill. Even Die...

It was a beautiful fall day in Tehran, the trees exploding in bright shades of yellow and orange. Abdullah was sitting on a rooftop pretending to feed the pigeons, but the machine gun sitting next to him indicated otherwise. In Iran and mostly on the south side of Tehran, many men's hobby was to train pigeons. They would have large cages made of wires on the rooftop, and they would fly their pigeons almost on a daily basis.

An exciting part for them was when their pigeons recruited another and brought her along. They had a name for many of their pigeons that was based on how high they fly and how many other pigeons they recruited. On the rooftop where Abdullah was hiding and observing the masque several hundred yards away and a few other rooftops, there were a few large cages with many pigeons flying around.

Abdullah would occasionally glance at the nearby mosque with its loudspeaker blaring, but it was the pigeons that had captured his attention, or at least that was the impression he had hoped to give.

Abdullah had chosen the roof with care for its location. The mosque had two monuments that could only be seen from his vantage point. Rules and decision-making about policies for running the country had originated from the mosques that initiated a post-revolution regulation that mosques were to be hidden from view for safety. These days, if you wanted to get promoted to a better position in your job or to save whatever position you had, you had to be visible from the mosque.

The new trend was the essential short beard and sloppy shirt with absolutely no tie, something completely different from the Shah's times. Appearance was important in order not to be marked as westernized, a modernist, or imperialist, and the strict traditions were becoming a growing burden to the people of Iran.

Abdullah's attention cut to Cyrus's car, parked by the alley's entrance on the far side of the mosque. Like the rooftop, the alley connecting the two main streets to one another had been chosen for a reason, its location. Roxanna sat next to Cyrus, dressed in traditional female Muslim garb, wearing a scarf and sunglasses.

It was a strange time for friends in Iran. All were in hiding and had no choice but to become part of the underground. Cyrus had finally received the message from Hussein he'd been waiting for, telling him where they should meet so he could pass along information about the safe place he had taken Assad.

Meetings weren't safe anywhere, but a meeting with Hussein was especially dangerous; Hussein was the ex-president Banisader's foreign adviser. He was also one of the most famous political columnists for Banisader's own paper, "ANGHELAB-a-ESLAMI." But, when Banisadr had to escape with the head of the Mujaheddin Massoud Rajavi to France, along with a few others, Hussein had refused to join them. Now with a price on his head, the guards had arrested his father.

Every day they would torture the old man in hopes that he would tell them where Hussein was, but the old man refused to talk. He knew deep inside that he had been an abusive father and believed that he had driven Hussein to this end. He had beaten his sons with his belt regularly; this was the main reason Hussein left Iran for America and joined the anti-Iranian government groups in Los Angeles. Accepting his part in what had happened, Hussein's father would have rather died than give his son up to the authorities.

Cyrus knew the entire Iranian secret police were after his people, especially Hussein. And thanks to Saeed, who had become his number one enemy, being around Hussein meant being with a time bomb that could explode at any time; a fact that meant nothing to Cyrus, who was willing to risk everything for Assad's safety. He playfully tossed his keys at Roxanna and gave her instructions, "Do not leave the car. If something happens, drive away. Don't wait for me. Go to the Swedish Embassy... even if you have to crash, land inside."

Roxanna nodded, wondering how Cyrus could smile while saying something so frightening. She was hoping the meeting was about her father and not about getting her out of Iran. She knew when she left Dorian that it was already too late for that. She had become one of them, part of the struggle just like her father, and for that reason alone, leaving was not an option.

Roxanna knew that Cyrus had the special power of dreams and visions and wondered if he was keeping anything from her, but before she could ask, he looked around and checked their surroundings, "No, I did not have a new dream, and I do not know that anything is about to happen, but things are not normal these days. Nothing looks normal, not even my dreams."

He looked down, embarrassed, "I worry... I am just saying you must be careful. I want to be sure of your safety." Cyrus headed for the mosque then turned, "Please, you do not have to be tough...or a hero. I have to see Hussein, and then we will leave for your father but, again, if you see something suspicious, just take off. Do not wait for me. I will find you."

Cyrus headed down the alley toward the mosque as the loudspeakers began to broadcast prayers. Roxanna watched his every step as she fixed her scarf, becoming distracted by a young couple up the street being held at gunpoint.

Several guards searched their car before slapping the man and forcing them both inside the back of the guards' car, which was now heading in her direction. Roxanna turned away as they sped past, hoping not to bring attention to herself. Looking back towards Cyrus, she was sickened by what she had allowed to happen. She had looked away just long enough to lose sight of him. He had disappeared.

*****

In the middle of the alley leading to the mosque, Cyrus waited behind the door of the house which he was to enter. When the door opened, and he saw a young man who knew him and welcomed him with a smile, he entered. Cyrus followed the young man; they passed a pool in the middle of a courtyard and reached a building several yards away.

The young man climbed up the tall window that reached to his chest and entered the room. He hurriedly joined the other three playing cards but did not see Hussein. By the open window, Hussein appeared on the doorstep of the entry door, the two old friends looked at each other, and their silence spoke to them.

Hussein went down three to four steps, walked to the pool, and sat by the faucet. He opened the valve and began to splash water on his face. It seemed as though he was washing his guilt off. Cyrus went to the pool, where he could clearly see Hussein, and sat on the other side of the pool's edge, watching Hussein, waiting for him to speak.

Somehow, they knew in their hearts they would get to Assad's whereabouts soon enough, but first, they had to resolve the tensions that had developed between them. Each blamed the other for the mess they were in. Although Cyrus rarely showed his feelings, he was angry with Hussein for putting Roxanna's life in danger by involving her in the country's turmoil, but he never spoke about his feelings to Hussein.

Hussein, in turn, used to blame Cyrus for what he considered a lack of commitment towards their cause and for not doing enough for his people. And now, sitting face to face, they were about to put their long friendship to the test, each determined to wait the other out.

Finally, it was Hussein who broke the long silence. "I've always wondered ... how does it feel to have a real wife, to have a child? Be a family man. Come to them every night. Hug your children. Yell at them… how I would feel…? Perhaps I was better off…!" Hussein stared at the water and, with deep feeling, whispered, "I know for sure; I would never raise my hand to my children. I would give them love." Hussein continued.

"I don't have a child yet, but as for a wife...I guess it's unexplainable, sort of holy, and at the same time, a bit confusing. At least my marriage is . . ."

Hussein was staring at the water, reminiscing about their early years, "It seems like yesterday that you wanted to be a professional soccer player. Saeed wanted to be a lawyer … and Nader wanted to be a wrestler. I wanted to be a basketball player."

He splashed some water on his face to cool off, "And here we are. You are lost to America with an American wife. All I have left is this worn-out pair of pants. I am homeless, fearing for my life, and afraid to sleep. Nader got burned to death by our best friend, Saeed, and whatever happened to Saeed, I do not know. And I am homeless, displaced, afraid of living, and afraid of sleeping ... how can it be just accepted that Nader was set on fire by our best friend, Saeed? How could a person do that? Change like that? Maybe he was what he is, but now he's taken the mask off his face..."

Hussein could not help but stare at Cyrus's new jeans, "If I do not give any credit to The Americans on anything, I must give them credit for their jeans. They last forever, the only thing I have left are these worn out and torn jeans..."

Cyrus began to take off his pants, "It's a bit short for you, but it works and does the job. Here, I have another pair at the house." Cyrus took off his pants, they exchanged glances, and then Hussein took his off, and they exchanged pants. Hussein continued, "Now, if I do not have you around, your memory will always be with me."

Hussein's eyes catch Abdullah's, who was watching from the rooftop, then turned to Cyrus," Do you realize that every time we see each other could be the last?"

Cyrus knew Hussein and Pary were in hiding, but that was pretty much the same for everyone. They, however, had a price on their heads. The government was looking for them everywhere, and it was only a matter of time before they were seen, or someone talked to save his own skin.

Cyrus knew that if the guards found him, he too would be arrested and tortured to get information on where Hussein was hiding. What caused him the greatest pain was knowing that their worst enemy was one of their oldest and best friends.

Cyrus was beginning to feel agitated. It was too dangerous to be around Hussein, and just as soon as he found out where Assad was hiding, he intended to leave. Cyrus's first priority was getting back to Roxanna, and he was there to find Pary so that he could take her with them and keep them from danger. But Hussein had no intention of getting to the point of where Pary was. He just said she is on her way to Hussein's. He had opened the floodgates and was pouring his heart out, and there was nothing Cyrus could do but let him finish.

" Pary has not been able to handle things since she heard about what happened to Nader. She is out for revenge. More than I am. Life doesn't mean anything or have any value for either of us… I went along with her at first, but now I am rethinking things. She is willing to give up everything. But she must stay alive; her family needs her. I have no one to be worried about. When the time is right and the opportunity presents itself, I will deal with Saeed. But it is Pary that I worry about. But I feel it is too late for Pary to be saved."

Cyrus did not like what he was hearing, "What in hell are you talking about? Where can I find her? What is Pary up to?"

Hussein rose, lost and confused, staring at Cyrus a bit, "I have always thought freedom doesn't come easy. There are always sacrifices that must be made. Our lives are not important. What is important is the cause? The revolution is over, but this is just the beginning of the sacrifice. The clergy is a much worse enemy than the Shah. All we did was repeat history, replacing one dictator for another one who is much worse."

All Cyrus wanted was an answer, "Where can I find Pary? What is Pary up to?!"

*****

It was way more than the few minutes Cyrus was supposed to be gone, and there was still no sign of Cyrus. Roxanna wasn't sure if it was time to worry or not, and that, in itself, caused her to worry. She looked around for anything suspicious but was distracted by a flock of pigeons flying just above the rooftops. She watched as they headed for their handler, a middle-aged man tending to his pigeons in cages on a roof near the mosque.

The pigeons were about to land until they were startled by the sudden, jarring sound of prayers coming from the mosque's loudspeaker. Instead, they circled back and flew over a group of small kids and teenagers, marching down the sidewalk in an organized line. Roxanna watched, intrigued by the birds in flight, casting elongated shadows on the ground.

It was a separate group of rowdy children headed her way that finally grabbed her attention. They were surprisingly young for the disturbing commotion they were making, ranging in age from about eight to fifteen years old. As they ran past, Roxanna could see that they were wearing green Army uniforms and carrying guns, singing propaganda songs, "I die for Islam, I die for Imam Khomeini."

It was a moment that would be frozen in Roxanna's memory, forever. She recalled, there had been a group of young boys before the Revolution running along the sidewalk yelling 'Allah Hoo Akbaar, Khomeini rehabber," which translated to 'God is great, and Khomeini is the leader.' Unlike that time, Roxanna made no move or attempted to follow them. She remained in Cyrus's car, not wanting to hear, see or appear to be part of their performance.

Recalling Cyrus's warning, her eyes followed a suspicious woman who was walking past the boys towards her, wearing a familiar Islamic outfit like one she used to wear with Pary with only her eyes visible. The woman was making Roxanna extremely nervous the way she would stare at her, stops, turned to look at the mosque and then looked back at her. Finally, knowing she would never drive away and leave Cyrus in a dangerous situation, she reached under his seat and found his handgun, hiding it underneath her jacket. No one knew she had a handgun but Pary, who gave her one.

The veiled woman finally approached and looked at Roxanna as if she knew her, "I have always tried to be as good a daughter as my parents would want me to be. It just happens that I can't be a normal woman with a husband and many children." It was Pary's voice. Roxanna was so elated she started to get out of the car, "We are here to find and take you with us…" But Pary pushed the door closed with her hip. "Stay inside. How many times do I have to tell you to go back home? This is not your fight. If I had a choice now to be in your place or mine, I would choose yours, and I would leave and leave this place right away."

The two friends were distracted for a few moments by a boy who dashed up and stole another boy's balloon. The boy took off in hot pursuit and caught up with the second boy, who was still holding on to the balloon. A fight broke out, and soon other boys gathered to cheer them on. The red balloon was lost in the scuffle, floating high up into the air.

Pary's attention was distracted as she noticed, at that moment, several clergymen and their bodyguards exited the mosque near the far end of the alley. Among them was the same stout clergyman who led the raids on the newspaper office and Cyrus's house. Roxanna used Pary's distraction to her advantage and got out of the car, was shocked to see the stout Clergyman walking toward them.

Turning to Pary, she watched as her friend gazed at Saeed with a painful expression. It was obvious this was the time to worry. Roxanna was unable to focus her eyes on the fat clergy and Saeed, their figures distorted by visions of Nader in flames flashing in her mind, along with the memory of the little girl.

Pary, too, was overcome by the image of tall flames devouring Nader as she watched Saeed and his familiar, stout clergyman walk down the alley towards them, escorted by bodyguards with machine guns and smiling as though they were blessed by God. The gang stopped, talking to a few others who approached them at the alley.

Then Roxanna was more shocked to see Saeed walking out of the mosque with a few bodyguards and head toward the stout clergyman. The loudspeaker wailed in the background as Pary adjusted her Hijab, trying not to be recognized.

"It seems you are in the wrong place at the wrong time, again. You'd better take off, and you had better listen this time, or you will never see your father again. We are sorry about what happened to your father. We would not let it go without revenge..."

Pary took a few steps before stopping and looking at Roxanna with conviction. "Do something for your friends when you get back to the States. Tell them to look in the mirror and ask themselves, what if everything was reversed? What if Iran did to America what America did to us? What if we caused your people such hardship and pain with no regard for human life?

"Ask them for me. Ask them if changing a government by force to get cheap oil, if killing children and woman and causing suffering is human?! Is right? Ask them if this is what Christianity, Judaism, Islam, or any religion stands for! Ask them! Is it right to cause hardship and pain to others for your own personal comfort? Please, just ask them." With that, Pary turned and walked down the alley, calmly toward Saeed and the stout clergyman.

Roxanna looked around, desperately, for Cyrus, unsure of what she should do. If she ran after Pary, exposing her, they would both be arrested and killed. But if she did nothing, what would that solve? She knew her friend well enough to know that something terrible was about to happen. Pary was putting herself at greater risk than she had ever done, and if she died because of her inaction, Roxanna wouldn't be able to live with the guilt. She ran after Parry.

"Pary! Stop! Damn it! Stop!"

Furious, Pary pulled Roxanna into a doorway hidden from view and shoved her against the wall, "You are going to get me, you, and everyone else killed! Don't you get it? Go away! You are going to expose us all and get us all killed. How many times should I tell you? This is not your battle! Go before it is too late! Go!"

But Roxanna refused to listen, "Bullshit! It's as much my fight as it is yours. If you are in it, I am in it. If you die, I die .?" Pary held her against a door so tight she could feel her heart beating. "I have nothing in this world to give to anyone except my life to my country, my soul to our people, and my friendship to you. Stay alive and tell the world what is happening in this country. That is what you must do."

Pary pushed the door open and handed Roxanna over to a very surprised young woman who has been trying to eavesdrop, "Keep her inside; she is in danger!"

Pary headed down the alley while the young girl's family held Roxanna tight, close enough to watch but far enough away to remain safe. An eerie quiet hung in the air like swamp moss, warning intruders of impending doom. All eyes were on Pary as she zeroed in on the stout clergyman and Saeed with determination, adjusting something under her outfit. She looked up towards Abdullah, who was standing guard on the rooftop of Hussein's place and gave him a sign.

Inside the stairway, still holding on, Roxanna wanted to scream out but heard Pary's warning play over and over in her head; she remained silent.

Across the street, as if straight out of a Hitchcock movie, six black ravens landed on the rooftop, and they began to sing.

Roxanna tried, once again, to get away, but the young girl's mother slapped her, hard, across the face and yelled at her, "What do you think you will accomplish by getting killed? Think about your poor mother!"

*****

Meanwhile, by the fountain, Hussein continued to distract Cyrus with stories of their youth. It wasn't until Abdullah left his post on the roof and showed up in the courtyard carrying his machine gun that Cyrus realized something was about to go down! Abdullah yelled to Hussein, "She is really going after them! She is doing it now!"

A feeling of intense dread came over Cyrus, "What is he talking about!?" Not wanting to answer, Hussein jumped in through the window to the annoyance of his friends who were still playing cards and grabbed his gun before jumping back out the same way he entered. All hell was about to break loose, and he realized that he still hadn't told Cyrus where Assad was staying.

"It's too late to save Pary… you had better go. It is not safe here. Take Roxy away. Now! At least save her. Assad is at my late mother's house by the river. Tell Roxanna I am sorry for getting her involved with this mess! I was wrong. Go fast, or you will get her killed." Fearing the worst, Cyrus's eyes searched for his childhood friend, "What about Pary!?"

"I just told you! It is too late to save her. Leave! When you get out, do not look to the right. Just go to the car and get in and drive away—no matter what." Hussein pointed up towards the rooftops. "We will cover you. You do not need to be a hero, Cyrus. Just take Roxanna away. Remember, you are a writer, not a fighter!"

Cyrus had known his friend long enough to respect his judgment. He exited onto the alley, just when Pary had passed the house going toward Saeed. He hurried towards his car without turning to look in the direction of Saeed or the clergyman. Up ahead, he noticed a woman being held back in a doorway. It was Roxanna, a look of terror in her eyes as she stared down the alley.

The moment Cyrus saw Roxanna, he knew something was wrong. He immediately turned and looked toward the end of the alley and saw a woman in an Islamic hijab walking toward Saeed. He knew it was Pary. Cyrus was taken aback by the scene unfolding before his eyes. People were pushing in front of her, going up to the stout clergyman to kiss his hand as others approached, handing letters to him. Hussein and Abdullah exited the house and began to head towards Cyrus and away from Pary at a rapid pace.

Suddenly understanding the seriousness of the situation, Cyrus had two choices; go and help Pary or save Roxanna's life. The choice was clear; he realized Hussein was right, it was too late to save Pary, and his concern must be on saving Roxanna.

He rushed towards her, grabbed her hand, and pushed her away from the mother and daughter, "Didn't I ask you to stay in the car no matter what? When are you going to listen!" Then he gave a nod of appreciation to the family, who motioned for Roxanna to go. They took off as Roxanna was pushing to go towards Pary, "Pary, we must help Pary,"

But Cyrus pushed back, "I am really getting tired of this nonsense, be quiet. You are going to get us killed. It is too late to help Pary. Save your own ass." Cyrus was holding Roxanna's hand firmly and pushing her away from Pary, but she would not take her eyes off of her.

Watching, Pary stopped and took one last look around as if she was assessing the situation. Her eyes cut to Roxanna's. The two friends were saying goodbye. Then Pary turned away from Roxanna towards Saeed. Roxanna knew in her heart; Pary had decided to walk straight into the wraith.

Pary had been waiting for Saeed to close the gap between himself and the clergyman. Her goal was to get to Saeed. Pary ducked past the guards, pretending to give The Sheik Assef a note, and then passed him casually to get to Saeed. But she noticed Saeed was alerted to her presence and was staring directly at her. Sheik Assef reached his hand toward Pary to kiss it; Pary knew if she didn't act immediately, she would lose her chance to get to either him or Saeed. Within seconds she grabbed Sheik Assef's hand and placed handcuffs on his right wrist, the other side locked on to hers, then she revealed a hand grenade, pushing him toward Saeed.

Now the two were handcuffed to one another, and he has no way to run. She pulled the pin, dropped her veil, and pulled off her scarf. Her long black hair flew into the wind, her beautiful body in a loose dress covered with explosives. Cyrus had never realized how beautiful she was.

Suddenly everyone panicked, and guards closed in, their guns pointed at her. Bystanders were screaming for people to get back. The bullhorn of the mosque blared even louder, prayers cutting through the air like a razor-sharp knife. Pary held the clergyman's hand in a death grip. Saeed tried to move away, but Pary aggressively shoved the clergyman toward him.

Cyrus stopped, watching Pary in pain. He knew it was too late to save Pary. But Roxanna refused to remain on the sidelines any longer. She freed herself and raced toward Cyrus, intent on reaching Pary, who was still clutching Shaykh Aasef and trying to move toward Saeed at the same time.

Pandemonium and chaos broke out everywhere. Neighbors began opening windows and climbing to the rooftops, cheering in their hearts for

Pary, who had one arm locked around the clergyman's throat, the other hand holding the grenade to his head.

The black ravens were now singing louder, and it seemed they were in competition with the mosque bullhorn. All the pigeons were landing on the rooftop and watching in silence.

Pary had been waiting for this moment since her brother's death. She knew the fat clergyman was one of those watching as Saeed threw a match at her brother, setting him on fire. Pary had hoped to get close enough to Saeed to blow them both away, but the coward had already abandoned his friend.

It was the moment Pary had lived for. She began reciting the names of people executed by the clergy's order as she pivoted the fat man back and forth, extending his life long enough to watch him sweat. The guards followed her around, desperately waiting for an opening they would never get. She was pleased that the event was going down as smoothly as planned. Shaykh Assef was shaking, his face twitching, as he signaled to the guards not to shoot, just in case they missed.

"In the memory of Nader, Fatemeh Nouri, Akbaar Rahimi, Akbaar Mohammedi, Aflaton Ghasemi, Amir Abbas Hoveyda, General Ali Neshat, General Mehdi Rahimi . . ." Pary was amazed at how easy it was to drag the Shaykh Assef away from the guards and towards the center of the street where Saeed had stopped to watch, all the while holding the grenade to his pudgy face. The guards had backed away without argument, dumbfounded by the brazenness of the strange woman in Islamic attire.

Shaykh Assef kept yelling, "No one shoot!" Saeed, cowering like the dog, waiting for the opportunity to act, he was, crouched behind the guards, hoping when Pary actually did pull the pin on the grenade before she gets to him, he was far enough away so that at worst, he would be injured and not killed. Tears streamed down Pary's face as she continued delivering her memorial to the dead, "For all innocent, brave people of Iran, all who were executed unlawfully and unjustly by you and your colleagues . . . In their names and acting on behalf of the court of the true Iranian people, I hereby render their justice and sentence you to die by execution."

Pary turned and looked at Cyrus and Roxanna in the distance and directed her speech to them, proudly, "Death to dictators! Death to mullahs!" With that, she shoved Shaykh Assef toward Saeed and raised her hand in defiance, still not taking her eyes off Cyrus and Roxanna, discharging the grenade. Both were shocked and surprised to hear Pary called the name of The Shah's army generals and prime minister; that was a message to confess her mistake of supporting Khomeini.

The sound was deafening, powerful enough to bring many bystanders to their knees. A huge flash of fire radiated from the center of the explosion, smoke rising into the air like it had erupted from a spewing volcano. Shards of glass, metal, body parts, and blood were propelled in all directions, slamming against the walls surrounding the alley as if they were paintballs exploding on impact. The entire mosque cleared out, but the bullhorn horn was still playing loud.

A mass of Pigeons flew helter-skelter, their flight pattern in chaos as they lost their way amidst the smoke and flying debris; their erratic behavior, a mirror image of what was transpiring far below them on the ground. Pary's beautiful body was scattered around in pieces, unrecognizable, among the trash of murderers who took the lives of so many innocent people. Her death, a price she had been willing to pay.

Cyrus looked around desperately for Roxanna and noticed her, dazed, running toward the blast site. Cyrus took off after her, desperately trying to get to her and stop her. In her pocket, Roxanna held his gun, knowing, for the first time in her life, she might have to make a decision she never imagined. Could she kill? Cyrus launched toward her.

The mass of guards began to run around with their machine guns, ready to shoot and kill. Saeed rose from the ground covered in blood. He immediately noticed Roxanna, and now was like an angry snake, injured and willing to kill. He immediately ordered his men to rush toward her, a gun battle erupted.

Hussein, Abdullah, and many of their friends who had remained in the background, hiding their identity, moved in and fired at the guards to cover Cyrus as he continued his way toward Roxanna. Pigeons, scared off their perches, circled above as if it was their obligation to witness the horrible scene being played out on the ground.

Smoke lingered with its acrid scent for what seemed like an eternity. The bullhorn at the mosque began to play louder, calling for the shocked bystanders to rise and join the Jihad against the evil of the enemy of Islam and the agent of American imperialism. The message was the same. Kill, kill, kill, in the name of Allah, the Allah, which was known only to the clergy, not to the people.

Hussein, who had been focusing his attention on Cyrus, turned just in time to see a guard aiming directly at Roxanna. Raising his gun, he killed him before she even knew she was in danger.

Hussein had no idea how much Roxanna despised him until he grabbed her and tried to pull her away. Resisting his efforts to protect her, she fought him off like a wild animal caught in a trap. "Are you crazy? That's suicide out there!" But Roxanna hated Hussein for using her to his own advantage and wasn't about to do one more thing that he tried to force her to do. She would die first!

Although it was almost impossible to express herself during the struggle, she still managed to let him know exactly how she felt. "In the name of the Revolution, young girls are certainly attracted to men of conviction. Damn you! You really believe you're the sole proprietor of truth! You're no hero. You're an animal!" Her words shocked him just enough, so he loosened his grip, allowing her to free one hand and slap him as hard as she could. Hussein flashed back to the last time his face throbbed from being slapped …by Roxanna's mother.

Cyrus finally reached Roxanna but not before getting hit by a bullet on his hand. He grabbed her, pulling her away, towards the car. But it was not easy. Hussein could feel the fight draining from Roxanna as their eyes met. Seeing blood seeping through Cyrus's shirt, she allowed Hussein to hustle her towards him. Hussein knew Cyrus was shot. Finally, together, Cyrus placed his cheek next to hers and, in a soft but firm voice, reprimanded her for her childish behavior. "There is time later for your judgments. If you stay alive! Now's the time to save your ass!"

But Roxanna was not thinking about her life; she was overcome with a grief that was beyond comprehension. She was thinking about Pary, her best friend, no longer alive. She was not just a friend but a sister. She turned towards Hussein and made sure she had the last word. "You coward! You use people for your dirty work."

Even after the explosion, Saeed, who was severely wounded and covered with blood, managed to stay on his feet and chase Cyrus and Roxanna. Like a character in a sinister novel, he and his men ran towards them, shooting in their direction as well as arbitrarily shooting into the crowd, causing panic amidst people exiting the mosque. Cyrus managed to get Roxanna in the car as Hussein and Abdullah gave them cover. Then he drove towards Hussein in hopes of helping him escape. "Let's go, Hussein! Get in!"

Several guards approached and were closing in on Cyrus's car, leaving Hussein, Abdullah, and their friends no choice but to start fighting in the streets to create a distraction. Hussein began yelling, "Get her out of here, Cyrus! Go! Go!" Instead, Cyrus pushed Roxanna down, below the window, in an effort to keep her safe while, at the same time, throwing the car into reverse, hoping there was still a chance to grab Hussein before they left.

Saeed directed a rain of firepower toward their car, creating a series of loud metallic blasts as it was repeatedly hit. Cyrus reached for the lever and popped the trunk, yelling for Hussein to get in a while, at the same time, Roxanna, still curled in the passenger side well, felt something cold and hard and inviting in her pocket, her gun. Much to Cyrus's chagrin, she bolted up and surveyed the surrounding area looking for a reason to use it.

Circumstance had, indeed, transformed Roxanna from a gentle, young girl to a formidable woman of courage. She stared, defiantly, into the faces of the approaching clergy with fierceness and conviction, daring them to come any closer. She saw three guards aiming directly at Cyrus and, without hesitation, began shooting, emptying one round after another. Next, she focused on the approaching clergy who had taken over the front position, leading the others. Holding the gun in both hands, she closed one eye to sharpen her aim and pulled the trigger repeatedly. She proved to

Cyrus and the world that she was truly Iranian, willing to do anything to protect her friends, anything to buy them time to secure a safe foothold. Even kill. Even die.

Hussein raced towards Cyrus's car, running from left to right, trying not to make himself an easy target, but even then, bullets found their mark as he sprinted and dove into the open trunk. His body riddled with holes; he could do nothing but hold on for his life. To avoid crashing into an unexpected traffic jam, Cyrus's car went over the curb and became airborne. Hussein lost his grip and was thrown from the trunk, landing face down in a small, running creek close to a small bridge.

Before he was able to gain control, Cyrus drove over a small bridge and onto the sidewalk, crashing through several book displays as terrified pedestrians nose-dived to the side, cursing. Checking his rearview mirror for Hussein, he saw nothing but guards gaining on him, and given no choice, he swerved back into traffic only to be stopped by some sort of confrontation in front of him. Fortunately for Cyrus, the two Revolutionary Guard cars that had been following him tried unsuccessfully to attempt the same maneuver and crashed into a bus, causing a six-car pile-up.

It took all of Hussein's strength to pull his wounded body up from the creek, his eyes searching for his friend. He pulled himself under the bridge hidden from the view. Things were happening so fast that people around were running for their lives, so Hussein went unnoticed. He looked up, searching for Abdullah through his own blood as it mixed with the running water staining it red.

He was too late to do anything but watch through bloody eyes. Not far away, he saw Abdullah, face down on the ground surrounded by guards, like a wounded, hunted animal. He lay still, covered in blood, life pouring out of his body, still being beaten by ruthless guards. Still holding his gun, Abdullah didn't take his eyes off Saeed, who was approaching from the distance. He raised his gun slightly, pointing it directly into Saeed's heart, but he was weak, and his reactions were slow. Before he could pull his trigger, Saeed shot his old friend until he was out of bullets. He looked up from Abdullah's riddled body with the pride of a big game hunter, his eyes searching the crowd for praise.

Saeed was furious Abdullah had turned a blind eye to him and did not share Saeed's pride and joy at hunting and killing him. Instead, Abdullah's eyes were locked on the eyes of a little boy who squatted a few meters down the street, with his hands under his chin, staring at him lost in astonishment at what was happening. Abdullah's eyes closed as he watched tears fall down the little boy's face. Now Saeed was looking for Hussein, Cyrus, and Roxanna. He was enraged, shoot to kill was his mode, no matter if you were friend or foe.

Hussein kept his eyes closed under the bridge. He preferred not to see anything anymore. He knew he had to wait for a suitable situation to get out and escape safely. Although he knew he had been badly injured, he had no choice but to endure it for at least a few hours until darkness replaced the light. What he didn't know was that one of his friends had skillfully hidden his gun for him. He had been waiting for the right opportunity to get Hussein out of there. He has also called a few friends for help. When the coast was clear, they moved Hussein out cautiously to one of their friends' houses outside of the city, who also happened to be a doctor. His injuries were not serious, but he had to hide and rest for a while.

*****

It was early evening, near the outskirts of the city. Cyrus turned onto an empty road, the sunset reflecting orange and red against his car. Roxanna sat next to him, still holding his gun, letting it be known that nothing in their world had returned to normal. Suddenly, without warning, the winding road and lack of sleep caught up with him, and he lost control. The car skidded into a bumpy, dried-out field and down a gully, finally coming to a stop in one of the many beautiful creeks that laced across outside Tehran.

Haunted by terrifying images, Cyrus began to punch the dashboard, the steering wheel, and the windows, his mouth wide open, throat cut off, strangled by death's gnarled and ugly grip. As his hand was dancing up and down, beating up the car, blood from a new and old gash in Cyrus's arm had splattered all over the car and onto Roxanna's face. As he watched Abdullah die, Cyrus's screams were truly silent, locked inside a vortex of unrelentless pain.

When Cyrus finally regained his voice, it came out as sound without words; a primal scream, an exploding cyst of raw emotion that had been festering for what felt like an eternity. Cyrus could not believe what he had done! Finding no one else to blame, he turned to God, with a whispering cry, "Is there no God in the sky over this land? What is this? How much more bloodshed? Where are we going? Where are you, God?"

Roxanna reached over and gently touched the back of his neck, sending her own electric shock through Cyrus's body. Falling into Roxanna's arms, he wept endless tears for his shattered dreams. His country, once again, on the verge of destruction.

Life was never smooth in his world, but Cyrus thought he had learned to brace himself for unknown disaster. Not this time. He felt his life spiraling out of control at the realization of what had just happened. He had left his best friends, one dead, the other, dying, in the streets. It was inconceivable. Pary? A suicide bomber? How could it have happened? Who was to blame? How could he have not known?

*****

Chapter 39

When the Silence is Kissed by its Haunting Melody... the Light Finally Shines...

On this day of fall in the empty, quiet countryside of south Iran, a gentle breeze was blowing through the car window, caressing Roxanna's face. She marveled at how the electrical posts lining either side of the road seemed to dissolve into infinity, a metaphor for her time in Iran. She had come to the country with one objective, to find her father, only to get manipulated and used, caught up in a maze of horrible events which spiraled out of control and, like the electrical poles, seemed to never end.

The realization that Roxanna was finally on her way to meet her father was almost too much for her to comprehend. Her plan had been to stay about 6 months in Iran to search for her father. It was Hussein who has initiated her departure, telling her that her father was alive. He had even promised to have his friends take care of her while she was in Iran and help her find her father.

It wasn't long before Roxanna realized that everything Hussein had said was "Smoke and Mirrors." In a country on the verge of revolution, the truth was a rare commodity. And the fact that she had been deceived by someone she thought she was in love with made it all the more devastating and remarkable that hopefully, her journey to find her father would finally come to an end.

Roxanna's eyes followed the horizon where the endless sky bent down and kissed the earth. As she settled back in her seat, she stared out into nothingness, into the web of lies that were consuming her, knowing only one truth. She was still alive. Anything more than that was a gift.

Before they knew it, the sun had eclipsed the day; a vibrant amethyst sunset escaping into the sky as if on horseback, boldly highlighting the rolling hills and tree-lined path that paralleled some untamed river next to them. Roxanna sat motionless, mesmerized by the yellow, orange, and gold leaves as they danced in the current, mixing with errant logs, searching for still waters.

Suddenly, and without warning, Cyrus hit the brakes, jolting Roxanna from her reverie. A short distance from the river, they saw a house nestled in a grove of trees, their leaves, the honey-yellow jewels of fall, blanketing the ground around them.

She looked to Cyrus for hope, some sort of confirmation, but all he did was lift an eyebrow. He exited the car and began to observe the surroundings to be sure everything was safe and sound. He knew they were at the right place because he was there before with Hussein a few times. Cyrus relaxed when he noticed Akbaar standing on the porch, waving a friendly hello.

Cyrus walked around and opened Roxanna's door, nodding for her to go to the man sleeping under the tree by the running river.

Exiting the car, Roxanna recognized Akbaar standing on the porch. Her gaze moved from Akbaar waving on the porch to the man napping by the fire.

Looking towards the river, Roxanna spotted an older man who appeared to be resting his back against the trunk of a tree. Next to him, a small fire was burning with two teapots strategically placed near its warmth.

A young boy named Samad had been collecting leaves while several sheep grazed placidly, nearby, but when he looked up and saw the strangers, he raised a stick, defensively. His playmate was a black and white dog whose only reaction to the stick was to try and tug it away.

Samad relaxed when he noticed Akbaar standing on the porch, waving a friendly hello. He shrugs, finally nodding towards a figure in the distance.

A nervous calm flooded Roxanna as she began walking down the small hill, the dry brown leaves crunching beneath her feet at every step, like a clock ticking, marking off the seconds before she would finally meet her father.

She was thankful she hadn't wakened him. She used that magical, quiet moment to commit the scene to memory, looking in every direction, slowly studying, memorizing the finest details, painting a picture that she would treasure, forever, in her mind.

A feeling of warmth flowed through her, a love so profound it transcended the living hell her life had become since her arrival in Iran. Her Baba was in front of her, and soon she would touch him, be held in his arms. Then, for a horrible brief second, she was afraid he was dead.

She had faced too much tragedy the past few months not to assume the worst. But there was no possible way fate could be that cruel! Roxanna noticed the chain of Assad's pocket watch that normally hung from his jacket was hanging on a nearby tree. Quietly she reached out and pulled on it. It was an Assad's old pocket watch.

Samad and his dog sat watching the strange meeting, enchanted by this beautiful young woman who had appeared out of nowhere. Although the young boy had no idea what was happening, he took his cue from Akbaar and smiled warmly, his heart-melting. From the porch, Cyrus and Akbaar watched in wonder as the curtain rose on this final act, a love story like no other.

Roxanna opened the pocket watch, cherishing the picture of her young father, lovingly holding her as a baby in his arms, the silence gently kissed by its haunting melody, "Hush Little Baby ..." Softly, she whispered "Baba" as she began to half-sing, half-whisper, along with the music.

Assad opened his eyes to a sight more precious to him than freedom or life. His daughter. Afraid he was still dreaming, confused, he poured the tea in the cup and held it up to her. The last rays of sunset turned pale in the distance in comparison with his daughter's beauty. Assad was old and bent, weighed down by a heavy heart. No more. No more.

Assad chastised himself for spending a lifetime searching for the meaning of life in the unattainable, a way to fix a country broken by greed, the most formidable of adversaries. And all the while, the true meaning had been right there, within reach. Standing before him was the answer to his prayers, his reason for living. It was his daughter that had opened his eyes to the meaning of life; to love and be loved. Roxanna knelt beside her father, takes the tea, and places it down, then held his hand, singing the song he used to sing to her, "Hush, little baby, don't say a word. Baba's gonna buy you a mockingbird. La la la la la la la . . ." They held each other in their arms, their cheeks pressed together, their tears, like tributaries, joining to form a river of love and strength.

*****

Assad's heart filled with memories of life in West Germany which he joyously shared with Roxanna. Lapsing into sentimentality, he recalled a time when he was as young as she. He was playing his tar and singing an Iranian lullaby to baby Roxanna as she lay in his arms, staring up at him in rapture at the sound of his voice. Linda entered and began to sing as well, serenading their precious Roxanna. "Hush, little baby, don't say a word. Baba's gonna buy you a mockingbird..." As he told the story and sang, Assad changed the "Hush, Little Baby" to the Farsi version of the lullaby, "La llaye Koon. (Which meant fall in deep peaceful sleep...)"

A feeling of lightness came over Roxanna as if a wonderous rain had cleansed her world, leaving behind nothing but essentials, fresh air, nature's bounty, and love. She literally hopped to her feet and shook the branches above Assad, giggling as yellow and reddish leaves fluttered down like butterflies. Magically, as if the sheep felt the power and pull of this long-awaited joining, they moved in unison, surrounding them, and quietly began to nibble the leaves. Although Cyrus felt the moment was sacred and meant to be shared between father and daughter, he let his playful personality gets the best of him. It was just before dusk. A time for fairytales. His harmonica came alive, music traveling through the air, mixing with the soft breeze and the sounds of the wild, running river. He was working his magic. Soon they would be dancing.

Assad realized that she hadn't had her tea yet, but as he tried to reach for the pot, Roxanna put her hand in his and gently helped him up. Scooping the earthy leaves and tossing them in the air, she began dancing and twirling as the leaves circled, magically, to the ground around them. Assad, although older and more cautious, joined his daughter, moving to the rhythm of the music and their beating hearts. Their struggle was finally over. No force, no matter how strong, could take this precious memory from them.

Roxanna murmured softly, again and again, "Baba. I have found you."

*****

Chapter 40

When Your Medicine, Your Peaceful elixir, is the One You Love... and Love is divided...

Nature, being a most perfect artist, could not have blessed them with a more beautiful backdrop than what the eyes could see on that day. Assad sat on the small balcony on the second floor, savoring the new, almost exotic feelings that had come over him since Roxanna's arrival. In all the years since he left Linda and his baby daughter behind, this was the first time he felt such happiness. He was overcome with feelings of calmness and wholeness.

Reflecting back on those lost years, he couldn't help but feel regret, wondering if it had been worth the huge sacrifice. He had given up everything that mattered for his country, for what turned out to be a failed attempt to change the plight and direction of his people for the better. He was contemplating what went wrong. How could they have been so naive about the power and agenda of Khomeini?

On the porch below, Roxanna sat next to Cyrus as he checked and rechecked his gun, looking through the barrel to be sure it was spotless, making sure it was in perfect firing condition. Roxanna, who suddenly found herself a veteran, asked, "Have you ever shot a gun?" Cyrus shook his head but said nothing as he looked down the barrel and into the trees, perpetually searching for unwelcome guests. It was just a matter of time…

He was very aware of his surroundings. Anything out of place or anyone unfamiliar to him would immediately catch his attention. He was worried and unable to sleep, not just because of any possible threat but because of a general feeling of angst. He knew sooner or later they would find Assad, and it would be up to him, alone, to stop the massacre.

Unfortunately, Cyrus knew Saeed's nature all too well. He was an evil snake, a wounded animal, injured and out for revenge. He would stop at nothing to make everyone he perceived to have hurt him suffer without mercy. And unfortunately, having risen to the top of the organization, Saeed had the financial, manpower, and political clout to make it happen.

Cyrus was also concerned because he and Roxanna had been cut off from the mainstream while staying with Assad, and it was impossible to get details on daily activities as they occurred. Although he never spoke of it to anyone, Cyrus was also very concerned about his wife in America. It had been over a month since he had contacted her, and he knew she would be sick with worry.

All he could do was deal with the moment, which meant Assad and Roxanna were his first priority. If it weren't for them, he could have left his life behind and returned to America. But Assad was his moral compass and Roxanna, his medicine, a peaceful elixir. He would never walk away. Now his mission is to take them with him, to save their life.

*****

Each new day was met with feelings of trepidation, bracing for something demanding attention, slicing into moments of calm. While Cyrus had gone to the city early in the morning to get some news and contact Akbaar, Assad was busy planting a cherry tree by the riverbank, hoping this last part of his life he may do something good for the future living. Samad and his dog raced past the two as they headed up the driveway to deliver Assad's medicines.

He did not like it, but the dog knew to wait on the porch while Samad entered the house, placing Assad's medicine where he was supposed to. He quietly looked around for Roxanna, hoping she would show up. Love doesn't discriminate between young or old; Samad had developed a crush on Roxanna and was doing his best to announce his arrival on his way out by letting the door slam behind him in hopes of seeing her. But the minute he would see her, he was overwhelmed with embarrassment and lowered his head.

As Assad was planting his Cherry tree, quietly, he was watching Samad and his dog, seeing how happy and excited the dog was about Samad's return, standing motionless and watching the dog tend to Samad, thinking how good it would be if humans adopted a dog's ideology. Loyal and loving to their owners, defended and protected, and it made no difference if they were rich or poor.

Just as he did at the end of every visit, Samad admired a bicycle Assad had propped up against the wall at the top of the stairs. It seemed as if just having the opportunity to touch the bike was enough to bring him happiness. Assad had been using this bike for about ten years, and now Akbaar had brought it here from Assad's house so that she could use it if he wanted to go to the city. Staring at the bicycle and imagining he was riding it and feeling the breeze was his routine every time Samad would see it.

As always, Assad was watching the young boy and his love affair with his bicycle. To put an even bigger smile on the young boy's face, Roxanna exited the house carrying a tray with teas and pastry. She offered Samad a sweet and big hug before traveling through trees and setting the tray down by her father, where he was planting the tree. She held the small tree straight while her father shoveled dirt around it, finally securing it to a post. To Roxanna, the planting of the tree was symbolic as it represented new life, memorializing this moment in their shared history.

Breaking the silence, she whispered, "I only know what mom told me..." Assad looked at her realizing it was time to share his side of the story. "It was a long time ago, and you were just a baby. But I never lost the hope of seeing you again." He paused a moment to gather his thoughts.

"Not having you in my life was a huge sacrifice, one I never dreamed I would have to make, but then, life doesn't always go as planned.

I wasn't there for you growing up, to help you and guide you, and that is my biggest regret. I didn't see you become the beautiful, courageous woman you are." Assad turned and gazed into the woods, then turned back to look into her eyes. But the smile had left his face. "I am so very proud of the beautiful woman you have become. If today was to be my last day on earth, my eyes would close in peace knowing that you walk this earth, and it is a better place because you are here."

Roxanna handed him a cup of tea as he asked her about her schooling, which he felt was the most important part of a child's upbringing outside of the family. "I went right from high school to UCLA. I always wanted to study economics, but I changed to political science, then art. You know what I ended up with? Being an architect."

Assad couldn't have been more surprised, "Architect?"

Roxanna nodded, "Yes, an architect! Mom didn't like that a bit! She wanted me to study music, play the piano and become a tennis player. All of the above! Mom and I used to fight, and we still do, I guess…but mostly it was when I'd ask about you. Then she'd get really mad."

Roxanna handed the small plate of pastries to her father, "I have to tell you something about Mom. I know one thing for certain. She really did love you. I didn't know until I came here, but it's true. And she still does. I thought she hated you, but then I realized it was the only way she could protect herself from the hurt of loving you so much. She never got married again. Did you know that?"

Assad fell silent, wondering about what might have been and if it was too late to change the future. Although Roxanna wanted to know more about his relationship with her mother, she did not wish to be disrespectful or put him in an uncomfortable position. But after a few moments, she decided to ask, anyway, "Did you love her?"

Unable to respond, he turned his attention towards the tree he had just planted, "You know, finally, I'm doing something right. People will benefit from your shade . . . and fruit." Roxanna refused to be ignored,

"Did you love her?" It had been a long, long time since Assad had thought about love in that way. And now, suddenly, he was put on the spot by the one he loved most, with a question that had not crossed his mind for an eternity.

He could not have afforded the luxury of sentimentality at the time he left Germany, leaving his wife and baby behind. It had been so long ago. To Assad, there had been no greater calling than to offer his life and his love to his country and its people, to improve the life of the poor, of people who had little or nothing to sustain themselves and even more tragic, little hope that the future would be brighter or maybe no hope. He had rationalized that by leaving Roxanna and Linda plenty of money to live on, they were better off than most people when, in reality, everything he had done had been achieved through the personal sacrifice of his wife and daughter. It was country first.

Now, after all these years, he was sitting in front of his most precious daughter, who wanted and clearly deserved answers to questions that he hadn't even had the nerve to ask himself. The reality was if Assad could have moved the clock backward, how differently things may have turned out. Assad spoke softly, "That . . . that was a very long time ago, and so much has happened . . . changed, since then."

Roxanna cut him off. "What about your Iranian wife? Do you love her?" Roxanna had no way of knowing that this was the hardest question that she could have asked her father. At that time in Iran, men would not talk about their feelings. It was not manly; you showed how you felt through your actions and behavior.

Assad had been raised in that culture, and as a result, he found himself being intimidated by his daughter's questions. Still, he was committed to trying to find the words to answer. "I'm not sure I really remember what spousal love is. Perhaps if I could live another forty years, I may learn." It seemed that every time he opened his mouth, he got himself in deeper trouble.

Roxanna couldn't help thinking about Cyrus when her father talked about spousal love, "Doesn't anybody love their wife here?" He rubbed his forehead, deep in thought. "There's no difference between us and others. When you get caught up in a crisis, love, children, wives all get mixed up and carried along into one tormented struggle. But you never stop loving the soul who gave you such wonderful fruit. I mean a child like you..."

Roxanna's mind filled with questions. If her father couldn't come out and say he loved her mother or his new wife, how could he say he loved her? Why was it acceptable to love a child but not the woman who gave birth to that child or the woman you slept next to every night? She wanted to know how he could have taken such a simple woman for his new wife.

How did he feel about the difference between her mother and his new wife, who was just a kind and pretty villager with no education? Her father had a Ph.D. in economics from Germany. How could they communicate? And about what? Knowing that any one of those questions would upset her father even further, she remained silent.

Cyrus was back from the city; his return was great timing, something that Roxanna needed to lean her mind and attention into so she could leave her father alone. She turned her gaze to Cyrus and tried to put her life in perspective. There was no doubt she loved Cyrus but was it a love worth sacrificing her happiness for? They had never spoken the word, but every time he disappeared, there was an endless longing in her heart. She never knew when he was leaving or "if or when" she would ever see him again. And all she dwelled upon during those long and lonely days that would inevitably turn into weeks was his return to her arms.

*****

Chapter 41

Marrying Because of Guilt, to Stay Alive Under the Radar...

The unrelenting rain beat down on the roof of Assad's house, keeping Roxanna from sleep. She was listening closely to its rhythm as it pounded in waves created by with the high winds. It was a sound she loved. And like so many of nature's miracles, it had a language all its own. She lay on the bed with her eyes wide open, seeing nothing, her head swirling with questions that had no answers.

She had always assumed that after finding her father, she would go back to Los Angeles, but now that her mission was over, she had mixed feelings about so many things. Of one thing she was certain, leaving Tehran was no longer an option. Even if she wanted to return to her safe, secure, unremarkable life in Los Angeles, she still had no passport. But now that she was finally with her father, she knew she didn't need one.

For the first time in her life, she felt complete. She had even arranged to have the bedroom next to his on the second floor in case he needed her, while Cyrus had the room downstairs where he was always on guard, always watching. For no reason she could think of, she could not sleep. Something always worried her. But she also knew she needed her rest if what was rumored was true.

From what she could gather without being conspicuous, Cyrus and Akbaar were trying to manage an escape for both Roxanna and her father. That was all she knew. By now, she had gotten used to the necessity of secrets and learned not to ask too many questions. She knew for certain that no one was to be trusted after the revolution, not even your best friend. But she also knew she could trust Cyrus with her life, and that was all that was important.

She had hoped her presence would bring new energy into her father's life, but it was not to be. It caused her great pain to see him getting weaker every day as if the years of struggle had finally worn him down. Each morning her father or Cyrus would beat her to prepared hot tea and made some simple sweets to serve her as a gesture of love. There wasn't much to it, and they had everything ready before she had awakened.

Both were great cooks and took turns playing the role of chef. She loved when they challenged one another to see who made a better dish. They would ask Roxanna to be the judge to determine who was, in fact, the better cook, it was a task that required great diplomacy and tact, but no matter what the outcome, the evening always ended with delicious meals, delightful conversation, and boundless laughter.

Listening to the soft and gentle voice of her father was like music to Roxanna. He uses to play his tar and chant with his great voice. She hung on every word he said, every story he told as if each was a newly discovered treasure. She cherished the evenings when Cyrus would join Assad, and together they would entertain her ... singing, dancing, and playing musical instruments for her pleasure.

She would sit for hours listening to them as they harmonized in perfect pitch and unison. What was especially pleasing was when they would sing old traditional, spiritual songs. She found the friendship between the two particularly moving, and every moment they shared together filled her with joy.

But this particular night, there had been no such festivities. Cyrus had gone to town on one of his mysterious missions earlier in the day and still hadn't returned. Very much aware of the danger, Roxanna looked outside every chance she could, trying not to concern her father. Since their arrival, Cyrus quietly made it clear to Roxanna that Assad had been on the Savanna's hit list, which meant that he would now be on Savanna's hit list. And with Saeed one of Savana's top men, there was no question that Assad was now the # 1 Most Wanted man in Iran.

The longer Cyrus took to return, Roxanna's thoughts grew more terrifying. Perhaps Saeed's men had found him. What if the assassins were on their way? They were surely going to die! It was just that moment when she heard something outside, Cyrus's harmonica.

*****

The next afternoon, Roxanna decided to bake sweets! What better way to celebrate life and love and family? She stood in the kitchen chopping vegetables for her Persian stew while keeping a protective eye on Assad. As long as he didn't overdo it, she had agreed to let him chop wood for the fireplace.

Samad and his faithful pooch were on their way up the long drive to deliver Assad's medicine, stopping, as usual, to chat and laugh with her father. While they were visiting, two rams started fighting. Alerted by the commotion, Samad's dog started barking viciously and ran after them, knocking Assad's bike over in the scuffle. Samad dropped the bags and ran toward the rams. Hitting them with the wooden stick he always carried, he was finally able to separate them and pull them away from Assad.

Watching from the kitchen, Roxanna raced out and picked up the containers of medicine, putting everything back in the bag. It occurred to her that she had never seen one particular medicine bottle, but since she couldn't read Farsi, she had no idea what it was for. After handing the bag to Samad to put away, Roxanna helped her father to the porch. "I'm still breathing, my love. It is just because of old age." He smiled at Samad as the young boy came out of the house, "Samad, tell her I am okay."

"He is okay," the boy said, obediently but without conviction. Roxanna and Assad sat on the porch to catch their breath while Samad ran down to the rams and put them in the stable. Returning with a rag in one hand, the young boy went over to Assad's bike and started cleaning it. When it finally passed his inspection, he lifted it high over his head and carried it to the porch. Just as he was about to pass, the old man reached out and grabbed the wheel giving Samad no choice but to stop. The two stared at each other through the spokes, each waiting for the other to speak. Samad was worried if he had done something wrong?

He was relieved to hear the tender tone of Assad's voice. "I'm an old man, and I don't need to impress anyone anymore. You, however, are young and full of energy. You keep it; it is yours..." The young boy had no idea what Assad was referring to, so he looked towards Roxanna for help. "

Do you know how to ride it?" She asked. Soon, the shy Samad began to smile and nod his head. "It's yours! Let's see you ride it!" Samad carried the bike down the stairs.

Hesitating, he turned and looking at Assad and Roxanna for reassurance. It was too great a gift for a child who had received nothing in his short life outweighing necessity. Samad found himself at a loss for words, not knowing how to thank his kind friend for such a gesture other than by showing his appreciation. He held the handlebars and started running, finally jumping into the air, his feet and legs held out so high he felt like he was flying. He landed right on the seat just as he had done a thousand times in his dreams.

With his dog at his side, he peddled fast to build up speed and then started doing tricks, showing off. As he reached the top of the hill, he looked back at his audience to see if he still had their attention, but unfortunately, his dog chose that exact moment to run in front of his bike, causing him to unceremoniously crash! He looked up, embarrassed, but Roxanna just cheered him on. He brushed himself off and got right back on but not before yelling at his dog to watch where she was going and asking if she was blind to run in front of him like that!

Roxanna hugged her father tightly, thanking him for making young Samad so happy. "I needed to make something right." Assad searched for words to explain his feelings. "You asked me why I married again. I needed a wife, and she was available. I felt guilty... You see, she was married to the man who helped me to stay away from the Savak's radar. He was caught and taken to jail. He never talked...then he was released. He survived being in jail and the Savak, but on his way back to his village, he was killed in a bus accident.

"Three people were killed, and he was one of the three. After I heard the news, I went to visit his wife and his two children. The children were staring at me with fear and sadness all over their faces. I felt empty. I felt guilty. I do not know why I felt I was responsible for their father's death. I had no choice but to take care of them. Her parents came to Akbaar, and they asked if I would marry her and raise the children. I resisted at first, but somehow Akbaar and her parents persuaded me to marry her. She was young, much younger than me, but she did not care. I married her and moved them away from their village."

Roxanna listened, mesmerized, as Assad talked about her Iranian stepmother. Wanting him to tell her more, she chose not to mention that Cyrus had said anything. Roxanna nodded. "I love them even more, now. And they are welcome to come to the States with us. I always wished I had a large family. I will take them with me when the time comes."

Assad held her tight and whispered so quietly that only he could hear, "My lovely girl . . ."

*****

Chapter 42

When Life Doesn't Go as Planned...and Love is divided...

Greek chorus commenting on the state of Iran, black thundering skies forewarned its people of evil deeds brewing in the night, conjuring exclamation marks from lightning bolts, mercilessly cutting the sky to shreds. Assad had spent the dark, wet day at the doctor's and was now sipping tea on the porch of his hideaway with Akbaar and Cyrus.

Inside, Assad's children sat on the floor, laughing as they played some sort of game. Sara knew that if her little brother didn't win, he would be reduced to inconsolable tears, so the outcome was always the same. Lovers of laughter, like their father, the girls would always throw the game in his direction.

Shahnaz, the littlest one, headed upstairs and wandered the hallway, sticking her little nose in each room as she passed until she found Roxanna, which had been her goal all along. Roxanna, who always slept fully dressed, was lying on her bed, ready to respond to anything at a moment's notice. Little Shahnaz entered quietly and stood by the edge, staring at Roxanna like she was a fairytale princess waiting for her prince charming to wake her from a spell. Finally, as if she could wait no longer, Shahnaz reached out and touched Roxanna's hair, twirling it around her fingers.

Roxanna had been dreaming, using sleep as an escape from the constant mental and emotional stress she had created by her actions. She knew that by searching for her father, she may have disclosed his whereabouts to Saeed and the Savanna, and it was eating at her gut. Each day was a continuous waiting game. She knew they couldn't hide forever, and Assad was too old and sick to be on the constant run.

On good nights, sweet dreams would take her to a time and place she could only imagine, a fantasy where her parents would be together and she and Cyrus would be inseparable. She would dream of being in Cyrus's arms, feeling their hearts beating as one. Then, something, someone would jolt her right back to the real-life nightmare she had walked into, so innocently, not so very long ago.

Roxanna reached out and gathered little Shahnaz into her arms and hugged her close, the tender moment interrupted by Akbaar's harsh voice coming from the porch below.

"Stop being stubborn, you must move to a new safe house and stop writing these letters, or you will get us all killed. If the clergy doesn't care about Islam, how can you expect them to care about their people or their country or new ideas which would elevate Iran to a world power? It is too late to make a difference. Iran's future has been set in stone by men whose hearts were carved of stone. Nothing, not even God, can bring our country back to the way it was before the Shah. Please, Assad, from now on, your time should be devoted to your family."

It was Assad's turn to be firm, "Just deliver my letter. It will settle everything. Let us go inside. I must spend some time with my children before they leave."

Roxanna froze, stunned by what she had just heard. Too young to have any comprehension of what was happening, Shahnaz kneeled on the bed, placing kisses on her sister's cheeks as the hard rain grew louder, pounding out its unrelenting message of doom. Knowing that Assad would be calling her down soon, Roxanna fixed Shahnaz's hair. Taking her hand, they started walking down the stairs.

Coming in from the rain, the men looked up, their eyes riveted on Roxanna and her little sister as they descended, so many years apart but so alike in their beauty. Akbaar took a step back to take it all in.

"I hope you're finally finding a few moments of peace and pleasure in this beautiful country," Akbaar said to his niece. Sara, the older stepsister, gave Roxanna a strong hug. Overwhelmed with affection, Roxanna lifted the littlest girl in her arms and kissed her chubby, rosy cheeks, saying, "I love you!" Her shy half-brother, Ahmad, looked up at her with soft black eyes and gently extended his hand to touch hers in a loving gesture. To Assad, the moment was magical, beyond his wildest dreams.

*****

Cyrus felt a strange emptiness come over him as he watched Assad, Roxanna, and all the children together, perhaps for the last time. His heart filled with sadness as his thoughts turned to his wife in America; his mind was traveling into the future, wondering if one day he would have children. And if he did, perhaps his life would be no different than Assad's, unable to be there for them, to share their lives, to watch them grow. He was overcome with guilt just thinking about how dangerous he had become to himself and those he loved. Words like guilt, judgment, blame, and abandonment haunted him.

His thoughts flew; like hummingbirds from one flower to another. How had it happened that his mother, who had raised him, cared for him when he was sick, taught him right from wrong, and given him a sense of identity could have been kicked out of the house she had lived in for fifty years? Forced out by Cyrus's old friend, Saeed, a friend he had once supported?

How fair was it to his American wife, the woman who loved him, the woman he'd promised to be with, in sadness and happiness, to leave her alone in the States? His answer could have lifetime consequences. His decision could require him to ignore everything he had lived and fought for, to turn his back on everyone he loved. But that would mean leaving Roxanna all alone in a dangerous country without a passport. And what of his responsibility to his other friends and to his loved ones, those who had been there for him all his life? How could he leave for America when they were suffering?

It was a heavy burden for Cyrus to carry on his shoulders; he felt as if the people of his homeland, those who had suffered and died to protect her, were passing the honor and the torch on to him. His assignment was to guard the land for future generations so it may be gifted to them, unencumbered, and to preserve Iran and its heritage; preserve the earth upon which Cyrus the Great walked, the land of King Cyrus the Great, founder of the first Declaration of Human Rights, which had inspired the genius of Khayyam, Saadi, Ferdowsi, Rumi, and so many others. How could he pretend not to see the hardships suffered by people affected by the greed and power of rogue nations, wishing to strip this beautiful land of her natural resources, placed there by God.

*****

Akbaar looked at his watch, wearily, as he began to collect his belongings, at the same time refusing to give up his attempt to appeal to his brother's sense of logic. It was not too late to take Assad away from Iran if he would go. He had already made arrangements to get him and Roxanna to the Iranian-Pakistani or Turkish borders, where he had a team ready to walk him over to Pakistan or Turkey. There was only one thing standing in his way. Assad refused to leave. His home was Iran. And Roxanna would not leave without her father.

Assad always said he could not breathe anywhere else. All that he had done had been for the good of the people of his country. Despite a lifetime of effort, planning, and sacrifice, all his good intentions had been for nothing, leaving him immobile, weighed down by frustration and guilt over the unintended results and the hardships he had inflicted upon his family as well as the people of Iran. But to leave now would negate both his failures and his achievements, voiding his past, stripping it of value … discarding the history of a country in the throes of rebirth, reducing it to rubble.

The plan was to leave with the children at night, using the rain as a deterrent. Even if the Revolutionary Guards had found out about Assad's safe house, they would be a bit less likely to brave thunderous storms and lightning, opting to wait until the weather cleared before they continued their nefarious activities.

Akbaar had prepared everyone for their departure, each child holding a little bag while he held two larger packages of his own. It was time. He would take Assad's children back to their mother while doing his best to mask the truth; this would be the last time they would see their father.

Although they didn't understand the reality of the situation, Assad had tried to explain his upcoming absence in their lives by using his job and the excuse that he was transferred. Perhaps it would have been better to let the children leave, thinking their father would be home soon, but it was too late. The thought of leaving their father and especially Roxanna was devastating, and now they refused to leave. Crying, they took turns hugging their father and then Roxanna.

Shahnaz held on to Roxanna with all her might, wailing as if the end of the world had come. Roxanna picked her up and carried her outside as both sisters tried to change Roxanna's mind in chorus, "We love you! We don't want to say goodbye. Tell Baba we must stay together. Come with us. Please! Please, Roxanna, please."

Roxanna's heart was breaking along with the children's, her eyes cut Asaad's, Rosanna could see a broken man who has no strength left to move or do anything, she knew in heart Assad has no other choice than let the children go, she felt so much sorrow for a man, for a man who she took so many steps to meet and known and respect and loved as her beloved father, but she knew the look of determination in Assad's eyes. Nothing would change his decision.

Assad stood steady for what he thought was right. He would accept death before compromise. Assad knew he has no choice, to go with the children or to keep them there. It only would place them in danger of getting killed. He knew this time the enemy has no mercy for no one, not even for the ancient children. The only thing he could do holding his tears back from his children until they left. Respecting his decision, Akbaar hugged Assad one last time in silence. Little did they know that deep inside, their heart was breaking. The two grown men were crying in silence within, neither of them had any answer for what had happened to them, they only were agreed on one thing, life is like a wild running river that changes direction any time with no prior notice, and it will take anything it gets hold of in its path, and in the end, it'll sink deep into the ground and die, or they will become as steam against the hut and disappear into the air, and then it is gone, just like life.

The rain was now coming down in sheets. It was not easy for Akbaar to help Roxanna get little Shahnaz in the middle while her older sister and brother held on to her. She did not want to leave Roxanna. Once they were all secure, Roxanna stepped back to start giving distance to their departure. The sound of the slamming door and the pounding rain, along with Shahnaz's torment, wrenched her heart. With almost animal-like fury, the little girl clawed her way over her sister and pressed her tiny face against the window, her eyes pleading to Roxanna to save her.

Before Akbaar could get in, Roxanna approached him and gave him one last hug. "Be safe, Akbaar. Thank you for taking care of the children. One day I will take them back to the states." The two stared into each other's eyes. "Take care of yourself." Akbaar Said. "I'm more worried about you than about your father. You are too young and innocent to be involved in something as tragic as what is happening in our country."

Then Akbaar recalled he has something for her. He walked open the trunk and took one of the two large packages, and held it out to Roxanna. "I do not believe your father would mind for you to have this. It is his oldest and favorite Tar." She took the package but could not say a word. Lost in emotion, she watched Akbaar get inside the car, and soon, the car had disappeared in the fog of night. She could not stop her tears, her endless, salt tears falling like acid rain, burning her cheeks, forever scarring her heart.

Like magic, the raindrops turned into silent flakes of gentle snow, transforming the nightmare into a childlike fantasy. There was a sense of God in the air, sending a message of hope, letting them know that life is a continuous metamorphosis. She turned toward the house and noticed her father, Assad, was watching her from the window all along, being showered by rain, washing her sadness, but even the heavy rain could not succeed.

Back inside, Assad greeted her with red, swollen eyes and a shy smile. He had lost his youngest children forever, but the daughter he never knew had stayed by his side. He felt a sense of guilt for not making sure she left with the others, but Cyrus assured him that trying to send her away would have been an impossible task. The two men sat on either side of the couch as they watched Roxanna carefully untie the twine from around the heavy, tan mailing paper. Underneath, the gift was wrapped in the most beautiful, delicate tissue paper, decorated with colorful mosques that she had ever seen.

She gently unfolded one end and then the other to reveal Assad's old tar. Both Cyrus and Assad were taken aback at how beautiful Roxanna looked when her eyes gazed down on the ancient instrument. Love radiated from her as she held it out to her father. "Uncle Akbaar said you do not mind if I have this?" Tears in his eyes, choking with emotion, "This is the best ever your Uncle Akbaar has done yet."

"Then would you play it for me?"

Assad walked to her, looked at his old tar, this hauntingly beautiful percussion instrument that he'd had for decades. The sound from the animal skin wrapped tightly around the frame emitting such a unique tone; it is Iran, its heartbeat, its rhythm. Assad carefully lifted it and, holding it with one hand, placed his fingers on its body and began to gently tap it with finesse. The music of Assad's tar resonated throughout the house, carrying the problems of the world away, far from their safe haven.

In a rare moment that he attributed to Cyrus and Roxanna's presence, Assad sat on the sofa with his eyes closed, playing and chanting, totally absorbed at the moment. He was able to let his guard down because he knew he was protected, surrounded by love. For as long as he could remember, he had not known pleasure or joy, except from his children. He could not remember peace. It was with him now.

Mesmerized by the sound of the tar, Roxanna listened, watching the two men in her life. Assad had lived a life of frustration, unfinished endings, and sacrifices of huge proportions, only to find that, in the end, nothing had changed. Tyranny and oppression had won, regardless of the best efforts of the people who fought for a better life for their country.

He had never wavered in his fight to achieve his goals, and whether he achieved them or not, he held strong to his values and what he believed was best for his country. The only honor he felt was to know with certainty that he had fought for his strong values and had remained true to his convictions to the bitter end, for him, that was enough.

Cyrus, she desperately loved. But in an ironic twist of fate, she had lost him before he was ever hers to lose. If they had met in America, she would not have waited for him to make the first move. She would have been the aggressor, setting her sites on her man and taken him down. But they had met in Iran and under special circumstances.

How could it be that Cyrus went to Los Angeles and returned married? It was a dumb question, and she knew it. She understood exactly how it happened. Love was free in the United States, and everything moved at lightning speed, including relationships. Still, during long, sleepless nights, she found herself obsessing over the fact that somewhere a million miles away, there was a woman with a ring on her finger waiting for her husband's return.

Just like her mother had waited for Assad. But it wasn't her…Assad's festive mood filled the room, and Cyrus, too, began to chant as he joined in, playing his harmonica. Although words were never spoken, they were all too aware that their time together was marked in stolen moments, both priceless and irreplaceable.

Watching Cyrus as he moved his body, rhythmically, to the music in front of her, she could feel herself falling off a mountain. She knew she must enjoy this moment of beautiful truth with the two men she loved, knowing destiny would have the final word.

*****

Chapter 43

The Purpose of Dreaming is to Give Life Direction Until Reality Sets Your Course...

From her seat on the second-floor balcony, Roxanna gazed into the sky, alight with a thousand stars, marveling at the occasional shooting star, the entrancing beauty of eternity, sparkling like diamonds, before her very eyes. It was way past midnight, and unlike the two men in her life, she couldn't sleep. She was getting closer and more attached to her father with each passing day, and the thought of losing him, even from old age or perhaps sickness, was becoming unbearable.

Wrapped in a thick blanket, her gaze traveled from the star-filled sky to the tranquil river, and she shivered in spite of its warmth. She recalled sitting by the water, having a peaceful moment away from the storm that was hunting them. Knowing their time together was limited, she forced herself to ask the question she had been dreading ... but had traveled halfway around the world to find the answer to. "I sometimes wonder how you could leave a little girl and your wife who really needed you and loved you so much."

Assad spoke dryly, knowing that no matter how he said it, the response would fall flat on those he left behind. "The sick need a doctor to get well; building machinery cannot be done without engineers. I was an economist. My country needed a new age of economics and politics; that is what I studied for. That is why I had to return. When I was making the decision, it seemed to be the correct one."

His answer struck a chord deep within Roxanna, and she could not disguise the bitterness that crept into her voice. "So, it was okay to abandon your little daughter and wife who loved you?"

"We were all put on Earth for a purpose, to help others less fortunate. My thoughts at the time were of the millions of mothers here who were holding their hungry and destitute children. You and your mother were well cared for. I had to return and fight for the helpless—in the name of humanity. I always thought I would be able to be with you both in time.

"I made my decision to give up everything for a limited time in order to help because I could not justify living a luxurious life when my people did not have the basic necessities to survive. I never imagined not being allowed to leave Iran once I got here. Right or wrong, I walked down the path my heart led me. It was without my knowledge along the way that doors kept shutting behind me, and by the time I found out what had happened, it was too late. I woke up one day … a prisoner in my own country. But I accept responsibility and am forced to live with the consequences of the choices I made, no matter if they were the right ones or not, sad or happy, and even if I live each day carrying the burden of guilt, I realize it still does not change what was done."

Seeing the pain in his eyes, Roxanna reached out and held her father tightly, hugging him.

Roxanna was deep in thought, thinking ever since she was a little girl, a huge part of her was missing, and that part was her father. She needed to know it wasn't her fault. She always blamed herself and even her mom for driving him away. For the first time, she thought she understood. She thought there was no one to blame but the country and the politics. But she could not help but admire him for trying to bring goodness and happiness to others. She really loved him with his big, wonderful heart.

Then she noticed Cyrus's car was gone. She checked the house. Cyrus was nowhere to be found. He was gone like a ghost, once again, and only God knew when he would show up next. But this time, it was more painful and concerning for Roxanna, knowing both she and her father were in danger, and they were left alone.

*****

Chapter 44

When You Have No Choice but to Beg For Help From Someone You Don't Trust...

As the taxi approached a luxurious street on the North side of Tehran, the passengers realized they could hear a prayer reaching out to them in the distance, perhaps a mosque. Cars, mostly Mercedes and late-model luxury vehicles, were parked on both sides of the street. Older, less expensive cars were scarce or hidden from view.

The taxi stopped in front of Hajji Mohammad Zadeh's immaculate mansion on the North side; its large iron gate was open to allow entrance by invited guests. To most, the estate with its seven-foot-high wall was both mysterious and menacing, but not to Cyrus, who had been inside many times.

The only thing different was that previously he would have been driving his own car rather than showing up in a taxi. Much had changed since his last visit. Guests no longer arrived in suits or the latest western styles. Gone were the latest fashions from Paris or Italy. The best he could come up with to describe the latest fashion was…sloppy. Cyrus had refused to follow fashion in days past; that had not changed. He was true to himself and usually dressed in casual attire for comfort.

Standing by the gate, Cyrus was wondering if it was a good idea to go in when there was obviously some sort of event going on. During the Shah's time, Mohammad Zadeh was the one Cyrus would go to when he needed help for something that he didn't want his brother to know about. He had gone there to ask for his help getting Roxanna released from the Savak. But this time, he was there because Mohammad Zadeh had sent a message to see him.

Mohammad Zadeh had been a well-known lobbyist during the Shah's time. That had not changed. Cyrus knew he had been paid by the Savak to run a prayer ceremony and to identify people for the Savak. Now he was with the new men on the block, the clergy, and Savak. Not only had the name changed, but the people who were running it were also much more ruthless. The prayer ceremonies, which had been financed by the old Savak, had enabled Hajji Mohammad Zadeh to be well connected.

Now, with a small adjustment, funding was coming from the Savak. His job remained the same, only he now worked for the new regime. He had changed his loyalty the moment he realized the Shah would fall and Khomeini was coming into power. Fortunately, he had always liked Cyrus so much that he had tried to interest him in his daughter with the hopes of having him as his son-in-law still did not lose hope.

Realizing he had no choice but to go in quietly, he entered the gate on foot, surprised to find that valet parking had been replaced by bearded guards holding machine guns. Cyrus was trying to keep a low profile to hide his identity when suddenly a Mercedes charged through the gate and forced him into the flower garden to keep from being run over. Having no idea why a crowd of people had gathered closer to the house, he decided to stay where he was and watch.

When the Mercedes stopped in front of the mansion, the driver jumped out and held the door for the two clergymen sitting in the back, both dressed in Arabic outfits, one in a yellowish color, the other in gray. A man called a prayer, and people answered, each trying to yell louder than the next, as a way of showing their respect. Unable to make their way through the crowd, a guard approached and cleared the way into the building. Cyrus continued to observe from the flower bed as two more

Mercedes drove in, drawing an even bigger crowd, finally giving Cyrus the opportunity to mix in and avoid being questioned by the guards as he entered.

Passing through the entry, he was greeted by religious songs, crying. Being there many times, the first thing that caught his attention was that it seemed like everything, and the people were wearing black outfits, crying and mourning and having just tea and a sweet they call halva. The big difference than before was that there was laughing, joking, dancing, colorful clothing, food and fruit everywhere with servers to serve all equally. Being very familiar with the layout of the house, he forced his way through the crowds of people, winding his way up the staircase, passing two guards who controlled who goes upstairs and through the hallway.

Of course, he announced to the guard that he is Mohamad Zadeh's special guest, and they believed him. Far away from the noise of the mourning, he could smell the strong odor of opium. He passed elaborate private rooms filled with important people sitting around smoking opium and eating massive amounts of delicacies from silver platters, fruits and pastry. Much different than the average attendant downstairs.

Searching for Mohammad Zadeh without success, he finally asked a man carrying platters of miniature kabobs for help. The man motioned for Cyrus to follow him to an area previously reserved for ministers and powerful government officials during the Shah's time; a private place where they would smoke opium while entertaining beautiful women. Two guards, cradling machine guns, stood in front of the door. Cyrus waited nervously while the server walked past the guards, asking his name. Cyrus called it out, and a familiar voice told him to enter.

Inside, Cyrus found Mohammad Zadeh wearing a collarless shirt and sporting a beard, holding beads, and sitting with several high-ranking clergy and a few other men. The smell of opium hit his nose with such force he was unable to handle its effect on him. Cyrus was overly sensitive to opium because of his father's addiction and, for that reason, always stayed away from the drugs

The first thing he noticed was that Mohammad Zadeh had now added one more title to his name so as to better fit into his new crowd: Hajji Mohammad Zadeh. He had hardly used the title "Hajji" in the past even though he had visited the house of God in Mecca several times. Cyrus knew from his mother when you go to Mecca and visit the house of God in Saudi Arabia, you become a Hajji.

Hajji Mohammad Zadeh smiled when he saw Cyrus standing in the doorway and placed his arm around his shoulder as if he were the son he'd never had. He had three daughters, any of which he would have liked to marry off to Cyrus, and one son who had died in an accident. He excused himself from the others and escorted Cyrus to a private room in the back that he used as his personal office.

He was especially fond of that particular room because it overlooked the living room, and he was able to observe his guests unnoticed. Several small wooden boxes were piled up next to the most luxurious gold couch Cyrus had ever seen. He was used to opulence, but the workmanship on the carved wood trim was impeccable museum quality.

Hajji Mohammad Zadeh sat first, staring at Cyrus' beard, amused. He remembered Cyrus wearing a trimmed, stylish beard all the time, but he had shaved it after the revolution when having a sloppy one; the short beard had become a fashion and symbol of being a believer of Islam and for Khomeini and anti-American imperialism. He wondered what kind of message Cyrus was trying to send by letting his beard grow again, but the reason was simple. To Cyrus, shaving was unimportant in the scheme of things.

Hajji Mohammad Zadeh knew Cyrus was waiting for him to speak first. "I am sorry about your brother and especially your mother. I wanted to help, but I was too late for them. But I can help you, and you need my help. It seems you have lots of enemies and the main one is your best friend, Saeed. Personally, I did not like him when you came to me before and asked me to help him to get the young woman released. I like him even less now!"

Hajji Mohammad Zadeh thought for a moment, then continued, "I know many things are troubling you now, and I can help. Just between you and I, I have frequent visits with Khomeini and talk to him regularly. So, as you know, I am powerful enough to help . . . like save your life."

Cyrus looked up for the first time and stared into his eyes. He was speechless. He knew that Saeed was looking for them, but he didn't realize that there was an actual hit list out there that he and Roxanna were on. "Then, if you could help to save my life, for sure you could save a few others, also." Hajji Mohammad Zadeh gazed at Cyrus shrewdly, waiting for him to talk. "I need to get someone over the border; I need your help and some money. I will pay you when I get back to America. I am flat broke."

Hajji Mohammad Zadeh's greedy smile morphed into an evil grin. That was not what he had hoped to hear, but he was rich, and money meant nothing to him, so what did it matter? Cyrus was like a son to him, and that was the bottom line. Perhaps he could use the favor as leverage to get him to marry his daughter and take her to America. He did not know Cyrus was already married.

He opened a safe and removed three envelopes, handing them to Cyrus, "You do not have to pay me back. I never touched the money you paid me for the young woman. Your family has always helped me, and I always liked you, like my lost son. You know your name is on the list at all the borders; you cannot simply leave the country, you will be arrested, but you would not have to deal with all of these problems. As I said, I could help you to clear all your problems, and you could come and go as you wish and also take your friend, the American girl, out of the country with no problem."

"And what would I have to do in return?" Cyrus was wary of this sudden turn of events.

"Trust me and meet with your friend, Saeed. We will discuss this between the three of us." Hearing Saeed's name distressed Cyrus, and he was suddenly unsure if he could trust Hajji Mohammad Zadeh.

A sharp knock on the door startled Cyrus, but Hajji Mohammad Zadeh seemed to be expecting the interruption. Two men entered, carrying two huge wooden boxes that they placed with the others. Cyrus didn't have to be told. He could guess what was in them — donations by the people for the Imam, for Khomeini, and the collector was Hajji Mohammad Zadeh.

Once the men left, Hajji Mohammad Zadeh opened one of the boxes to show Cyrus it was full of money and jewelry. "I am the beneficiary. It is my job to collect the donations for five mosques. This is from Giyahy's mosque on the corner of Saadabad Street. I get my share no matter what. The rest goes to several different clergy and multiple other foundations.

"That is what life is all about here. Nothing has changed. I told your brother to tell the Shah to increase the salary of the clergy and to learn from the English. He did not listen, and who is in power now? The clergy! They will take everything and continue to rob and steal the resources of our country."

He leaned over towards Cyrus and quietly whispered into his ear, "They have no mercy, and they do not care how many people they kill. They are here to stay, and they have no shame. Their levels of hubris are so insane. These are men without reason. They are angry and power-hungry.

"Revenge guides their every decision. Islam means very little, even to the clergy, now. Their goal is to create fear and dominate a country brought to its knees by murder and violence. Listen to me, you must save yourself. You must make a deal with them."

Cyrus was lost in thought, wondering what he should do and if he could any longer trust Hajji Mohamad Zadeh. At the same time, he had no one else to ask for help.

*****

Chapter 45

When You Have No Way Out, and You Are Forced to Face and Talk with Your Worst Enemy...?

It was many nights later, under a crescent moon, that Cyrus made his attempt to slip out of Tehran, unnoticed. He debated for several hours whether he should see Saeed first, but, in the end, he found himself heading toward Assad. The debate of what to do and what not to do raged in his mind over the ten-hour drive left back to the small town where Assad was hiding.

Cyrus was still puzzled as to why Hajji Mohammad Zadeh had sent for him. He had told Cyrus he could save his life, but Cyrus knew it had to be more than that. To marry his daughter, perhaps? Cyrus was relieved to have borrowed some money from him as long as he was there...but more importantly, he needed help getting Assad and Roxanna out of Iran. The man's response was for Cyrus to meet with Saeed directly, something Cyrus couldn't bring himself to do. Just the mention of Saeed's name created doubts in Cyrus's mind about his intentions.

While driving toward Assad's cottage, he concluded that he would have been better off going directly to Saeed and not contacting Hajji

Mohammad Zadeh at all. The fewer people involved, the better. But what was done was done.

Cyrus saw the night slowly fade to black and white as the world around him filled with large snowflakes, splashing and melting into the windshield, each one its own "one of a kind" visual masterpiece. Cyrus suddenly wanted to pull over and rejoice in the work that went into each and every one before being cast off by the wiper blades.

But the hour was late, and he was trying to race the clock. He was approaching another of the many small, unremarkable cities he had driven through since leaving Tehran. His eyes searched for a phone booth, but in small villages like the one he was in, they didn't exist. Finally parking a few blocks away, he walked to the telephone company, but as he feared, it had been closed for hours.

After much help from an evening street cleaner whose job it was to know everyone and everything that went on after hours in his quaint little village, Cyrus managed to pay what he considered a small fortune to get some guy to open the telephone company office for him. The call was incredibly more painful than he could have ever imagined.

Cyrus found himself dialing the same number he had used to call his mother his entire life. But this time, he was calling Saeed, the same Saeed who had orchestrated the massive assault on his childhood home and thrown his mother out onto the streets; The same Saeed that had destroyed Hajji Khanoum's life and taken over her house and the family's possessions as his own. Cyrus began to shake with anger when he heard Saeed's triumphant voice through the receiver.

"It must be very important for you to wish to talk to your enemy." Cyrus took a deep breath, picturing Saeed sitting on his mother's needlepoint couch, his feet resting on her precious, rosewood table, smiling smugly as they talked. He tried to distract himself by recalling past memories of their younger years. It seemed like yesterday that they had been inseparable, Saeed, Cyrus, Nader, and Hussein. Comrades. Drinking, smoking, partying, and traveling together, Cyrus could not help but let his mind travel to their past.

It was not so long ago that they were vacationing in a luxury villa overlooking the Caspian Sea, a large, ice-blue pool tempting them from their patio. In their late teens, Nader and Cyrus were partying, listening intently to the distinct sound of moaning and groaning coming from a bedroom. As the moans grew louder, the three took great pleasure in spying on the occupants. A moment later, one final loud groan, followed by silence.

Cyrus and Nader opened the door wide, announcing their approval to Saeed, who was lying on the bedspread out like a naked butterfly, his grinning face covered with lipstick. A bored young overweight woman leaned against the headboard, lighting a cigarette. 'He is no longer a virgin, and that cost extra. Who is next?" She was eyeing Hussein.

Nader and Cyrus began to sing "Happy Birthday" in between fits of laughter as Saeed pulled himself up and strutted past them like some superhero. They watched as he made his way to the pool and fell in, naked.

He thought back to his past, thinking about how life is short, and you can never predict what the future has in store for you. Cyrus held the receiver next to his ear and breathed slowly, collecting his thoughts. "Enemies are created in the mind. And minds can be changed. Friendship is born in the soul. And the soul is eternal." Cyrus peeked out from his booth to see if anyone was listening. As he had hoped, he was alone. "I need your help to get a few people out of Iran… Whatever it costs. I will find a way to pay you."

The silence on the other end was deafening. Cyrus did not need to mention whom; Saeed knew he meant Roxanna and Assad. Cyrus could feel himself getting dizzy. He knew Saeed was making him wait on purpose.

"His life for yours. You must poison him. Then I let you and the girl leave…" Cyrus could not believe what he had just heard; the demand was inconceivable. He was to poison Assad. Kill him! It was a vicious, evil request, made even worse, by the pleasure Cyrus could hear in Saeed's voice as he spelled out his demands. No man could be so ruthless. Cyrus knew then, he was dealing with a monster.

Cyrus seethed with fury, forcing himself not to give in to his desire to tell Saeed how he would like to grab him through the phone and choke him. He knew he had no choice but to continue playing the game and hope he drew a better hand later down the line and buy himself some time to find a way to get them out.

Saeed chose to let Cyrus sweat for a very long time before continuing. "As I have said. We trade. Assad's life for hers... and yours. A deal is being made as we speak. Assad has already offered to trade his life for the safe return of Roxanna to America. And as for you ... I will give you the honor of killing Assad. You have two days.

"In return, I will see to it that you and Roxanna make it back, safely, to the US. If my men, do it, be assured, it will be a blood bath. And you and she will be drowned in the blood as well. If I were you, I would take the deal and save myself...? He is dead, anyway... I am just trying to save your life... my old friend..."

Paralyzed with fear, it took Cyrus a moment, and then he whispered, "I will get back to you..." Cyrus let the phone drop to the desk. There was nothing left to say. Slowly, he walked out into the blizzard where he found the man with the key to the telephone company waiting to lock up, half asleep and covered with snow. Cyrus reached in his pocket and handed him some money, thanking him before slowly making his way down the desolate street towards his car. He wished he had dressed warmer but knew that was the least of his problems. He stopped and leaned against a streetlight, trying to make sense of what was happening while at the same time assessing his situation. It was quiet, too quiet. He checks around him. Did he see something move, or was it just his nerves playing tricks on him? The sound of howling wolves, though, was unmistakably real. As he looked toward the hills, his eyes caught a glimpse of something suspicious, partially hidden from view. Was it a man? A wolf? Or just a shadow? He made it to his car and locked the doors, watching for confirmation of his worst fears in his rearview mirror.

He attempted to block out the feeling of dread that was consuming him by letting his thoughts wander as he drove. His mind was at war with his soul. He was disgusted with himself. Even if he meant well, why was he risking his life to help Roxanna and Assad when he had his wife, Julia, in America? And why had he gotten married to a woman he was not being honest with? And most importantly, what was he doing getting involved in something as uncontrollable and dangerous as politics?

For what purpose had he given everything up? For this land called Iran? What had he received in return? Inside him were only heartbreak and devastating loss, compounded further by the sickening realization that he had inadvertently contributed to the further destruction of his country.

Even more heartbreaking and beyond comprehension was the task that he had been ordered to perform by Saeed, whose position of power and authority could not be denied. He had been given a directive to murder Assad, who he respected as a man and loved as a father, to save his own life and Roxanna's. There was only one tragic outcome; death and a cementing of the new face of Iran as a country that was amoral.

*****

The snow was falling harder, blinding him, adding to the loneliness of the empty road. He could feel his thoughts sucking him in like quicksand, tormenting him. Memories, images, horrors he wished to never recall, the blood-soaked bodies of friends and children he loved, were flashing through his mind, cycling over and over, like a movie in an endless loop.

Allowing his mind to wander, Cyrus's car entered an icy, snow-covered curve too fast and skidded into a hole facing the wild, running river. The tires kept spinning, but the car was trapped between the road, a huge rock, and the riverbank. He immediately turned off the car and the lights, hoping not to draw attention to his predicament. Hearing Saeed's voice echoing in his ears, he wasted no time leaping out, intending to head towards the safe house where Roxanna and Assad were staying.

He continually moved his eyes back and forth, studying the snow-covered trees for any signs of movement, wondering if perhaps someone was watching him. He had taken every precaution not to be followed, but as long as people knew he was alive, they would be looking for him. And now that he had a price on his head, he was fair game; he could trust no one. Not even Hajji Mohamad Zadeh. In fact, Cyrus was concerned and afraid he betrayed their trust and friendship and that he gave him up to Saeed.

He took off on foot. He crossed from tree to tree, finally stopping at the top of the hill in clear view of the cottage where Assad and Roxanna were staying. After resting for a moment, he continued on, climbing the porch and looking inside through the window. It appeared empty and dark inside, sending a chill of dread over him.

A moment later, Assad appeared like a ghost from the kitchen wearing what appeared to be an apron. It was four in the morning, and he was cooking! He didn't care if Assad was going out of his mind, whatever his reason for cooking so late, at least he was alive. Knowing they were safe, Cyrus chose to remain outside, on guard. He sat on the porch and watched through the curtain of falling snow, waiting for the final Act, but nothing seemed amiss. He could feel something was wrong with this night.

Behind the window, looking out, Assad, himself on watch, found Cyrus on the porch, his head resting against the freezing wall, exhausted. A few minutes later, he exited the house with steaming tea and sat by Cyrus, handing him a cup. They sipped the tea in silence, not wanting to wake Roxanna, and watched as the snow blanketed the earth. It was as if they had magically entered a snow globe, transported to a different time, another world, a place that you could call heaven.

It felt almost as if some outside force had brought them together as if they had lived the same life. Both came from wealthy families and had been pushed into the political world, wanting only what was right for the land that they both loved. They never set out to try and change the world, but circumstance called to them. When the poor worked so hard, only to become slaves to propaganda with little or no education, when they were caught in the lies and deception of politics, it was hard to turn and walk away, to pretend it wasn't real.

Assad and Cyrus were among the few who cared enough to even try to make a difference, but the harder they tried, the more complicated their predicament had become. In the final analysis, they realized they had sacrificed their family, friends, and their own personal lives and, in the end, to find out nothing had changed. What they learned was that they had no real control, that the events of 1953 had been repeated again.

This time Mossad Israeli intelligence agencies led the CIA and tricked President Carter into supporting the Iranian Revolution. Men like Assad and Cyrus were left riddled with guilt as they watched their beloved Iran descend into a vicious cycle of suffering, knowing that once the wheels had begun to turn, there was no stopping the destruction.

Assad had once wished for Cyrus and Roxanna to get married, but as time went on, he was having second thoughts. As much as he had grown to love Cyrus, he was too much like himself. It would have broken his heart to see Roxanna end up like her mother. Both men sat side by side, quietly playing back what went wrong in their fight. The great tragedy was that they both felt so close to victory after the revolution, not knowing it was all smoke and mirrors. They were just beginning to realize that without a powerful base of support by the majority of those you wish to help, everything is lost.

They took a silent moment to do nothing but take in their surroundings, watching the giant snowflakes blanket their world as they breathed in the icy air, tinged with smoke from the wood-burning stove.

Cyrus took a sip from his tea, staring into the cold, snowy fog, and finally broke the silence, "What went wrong this time? Why couldn't we get it right this time?" Assad no longer worried himself with such questions, "This is too late for me to look for the reason or truth… to find what went wrong?

"I am sure our young and passionate brothers and sisters will wake up one day and will get there someday. They will expose the truth. It will be a nightmare that will haunt the clergy and the west." He drew a deep breath. "They have to, eventually, don't they? Isn't change the only thing we can hope for?"

Assad realized he was out of tea, but continued, "The fact is, this regime, the clergy, in particular, places no value on human lives, God or

Islam... they would sell all to stay in power and rule the people... the only language the clergy understands to stay in power in Iran is by utilizing the power of corruption, the force of fear and dictatorship directed by the megalomaniacs who hide under the false Islam and God.

"The end result would be the destruction of the image of Islam in the world's opinion, and the fastest-growing religion will become the most disliked and unpopular. And eventually, it will backfire, and the Islamic Republic of corruption will be crushed by the will of the people, women, and younger generations, and Islam would not have any more influence in Iran. And that is the best this revolution can give to Iran..."

The damp, heavy snow building up on the edge of the rooftop broke free and came crashing down, shaking the entire house, bringing both Cyrus and Assad back to the moment. Seeing the tears that had appeared in Assad's eyes, Cyrus was painfully aware that Assad could not handle even thinking about Iran's future or that he had sacrificed his life and family for literally nothing. The very people for whom he had been willing to die were the same who betrayed him and would watch him die, unmoved. Making it all the more frustrating was that he held tremendous guilt inside because his participation had hurt the most vulnerable; the innocents, the children of Iran for whom he wanted a brighter future.

Cyrus looked at his empty cup. He knew there was no right time to bring up Saeed, but he would have to do it sooner or later. "I didn't go to Saeed. I went to Hajji Mohammad Zadeh and asked for his help in getting you and Roxanna out of Iran."

Assad nodded, not at all surprised, "And I assume he sent you to Saeed?"

Cyrus felt guilty for not doing as he asked. He shook his head, a beaten man. It was as if everything was spiraling out of his control. "I called Saeed. He said you made a deal with them. How could you trust the enemy to let them know where you are?"

The expression on Assad's face remained constant. "I do not trust them, and I did not tell them where I stay. I just offered them a deal. You were supposed to get their answer. That is why I asked you to meet with Saeed in the beginning."

Cyrus stood up, looking at the fallen snow, glad now that he hadn't seen Saeed in person, or he might have inadvertently led him to Assad. But suddenly realized the dynamics of what had happened. Saeed and Hajji Mohammad Zadeh must be working together. Otherwise, why had Hajji Mohamad Zadeh asked him to see Saeed? So, Saeed's men must have been at Hajji Mohamad Zadeh's house the night Cyrus met him. Now he was certain they must have followed him to Assad's location. It had been a set-up, and he fell for it. His eyes combed the area for any signs of movement. He was debating whether it was just a matter of time…

Cyrus stood up and opened the back door allowing the biting wind and snow to whip in, fanning the flames. The winter winds were so strong that Cyrus had to use his shoulder to shut the door, the fierce ice storm already whistling through the fragile cottage walls. But that was the least of Cyrus's worries. "We must move you out before they find us. I have a feeling they have followed me."

Assad shrugged, unafraid. "I am dying. It is for the best. If they have me, they must allow Roxanna to leave freely. And if they do not, I have faith in you to get her to safety. As long as they see that I am here, it will give you a chance to move her away. I almost forgot. It is her birthday." He smiled sadly. "She doesn't know I still remember her birthday. We will celebrate. And then you must promise to take her away before first light … or we will all be dead."

*****

Chapter 46

When the Hope for Survival Means Hiding the Truth...

It was past midnight, too late for any sane man to be playing his tar with guests in his house, but to Assad, it was the perfect time. Like the Pied Piper, his music reached Roxanna's ears, waking her from her sleep and drew her towards him. She appeared on the stairs in her usual sleeping attire, light blue jeans, and a baggy shirt, surprised to see the living room decorated for a birthday party, lit only by candles, burning everywhere. Assad smiled adoringly at his daughter as he played his tar under a homemade paper banner that read, "Happy Birthday, Roxanna!"

Cyrus was waiting in the kitchen with nervous anticipation. When he heard her sweet laughter, he quietly surprised her, carrying a small homemade yogurt cake with a red candle stuck in it, chanting happy birthday in Farsi and English. Roxanna felt her stomach do a flip-flop at the sight of Cyrus, and it took every ounce of restraint she had not to run to him and jump into his arms. The fear and loneliness that had been her constant companion suddenly dissolved, replaced by a warm glow.

Assad playfully joined Cyrus as they sang "Happy Birthday" together in Farsi and English. Roxanna was so taken by the love she felt that she was unable to hold back her tears. She had completely forgotten about her own birthday, but her father had not. Cyrus held out the cake for her, and she blew out the candle. The concept of using homemade yogurt as a birthday cake was the most interesting part of the birthday party for her.

Trying not to be too obvious, Cyrus excused himself for a moment and went out on the porch. Heavy fog and snow blocked the moon, limiting visibility, creating a silent sense of foreboding, turning the landscape into a muted, dreamlike work of art. Cyrus searched the horizon with trepidation... hoping for a few more hours.

*****

After a delightful treat of yogurt cake and tea, Assad motioned for Roxanna to sit next to him as he continued his serenade, playing his tar and chanting. Hiding his anxiety, Cyrus joined in with his harmonica, dancing his way over to Roxanna and inviting her to join him on the makeshift dance floor. Together, they laughed and swayed to the music.

After every third or fourth song, the men would switch; Cyrus going back to playing his harmonica while Assad joined Roxanna on the dance floor. Laughter echoed throughout the house, and for a brief moment in time, the outside world didn't exist. The pleasure and love they shared together transcended all anxiety.

It was Roxanna who noticed that Assad was breathing heavily and motioned to Cyrus to stop playing his harmonica. Her father smiled, relieved, "I'm too old for staying up all night. I must rest before another day is upon us." He turned to Roxanna and took her in his arms. "Happy birthday, baby." He said quietly.

Roxanna hugged him close, never imagining it would be the last time she would see her father. "It was the perfect birthday! Thank you, Dad."

" Baba . . . I like Baba better."

"Thank you, Baba. I love you..."

"You are my daughter... You are duty-bound to respect my wishes as long as you are in Iran." Roxanna was surprised by the severity of his words, but she nodded her head out of respect.

"I want you to promise me you will listen to Cyrus and do whatever he says. I trust him like my son."

Roxanna glanced at Cyrus, puzzled, but he was of no help as his attention elsewhere, searching for the enemy. But all he saw were achromatic shades of black and grey through the glistening snow. Roxanna looked back to her father. "I promise. Thank you, Baba, for a wonderful birthday."

Assad kissed her forehead. "It is getting late for prayers, and I must sleep." With that, he took Roxanna in his arms and hugged her. "Perhaps you can help Cyrus while I pray. His car is stuck by the river, and it would be best to get it out before the snow gets any deeper. I am an old man and of little help. No longer of use to this world."

Roxanna was stricken by her father's words. "Oh, Baba, don't say that! You rest. You go pray and rest. I can help him!"

Cyrus glanced back towards Assad with a concerned look on his face. Both men knew this would be the last time Roxanna would see her father. Assad had tried to make the moment perfect, but nothing is perfect, which ends in goodbye. Completely unaware of the conversation that had gone on between the two most important men in her life earlier in the evening, Roxanna was overflowing with feelings of love and happiness.

She had never felt more safe and secure. It pained both men to think of the day not so far away when she would look back at the tragedy and cry for her Baba. But until then, if there was any hope for survival for any of them, Cyrus no choice but take Roxanna away before light. Assad hugged his daughter one last time and slowly climbed the stairs to his room.

Cyrus picked up his heavy jacket and gestured for Roxanna to do the same. "I took a turn too fast and landed in the river. Well, almost in the river." Cyrus confided sheepishly. "I can dig it out but come along and keep me company."

He grabbed some blankets and a bag he had prepared before. "Take your purse. We may head to the city afterward to stock up on food." He could see that Roxanna thought he was absolutely out of his mind and was about to tell him so. He held up his hand to halt her words as she opened her mouth to speak. "Please do not question me. I need your help to arrange our escape."

As Roxanna disappeared to get her things, Cyrus's eyes landed on the case to Assad's tar. He found some beautiful tissue paper and gently wrapped the tar before placing it inside for safekeeping. He threw a blanket around it and placed it on his stuff to take with them. Just as Roxanna reappeared, he nodded towards Roxanna. It was time. She looked at him, frightened, but didn't say a word. Twice she had placed their lives in jeopardy; she knew better than to do it again. Silently, she followed Cyrus into the cold unknown.

*****

The sound of woeful howling hung heavy in the distance. Concerned, Assad was already standing on the small upstairs balcony, watching stoically, as the young couple walked away from the house and disappeared into the fog and snow. He knew the enemy might already be observing them, and he wanted to be a visible distraction, hoping to enable Cyrus and Roxanna time to escape.

He knew he was their number one priority and, if forced to make a choice, they would go after him first. After fifteen very cold minutes had passed, he finally felt comfortable to start to wash his face pouring water from the water jar he brought with himself, getting ready for his prayers. The sound of woeful howling could be heard louder and louder. The wolves were hungry or perhaps mad.

*****

Loaded down with heavy blankets, Cyrus trudged through the shimmering snow, making deep tracks as he went, so Roxanna could more easily follow in his footsteps carrying the tar with her. Because she was focused on watching each step and not falling, it hadn't occurred to her why Cyrus was rushing, or there could be danger in the area until she noticed Cyrus constantly looking from side to side, assessing their situation. She stopped and followed his eyes to see if she could see anything that might be of concern. Was it her imagination, or were those wolves lurking from behind the trees? She called to Cyrus. "What is it?"

"Wolves. Hurry up… do not stop…" Cyrus whispered, hurrying Roxanna following Cyrus.

*****

Assad was drying his face. He was sure Allah would forgive him for postponing his prayers until he had one last glimpse of his daughter. She and Cyrus had disappeared into the trees but not from his mind. Even when he closed his eyes, she was there. Assad could feel the devil of death needling him in the icy wind. It brought a gentle calmness with it as if he had resigned himself to slowly freezing to death.

Almost as if his life was playing in reverse before death, he held out his arm like a small child and watched as snowflakes settled on his coat and frozen hand. He turned his head up and let the snowflakes sting his face and eyes. He stuck out his tongue and tried to taste them, all the while listening to the wolves.

His mind was quickly traveling backward, running out of time. Roxanna was a baby now, crying in his arms. As if a spirit had moved in to guide him to safety, Assad turned and went back into the warmth, softly singing, "Hush, Little Baby," switching back and forth between the Farsi and English versions of the song. He gazed at his reflection in the small mirror hanging on the wall, continuing to sing his daughter's lullaby. Although there was nothing in his arms, he went through the motions of laying baby Roxanna down next to his prayer rug. Just as he was about to kneel for his prayer, he looked up to God, hoping that his just, kind, and loving God was thinking of his precious daughter and protecting her. Tears began to stream from the corners of his eyes and trail down his cold cheeks; his sadness, so dark and heavy, was burying him before death.

*****

Roxanna held on tightly to Cyrus's coat as he pulled her through the deep snow and up towards the last hill before heading down towards the partially frozen river where Cyrus's car was. He stopped to rearrange the blankets, making it easier for Roxanna to grab hold of the crook of his arm. Cyrus could feel the penetrating eyes of many wolves searing him; hungry shadows on the move from every direction.

Now, he knew these shadows could not be just the regular wolves; he was sure they had followed him. Hearts pounding and out of breath, they finally reached the car. Cyrus opened the back door and dropped the blankets inside, then took what she was carrying and placed it inside. Roxanna was holding the tar as she got in the front. Concerned, Cyrus looked back toward the house, then turned to Roxanna and asked her to wait in the car for him.

He then walked up the small hill, stopped at the crest, and looked towards the house, hoping all would be still. But it was not so. To his horror, flashlights sliced through every room, signaling that the guards were storming the house, and they were inside with Assad. He had no idea how or if he could save Assad, but he knew one thing, he would die trying. Without any reservations, he took off towards the house to see if he was right.

No longer willing to stay behind, Roxanna exited the car. She looked up for Cyrus but unable to see him, she dropped the tar inside and took off after Cyrus, falling in the snow and getting back up, again and again; the ferocious winds forcing jagged particles of icy snow into her face, burning her eyes, inflaming her nostrils with each breath.

The howling wolves were silenced by the harsh smell of evil erupting in the distance. It was time to listen and assess the human threat.

*****

Surrounded by chaos, smashed windows, and doors, Saeed's own men entered with machine guns pointed in every direction, searching through the house.

Several armed men ran upstairs, shining their flashlights on the walls and ceiling, anywhere they might find something of value to steal. Entering Assad's room, they stopped dead, frozen with fear. It was as if they had come face to face with a crouching lion. Over the years, their pursuit of Assad had become more desperate with time.

So, when suddenly, they found him kneeling on his prayer rug, their first response was disbelief, and then to shoot, but none did. To the guards, he had become bigger than life, the greatest prize of all, their trophy kills. Finally, there he was. Cornered ... alone, unattended, unprotected, kneeling on his prayer rug. They were paralyzed. Several more men entered, directing their machine guns at Assad's head, waiting for the order to shoot. Finally, Saeed came strutting through the door like the alpha wolf he was, so pleased that he had reached the level in life where all eyes were finally on him. He was the star and everyone else, bit players.

Assad sat on his praying rug in peace, praying. Surrounded by chaos, he remained stoic as the "The legged wolves" methodically tore apart his domain. He placed his forehead on the prayer rug and began to pray softly. Saeed knew that all the guards were studying him to see how he was going to react to being ignored by Assad. Each stood with his gun pointed at Assad's head, hoping he was going to be given the order to shoot.

In a move that would have been unheard of, even in the Savak, Saeed decided to interrupt Assad's prayers by slowly lifting his foot and slamming Assad to the floor with his heavy boot, breaking Assad away from his prayer. It was a move that horrified Assad. He remembered it had only been a short time ago when he was surrounded by the Savak's men. They had waited and allowed him to finish his prayer. Now he was at the mercy of their replacements, men who claimed to be the secret force of Islam. These supposed men of God did not even let him finish his prayer to the God they pretended to honor.

In defiance, Assad's voice once more echoed in the room. Choosing peace, this time, he began to chant one of Rumi's poems but not the Namaz; too late for prayers. That was his protest and insult to Saeed and his men, who called themselves the Army of Islam. But they were not. He had always known his future. He just never knew Roxanna would play such an important part in making death so easy. As long as she was safe, he was at peace.

In a move so fast that to most, it was a blur, Saeed swung his foot and kicked Assad so hard in his face that he broke all of Assad's teeth, knocking him flat on the floor. Assad spit out his broken teeth as blood spurted from his mouth. And still, he managed to continue chanting Rumi. Saeed let him lie on the floor, giving him time to regret his insolence. He shined his flashlight around the room, watching as his men collected any valuables they could find and placed them in a box.

The light beam stopped on a picture of Cyrus and Roxanna, picked up the picture, and looked around like a hungry lion in shifting winds, getting the scent of raw meat. "They are here! Keep looking! They are in this house!" Only one of his guards had the nerve to respond. "We have searched the whole house. It is only him, Saeed."

Saeed walked out onto the balcony and shined his light into the woods, his eyes searching for any signs of movement. "They are here. Find them!" He went back in and stood over Assad, who was continuing to chant from Rumi through his bloodied mouth. Saeed made a swift hand gesture towards his men. It was one they had seen many times in the past. A guard walked up and slowly poured gasoline over Assad's head, letting the harsh liquid run into the old man's eyes and mouth, choking him, saving some to pour around the room.

"I see you are experienced at what you do. Is this how you burned all those innocent people at the Rex Movie Theater in Abadan?" Assad asked, choking and coughing from the fumes. "And your best friend, Nader?" Saeed was not amused. He lit a candle and held it up, studying him through the flames. Assad's eyes were staring at Saeed, smiling in peace. Stinging from the fuel, his head throbbed in excruciating pain, but at no time did he beg for his life.

Infuriated, Saeed threw the candle on Assad, and within seconds he was engulfed in flames, chanting until the very end. Soon the entire room exploded into flames, devouring everything in its path, leaving nothing but the smell of burning flesh as evidence.

*****

Finding it harder and harder to walk through the snow without Cyrus's footsteps to pack it down in front of her, Roxanna was forced to stop and try to catch her breath, the smell of death contaminating the air, creating a terminal fog, almost impossible to breathe. She could feel the vomit rising in her throat.

Out of nowhere, in a sudden move, she was tackled to the ground. She crouched down, motionless, realizing it was Cyrus. The weight of his body held her down, out of sight. With one hand, he pulled her face sideways, their cheeks pressed together, as he whispered with authority.

"They are all over, be quiet, please. We must leave." Cyrus was aggressive, almost to the point of violence. Roxanna had never seen him act aggressively towards anyone, so to see him act that way towards her was terrifying. She loved him enough to trust him in any situation, so her first reaction was to obey. But this wasn't "any situation." Her father was in that burning house! It also appeared that the stables were burning.

Ignoring the cries of the animals, the guards put down their machine guns and, like scavengers, began filling their cars with everything they had managed to steal during the raid. On top of the hill, Yousef, Amir's old driver, had been watching the events as they unfolded, his heartbreaking, knowing Assad was inside.

By the time Yousef turned his attention to the stables, it was too late to open the doors. He fired his gun at the locks hoping the animals could push their way out, but all that was heard was the sound of hooves beating against the stalls and the panicked cries of the horses, goats, and sheep that Roxanna had loved and tended during her stay.

Saeed exited the house, joining his men. He stood by his car and stared into the hills, grinning at the magnitude of the destruction he had caused. Yousef had seen the look in his eyes on more and more occasions, the look of a madman. It was all Yousef could do to hide his hatred for this evil excuse for a man, who had forced him to be his driver after Amir's death.

Saeed turned to his personal guards and chastised them for standing around and not continuing their search for Cyrus and Roxanna. They immediately set out on foot, yelling to their fellow guards to join them. Flashlight beams shined in every direction, cutting through trees, bouncing off the ice blue snow, moving away from the destruction.

The longer Cyrus held her, the more she fought. If something terrible was happening to her father, she would witness it to the end. If he was still inside, she would watch until there was nothing left to burn. She didn't want her last memory to be a fake smile as he waved goodbye! She wanted to remember the man who stood for his beliefs and died with his dreams! And she was willing to die along with him.

Cyrus held Roxanna's head firmly in the snow, his hands covering her mouth. Sobbing, tears streamed sideways across her face as her lips and chin quivered uncontrollably. Although her anguished screams were muffled by Cyrus, his gloved hand pressing on her lips, her words could be heard, faint but clear, "I love you, Baba! You will be with me in every flame I see, every burning candle, every flame from every oil field, until the day I die!"

Roxanna had witnessed too many deaths since coming to Iran to care about dying. She, herself, was on a hit list, so perhaps it would be better if she made her own decision when to die instead of being chased down like an animal. But what had she done to Cyrus? Once again, she had placed his life in jeopardy. She searched his eyes for any signs of anger, of hate, or regret, but all she saw was love.

He whispered, "We must go." Cyrus helped her up and pulled her towards the trees just as flashlight beams started crisscrossing through the branches overhead. Once again, he forced her to the ground and got on top, hiding her from view, speaking quietly and as fast as he could. He knew they did not have much time to save their lives.

"He knew they were coming. He traded his life for yours so you could survive. You must stay alive to honor his wish! They'll kill us both! It's over . . . Do you understand? He is gone." Their eyes locked, knowing Assad had disappeared into the flames. For a brief moment, sharing the inconsolable pain of loss, their hearts became one.

Finally, Cyrus pulled her away, and they begin to rush through the woods, Roxanna still looking back, watching the flames reaching into the sky burning her father alive, her eyes tearing in the snow. Racing to their car, Cyrus and Roxanna were thrown to the ground by one final explosion. Looking back, they could see flashlight beams dancing through the woods, closing in on them.

Cyrus grabbed the extra coats and blankets and tossed them in the car while Roxanna climbed in the front seat holding tight to her father's Tar. The heavy snows had hidden his tire tracks long ago, making it harder for the guards to find them but also making it harder for Cyrus to dig them out. Although the fog made it almost impossible to see, Cyrus knew the front of the car sat just a few yards from the raging river, which left them between a rock and a hard spot. Without a miracle, they were doomed! He hunted in the snow and started digging. His eyes were focused on the top of the small hill, watching.

Flashlight beams were closing in, the yelling louder. They were moments away from getting shot. Cyrus opened the driver's door and shifted into neutral as he tried to push the car towards the river. Roxanna jumped out and began pushing on her side. The car started to move, an inch at a time, but far from the front tires reaching the water; the sound of a splash and then silence. The car suddenly felt heavy and came to a stop, and would not move. Horrified, Cyrus looked around for Roxanna, but she had vanished. He ran to the back of the car and around the other side and found her in the raging river, trying desperately to pull herself out. She had lost her footing and slipped just far enough away to wind up soaking wet and terrified.

She tried to reach towards Cyrus with one hand but lost her balance and wound up even deeper in the water. Cyrus held tight to the front bumper and grabbed a tree branch with his other hand, positioning himself to reach Roxanna. Terrified of losing her footing, she remained frozen until Cyrus, balancing on one foot, was able to swing his leg in her direction.

She dove toward it and held on while he bent his knee, pulling her towards him and out of the river. Relieved, he lifted her in his arms and carried her frozen body back to the car, covering her with every blanket and coat he had.

Lights were getting brighter, cars closer, voices louder. Cyrus was afraid to turn around and face the approaching headlights, but he had no choice. His heart skipped a beat when the car stopped inches from his, its high beams directed at his face. He reached for his handgun, got out, and looked into the blinding light, knowing it was Saeed. But it was not. It was Yousef.

He immediately turned his lights off so as not to draw unwanted attention, leaving Cyrus speechless. They could hear the sounds of other men working their way towards them. Cyrus was unsure of where Yousef's loyalties stood but knew he would do whatever Yousef said unless it put Roxanna in danger. It was a clear and simple order. "Stand back."

Cyrus motioned for Roxanna, who was shaking badly, to stay down as he took three steps away. Yousef drove his car into the back of Cyrus's car and pushed it far enough into the river for it to start to float. Cyrus and Roxanna had found their miracle in Yousef. He caught up with his car and managed to climb in before water started pouring in, all the while thanking God and Yousef! All that was left was for Cyrus to guide his car into the wild, strong current and let it carry them to freedom.

Minutes later, Saeed arrived, yelling ferociously at Yousef. Surprised, he turned and apologized, profusely, for leaving him behind to join the search and then making a wrong turn because he had kept his lights off, almost winding up in the river. Cold and shaking, Yousef couldn't have been more convincing.

*****

Covered with all the blankets, shaking as bad as anyone could, fighting to stay awake, Roxanna watched. Cyrus was in a fight with the wild river. As hard as Cyrus tried to maneuver the car away from rocks and giant logs, he had little control over where the current was carrying them. His eyes focused on a huge log heading in his direction, but all he could do was duck as it slammed into the windshield with the force of a locomotive, shattering the glass and letting the icy water pour inside. Both Roxanna and Cyrus had accepted their fate, consoled by the fact that Saeed would not have the pleasure of watching them die.

A few miles downstream, the river widened, slowing the water to a quiet calm and giving them a chance to take a deep breath. They were soaking wet but alive. Cyrus reached around and gently touched Roxanna's leg to let her know things were getting better. She was curled up into a ball, her entire body drenched and shivering.

Cyrus climbed over the back seat, searching the floor for anything even half dry to put over her, leaving the car to drift towards the riverbank, finally lodging itself behind a huge rock. His only concern was for Roxanna. He wiped her face with his cold, numb hands, hoping to share what little warmth was his; their bodies pressed together, keeping her alive. Even the birds and forest animals fell silent in reverence. It was time to cry.

Roxanna's body temperature was falling dangerously low. She was shivering uncontrollably, sweating with fever, her skin hot and flushed. It would be hours, if at all, before the sun would break through and fight the cloud cover, warming the couple. By then, it would be too late.

Cyrus was losing faith. He gently removed her wet clothes and wrapped her in a damp blanket, his eyes searching for another miracle; dry leaves, a dead animal carcass, something to cover her with. There was nothing. Removing his coat, he tucked it around her to help hold in her body. Looking out, he was concerned whether he could see any beam of Saeed and his men's flashlights. He could not see any. It would be better to stay where they were, partially hidden and hope Saeed had thought them dead.

But he knew he had to wait for a miracle to save Roxana's life. At the same time, Cyrus was terrified when he heard the slightest sound from outside, and he removed the blanket from his face and inspected the surroundings. He was looking for a dance, the light of flashlights, or the shadow of hungry wolves. But he does not see anything. To some extent, his anxiety subsided, and he covered his head and started warming up and talking to Roxana.

Once he had a thought, he hurriedly moved Roxanna toward the front seat of the car and left her. Then he waded towards the back part and attempted to open the cover that was covering the trunk. It wasn't easy; he had no choice but to use a knife to break part of it and create a hole big enough for his hand to go through, and soon, his hand was searching what he was looking for. His fingers were numb with frostbite and of little use, but after a few failed attempts, he found what he was looking for…a small package wrapped in a dirty rag containing two bottles of hard liquor.

Cyrus knew that Roxanna was already slipping into hypothermia, and he was depending on the vodka to warm her insides. He got back to Roxanna, removed his clothes, and slipped beneath the blanket, pressing his body against hers, and like two sticks being rubbed together, they began to generate an intense heat. Cyrus took a swig from the bottle and held it to her lips, letting the biting liquid drip down into the corner of her mouth.

*****

They were in imminent danger. Unless they were wrong about Saeed, his guards were already within hearing distance…but the future was of no consequence to them. Roxanna had almost frozen to death, yet all she could think about was the warmth of his body next to hers, the way his chest moved when he breathed, his touch…his masculine, raw scent. She was consumed by his essence, submitting to the will of a powerful yearning, clawing to be set free.

Their passion, stronger than any fears that loomed ahead, released itself as they lay entwined among the wolves. Roxanna's beautiful, perfect breasts responded to his gentle touch. She could feel his chest rise and fall against hers, each breath becoming deeper, more jagged, intensifying with desire. They tasted love, sipping at first, then drinking it in like fine wine.

Filled with a desire fanned by urgency, the embers smoldered, catching fire and burning out of control. Their bodies joined together, becoming one, the rhythm of their movements, a symphony only their hearts could hear.

*****

Awakened by the sound of a lonely cry, Cyrus chastised himself for falling asleep. In the distance, he saw a pack of wolves huddled against a curtain of freshly fallen snow. Almost as if by magic, five inches had fallen as they slept, blanketing their world in a gentle calmness. It was as if Mother Nature had waved her magic wand and erased the past, eradicating all fear, creating a blank canvas, a new world untouched and filled with promise.

Cyrus reached out to find his handgun in case he needed to use it, held Roxanna tenderly as she slept, mesmerized by the family of wolves sharing their space. The female held her head high and kept a watchful eye over everything in his sight. After a time, she got up and paced back and forth at a safe distance, stopping to watch Cyrus and Roxanna, wondering. Waiting. Satisfied that all was well, she would lie back down in the snow.

The others followed, lying down by her side, yelping. Awakened by the howling of wolves communicating with each other, Roxanna looked into Cyrus's eyes to see if she could sense any danger in his. He pointed towards the families of beautiful wolves with their thick winter coats watching over them, and they both smiled. Roxanna was too weak and sick to move.

*****

The sound of a gunshot slammed them, head-first, into reality; the two-legged predators were closing in. The horrible events of the previous night hit Roxanna full force. Her head swirled around for confirmation, her eyes searching for any sign of the house that went up in flames, taking her father's life along with it. But strong currents and heavy winds had driven them far beyond the evidence. All they could see was snow, the truth buried so deep it was as if it had never happened.

Still, she needed something tangible, an acknowledgment of the enormous loss she suffered, something to validate her emptiness. She reached for her father's Tar. Although the blanket was gone, it was still in its case, wrapped in white tissue paper covered with brightly colored mosques. It was safe! And it was real. Roxanna looked into Cyrus's eyes, but for the first time since they'd met, he wasn't looking back. She slipped back into his arms and pulled the blankets over them, feeling a cold chill like she had never felt before. Cyrus was lost in thought. For him, his task has just begun, and it was the hardest task he would ever be assigned; to take Roxanna somewhere safe until he could devise a plan to get her out of Iran. It would not be easy. They had no friends left.

The female wolf howled and gathered her pack around her, a sign that someone was approaching. Cyrus grabbed his gun again and pointed it towards a figure in the distance, trudging through the snow. Something familiar told him to hold off… A sense of great relief came over him when he realized it was Samad, the young boy with his dog. It was the dog who helped Samad to locate them.

If Roxanna had any hope of waking up from her nightmare, the young boy ended it. With tears streaming down his face, he told them he went to the house to deliver food and what he had seen. There was nothing left of the burned-out house but a pile of glowing embers and hot white ash, harsh against the new-fallen snow.

"Where is Assad? Did they burn him? Where is God? Is there no God?" Samad was practically crying and could hardly talk through his tears as he continued, "I went to the house … there was no house… few guards surrounded me, and they want to know where about you guys are? I told them perhaps you guys left at nighttime… one said 'they cannot leave because we were around the road.' I told them you generally use the hill to come and go, so they left me and took off toward the hill… I knew you guys must be around. That is why I was looking all morning for you… my dog found you… he smelled you… we must go before it is late…" Neither Cyrus nor Roxanna had an answer for the crying child.

The lone wolf howled, accepting Roxanna and Cyrus into her pack, becoming their protector. They all looked up to see the majestic animal standing, alone, on the hill; a messenger. She howled again. Cyrus nodded knowingly, finally looking Roxanna in the eyes. "Neither of us is safe as long as Saeed has a breath of life in him..."

*****

With Roxanna too weak to travel, it was Samad that braved the snow and ice to get help and move them to a safe location to recover until Akbaar reached them. Akbaar's truck was parked far enough away to offer privacy for their last goodbye. Both Roxanna and Akbaar had changed their identities for their trip ahead. There were only the friendly wolves on the hill watching them. Akbaar was sitting in the driver's seat to give Roxanna and Cyrus privacy to say goodbye.

Leaning against the bed of the truck looking into the hill, watching the wolves, neither of them wanted to let go, to say goodbye. Roxanna gazed into his soulful eyes, her image reflecting in his tears, whispered.

"I want you to know... I don't regret coming here?"

Cyrus, in deep pain, whispered, "I know. Please, you are not safe here any longer. Go back home."

Roxanna lost into the hill, watching the nature and the peaceful wolves, "Your home is where your heart is. I am home..." Then she continued, "I struggle to understand why sometimes love is your worst enemy? Why does it bring sadness and pain? When it meant to bring happiness?"

Cyrus responded in more pain, "Maybe it is meant to be forbidden all along. So, it would never die." Cyrus continues, "If I die, it is up to you to carry on my work. Document our tragedy. Expose the truth. Let the world know what is happening here."

Roxanna gazed into his soulful eyes, her image reflecting in his tears, "You must stay alive. This is your job to write and document the event... you belong to them... just like my father was..."

Then, tearfully she reached and hugged him tightly. Then she opened the front door to get in, stopped, and turned, "I am wondering why the final words always had to be goodbye?"

She gets in closed the door. Akbaar reached around and grabbed Assad's Tar, holding it until she got in, then handed it to her, placing it in her lap. Akbaar started driving slowly towards the horizon, ripping Cyrus's heart out with it as it went. Alone, like a statue covered in white snow, Cyrus stood and watched for what felt like an eternity, everything he lived for, loved for, fading into blinding white.

Almost as if she was by his side, he could hear Roxanna's voice, overcome with disappointment, anger, and sadness…as she would begin the task Cyrus had put to her; to expose man's inhumanity towards man…

*****

'I struggle to understand how we can justify interfering in the business of ruling other countries, ruining them by imposing and manipulating dictators who oppress their people in the name of black gold. We foreigners have masked our greed, our lust for oil, by hiding it under the cloak of democracy. It is time to ask ourselves what we would do if it were happening to us! What if those suffering injustices were our brothers, sisters, mothers, fathers, children? Ask yourselves if what our country is doing to Iran is humane! Is what we have done Christian? Jewish? Muslim? Is this the world we would want for our loved ones?"

*****

Chapter 47

The Sound of the Tar Haunts a Soul...

The clouds hung low and threatening as if Assad's tragic death had thrown a heavy, grey blanket over Tehran, smothering all that was good. Saeed had hardly been seen outside of Cyrus' mother's house since the day he threw Hajji Khanoum out onto the street and moved in. This day, he was standing in the glass door of her bedroom, now his own, looking out onto the balcony where she used to feed her birds. Since his takeover, Saeed had continued to throw seeds out to attract the birds and then shoot ... to hunt them. There was nothing more he enjoyed than eating the innocent little birds.

Saeed held a gun in one hand while holding the phone up to his ear with the other, listening to Cyrus's voice coming through the receiver. He had an evil, threatening look on his face, not liking what Cyrus was saying. "I am watching you... every day ... every night..."

Saeed stepped further out onto the balcony, daring him to back up his words, waiting to hear if Cyrus knew where he was standing. But if he saw him, he wasn't letting on. Cyrus's comment was followed by a long silence that Saeed was enjoying. Cyrus had been the one to call him. It was up to him to say what was on his mind.

Saeed could only guess, but it was a good guess. Still, he wanted to hear it from Cyrus's mouth. He wanted to hear Cyrus beg for his life, for the life of that American girl he was involved with. He wanted to hear his old friend beg for mercy. And it would be more enjoyable for him to kill Cyrus after he begged for his life.

Finally bored with the endless silence, Saeed put the phone down on the railing, raised his gun, and aimed, shooting one of Hajji Khanoum's beloved birds out of the sky. It was a direct hit, feathers flying everywhere, bloody pieces of the gentle bird falling to the balcony deck. He raised his gun and shot, again, this time hitting a small dove trying to fly away, its tiny bloody body spiraling downward, slamming onto the deck. "I don't like being watched." Saeed seethed, into the phone, hoping Cyrus was watching his every action.

Far in the distance, the lone wolf stood in the snow and howled in anger, her heart bleeding for what she had been made witness to. Cyrus remained on the phone, appalled by Saeed's inhumane act towards his mother's innocent birds. There were no words to express Cyrus' feelings towards his long-ago friend. How could he have turned into this monstrous, savage murderer standing before him?

Angered by the thought that Cyrus could be playing some sort of game with him, Saeed threw the phone back into the house, ending the call. He looked at the dead birds on the balcony and kicked each one before looking in the air and waving his gun, "Soon, you will all be dead." Something caught his eye. Did he see a light reflected from the window across the way, or were his nerves playing tricks on him? His evil grin melted from his face when he realized it was Cyrus, opening the window directly across from his balcony, his body in full view. He was holding a gun, his face expressionless.

After a moment's thought, Saeed found the situation amusing. There was nothing in the world less terrifying than Cyrus. He spoke up, sending his words in Cyrus' direction, "You have no heart to shoot… to kill… You are not a killer…" He found Cyrus's attempt to scare him completely ridiculous, "You are a lover, lover of peace…and American women."

And before he could raise his gun to shoot, a bullet pierced Saeed's heart. Feeling his legs begin to weaken, Saeed grabbed the white, iron railing and slowly fell to his knees, his bloody hands staining the bars holding him in; a prison cell. The lone wolf howled louder, lending her support to Cyrus.

Saeed was amazed that he was able to find irony in his own death. He just got a huge dose of his own medicine from the last person he thought capable of giving it to him, Cyrus. He was going to die at the hands of his best friend, the only person he had never seen hold a gun. Saeed could only whisper, making sure Cyrus could read his lips, if not hear him, "Now there is no difference between you and me… We are both killers!"

Knowing Saeed's favorite sport was shooting Hajji Khanoum's birds, his guards had been unconcerned by the sound of gunshots coming from upstairs. It was long after dark before they finally went looking for him. They stood in Hajji Khanoum's old bedroom, surprisingly unmoved by the sight of Saeed's body spread out on the balcony in a mixture of blood, feathers, and dead birds. They looked around, but all they could see in the distance was a blanket of glistening snow, building.

The dark clouds had moved out, and a new beginning was about to dawn.

*****

Somewhere in the east of Iran, in the distance, a beautiful sunset highlighted the craggy mountains, accentuating the dangers awaiting anyone crazy enough to try to cross. Far below, a lone car appeared, traveling along a desolate road, flanked on either side by endless rows of power lines. Akbaar and Roxanna were in a Paykan, often referred to as the Iranian "chariot," a car that had intrigued Cyrus but was in very high demand and hard to come by, leaving him wishing.

Roxanna, now dressed in traditional Iranian attire, sat in the front seat, her long, slim, feminine hands cradling Assad's tar, protectively; the wind coming through the window, playing with the soft tissue paper. What had once been the source of Roxanna's greatest pleasure, dancing and laughing with her father and Cyrus, now lay on her lap, as dead as all the timeworn hands that had once made it come alive.

Wrapped in its paper shroud, itself a victim of unfathomable violence, it too, like the people of Iran, was silenced by Assad's death. She opened Assad's pocket watch and stared at the picture. "Hush, Little Baby" played as the car moved down the quiet road.

No matter what Roxanna's future held for her, the soft music of her father's tar and his gentle, wise, and loving voice would forever play in her memories. And as she promised, she would see his face in every flame.

"I dreamed that a candle burned with a tall flame. For a brief moment in time, I heard a million white doves take flight, and then they vanished into the dark night."

The car disappeared into the sunset, taking its passenger to the uncertain future.

*****

Somewhere safe in the wilderness, far away from what humans called "civilization," Cyrus's wolf howled, forging a new path through the icy blue snow; one lone wolf, reaching the crest, looking down on destruction. Again, she howled. "Man's inhumanity to man." She smelled something in the breeze that put her on alert, drawing her towards the ridge where the tragedy had occurred, her nose following the scent. Finally, up ahead, she saw him, her man.

Cyrus, freezing and covered with snow, sat alone, tears streaking his frozen face. She came to him and lay by his side, lending comfort to ease his pain.

What little had remained slowly faded away. Buried in the snow were Assad's ashes, the burned-out "safe" house, and soon, the wolf's paw prints, leading to eternity. Cyrus stared ahead, speaking to his wolf, his Roxanna, to the world,

"It is too late to cry, to yell, to fight ... too late to change what is already history. There is nothing left but to record it... so it just may others possibly learn from our mistakes..."

The End.

Main Characters Descriptions.

Assad: Roxana's father who went to Iran and never heard of.

Roxanna: An American Iranian, goes to Iran, searching for her lost father, Assad.

Linda: Roxanna's mother and Assad's wife.

Dorian MacGray: CIA Agent,

Peter: American priest living in Iran.

Katayoun: Peter the priest gypsy love.

Cyrus: Iranian filmmaker artist/falls in love with Roxanna.

Hussein: Roxanna's boyfriend. Cyrus's Best friend.

Nader: Hussein and Cyrus's best friend and classmate/ Savak's agent.

Pary: Nader's sister who is in love with Cyrus.

Saeed: Cyrus, Hussein, Nader's classmate.

Abdullah: Cyrus, Nader, Saeed, Hussein's friend.

Hajji Khanoum: Cyrus's mother.

Amir: Cyrus's brother and works for Savak.

Yousef: Amir's driver.

Akbaar: Assad's brother.

www.ingramcontent.com/pod-product-compliance
Lightning Source LLC
Chambersburg PA
CBHW070455120526
44590CB00013B/649